the Unofficial Guide™ to Childcare

Ann Douglas

Macmillan • USA

Macmillan General Reference
A Simon & Schuster Macmillan Company
1633 Broadway
New York, New York 10019-6785

The advice in this book is provided for information purposes only. It
does not guarantee that you will be able to avoid situations that
might be injurious to your child. The decision about whether a particular childcare situation is suitable for your child ultimately rests
with you.

This publication contains the opinions and ideas of its author[s] and
is designed to provide useful advice to the reader on the subject matter covered. All matters regarding your health require medical supervision. Consult your physician before adopting any suggestions in this
publication, as well as about any condition that may require medical
attention. Any references to any products or services do not consti-
tute or imply an endorsement or recommendation. The publisher and
the author[s] specifically disclaim any responsibility for any liability,
loss or risk (financial, personal or otherwise) which may be claimed or
incurred as a consequence, directly or indirectly, of the use and/or
application of any of the contents of this publication.

Certain terms mentioned in this book which are known or claimed to
be trademarks or service marks have been capitalized. Alpha Books
and Macmillan General Reference do not attest to the validity, accuracy or completeness of this information. Use of a term in this book
should not be regarded as affecting the validity of any trademark or
service mark.

Macmillan is a registered trademark of Macmillan, Inc.

ISBN: 0-02-862457-2

Manufactured in the United States of America

10 9 8 7 6 5 4 3 2 1

First edition

To Janice: For everything you did to help me to juggle my baby and my book.
To Neil: For once again assuming responsibility for every imaginable household task, so that I could spend an insane amount of time in front of my computer.

Acknowledgments

I want to thank the following individuals for their contributions to this book: Linda Viscardis, Facilitator, P.R.O.S.P.E.C.T.S., for sharing her knowledge of the unique childcare issues faced by families who have children with special needs; Christine Maniscalco, creator of the Life With Nanny Web site, for allowing us to reprint the superb in-home care work agreement that she has developed; and Abbey Griffith, Senior Associate, Zero to Three, for her detailed and tremendously helpful comments about the manuscript.

I also want to thank the following parents for generously sharing their childcare experiences with me prior to and during the writing of this book: Margaret Allan, Pat Carlson, Shannon Cates, Mara Cook, Jennifer Dawson, Diane Dobry, Katie Ellis, Janet Eye, Rosemary Forrest, Elizabeth Harris, Anne Hoover, Bridget Kelley, LeeAnne Lavender, Kim Michaud Wheelock, Jackie Patrick, Suzi Prokell, Justina Rigby, Dawn Ringel, Lianne Shea, Linda Viscardis, Ruth Ann Weidwall, and the many other parents who chose to share their experiences anonymously.

Contents

The *Unofficial Guide* Reader's Bill of Rights

We Give You More Than the Official Line

Welcome to the *Unofficial Guide* series of Lifestyles titles—books that deliver critical, unbiased information that other books can't or won't reveal—*the inside scoop*. Our goal is to provide you with the *most accessible, useful* information and advice possible. The recommendations we offer in these pages are not influenced by the corporate line of any organization or industry; we give you the hard facts, whether those institutions like them or not. If something is ill-advised or will cause a loss of time and/or money, we'll give you ample warning. And if it is a worthwhile option, we'll let you know that, too.

Armed and Ready

Our hand-picked authors confidently and critically report on a wide range of topics that matter to smart readers like you. Our authors are passionate about their subjects, but have distanced themselves enough from them to help you be armed and protected, and help you make educated decisions as you go through your process. It is our intent that, from

Why "Unofficial"?

having read this book, you will avoid the pitfalls everyone else falls into and get it right the first time.

Don't be fooled by cheap imitations; this is the genuine article *Unofficial Guide* series from Macmillan Publishing. You may be familiar with our proven track record of the travel *Unofficial Guides*, which have more than three million copies in print. Each year thousands of travelers—new and old—are armed with a brand new, fully updated edition of the flagship *Unofficial Guide to Walt Disney World*, by Bob Sehlinger. It is our intention here to provide you with the same level of objective authority that Mr. Sehlinger does in his brainchild.

The Unofficial Panel of Experts

Every work in the Lifestyle *Unofficial Guides* is intensively inspected by a team of three top professionals in their fields. These experts review the manuscript for factual accuracy, comprehensiveness, and an insider's determination as to whether the manuscript fulfills the credo in this Reader's Bill of Rights. In other words, our Panel ensures that you are, in fact, getting "the inside scoop."

Our Pledge

The authors, the editorial staff, and the Unofficial Panel of Experts assembled for *Unofficial Guides* are determined to lay out the most valuable alternatives available for our readers. This dictum means that our writers must be explicit, prescriptive, and above all, direct. We strive to be thorough and complete, but our goal is not necessarily to have the "most" or "all" of the information on a topic; this is not, after all, an encyclopedia. Our objective is to help you narrow down your options to the best of what is available, unbiased by affiliation with any industry or organization.

In each *Unofficial Guide* we give you:

- Comprehensive coverage of necessary and vital information
- Authoritative, rigidly fact-checked data
- The most up-to-date insights into trends
- Savvy, sophisticated writing that's also readable
- Sensible, applicable facts and secrets that only an insider knows

Special Features

Every book in our series offers the following six special sidebars in the margins that were devised to help you get things done cheaply, efficiently, and smartly.

1. "Timesaver"—tips and shortcuts that save you time.
2. "Moneysaver"—tips and shortcuts that save you money.
3. "Watch Out!"—more serious cautions and warnings.
4. "Bright Idea"—general tips and shortcuts to help you find an easier or smarter way to do something.
5. "Quote"—statements from real people that are intended to be prescriptive and valuable to you.
6. "Unofficially..."—an insider's fact or anecdote.

We also recognize your need to have quick information at your fingertips, and have thus provided the following comprehensive sections at the back of the book:

1. **Glossary**: Definitions of complicated terminology and jargon.

2. **Resource Guide**: Lists of relevant agencies, associations, institutions, Web sites, etc.

3. **Recommended Reading List**: Suggested titles that can help you get more in-depth information on related topics.

4. **Important Documents**: "Official" pieces of information you need to refer to, such as government forms.

5. **Important Statistics**: Facts and numbers presented at-a-glance for easy reference.

6. **Index.**

Letters, Comments, and Questions from Readers

We strive to continually improve the *Unofficial* series, and input from our readers is a valuable way for us to do that.

Many of those who have used the *Unofficial Guide* travel books write to the authors to ask questions, make comments, or share their own discoveries and lessons. For Lifestyle *Unofficial Guides*, we would also appreciate all such correspondence, both positive and critical, and we will make best efforts to incorporate appropriate readers' feedback and comments in revised editions of this work.

How to write to us:

Unofficial Guides
Macmillan Lifestyle Guides
Macmillan Publishing
1633 Broadway
New York, NY 10019
Attention: Reader's Comments

The *Unofficial Guide* Panel of Experts

The *Unofficial Guide* editorial team recognizes that you've purchased this book with the expectation of getting the most authoritative, carefully inspected information currently available. Toward that end, on each and every title in this series, we have selected a minimum of three "official" experts comprising the "Unofficial Panel" who painstakingly review the manuscripts to ensure: factual accuracy of all data; inclusion of the most up-to-date and relevant information; and that, from an insider's perspective, the authors have armed you with all the necessary facts you need—but the institutions don't want you to know.

For *The Unofficial Guide to Childcare,* we are proud to introduce the following panel of experts:

Beth Teitelman Beth Teitelman is presently the Director of the 92nd Street Y Parenting Center in New York City. The Y's Parenting Center is a nationwide model offering educational workshops and seminars in addition to recreational programs for parents, infants, toddlers, and pre-schoolers.

Ms. Teitelman is a consultant for parent education programs throughout the New York metropolitan area. She has served on the Tri-State Parenting Council of Channel 13/WNET and currently serves on the PTV-Ready to Learn Council.

Ms. Teitelman holds a Master's Degree in Education from the New York University School of Education, and has additional training from the Bank Street College of Education. Before joining the Y, Ms. Teitelman was an elementary school teacher and she developed curriculum materials. Her first book for parents and children, *Wonderplay,* was published in 1995 by Running Press. She writes for *New York Family Magazine, Children's Video Report,* and other family publications.

Anne Goldstein   Anne Goldstein has been a childcare professional for 24 years. She currently serves as the Director of the National Child Care Information Center (NCCIC) and has held this position since its inception in 1994. The NCCIC is a central source of information for childcare organizations, providers, parents, and the general public.

Prior to her work at NCCIC, Ms. Goldstein worked for a multi-site campus childcare program as teacher, Director, and Child Care Services Manager. During this period, she established and directed a county-wide Child Care Technical Assistance Office. Upon leaving this position, the Anne Goldstein Tribute

Scholarship was established for students majoring in early-childhood education.

Ms. Goldstein has been a childcare consultant for parents, providers, employers, corporations, and state and local governments. She has held several board positions with the Northern Virginia Association for the Education of Young Children.

Deena Lahn Deena Lahn is Executive Director of the Child Care Law Center, a non-profit legal services agency dedicated to promoting quality, affordable childcare. The Child Care Law Center provides free legal services, advocacy, training and technical assistance.

Prior to working at the Center, Ms. Lahn worked for seven years at the Office of Management and Budget in New York City. Her work there involved frequent negotiations with the State over health, mental health, social service, and education programs. She is also familiar with the challenges of caring for children, since she spent three years as a counselor at a residential treatment center for children and adolescents with severe emotional and behavioral problems.

Ms. Lahn received a BA from Yale University and a Master's degree from the University of Chicago.

Introduction: The Truth About America's Childcare Crisis

Arecent study of 400 American day-care centers concluded that 40 percent of the children in those centers were receiving care so lacking in quality that it actually threatened the children's health, safety, and ability to learn.

That, unfortunately, was the good news.

In a related finding that should send shivers down the spine of every American parent, researchers discovered that parents of the children in the study were totally oblivious to the conditions their children faced in the childcare environment. Ninety percent of the parents whose children were receiving substandard care rated that care as high quality—ignoring or failing to see shortcomings that quite literally put their children's lives in danger. The results of this study serve to hammer home an ugly truth about childcare in America: a shortage of high quality, affordable care is forcing American parents to settle for lower standards than their children deserve.

It's not that American parents are deliberately making poor childcare choices. It's simply that they feel there is no real option but to send their children to whatever childcare arrangements are available, whether the quality of care is good, bad, or indifferent.

Stephanie Coontz, a professor of history and family studies at Evergreen College in Olympia, Washington, recently told a CNN reporter that the shortage of high-quality childcare arrangements in America is forcing parents to put their children at risk. "It's a lottery. It's a total crap shoot. You may find the best or you may muddle through. But you're forced to play the lottery every time you do it."

The Ugly Truth

Two decades after women began to enter the workforce en masse, America continues to be ill-equipped to meet the needs of dual-income families. Our strategy when it comes to childcare has been to bury our heads in the sand and pretend that it's still the 1950s, that Ozzie and Harriet are still the norm, when, in fact, Harriet went back to work twenty years ago.

The mainstream media focuses on either the very best or very worst childcare situations, either painting glowing portraits of adorable children being doted over by their highly skilled childcare providers or zeroing in on those tragic instances when a child dies at the hands of his or her caregiver. What falls through the cracks is the experience of average American parents who are desperate to find quality, affordable care.

This is definitely a case when numbers speak louder than words. According to the United States Census Bureau, 53 percent of women with young children today work outside the home, and the majority of those women return to work within three months of giving birth. This means that there are just under 10 million children being cared for by approximately three million caregivers in a nation that still likes to pretend that being a stay-at-home parent is the norm.

Not surprisingly, our country is in the midst of a childcare crisis. According to a recent story in *Newsweek*, 30 percent of all American parents report having difficulty finding quality childcare. What's more, a further 32 percent indicate that they have been unable to find a job that allows them to work around the needs of their families by taking advantage of such workplace innovations as flex-time, telecommuting, and job sharing. It's a problem that parents are struggling with in every state and at every income level—although the working poor face the greatest difficulties.

It doesn't take a rocket scientist to figure out why the majority of working parents feel like they're caught between a rock and a hard place. They want to do what's best for their children, and yet they find themselves trapped in situations that leave them few—if any—options but to settle for whatever childcare arrangements they can cobble together.

Each working day in communities across the country, American parents scramble to patch together a childcare arrangement that will let them to head off to work with relative peace of mind. Unfortunately, the odds are against them. Consider the facts for yourself:

- According to the U.S. General Accounting Office, the demand for infant care exceeds the supply of infant care by anywhere from 16 to 67 percent in various parts of the county. As a result, many parents end up leaving their babies in unlicensed, unregulated environments.

- Only a fraction of childcare providers—anywhere from one in ten to one in three (according to the U.S. General Accounting Office) provide care outside of traditional working hours—a situation that leaves parents who work anything other than 9-to-5 struggling to patch together some kind of ad hoc childcare arrangement.

- A recent study of the childcare situation in Milwaukee, Wisconsin (a.k.a. Anytown, U.S.A.) revealed that only 77 percent of the 90,000 area children were being cared for in regulated situations. The remaining 21,000 children were being cared for in unlicensed or downright illegal childcare settings. (In some states, childcare isn't licensed, so a perfectly good day-care center can operate without a license. That same state may have maximums for the number of children a provider can care for; it's illegal if the provider exceeds that maximum.)

Show Us the Money

As if the supply and quality issues weren't damning enough, there's also the issue of cost. Childcare costs have increased dramatically in recent years, jumping by almost 10 percent between 1990 and 1993. According to the U.S. Census Bureau, the average weekly cost of care for a preschooler is $79. That cost jumps to $85 if you live in the Northeast or the West, or if you live in a large metropolitan area. If you have two children who require childcare and you live in a metropolitan area, you can expect to fork out $10,000 per year.

The cost of childcare almost makes the quality issue a moot point: what good is quality if you can't afford it?

The sad truth about childcare in America is that families who don't have the means to hire highly trained nannies or place their children in *la crème de la crème* of day-care centers or family day care homes are forced to rely on unlicensed—even illegal—childcare arrangements. A recent study showed that 55% of low income families rely on unlicensed childcare arrangements as opposed to 21 percent of upper and middle income families—proof positive that America's most vulnerable children get hit hardest when childcare is treated as a free market issue.

The Waiting Game

Families that are waiting for subsidized childcare spaces have a long wait indeed. Recent changes to welfare legislation that require most welfare recipients to work or train for work once their youngest child is three years old have created a big demand for childcare. In New Jersey alone, there are 15,000 children on a waiting list for the state's 30,000 subsidized daycare spaces. It doesn't take a genius to figure out that policies such as these wreak havoc on the childcare supply, causing headaches for all working parents, not just those who are at the bottom of the income ladder.

The states are doing what they can to up the supply of daycare spaces, but some of their strategies are worrisome to say the least. Some states actively encourage stay-at-home welfare mothers to care for the children of employed welfare mothers, requiring only that such childcare providers pass a criminal background check and meet some less-than-rigorous health and safety standards.

Wondering where quality fits into this picture?

It doesn't.

But wait. It gets worse. In New York state, "babysitting" (that is, informal care by relatives, neighbors, and friends) accounts for a full 80 percent of care funded by workfare. It's an appealing solution to cash-strapped governments because they can pay informal caregivers a fraction of the going rate for highly trained day-care center teachers. It's less appealing to those families who find themselves pressured into placing their children in substandard care arrangements because it's all they can afford. Clearly, there's cause for concern: A 1994 study of informal childcare arrangements showed that only nine percent of care arrangements actually enhanced a child's intellectual development while a full 35 percent actually retarded it—a situation that's appalling to say the least.

Other states are using more creative strategies to drum up more cash for the childcare coffers. In Massachusetts, for example, the state has dedicated the revenues from a special series of license plates to childcare training. The license plates are emblazoned with a message that says it all: "Invest in Children."

Here Today, Gone Tomorrow

Here's another distressing fact about childcare in America: even if you do manage to beat the odds and find a childcare situation you like at a price you can afford, there's no guarantee that you won't be looking for a new situation a few months down the road. Turnover in the childcare profession is legendary—a mind-boggling 30 percent per year. You can't blame caregivers for leaving a profession that pays highly qualified teachers as little as $12,058 per year and family childcare providers a pitiful $9,528 per year after expenses. When they do move on, they leave the families that have come to rely on them scrambling to piece together new care arrangements.

And that's the least of the problem. There's even more troubling fallout to the whole turnover issue: Children who are exposed to an ever-changing parade of caregivers don't have the opportunity to form healthy attachments—something that child development experts argue is critical during the first few years of life. The experts say that a child should have the same caregiver for his or her first two to three years of life—a recommendation that is quite simply pie in the sky for the majority of American infants who instead find themselves unwilling members of the Caregiver of the Month Club.

From Bad to Worse

Then there's the issue of abuse and other threats to children's well-being. Unless you've had your head buried in the sand for the past year or so—and frankly, who could blame you for wanting to tune out—you've no doubt heard about the British au pair charged with murdering the eight-month-old baby who was entrusted in her care or the crazed gunman who took 78 children and five adults hostage in a Texas day-care center.

It's enough to make you want to quit your job—assuming, of course, that you're lucky enough to have that choice.

How are American parents reacting to the child-care crisis?

With panic, that's how.

Sales of so-called nanny cams—hidden cameras that let parents check up on their children's care-givers—are soaring. Day-care centers are installing closed circuit television systems that let anxious parents monitor their children throughout the day via the Internet. And performing a background check on a potential nanny is becoming a routine part of the hiring process.

Clinton's Childcare Initiatives

The state of childcare in America is shameful—a fact that President Bill Clinton recognized in his recent State of the Union address. Following close on the heels of the first-ever White House Conference on Childcare, Clinton's address focussed on the very real need for childcare reform. "Not a single family should have to choose between the job they need and the children they love," he said. He then went on to propose a smorgasbord of childcare reforms—the first good news on childcare that American parents have heard for a very long time. Here are the highlights of Clinton's childcare agenda:

- $21.7 billion dollars would be devoted to child-care-related programs over a five year period.

- Twice as many American children—roughly two million—would receive childcare subsidies under the Childcare and Developmental Block Grant (the source of federal aid to the states).

- An additional half-million children per year would be given the opportunity to participate in after-school childcare programs developed by school-community partnerships funded under the 21st Century Community Learning Center program.

- The Child and Dependent Tax Credit would be extended to an additional three million working families to help offset the costs of childcare.

- Businesses that offer childcare services to their employees would receive a tax credit.

- Childcare safety and quality standards would be enhanced by supporting the enforcement of state childcare health and safety standards and providing scholarships to up to 50,000 childcare providers each year.

While there's no guarantee that these reforms will all make their way into the law books, at least childcare has finally made it on to the governmental agenda—even if it is about 20 years too late.

Earth to Corporate America: Parents Need Your Help

There are also some indications that the childcare issue is capturing the attention of corporate America. As you might expect, what's put it into the business plans of Fortune 500 companies is its effect on the bottom line.

A recent study by the Colorado Business Commission on Childcare Financing concluded that lost time and reduced productivity due to childcare problems is costing American businesses an estimated $3 billion dollars each year. This study—and others like it—have served as a wake-up call to corporate America. As a result, a growing number of forward-thinking companies are striving to find ways to make it easier for their employees to balance their conflicting work-and-family commitments. Here are some examples of family-friendly workplace innovations that were cited in a recent article in *Redbook* magazine:

- In Sioux Falls, South Dakota, working parents can drop off their sick children at the WeeCare sick child daycare center at McKennan Hospital.

- In Des Moines, Iowa, employees of the Principal Financial Group have access to both a childcare referral service and an on-site lactation center.

- In Raleigh-Durham, North Carolina, employees at Glaxo Wellcome can participate in a series of workplace-based wellness programs designed to help them to juggle their duelling responsibilities as parents and employees.

- In Seattle, Washington, employees of Immunex Corp (a biopharmaceutical company) can take advantage of paid paternity and adoption leave, job sharing, and a number of other family-friendly initiatives.

- In Tallahassee, Florida, employees of the Florida Department of Transportation are permitted to take one hour off per month to attend functions at their children's schools.

Do these examples of family-friendly initiatives mean that balancing work and family is becoming any easier? Unfortunately not.

While some significant strides have been made in certain workplaces, the vast majority of American parents continue to struggle to balance the needs of their children with the demands of their jobs—a task that is anything but easy but certainly not impossible.

Why You Need This Book

We've been convinced for some time that there's a need in the marketplace for a childcare book that tells it like it is—a book that refuses to whitewash the childcare situation in America, but rather gives parents and parents-to-be the inside scoop on finding a childcare arrangement that they and their children can live with.

The result is the book you're holding in your hands—a book unlike anything else you're likely to find on the bookstore shelf. Rather than handing you a token childcare checklist, patting you on the head, and setting you loose to play childcare roulette—something that far too many other childcare books do—we've chosen instead to arm you with the facts you'll need to make the best possible childcare decisions in America's less-than-perfect childcare environment.

Some of those facts are anything but pretty. We tackle ugly topics like child abuse, caregiver-employer accusations of sexual harassment, and more. But by refusing to whitewash a complex and critically important topic, we've managed to provide you with the information you need to make an informed and intelligent decision.

We've devoted an entire chapter to talking about what we call "The Dirty Little Secret"—how America's parents really feel about going to work and leaving their children in less-than-adequate childcare arrangements. It's a topic that few other childcare books are willing to broach—and for good reason. It's painfully gritty stuff that can have you lying in bed at 3:00 a.m. with your eyes wide open. It also happens to be real, which is why we put it in the book.

The chapter on finding childcare also goes into territory that other books don't tackle. We tell you where the childcare is—and what you need to do to find it. Rather than holding your hand and telling you to do the obvious, that is, "pick up the Yellow Pages and look under 'Childcare'!" we serve up a smorgasbord of alternative strategies designed to help you find the best possible childcare situation in the shortest possible time.

We take a similarly comprehensive approach when we tackle the topic of money: We tell you what you can expect to pay for childcare, when it does—and doesn't—make sense for you to work, what you need to know about subsidies and tax breaks, and why you shouldn't even consider paying your caregiver under the table. The book provides a thorough discussion of the two basic types of childcare: out-of-home childcare (daycare centers and family daycare homes) and in-home childcare (nannies, babysitters, au pairs, relative care, and other types of care arrangements). We tell you everything you need to know about each option, update you on what the experts have to say about them, and give you the tools you need to evaluate your options in as hard-nosed a manner as possible. We teach you what quality childcare really means in America and how you can tell if a particular daycare center is everything it claims to be. We tell you how to investigate each potential care situation with such rigor that you'll have even Mary Poppins shaking in her boots.

As you've probably gathered by now, we're not afraid to tackle subjects that other childcare books would prefer to leave unsaid. We spill the beans on all those sticky situations that arise when you're sharing your home with an in-home caregiver, including those situations which you can't possibly imagine until you're in the thick of things. We'll tell you what to do if your au pair decides that she wants to move in with her newfound American boyfriend or your nanny starts taking drugs. We take a similarly rigorous approach when examining your out-of-home childcare options. We explain why a license is no guarantee that a particular daycare center will deliver a quality program, and we show you how to tell whether the family daycare provider you're considering is really in it for the love of children.

We also provide you with a wealth of practical information and advice that you could spend hundreds of dollars on trying to track down on your own. We save you the bother and expense of hiring a lawyer to draft a work agreement between you and your nanny and eliminate the need for you to pay an accountant big bucks to teach you the ins and outs of payroll taxes. We also show you how to make your way through the maze of governmental red tape that goes along with being an employer—reason alone to purchase this book.

As we've said before, the emphasis throughout the book is on giving you the information and tools you need to find a childcare situation that works for your family. We provide you with detailed breast-feeding advice that you won't find anywhere else: where to pump, how to pump, and what to wear. We show you how to find a caregiver who will support—not patronize—your special needs child. And we arm you with powerful arguments that you can use to convince your employer of the merits of introducing family-friendly policies to your particular workplace.

The book is packed with useful and hard-to-find information: statistics on caregiver-child ratios for both the United States and Canada, the addresses of the hottest childcare-related Web sites, a comprehensive directory of childcare-related organizations on both sides of the border, the rules for using the services of an au pair, a sample work agreement for in-home caregivers, and much more.

By the time you finish reading this book, you should have a thorough understanding of what's involved in finding a suitable childcare arrangement for your child. Armed with the facts and a healthy amount of skepticism, and a little encouragement, too, you'll know when to take a caregiver's claims at face value—and when (and how) to dig a little deeper. We will have done our job if we've helped to transform you into the kind of parent who won't settle for anything less than the best for his or her child.

A Word on Gender

In the interests of political correctness—and in a desire to avoid those dreadful he/she, his/her constructions—we will alternate the gender of the pronouns used in this book. Certain chapters will assume that you are looking for care for your son; others will assume that you're looking for care for your daughter. We've also made a similar executive decision when it comes to the caregiver's gender. Because the vast majority of childcare workers are female, we've used feminine pronouns to describe them.

A Note About Terminology

Just a quick note about terminology before we plunge into the book: The term "daycare" is increasingly being used to describe the type of care that disabled adults receive in drop-in centers or from in-home attendants. As a result, childcare experts are increasingly using the term "childcare" to describe the type of care children receive while their parents are at work.

While childcare experts have already made the switch to the new terminology, most parents haven't. That's why we've decided to stick with the term "daycare"—at least for this edition of the book.

We use "daycare" as a general term to describe childcare provided by either "daycare centers" or "family daycare homes."

More specifically, "daycare" refers to center-based care for children; "family daycare" describes the type of care children receive in other people's homes.

Here are some other terms we've used in the book:

At-home care: Care that a child receives in his or her own home.

Relative care: Care that a child receives from one of his or her own relatives.

On-site care: Care that a child receives in a workplace-based daycare center.

You can find a more comprehensive list of childcare-related terminology in the glossary found in Appendix A.

The Facts About Childcare in America

GET THE SCOOP ON...
How you may feel about being a working parent
▪ How your child may feel about going
to daycare ▪ Making the best of a difficult situation ▪ Helping your child to cope with his
feelings ▪ Finding the environment that's right
for your child ▪ Reducing the stress of
being a working parent

PART I

The Dirty Little Secret

The spin doctors in advertising agencies across the country like to paint a rosy picture of what it's like to be a working parent. Flip through any glossy magazine or engage in a little channel surfing and you'll see stunningly attractive parents dropping their fashionably dressed children off at daycare centers that boast Martha Stewart-like decors. If you were paranoid, you might start to believe it's all part of an evil campaign to brainwash you into thinking you can have it all—a career and a family—without messy emotions like guilt and worry getting in the way.

Despite the glamorous image of parenthood advertising agencies would have us believe, the majority of working parents have an entirely different story to tell. Rather than feeling euphoric as they make the morning pitstop at daycare, many working parents feel so guilty about leaving their children in someone else's care and so worried about the quality of care their children are

receiving, that it is all they can do to force themselves to walk out the doors of the daycare center
each morning.

Unofficially...
In 1995, approx-
imately 60 per-
cent of American
infants, toddlers,
and preschoolers
were being cared
for regularly by
someone other
than their
parents.
Source: National
Household
Education Survey

But that's not the worst of it. Most working parents feel like they are part of a conspiracy of silence:
that they can't tell their co-workers how they're feeling about juggling their work and family commitments because it's something that no one wants to
talk about. And so it remains every working parent's
Dirty Little Secret.

In this chapter, I'm going to crack the code of
silence and talk about what it's really like to be a
working parent: how you may feel about leaving
your child in the care of someone else, how your
child may react to going to daycare, and what your
family can do to make the best of a difficult situation.

How you may feel about being a working parent

It isn't easy to be a working parent. You may feel like
you're trying to do two full-time jobs: your day job
and your "real" job—being a parent.

If you're like most working parents, you may
have days when you feel that your life is out of control—that you have too many balls in the air.
Perhaps you arrive at work and discover to your horror that the bottles of breast milk you dutifully
pumped for your child the day before are still sitting
in the back seat of the car. Or you are forced to walk
out of a critically important meeting to take a phone
call from your child's caregiver.

That's what it's like to be a working parent.
You're constantly struggling to play catch-up and to
anticipate the next curve ball that life's getting
ready to throw your way.

Guilt

As if the stress of trying to hold everything together wasn't enough to contend with, you've also got to deal with that mainstay of parental emotions: guilt.

Whether you've chosen to work for financial reasons or because you derive a lot of satisfaction from your career, you're likely to be hit with guilt feelings on a regular basis. Here are just a few of the things you may be feeling guilty about:

- being apart from your child

- leaving your child in someone else's care

- giving your baby formula rather than breast milk because it's too difficult to use a breast pump while you're at work

- not being there when your child takes his first steps or says his first words

- not being there if your child is ill or in need of a hug

- picking your child up later one day because you got held up in an important meeting at work

- forgetting to bring cupcakes to daycare on his birthday like all the other mothers at daycare seem to be able to manage to do

- not being able to take time off work to attend the daycare center's Halloween party—even though your child begged you to be there.

This list could go on and on. In fact, it could easily fill the remaining pages of this book. But rather than giving you more things to feel guilty about— things you might have neglected to put on your own guilt list—let's move on and talk about another perennial emotion for working parents: worry.

Watch Out!
Resist the temptation to overcompensate for your guilt feelings by showering your child with material goods. Instead of trying to buy your way out of your guilt feelings, look for ways to give your child what he or she really wants most: time with you!

Worry

Bet you never realized how many things there were to worry about until you became a parent. Life seems immeasurably more complicated and more fragile when you've been entrusted with the welfare of a tiny and vulnerable human being.

Here are just a few of the things you may be worrying about as you begin thinking about leaving your child in the care of someone else:

- whether your child will be well taken care of while you're gone
- whether he will cry the whole time you're at work
- whether he will like his caregiver
- whether his caregiver will like him
- whether he will like his caregiver more than he likes you
- whether the caregiver will be as nice to your child when you're away as she is when you're there
- whether the caregiver will supervise him appropriately throughout the day and ensure that he stays safe
- whether the caregiver will secretly abuse or mistreat him—or leave him in the care of someone else who might harm him
- whether the caregiver will follow your instructions about feeding your child, changing his diaper, administering his medications, and so on
- whether your child will be too sick to go to daycare on a day when you absolutely have to make it to the office

Unofficially...
Child development experts believe that babies need to have the opportunity to form attachments to the people who are caring for them. Your baby can't form such an attachment if he's passed around from caregiver to caregiver. That's why caregiver consistency is so important to your child's long term well-being.

■ whether your child's caregiver will suddenly decide to take a job elsewhere, leaving you in the lurch

As you can see, worry comes as naturally to working parents as guilt. It doesn't matter how well your child appears to have adjusted to daycare or how good you feel about the quality of care that he is receiving, you'll always find something to worry about. It goes with the turf.

Sadness

Some working parents are shocked to discover how sad they feel about leaving their children in the care of someone else. Even if you're fully committed to your career, you may find yourself feeling incredibly sad as you anticipate your first day back at the office. Brenda Sisson and Heather McDowall Black describe this phenomenon in their book *Choosing With Care:* "Even though you may have always planned to return to work, plans you made before the birth of your child don't seem quite as straightforward now that you have come to know and love your child."

■ you will miss your child

■ your child will miss you

■ you will miss out on some of your child's "firsts"—like his first smile

■ your return to work signals the end of the time you had at home with your child, however brief that time may have been.

Most parents find that feelings of sadness ease up considerably after the family gets into a predictable workday routine, but others—particularly those who are feeling ambivalent about leaving

> 66
> I cried on my way home from work every day during Willie's first week at daycare. Once I got to know his caregiver, however, I started feeling better about my decision to go back to work.
> —Jackie, recalling her baby's first week at daycare
> 99

their child in care—find that sadness is a permanent part of being a working parent.

Anger

Anger is another common emotion among working parents. You may find yourself feeling angry about your child's childcare situation if:

- you feel that you were forced into returning to work for financial or other reasons and would actually rather be at home with your baby

- you are frustrated by the lack of quality, affordable childcare in your community

- you resent the fact that your company doesn't cut working parents any slack by offering such family-friendly benefits as job sharing, telecommuting, or flex-time

- you feel that any childcare problems ultimately fall on your shoulders, regardless of how these problems may impact on your career

- you resent the fact that your partner refuses to share the myriad of tasks that go along with being a working parent, such as interviewing potential caregivers, packing and unpacking the change bag each night, and so on

You'll find some constructive tips on dealing with your anger elsewhere in this chapter.

Jealousy

Another emotion that is experienced by a lot of working parents—once again, by mothers in particular—is jealousy.

While most parents go to great pains to choose a caregiver who will provide their child with top quality care in their absence, they may be surprised by how jealous they feel when a bond begins to emerge between the child and the caregiver.

While pangs of jealousy can be painful to deal with, they're a good thing. They're proof positive that you've fallen head over heels in love with your baby.

Here are some reasons why you may be feeling jealous of your child's caregiver:

- your child spends more of his waking hours with her than with you during the week

- your child has become attached to her and may actually cry when it's time to go home— something that even the most secure of parents can find heart-wrenching

- your child's caregiver seems to get all the benefits of parenting (hugs, kisses, and cuddles galore) without the 3:00 a.m. wakeup calls

- your child's caregiver can be home with her preschool aged children and you're not able to be home with yours

An experienced caregiver will understand how you may be feeling about her relationship with your child and will attempt to handle the situation with a great deal of sensitivity. Ideally, she should spend some time reassuring you that the relationship that is blossoming between her and your child will never replace the bond between yourself and your child, and help you feel confident about your decision to work. This seems as good a time as any to sing the praises of those wonderful caregivers who make it possible for working parents to feel good about their decision to work. While I spend a lot of time in this book telling you how to avoid the bad guys, I don't want you to get the idea that they're all bad guys. There are a lot of loving and supportive caregivers out there, and your family has a good chance of finding one. You just need perseverance—and a little luck.

Relief

Perhaps the most difficult emotion for a working parent to admit to is relief. If you're not cut out for 24-hour-a-day diaper duty, you may feel guilty about feeling so relieved about returning to work. After all, don't "good mothers" feel bad about leaving their children in another person's care?

You may be feeling relieved that:

- you have an alternative to being a stay-at-home mom
- someone else can share the responsibility for caring for your child and dealing with those less-than-delightful stages like teething, toilet training, and so on
- you have an opportunity to have regular contact with adults—something you may have longed for during your parental leave

I'll be talking about ways to resolve these feelings later on in this chapter

How your child may feel about going to daycare

Up until now, I've been focusing on how you may be feeling about being a working parent; now it's time to consider how your child may react to this major upheaval in his life.

First of all, no two children are alike, and you have no way to predict how your child will react until you're right in the thick of things.

That said, you can expect your child to react in one of the following ways:

- with sadness
- with fear

Bright Idea
Send your child to daycare on a part-time basis a week or two before you have to return to work. That way, your child can adjust to his new daycare arrange-ment gradually and you can bank some extra hours at work—something that you'll no doubt find helpful when your child's first ear infection crops up.

- with complete and utter joy
- all of the above

Sadness

If you're unlucky enough to have to return to work when your child is experiencing his peak period of separation anxiety (eight to fourteen months of age), you could be in for a rough ride indeed. By this point in their lives, young children have formed a bond with one or more special people in their lives (typically Mom and Dad) and protest vehemently when one or both of these individuals tries to leave them with someone else.

What makes this stage particularly painful for both babies and their parents is the fact that children this age are too young to understand that their parents will return. When you wave goodbye to your sobbing ten-month-old, you might as well be walking away forever.

Fear

It's not unusual for young children to be afraid of strangers—and until your child begins to form a bond with his new caregiver that's exactly what she is: a stranger.

Complete and utter joy

Believe it or not, parents find it just as disconcerting to have to deal with a child who doesn't appear to care less about being left with a new caregiver as a child who cries his heart out. Your child's casual dismissal or bored yawn as you smother him with goodbye kisses can be disconcerting, but at the same time it should reassure you that your child is making a healthy adjustment to his new environment.

You're more likely to get this kind of a reaction if your child starts care when he is either very young

Unofficially...
The percentage of preschoolers of working mothers in selected care arrangements during 1993:

Centers: 30%
Family daycare (nonrelatives): 21%
Grandparents: 17%
Father: 16%
Other relatives: 9%
Other: 7%
Source: U.S. Census Bureau

(six months of age or younger) or well into his tod-dler years (eighteen months or older). The reason is simple: Separation anxiety is less of an issue for him at this stage in his development.

All of the above

Most children show a mix of emotions when they're placed in a new daycare situation. They may feel sad about being apart from you and a bit nervous about their new caregiver, but they may also be excited about being with other children and having lots of new sights and sounds to take in.

Your child's emotions may fluctuate from day to day—and even from minute to minute. One minute, he may be perfectly contented about being held by his new caregiver. The next, he may be crying for you. Many parents find this roller coaster ride of emotions more than a little challenging to deal with—particularly at 8:00 a.m.

Making the best of a difficult situation

Up until now, I've been talking about the various types of difficulties you and your child may face as you attempt to integrate yourselves into the world of childcare. Now it's time to toss out some solutions because that's the reason you purchased this book in the first place.

I'm going to start out by talking about how you can come to terms with your own feelings. Then I'll show you some tried-and-true methods for helping your child to work through his emotions, too.

As difficult as the smorgasbord of emotions can be to cope with at first, you will start to feel better as you and your child begin to adjust to your new rou-tine. Until that happens, however, you need to have some coping strategies in place. Here are some tips

Bright Idea
Look for a child-care environment that can grow with your child for at least the foreseeable future. The calm and peaceful environment that is so well-suited to a young infant may be less than ideal for an active toddler or highly social preschooler.

to deal with some of the conflicting emotions you're most likely to experience:

- Acknowledge your feelings. Don't bury them. Give yourself permission to feel worried, guilty, angry, sad, or relieved: whatever the case may be. There's no right or wrong way to feel about being a working parent.

- Come to terms with your decision. There's no point beating up yourself indefinitely about your decision to be a working parent. Whether you're working for financial or other reasons, it's important to accept your decision to work— and then move on.

- Talk to someone who understands—your spouse, a professional counselor, your family doctor, or another working parent. It's important for you to express your feelings to someone that will listen and reassure you that you will begin to feel better over time.

- Spend plenty of time with your child. Try to keep your weeknights and weekends free for at least the first few weeks so you can spend as much of your nonworking time as possible with your family.

- Be part of your child's childcare experience. Leave for work a little earlier than you absolutely need to so that you'll have a few minutes to play with him at the daycare center. Volunteer to accompany your child's group on an outing to the local library or fire station. The more you know about the people he is spending his days with, the better you'll feel about the entire situation.

- Establish a rapport with your child's caregiver. Getting to know her better can help you feel more comfortable about leaving your child with her and will let you to troubleshoot any problems that may arise more quickly and easily.

Helping your child to cope with his feelings

Like you, your child will most likely experience powerful emotions as he attempts to adjust to a new childcare situation. You may find it difficult to deal with his feelings when you're dealing with so many conflicting emotions of your own, but this is one time in his life when your child really needs your love and support.

Here are some tips on helping your child to cope with his emotions.

Watch Out!
Make sure that the books or videos you use to prepare your child for daycare are based on the particular daycare setting you've chosen. Otherwise, your child will wonder where the other 50 kids are when he arrives for his first day at family daycare.

- Prepare your child for his daycare experience by reading books or watching videos about daycare together. There are a number of excellent books and videos on the market. (See Appendix C.)

- Arrange for your child to meet his new caregiver ahead of time. In addition to giving your child the opportunity to meet his new caregiver in a safe environment (from the vantage point of your lap), visiting the daycare center or family daycare home can also help to eliminate any concerns he may have about his new care arrangement (will he be able to find the bathroom when the need arises?). Most caregivers and daycare centers understand the need for such a visit and will be more than willing to set aside some time to spend with you and your child. If they aren't, there's something wrong.

- Bring your child to daycare at least 15 minutes before you have to leave. That will give your child's caregiver enough time to get him engaged in an activity before you make your exit. Don't be alarmed if your child refuses to have anything to do with the caregiver while you're in sight; it's just his way of hammering home the fact that you're the one he really wants. Most likely he'll plunge into the game wholeheartedly as soon as the door closes behind you.

- Pack your child's special blanket, his favorite toy, or something that will remind him of you (a picture or an item of clothing that still has your smell on it). These comfort (or "transition") objects will help him to feel more secure while he's away from you.

- Try the buddy system. Enrolling a child with his best friend or an older sibling can help ease the transition from home to daycare.

- A few minutes before you actually have to leave, remind your child that you are about to go to work. While it may be easier to try to sneak off and avoid a scene, it's not fair to your child to do so. You can also set yourself up for many weeks of painful goodbyes if your child learns that Mommy or Daddy can—and do—disappear in the blink of an eye.

- Keep your good-byes short and sweet. Keep a smile on your face, even if your child is crying, and reassure him that you will be back at the end of the day.

- Be understanding of his feelings. Let him know that it's only normal to miss people you love

Unofficially...
You can make the transition to daycare easier on your baby by starting him or her in a new care situation either before or after the peak period of separation anxiety, which typically occurs at eight to fourteen months of age. You likely won't be able to sidestep the problem entirely, however, as separation anxiety recurs sporadically throughout a child's first few years of life. Difficult as separation anxiety can be to cope with, it's your baby's way of showing you how important you have become to him.

when you have to be away from them, and that you understand that it takes time to get used to new people and places. If your child is nonverbal, try to put his feelings into words for him: "You really miss Mommy when she's at work."

- Be prepared to make changes in your child's routine. Don't be surprised, for example, if a child who has been sleeping in his own bed for months suddenly wants to start sleeping with you. It's his way of ensuring that he gets to spend as much time as possible with you during your nonworking hours.

- Convey your feelings of confidence to your child. You can't expect him to buy into the idea that his new care arrangement is going to be terrific if you don't actually believe it yourself. Tell him what he can expect to experience each day, but do so in terms that he can understand: for example, "After breakfast, I'll take you to Jane's. You'll play, have lunch, and have a nap, and then Daddy will pick you up on his way home from work."

Even if your child is very young, it's important to have this "conversation." Your child may not understand the words you're using, but he'll pick up on the reassuring tone of your voice.

- If your child still hasn't settled within a reasonable period of time after starting a new care arrangement, you may have to consider finding a new caregiver for him.

Finding the environment that's right for your child

One of the best ways to ensure that your child can adjust to daycare as quickly and painlessly as possible is to choose a childcare environment that is suited to his age and his temperament.

Your child's age

Infants have very different needs than their toddler or preschool-aged siblings and vice versa. Here's a brief overview of what the experts believe children of various ages need from their caregivers and daycare environments:

Infants (from birth to eighteen months) need:

- a low caregiver-child ratio, ideally 1:1 but no more than 1:3

- a group size of three, if you can find it, but certainly no more than four

- continuity in care, so that they can establish strong attachments to their caregivers

- responsive caregivers who genuinely love babies and who are prepared to respond to their needs as quickly and effectively as possible

- a flexible environment in which they are free to eat and sleep in accordance with their individual needs (as opposed to trying to conform to their caregiver's schedule)

- a nurturing environment in which there are plenty of opportunities for cuddling, holding, and unhurried care

- a predictable environment in which they can feel secure

- a safe yet stimulating environment in which they are free to explore (as opposed to being confined to playpens or cribs for unreasonably long portions of the day)

Toddlers (eighteen months to three years) need:

Watch Out!
If your child has a difficult time adjusting to new situations, be careful about placing him in an age-based group in a daycare center. If the grouping rules are too rigid, he may be forced to readjust each time a child enters or leaves his group—something that can happen quite frequently if children are required to move to another group each time their birthdays roll around.

Unofficially...
Studies have shown that when babies and toddlers share the same caregiver, toddlers get the short end of the stick. Make sure that your child's caregiver can provide him with the time and attention he deserves if he is placed in a mixed group (a group that contains children of different ages) rather than an age-based group (one that consists of children of roughly the same age).

- a low caregiver-child ratio, ideally 1:3 or less, but certainly no more than 1:5

- a group size of four, if you can find it, but certainly no more than six

- caregivers who have the patience and energy to weather their ever-changing moods, and who have realistic expectations of their behavior

- a safe environment that encourages their natural love of physical activity and active exploration

- a setting in which they are given the opportunity to practice new skills, do things for themselves, and make simple choices

Preschoolers (three to six years) need:

- a low caregiver-child ratio, ideally 1:5 or less, but certainly no more than 1:8

- caregivers with the time and patience to field their endless questions

- an environment that provides them with access to age-appropriate activities and equipment

- opportunities to socialize with other children their own age and to build on their increasingly sophisticated language skills

I'll return to these points in future chapters as I evaluate specific childcare options.

Your child's temperament

Another important factor in determining how well your child will do in a particular childcare environment is his temperament.

If you were lucky enough to be blessed with a child who embraces new situations as a welcome challenge, smiles at everyone, and isn't overly sensitive to noise and activity, you've got it made. If, however, your child is clingy, fearful, and reluctant to let you go to the bathroom alone, you're probably in for a much rougher ride.

This is not to say that some kids are made for daycare and others aren't. It's not nearly that cut and dried. It's simply a matter of finding a daycare environment that will work for your child.

If your child is outgoing and relatively fearless, he'll most likely adapt equally well to either home-based or center-based care environments. If, however, your child is a bit more subdued and cautious, he might feel more secure dealing with a single caregiver and a relatively small number of children in either a one-to-one care arrangement in his own home or in a family daycare environment.

In all likelihood you'll be able to predict which environment is best suited to your child, but don't be afraid to test-drive your hypothesis. Bring your child along while you're investigating care situations and watch his body language carefully. If he clings to your leg and screams every time a toddler whizzes by on a scooter, the daycare environment may not be his cup of tea. Likewise, if he's terrified of men with beards, the family childcare provider's husband may seem downright frightening.

That said, it's important to remember that most children will go through some period of adjustment when they first enter a new care situation. So don't panic too much if it looks like the only caregiver your child will willingly embrace is you! That will likely change, given a bit of time and a lot of TLC from his new childcare provider.

Your child's special needs

If your child has special needs (i.e., a physical or mental disability; a visual or hearing impairment or perceptual problem; speech or language difficulties; or emotional disturbances, including behavioral problems or autism), you may need to find a caregiver who has the training and experience required to deal with your child's special needs. (You can find a list of useful resources in Appendix B.) Even if you decide to integrate your child into a mainstream daycare environment, you will need to consider such factors as whether or not the facility is wheelchair accessible and whether or not any specialized equipment needed by your child is available. You may also have to grapple with even more complex issues, such as monitoring for abuse in a non-verbal school-aged child—issues that most other parents simply don't have to deal with. We explore these issues in much greater depth in Chapter Eleven.

Ways to reduce the stress of being a working parent

One of the best ways to reduce the stress of being a working parent is to choose a daycare situation that is a good fit for your family: one that meshes well with your work schedule, is close to home or work, and that supports your parenting philosophies.

Your work schedule

One of the major stressors that working parents face is finding daycare that fits their working schedule. It's less of a problem if you work standard nine-to-five hours, but you can still find yourself showing up late for an early-morning meeting because the day-care center wasn't open in time or dashing out of an important late-afternoon meeting to avoid running up a hefty overtime bill at daycare.

Parents who work shifts, have fluctuating hours, or work on an "on call" basis, often have to patch

Moneysaver
Most daycare centers and family daycare providers charge an additional fee if you're late picking up your child. Make sure you find out about these charges up front so that you can factor them into your daycare budget.

together daycare arrangements that are less than ideal. A recent report by the federal Women's Bureau, *Care Around The Clock,* revealed that children in some communities are left sleeping in cars in factory parking lots while their parents work the late shifts. Parents in other communities opt for "tag team" parenting where one parent provides care while the other works—a solution that works well in the short run but can lead to marital problems over the long haul.

While you may luck out and find a daycare center that provides 24-hour care or a family daycare provider who is willing to provide care around the clock, your best bet is to find an in-home caregiver who's willing to work around your schedule.

Your work location

In a perfect world, your workplace would be situated directly across the street from your child's daycare center and just around the corner from your home. Alas, not many parents in the real world enjoy such a luxury. Therefore, the location of your child's caregiver or daycare center is yet another factor to consider when you're choosing childcare—and one that can either add to or eliminate a lot of the stress of being a working parent.

So what should you do if your partner works in the north end of town, you work in the south end, and your home is in the east end? It depends. If your partner is going to be responsible for dropping your child off and picking your child up from daycare, and for being "on call" in the event that your child becomes ill during the day and has to go home, it makes sense to choose a location near his workplace. If you're assuming these responsibilities, then you'll probably want to find a location near

Timesaver
When you're con-
sidering the
hours for which
you need care,
remember that it
will take you
longer to drop
your child off in
the morning and
pick him up in
the afternoon
than you might
initially antici-
pate. Factor in at
least an extra
half-hour for this
important
stopover at the
start and end of
each day. Be sure
it is long
enough to help
locate a missing
soother, get your
child involved in
an activity with
his caregiver, or
to dish out an
extra hug if your
child's having a
particularly bad
day.

your own workplace. If you'll be sharing these responsibilities, then it makes more sense to choose a location near your home.

Like everything else in this book, this formula is anything but cut and dried. If the best childcare environment in town is in the west end, then you'll most likely decide that the extra few minutes of driving there each day is time well spent. Once again, it's a decision that's best made by you and your partner, with the interests of your child in mind.

Your care expectations

Assuming that your work schedule and location allow you the luxury of choice, it's important to spend some time thinking about the type of childcare arrangement you would prefer for your child. You may want to consider such factors as the philosophy of your child's caregiver and or daycare center; your child's caregiver's age and training; whether you prefer center-based or home-based care; and—should you decide to opt for care in your own home—whether to invite your child's caregiver to live with you.

While most daycare centers and family daycare providers are quite forthright about their philosophies, you'll have to do a little bit of digging to figure out where a potential in-home caregiver is coming from, philosophically speaking. Now I'm not suggesting that you insist that the individual in question pass a three-hour ethics test to determine whether she is qualified to care for your two-year-old. What I am suggesting, however, is that you find out where she stands on each of the following potentially volatile issues:

- Feeding practices: If you intend to continue to breastfeed your baby after you return to work, will the caregiver support your choice? What are her thoughts on using food as bribes or rewards for older children? What does she consider to be an appropriate menu for a baby, toddler, or preschooler? Does she allow the children in her care to eat sugary foods? Will she cater to your child's vegetarian diet or other special food requirements?

- Sleep routines: Does she allow the children in her care to take naps whenever they please, or does she require that all children take a nap at the same predetermined time so that she can grab a few minutes for herself? What does she do if a child is clearly overtired and yet cannot settle down for a nap: cuddle the child or send him off to bed with a bottle of juice?

- Comfort objects: What are her feelings about such comfort objects as pacifiers, teddy bears, blankets, and thumbs? Does she allow children to carry them with them throughout the day or limit their use to naptime only?

- Diapering and dressing: How often does she change the babies and toddlers in her care? When does she expect toddlers and older children to be able to dress themselves?

- Toilet training: How does she handle toilet training? What are her expectations of children of various ages?

- House rules: What are her house rules about running in the house, making noise, and so on? Do these rules seem reasonable, given the age of your child?

- Discipline: What methods of discipline does she use? Are they age-appropriate? Are they

Watch Out!
Infants need to be held while they're drinking from a bottle. Never leave your baby with any caregiver who routinely props bottles. Your baby could choke if left unattended.

compatible with the methods that you use at home?

▪ Values: What values are important to this person? How do her values compare to your own?

After you've established whether you're on the same wavelength when it comes to child-rearing, you should also give some thought to the age, training, and experience of your child's caregiver. You may have strong feelings about the type of person you would like to have caring for your child: for example, a kindly grandmotherly type as opposed to a fully qualified early childhood educator in her early 20s. While you don't want to get hung up on a stereotype of the perfect caregiver, it doesn't hurt to have a rough idea of what you're after, provided you're prepared to compromise as circumstance demands.

The next issue that you need to grapple with is whether you want center-based or home-based care for your child. Most parents have very strong feelings either way. Some opt for center-based care because they feel reassured by the fact that their child will only be cared for by experienced professionals (an assumption that may or may not be true!). Others prefer the "hominess" of the family daycare environment and seek care for their children in their own or another person's home. Before you make any snap decisions, it's important to be sure you understand the pros and cons of each type of care. That means researching each option thoroughly, and deciding whether it's a good fit for you and your child—something I'll help you to do in the remaining chapters of this book.

If you're considering having someone care for your child in your own home, you have an additional decision to make: if you want to share your home with a stranger, or if you would prefer that she live elsewhere. Obviously, this is a very complex issue that will be affected by your work schedule, your partner's work schedule, the number and ages of children in your family, and the extent of your desire for privacy.

You're most likely to choose an in-home caregiver if

- you work nonstandard hours or rotating shifts

- you put in a lot of overtime

- your job requires that you go into work with minimal notice (for example, you are on call)

- you travel out of town on a regular basis

- you don't have family or friends who can pinch hit for you in the event that your child is ill on a day when you absolutely have to make it into work

- you have two or more children requiring childcare (either full-time or after school)

- you aren't opposed to sharing your home with a stranger

You're less likely to choose an out-of-home care arrangement if

- you work standard nine-to-five hours and are rarely required to work overtime or travel out of town

- you have only one child who requires childcare

- you have a solid support network (family and friends) who can come to your rescue if your child is ill and can't go to the daycare center or family daycare provider

Unofficially...
A group of Phoenix, Arizona area employers including Allstate, American Express, and IBM have banded together to recruit and train childcare providers to provide care to children of employees who work weekend and evening hours.

- you and your spouse value your privacy and would feel awkward having a caregiver working in your home on either a live-in or live-out basis

- you are reluctant to take on the responsibilities of being an employer—something that you automatically become if you hire an in-home caregiver

By finding a childcare arrangement that works well for your entire family, you'll be able to eliminate much of the stress of being a working parent.

Just the facts

- Be prepared to experience a range of emotions during your child's first few days in a new care arrangement: worry, guilt, jealousy, anger, sadness, and maybe even relief.

- You can help your child to come to terms with his own feelings about going to daycare by preparing him ahead of time and then listening while he expresses his feelings.

- When you are shopping around for a daycare arrangement for your child, make sure you find one that suits his age, temperament, and any special needs he might have.

- You can minimize your overall stress level by finding a daycare center or family daycare provider that offers care at the times you need it, is conveniently located, and that supports your own childrearing philosophies.

GET THE SCOOP ON...
The pros and cons of out-of-home childcare ▪
The pros and cons of in-home childcare ▪
When to start looking for childcare ▪ Where to
look ▪ Applications, restrictions, and waiting
lists ▪ Narrowing your options ▪ Making a
decision you can live with

Chapter 2

Where the Childcare Is . . .

It's every working mother's fantasy: You're sitting at the dinner table with your partner, discussing your need to find someone to take care of little Jason or Jennifer so that you can return to work. Suddenly there's a knock at the door. It's an attractive young woman with a British accent who is looking for employment as a nanny. She tells you that she's extremely good with children and comes highly recommended. You invite her in for coffee (she prefers tea, of course!) and you and your partner take turns reading the many glowing letters of recommendation that she pulls from her bag. Within a matter of minutes, you know that you've found the answer to your childcare prayers. You quickly extend an offer of employment to this charming young woman, and thank your lucky stars that she knocked on your door first, rather than any of the neighbors'.

Timesaver
Begin your
search for child-
care as soon as
your pregnancy
is well-
established—
ideally around
the start of your
third trimester.
It's never too
early to get your
name on the
waiting list for a
space at the
daycare center or
family daycare
home of your
choice.

Before you get the idea that this book is going to tell you how you can re-create this fantasy in your very own home, let me be perfectly honest. Scenarios like this are the stuff of which dreams (and soap operas) are made. They rarely happen in real life. The fact of the matter is that there is an acute shortage of nannies of the Mary Poppins variety.

So what's a working parent to do? Give up any hope of returning to work? Abandon your child to the clutches of any Tom, Dick, or Jane who hangs up a childcare shingle? Beg your aging parents to give up tennis and golf in favor of spending quality time with their precious grandchild?

Difficult as it can be to find quality childcare, the situation isn't quite as dismal as you might think. While you might have to set your sights short of finding a real-life Mary Poppins, you don't have to settle for any of the scary characters who regularly make the rounds of daytime talk shows. They aren't your average, run-of-the-mill childcare providers. I promise.

Regardless of where you live, there are two basic options when it comes to childcare: out-of-home childcare and in-home childcare. In this chapter, I'll discuss the pros and cons of both out-of-home and in-home childcare; tell you when to start looking and where to find each type of childcare in your community, and give you the inside scoop on applications, restrictions, waiting lists and more. Then I'll give you some pointers on researching your options and coming to a decision that you can live with.

The pros and cons of out-of-home childcare

Out-of-home childcare is childcare that takes place somewhere other than in your own home (in a day-care center, a nursery school, or in a family daycare home, for example). As you no doubt realize, there are both advantages and disadvantages to out-of-home childcare arrangements. Let's take a quick look at the pros and cons.

Pros of out-of-home childcare:

▪ You don't have to share your home with a stranger—something that goes with the territory if you opt for an in-home caregiver. So, if your housekeeping standards are somewhat less than those of Martha Stewart and you have strong feelings about privacy, an out-of-home care arrangement is likely to be your best bet.

▪ You don't have to take out a second mortgage to pay someone to care for your child. There's no getting around it: In-home care is expensive. While you can still pay a small fortune for out-of-home care, you are more likely to find this kind of arrangement more suitable to your needs and budget.

▪ Your child will have the opportunity to be with other children her own age. While this might not seem important while she's an infant, the opportunity to socialize with her age mates will take on increasing importance as she enters the toddler and preschool years.

Cons of out-of-home childcare:

▪ Taking your child to a daycare center or family daycare setting is not nearly as convenient as having someone come into your home. Don't

Watch Out!
The benefits of a
low caregiver-
child ratio can
be lost if the
group size is too
large. Just as
you wouldn't
expect to enjoy
quality one-on-
one time with
your spouse in a
football stadium,
you shouldn't
expect your child
to enjoy quality
time with her
caregiver in a
room full of chil-
dren. Children
who are placed
in overly large
groups don't
receive the care
and attention
they deserve.

believe me? Just wait until the first time the entire family sleeps in on a day when you have an important meeting at 8:00 a.m.!

■ Your child is more likely to be exposed to illness if she's in an out-of-home care arrangement. Children in daycare centers and family daycare settings have a tendency to pass around the virus du jour, be it chicken pox, pink eye, or the common cold.

■ Caregiver consistency can be a problem due to high levels of turnover in the childcare profession. Your child's caregiver may decide to leave the daycare center or close up her family daycare business after your child has become attached to her. Then you're back at square one.

■ Out-of-home care becomes expensive if you're purchasing services for more than one child. If you've got two or more children needing childcare, you might want to give serious thought to having someone care for them in your own home.

■ You will still need a backup plan in case your child becomes ill. Vomiting, feverish, and otherwise seriously ill children should stay at home until they are well enough to return to daycare.

The pros and cons of in-home care

Now let's consider the pros and cons of in-home care.

Pros of in-home care:

■ Your child will be cared for by the same person day after day. Because caregiver consistency is so important for infants, in-home care can be an ideal form of childcare if you're returning to work while your child is still very young.

■ Your child will receive one-on-one care (unless, of course, she has siblings, in which case she'll have to share her caregiver with her brothers and sisters). While daycare providers and the staff of daycare centers do their best to keep their staff-child ratios low, most start at 1:3 and work their way up.

■ You can start your day in a relatively sane fashion because your childcare provider is coming to you. There's no need to drag your child out of bed before she's ready.

■ Your child can stick to her own schedule when it comes to eating, sleeping, and playing. This type of flexibility is much harder to find in a large group setting.

■ An in-home caregiver is generally better able to accommodate your erratic work schedule than the staff of either a daycare center or at family daycare. If you have to work into the evening hours to meet a pressing deadline, your in-home caregiver may be willing to assume responsibility for feeding your child dinner and putting her to bed.

■ There aren't any (or at least as many) runny-nosed kids to share toys with, so your child won't pick up as many illnesses as she would if she were being cared for in a large group setting.

Cons of in-home care:

■ In-home care is the most expensive type of childcare. Many families don't have the

Moneysaver
If you can't afford to hire an in-home caregiver on your own, consider sharing one with another family. If both families need part-time care, she can come to different houses on different days of the week. If you both need full-time care, she can either care for the children in one or the other houses on an ongoing basis, or rotate from house to house every couple of weeks.

incomes required to hire caregivers to come into their own homes.

- Because you have an employer-employee relationship with your child's caregiver, you have to make your way through all kinds of governmental red tape. In the blink of an eye, the employer-employee relationship transforms your home into someone else's workplace.

- Your in-home caregiver is unlikely to have a backup in the event that she is ill. If she comes down with the flu, you're on your own.

- The stress of caring for young children in relative isolation can lead to high levels of burnout among in-home caregivers. As a result, turnover can be a problem.

- Your home may not be large enough to provide adequate privacy for an in-home caregiver. The last thing you need as you're getting ready to go to work is a line outside the bathroom!

- If your child is alone at home with your caregiver, she may miss out on the chance to interact with other children her own age—something that is particularly important during the preschool years.

- It's hard enough to share your child with a caregiver without having to share your home with that person as well. Jealousy of the caregiver's relationship with your child can be a major issue for many working parents, especially mothers.

- In-home care arrangements aren't licensed by any level of government, so you're on your own when it comes to supervising the quality of care that your child receives.

■ Unless you have an exceptionally large toy budget, your home is likely to lack some of the bells and whistles that your child would be exposed to at a daycare center.

When to start looking for childcare

Timing is everything when it comes to looking for childcare. If you start your search too early, the vacancies you find may no longer be available by the time you need them. If you start your search too late, you might not find a suitable arrangement in time to go back to work.

While you may need to start your search a little earlier if childcare in your community is in exceptionally short supply, the following guidelines should help you to decide how soon to start your search.

■ If you're looking for a space in a family daycare setting, six to eight weeks is plenty of lead time for your search because most care providers don't know in advance whether they'll have an opening.

■ If you're looking for a spot in a daycare center, you should start looking at least a year before your child will start care. This is because full-time openings for infants and toddlers are in short supply and are typically reserved for families who already have children enrolled at the center.

■ If you're looking for a part-time daycare arrangement (a preschool or nursery school program for a three- to five-year-old, for example), you should plan to sign up your child during the winter or spring if you want to secure a space in a program starting in the fall.

Bright Idea
Toy libraries are an excellent resource for families whose children are being cared for at home. Besides lending out the latest and greatest toys, they're also a source of larger pieces of kid equipment like easels, slides, and ride-on toys. What's more, they cost next to nothing to join—typically as little as $20 per year. If there isn't a toy library up and running in your community, why not consider starting one?

- If you're looking for an in-home caregiver, you should allow yourself eight weeks to find a live-out caregiver and four months or longer to find an in-home caregiver. If you're planning to recruit a nanny or an au pair from overseas, you might need as much as nine months to a year of lead time.

Where to look

Now that I've reviewed your basic childcare options and discussed the pros and cons of both out-of-home and in-home care, let's talk about what you can do to find childcare in your community.

As you know from reading this book and listening to the news, there is a shortage of quality, affordable childcare across the United States. While you may be tempted to take the first childcare space you find, you owe it to your child to investigate a number of different childcare situations and then select the best one.

In subsequent chapters, I'll give you some pointers on evaluating various out-of-home and in-home childcare options. For now, I'll focus on the logistics of finding childcare in your community.

One quick disclaimer before I plunge into the heart of this discussion: You'll notice that I've skipped over some of the more obvious strategies for finding childcare, like looking up "Daycare Centers" and "Domestic Agencies" in the Yellow Pages. Instead, I suggest zeroing in on some of the less obvious places to look for leads on childcare. Some will only prove useful if you're looking for an in-home caregiver, and others will only help you out if you're looking for out-of-home care, but hopefully this list will enable you to cut to the chase as you engage in a little detective work of your own.

Friends and family

Friends and family are an excellent source of leads on all types of childcare arrangements. They may know of a vacancy at a daycare center or have a neighbor who is thinking of starting her own family daycare business. As helpful as their recommendations may be, however, you're the only one who can decide about the suitability of a particular childcare environment for your particular child. The very same childcare arrangement that is perfect for your sister's active toddler might be a bit too rambunctious for your brand new baby.

The "nanny network"

Don't neglect the so-called "nanny network." If some of your friends have nannies (or full-time babysitters), ask them for leads. They may be able to put you in touch with a wonderful caregiver who's looking for work in your community.

Your local family daycare network

In some communities, family daycare providers have banded together to exchange information and offer one another support. Contact your local family daycare network to find out if any of its members have vacancies at this time. Call the National Association of Family Child Care at 1-800-359-3817 to find out whether there's such a network up and running in your community.

It's a good idea to try to find a caregiver who's tapped into this type of network. Caregivers who belong to family childcare networks are more committed to their professions and at a far less risk of suffering from isolation and burnout—two of the major reasons why turnover is so high in this particular profession.

Timesaver
Child Care Resource and Referral Centers (CCR&R) can assist you in finding childcare in your area. Because they aren't in the childcare business themselves, you can rely on them to provide you with impartial information about your childcare choices. To locate a CCR&R in your area, contact Child Care Aware, 2116 Campus Drive S.E., Rochester, MN 55904, (507) 287-2220, 1-800-424-2246. You can also find more information about CCR&Rs at www.childcare-experts.org/ccx2.html.

Your child's pediatrician

Most pediatricians' offices have bulletin boards packed with useful information, including childcare information. You might find a posting from a caregiver who is looking for work or an advertisement from a daycare center that has some vacancies. Even if you can't find anything posted on the bulletin board, your pediatrician or his staff may be able to provide you with leads on childcare vacancies in your community.

Bulletin boards

The bulletin boards at your local library, YMCA, food co-op, laundromat, consignment store, gym, coffee-shop, or favorite family restaurant can be a gold mine when it comes to uncovering leads on childcare. You can find everything from daycare brochures to "nanny available" advertisements to notices about the next meeting of your local nanny association or family daycare association. You can also post your own ad, of course.

Community organizations

The staff of the children's department at your local library or other family-focused community organizations work with in-home caregivers and the staff of daycare centers on a regular basis. A quick phone call to one of these organizations could provide you with leads on both in-home and out-of-home childcare vacancies in your community. What's more, a growing number of community organizations are offering after-school childcare programs.

Newspapers, magazines, and newsletters

Don't neglect the power of the printed word. Caregivers who are looking for work frequently advertise in the "employment wanted" sections of local newspapers, magazines, and newsletters, and daycare centers often advertise their vacancies as well.

If you decide to advertise for a caregiver, however, be prepared to be flooded with responses. One New York executive received well over 100 phone calls on the night her "nanny wanted" ad hit the street. "We only managed to return the phone calls of the most qualified applicants," she admits.

The Internet

There are numerous online directories, newsgroups, and mailing lists devoted to childcare. You can use these as a tool for finding a caregiver for your child by either searching through some of the directories or posting a "childcare wanted" notice to a newsgroup or mailing list. (Just a quick word of caution: Things aren't always what they seem in cyberspace, so examine the credentials of anyone you recruit this way with the utmost care.) One family took things a step further and created a Web page describing what they were looking for in a caregiver for their as-yet-unborn child. While they haven't managed to find an online Mary Poppins yet, they're still optimistic that she'll surf by their Web site before it's time to head off to labor and delivery.

Religious or ecumenical groups

Religious groups are another excellent source of leads and many operate nursery schools and daycare centers. Others offer "drop-in" programs that are designed to give stay-at-home moms a much-needed break, but that can also double as emergency childcare for moms who are in the paid workforce.

Other people in the know

Real estate agents, small business consultants, and the presidents of business clubs (the local women's business network, for example) are other excellent sources of leads on childcare. Make a point of telling everyone that you know that you're looking for childcare.

The local small business office

Timesaver
Call Childcare Aware—a national non-profit group—for leads on quality childcare in your community. The number is 1-800-424-2246.

The small business or economic development office in your community may be able to put you in touch with clients who are in the process of launching their own home-based or center-based daycare businesses. Getting the inside scoop on these types of businesses before they start advertising their vacancies is often the key to finding a childcare space in a community with an impossibly tight childcare market.

Nanny schools

Because highly trained nannies are in such short supply, often your best bet for finding one is to scoop up a nanny who is about to graduate from nanny school. There are a number of different nanny schools in operation nationwide. You can find the contact information for some of the best-known schools in Appendix B.

Colleges and universities

Some colleges and universities that offer programs in early childhood education operate model daycare centers to enable their students to obtain hands-on experience. These programs are high quality, because they are typically directly supervised by faculty members; and budget-friendly, because they are typically subsidized by the university to provide this unique placement opportunity to students. The only downside is that your child may be cared for by an ever-changing parade of caregivers as one class of students is replaced by the next. (However, there is usually a stable core of staff in these excellent day-care facilities.) Nonetheless, if your child is very young or has difficulty adjusting to change, this may be reason enough to pass on the opportunity to enroll your child in a model daycare center.

Even if it doesn't offer an onsite daycare program, your local college and university can provide you with leads on childcare. The staff of the career placement center may be able to put you in touch with recent graduates who are looking for work as in-home caregivers or give you an idea of which daycare centers and family daycare providers in the area are expanding their programs.

Educational community

Your child's teacher, principal, school superintendent, or parent-teacher association president may be able to assist you in your search for childcare—particularly after-school programs. Because these people are in constant contact with large numbers of parents, they are often well placed to tap into the childcare grapevine.

Large employers in your community

A growing number of large companies are building onsite daycare centers for the use of their employees. When vacancies are available, members of the community are often allowed to enroll their children at the center too. Workplace-based childcare usually is high quality. The types of companies that decide to offer onsite childcare are the ones with the means to do things right. Because their corporate image is on the line, they typically provide top

66

I was surprised how quickly our name moved up the waiting list at the daycare center at the local university. The rate of turnover is high because students graduate and move on, so my son's name moved to the top of the list much sooner than I thought it would. —Ann, mother of four

99

quality facilities for their employees' children. There are also liability issues involved in offering childcare services, so most companies ensure that whatever childcare services they are providing or endorsing are first rate.

Your local chamber of commerce

The staff of your local chamber of commerce can tell you about vacancies at local daycare centers or assist you in tracking down the contact information for the local family daycare network or nanny association.

Your human resources department at work

Unofficially . . .
The Massachusetts Bay Transportation Authority purchases childcare services from 32 different daycare centers to ensure that their employees obtain quality, affordable childcare.

Your human resources department can be an excellent source of assistance. Many companies maintain lists of agencies that specialize in finding in-home caregivers. Some companies retain the services of work and family consultants, who are available to assist employees in finding childcare. Others purchase spaces in daycare centers and make them available to employees at a reduced price.

The local employment office

Your city or state employment office can hook you up with caregivers who are looking for work. The only problem with posting a job listing with your local employment office is that you're likely to be flooded with responses from under-qualified candidates. To cut down on the number of responses, be as specific as possible about the experience and training you require and the salary range you're offering. You might also want to insist that interested candidates apply in writing—a guaranteed way to weed out the least qualified applicants.

Government offices

Your state or local childcare licensing authority can provide you with the names of daycare centers and family daycare providers in your area. They can also provide you with detailed information about licensing requirements that may prove invaluable as you go about evaluating your various options. They can also give you the scoop on any childcare subsidies that may be available to you.

Applications, restrictions, and waiting lists

While you're researching your options, you'll want to make sure you get the scoop on three words you would probably like to live without: applications, restrictions, and waiting lists.

Applications

Most daycare centers and family daycare providers require that you fill out an application form prior to entering care. In most cases, you will be asked to supply the following information:

- your child's legal name and his preferred name
- your child's gender
- your child's birth date (or your due date, if you are pregnant)
- your preferred month of enrollment
- whether you require care for any additional siblings (in which case you will be asked to complete a separate application form for each additional child)
- the days when you will require care
- your anticipated pickup and drop-off times

- the names and ages of your child's older siblings (so that your child's caregiver will know a bit about his family situation)

- the details about any previous childcare arrangements that your child has used (type of care arrangement, name and phone number of caregiver, reason for leaving)

- your marital status

- details about you and your partner's employment (place of employment, position, contact information at work, and so on)

- details about any custodial arrangements for your child (does your child live with you, your partner, or both of you)

66

I attached a page to the application form and wrote out everything I could think of about Tyler: his favorite songs and toys, his personality, his daily routine. The staff at the daycare center found this very helpful.
—Kathy, mother of two

99

You may also be asked to answer other questions to determine your eligibility for any special grants or subsidies (if you are employed by a particular organization, if your child has any special needs, if your household income falls below a certain level, and so on).

Many daycare centers and family daycare providers insist that the application form be accompanied with a fee ($25 and up) which is used to offset the administrative costs associated with your child's application. Some centers will even insist that you fill out an application form and pay a fee to have your name placed on their waiting list.

Restrictions

There are a number of different types of restrictions that could complicate your childcare search. Some relate to the age of your child; others concern the population that a particular daycare facility is mandated to serve.

Daycare centers and family daycare providers are licensed to provide care for a limited number of children belonging to a particular age range. This means that they have a restricted number of infant spaces, a certain number of toddler spaces, and so on. Because infant spaces are in short supply, daycare centers and family daycare providers offer these spaces to families who are already using their services before they make them available to the general public. This can make it extremely difficult to find a space for a first-born child. The odds of finding two infant spaces in the same licensed daycare facility are next to none, so parents of twins and triplets are often forced to send their babies to different daycare settings or to turn to the informal (and often unlicensed) world of daycare.

While age-related restrictions are a fact of life in most daycare centers and family daycare settings, certain daycare facilities operate under some additional restrictions:

- Some are mandated to allocate a certain percentage of spaces to children with special needs or from low-income families.

- Others—particularly worksite-based daycare centers—are in business to provide childcare to employees from a particular company only.

It's important to inquire about these types of restrictions before you get your heart set on a particular daycare center that may end up being, for all intents and purposes, off limits to you and your child.

Waiting Lists

The waiting lists for spaces in the best daycare centers or family daycare settings can be unbelievably

Moneysaver
Be sure to find out if your company provides childcare subsidies to its employees. Companies can go two routes when it comes to helping working parents: either building workplace-based daycare centers or purchasing a certain number of spaces in area daycare centers or family daycare settings and making these spaces available to their employees for a fraction of their usual cost.

long. It's important to get your name on the list as early as possible, even if it will be a few more months before you actually need childcare.

Unfortunately, getting your name on a waiting list early is no guarantee that a space will come up at the appropriate time. That's why you need to have a backup plan—or two—in place at all times.

Narrowing your options

After you've compiled a list of leads on daycare centers, family daycare providers, and in-home caregivers, you'll want to do some research to find out which ones are likely to pan out and which ones aren't.

Because personal interviews and visits can be incredibly time-consuming and stressful, it's important to eliminate options that won't meet your needs.

When you're researching a daycare center or family daycare setting, you should find out:

- what age(s) of children the daycare center or family daycare provider accepts

- whether there are any openings at this time and, if not, how long the waiting list is

- what the standard hours of operation are—and whether there's any flexibility concerning those hours

- what fees the daycare center or family daycare provider charges for infants, toddlers, and preschoolers

- whether the daycare center or family daycare provider accepts families who need part-time care and, if so, what types of fees these families can expect to pay

- where the daycare center or family daycare setting is located.

When you're making preliminary contact with a potential in-home caregiver, you should find out

- whether the caregiver is interested in caring for a baby, toddler, or preschooler (whatever the case may be)

- how soon she would be available to care for your children, and whether she would be prepared to commit to working for your family for one or more years

- what hours she is available to work—and whether there is any flexibility to those hours

- whether she is most interested in a live-in or live-out arrangement

- what her salary expectations are, and what benefits, if any, she is hoping for

- whether she would be willing to work less than full-time hours (assuming, of course, that this is an option for your family)

- whether she has her own transportation, or whether she would be relying on you to pick her up at the start of each working day or provide her with the use of a vehicle

Conducting this preliminary screening by phone will enable you to bring your total number of choices down to a manageable number.

Because you will be dealing with a lot of information, it's important to stay organized throughout the research process. Here are a few pointers on preventing information overload:

- Make photocopies of the out-of-home care checklist in Appendix B and use this checklist to record the details of your research.

Bright Idea
Find out about the childcare situation in your state by checking out the National Childcare Information Center Web site at http://ericps.crc.uiuc.edu/nccic/statepro.html.

■ Store your childcare checklists, center brochures, reference notes, and other childcare-
   related material in either a large three-ring
   binder or a series of file folders.

■ Date each item in your binder so that you can
   use your notes as a starting point for a subsequent childcare search.

Watch Out!
While it's impor-
tant for your
child to relate
well to his care-
giver, you need
to relate well
to her, too.
Otherwise small
differences in
childrearing
approaches can
quickly escalate
into major
conflicts.

If you still feel overwhelmed by the sheer quantity of the information you've gathered, boil down
each option to the few key points that matter most
to you: for example, how your child related to the
caregiver, whether the environment appeared to be
safe and stimulating, the hours of operation, the
fees, the location, and so on. Using this method to
evaluate your options will enable you to compare
apples to apples and hopefully help you to zero in
on the right choice for you and your child.

Making a decision that meets your needs

After you've finished conducting your research, it's
time to make your final decision. To assist you in
sorting through your various options, you might
want to use this simple method:

■ Make a chart. Across the top, list the names of
   the various daycare centers or family daycare
   providers you are evaluating. Down the side, list
   your criteria in order of importance (i.e., suitability of caregiver, location, cost, etc.)

■ Assign each center a number from one to ten
   that indicates how well it measures up to each of
   your criteria. If you feel more comfortable
   assigning letter grades, go for it.

■ Immediately eliminate any center that fails to
   meet your top three criteria.

- If you still have a large number of choices remaining, you'll need to evaluate their relative strengths and weaknesses to whittle down your choices to a more manageable number.

- You may be able to make your decision at this point; if not, make another unscheduled visit to each of your remaining choices and attempt to reach a final decision.

- If some of your top choices have waiting lists and you have the luxury of time, get on as many waiting lists as possible. You never know what spaces will be available when you need them.

If you're lucky, and I mean really lucky, when you sit down with your partner and talk about the various childcare options available to your child, your choice will be obvious.

A more likely scenario, however, is that you'll either disagree about which of the choices is best for your child, or you'll be discouraged by the fact that none of the caregivers that you've interviewed is ideal.

If you're faced with the first dilemma, you might find it helpful to pay a final visit to your two top choices—and to do so together. Try to be open-minded and listen to what your partner has to say about his or her top choice. Then, express yourself clearly (and as unemotionally as possible) as you, in turn, describe the merits of your top choice. Remember: The goal is not to win this particular battle; it's to come up with a decision that's best for your child.

A quick word of caution: It's easy to be turned off by little things that really have no bearing on the quality of care your child will receive. Maybe the secretary at the daycare center is obnoxious, or the

Bright Idea
When you're shopping around for childcare, look for a caregiver who's willing to commit to caring for your child for the long term. Studies have shown that young children will grieve the loss of a caregiver to whom they have become attached when the time comes to part ways.

kitchen of the family daycare home you visited could use a fresh coat of paint. Neither of these factors is likely to affect the number of cuddles or amount of stimulation your child receives, so do yourself a favor and stop sweating the small stuff.

You might even find yourself in the rather distressing position of not particularly liking your child's caregiver—but realize that she and your child are a match made in heaven. Once again, if it's a minor personality conflict between you and her and it's obvious your child adores her, you might want to consider whether you can live with your own reservations for the foreseeable future, if it means your child will be excited about going to daycare.

Just the facts

- Out-of-home childcare is more affordable than in-home childcare, but it's also less convenient. The size of your family, the age of your children, and your ideas about the merits of out-of-home childcare versus in-home childcare will influence your childcare choice.

- Start looking for childcare at least two months before you need it. You'll need to give yourself considerably more lead time if you are looking for space in an infant daycare center or if you plan to hire a nanny from a different country.

- Leave no stone unturned as you begin your search for childcare. Tell everyone you know what type of childcare arrangement you're seeking, and ask them to let you know of any suitable vacancies.

- Try to eliminate the least suitable alternatives right away so that you won't waste time researching childcare arrangements that aren't likely to pan out.

GET THE SCOOP ON...

What you can expect to pay for childcare ▪
Childcare costs versus a second income ▪
The economics of second and subsequent children ▪ What you need to know about government childcare subsidies ▪ What you need to
know about private childcare subsidies ▪ The
Child and Dependent Care Credit ▪
The Child Tax Credit ▪ The real cost of
"under the table" childcare

Chapter 3

And What It Costs

As you've no doubt gathered from talking with other parents, childcare doesn't come cheap. What you might not realize, however, is just how expensive it can get—particularly if you have more than one child. Consider the numbers for yourself:

- If your baby is cared for in a family daycare home, you can expect to pay approximately $420 per month for care—and considerably more if you live in an urban area.

- If she's cared for in a daycare center or at home by an au pair, the cost creeps up to about $500 per month (and that doesn't include the hidden costs of having an au pair, such as room and board).

- If she's cared for at home by an au pair, you can expect to pay approximately $500 per month (plus your au pair's room and board).

Timesaver
Wondering what childcare costs will do to your budget, but don't want to spend an entire day crunching numbers on your calculator? Swing by www.smartcalc.com/cgi-bin/smartcalc/BUD7.cgi/FinanCenter to find out what you can expect to pay to raise your child to age 18. The online calculator lets you to plug in your own figures or use the default values if you prefer.

- If she's cared for by an in-home caregiver without any specialized training in child development, you can expect to pay $850 or more per month.

- And if she's cared for by a professionally trained nanny, the cost skyrockets to an eye-popping $2,000 to $4,000 per month.

As you can see, childcare is a major expense for most American parents. It's also an area where you can't afford to cut corners.

In this chapter, the focus is on the financial side of childcare. I'll tell you what you can expect to pay for childcare in your community, whether it makes economic sense for you to work outside the home, and what having a second or subsequent child may do to your childcare budget. I'll also provide you with the lowdown on both government and private subsidies and tax breaks—hard-to-find information that no working parent should be without. Then I'll wrap up the chapter by telling you exactly why you can't afford to pay for childcare that's anything other than above board.

What you can expect to pay for childcare

Before I plunge into a detailed discussion of dollars and cents, you need to understand a few basic truths about childcare:

- Childcare is more expensive than you might think. It's likely to be one of your family's largest expenses—at least until your kids are ready for school.

- Childcare is more expensive in small rural communities, where it is in short supply, and large urban centers, where it is in peak demand.

- Childcare is pricier in the North and the East. While parents in Dallas get away with paying an average of $4,210 per year for full-time child-care for a three-year-old, parents in Boston end up cleaning out their wallets to the tune of $8,840 per year. According to the Children's Defense Fund—the source of these statistics— the corresponding figures for Boulder, CO, Oakland, CA, and Minneapolis, MN are $6,240, $6,500, and $6,030, respectively.

- Your childcare costs will be slightly higher for an infant or a toddler than for a preschooler or older child because of government regulations limiting the number of infants that can be cared for by a single individual.

- In-home childcare is generally the most expensive type of childcare available (unless you have a large family, in which case it can work out to be cheaper on a per child basis). You can expect to pay anything from minimum wage up, depending on the skill of your in-home caregiver.

- Live-in caregivers receive roughly the same monthly salary as live-out caregivers, except that you're also picking up the tab for room and board.

- There are almost as many hidden fees on your average childcare fee schedule as in your standard new car price quote. Late charges can clock in at a dollar a minute or more—reason enough to justify getting a speeding ticket on your way to pick up your child from care.

Out-of-home childcare options

Out-of-home childcare continues to be the more affordable option for most American families—but it's still anything but cheap. Let's consider what you might expect to pay for full-time childcare—per week—in your typical daycare center or family daycare setting for children of various ages (see Table 3.1).

TABLE 3.1: WHAT YOU CAN EXPECT TO PAY

	Daycare Center	Family Daycare Setting
Infants	$125	$105
Toddlers	$110	$90
Preschoolers	$90	$75

If you think that working part-time is going to put a lot of money back in your pocket, think again. While working part-time will help to reduce your overall costs, the daily or hourly childcare rates go through the roof.

Confused?

Let me explain.

If you're looking for part-time care, you can expect to pay approximately $30 per day for an infant, $28 per day for a toddler, and $24 per day for a preschooler. If you're paying by the hour, however, you should expect to hand over $5.50 per hour for an infant, $5.00 per hour for a toddler, and $4.50 per hour for a preschooler. Half-day preschool programs come in at around $15 per day. The reason for the discrepancy is obvious. The daycare provider may not be able to line up another family to pay for the days or hours when your child is absent from care. Because many daycare centers and family daycare homes are, at best, break-even ventures, they need to charge their part-timers a slightly higher rate to make up for the fact that they aren't full-time users of the service.

The only tried-and-true method of reducing your part-time costs is to find another family who is willing to split daycare space with you. If you use the space Monday, Wednesday, and Friday, and they use the space Tuesday and Thursday, the daycare center or family daycare provider's financial woes are lessened. While you may still have to pay a small administrative fee for doubling the director or provider's paperwork, you're less likely to be hit with the type of part-time rates that you could otherwise expect to pay.

Just a few more words of wisdom before I move on: Don't even think about signing a childcare contract until you've figured out whether you qualify for any special discounts. A number of daycare centers and family daycare providers offer special discounts to families with more than one child. At the Penn State University Childcare Center, for example, parents are entitled to a 25 percent discount on the fees of their older child if two children are enrolled and a 30 percent discount if three or more children are enrolled. Other centers offer discounts to employees of certain companies or members of certain community organizations. If your local YMCA operates a daycare center, for example, your membership at the gym could be your ticket to considerable savings on daycare.

In-home care options

Professionally trained nannies are the most expensive type of in-home caregiver—but are worth every penny, if you're lucky enough to get a good one. Their fees range from $2,000 to $4,000 per month (plus room and board, if applicable). Many will also

Moneysaver
Find out whether your company is willing to reimburse you for any overnight childcare expenses incurred while you are away on a business trip. A growing number of companies are offering this benefit to employees who travel frequently for work-related reasons.

expect you to provide them with a car allowance or the use of the family vehicle—an issue I discuss further in Chapter 9.

Au pairs provide up to 45 hours of childcare per week. On top of room and board, they generally receive approximately $115 to $125 per week. That's not the whole picture, however: Families are also responsible for paying $500 per year toward an au pair's tuition costs and $3,950 to participate in the program—a fee that covers recruitment expenses, air transportation, training, insurance, and support from a community counsellor.

Full-time caregivers without any specialized training in early childhood education receive minimum wage (although they can demand more in areas where in-home services are in particularly short supply).

Because wages vary widely from state to state and even community to community, it's important to find out the going rate for childcare in your area before you talk salary with your caregiver. Otherwise you could risk losing out on a top calibre caregiver just because you're unaware of what good childcare is really worth.

If you want to find out more about childcare costs, check *"What Does It Cost to Mind Our Preschoolers?"* a Census Bureau report that is available online at www.census.gov/population/www/socdemo/child/p7053.html. The report, which analyzes childcare fee information collected in the fall of 1993, is also available for purchase by calling the Bureau of the Census' Population Division at (301) 457-2422.

> **"**
> We called the state employment office to find out what the going rate for nannies was in our community. In the end, we decided to offer slightly more than the going rate in the hope of attracting a better calibre of candidate.
> —Jennifer, mother of one
> **"**

Childcare costs versus a second income

Because childcare is a significant cost for most families (in most cases surpassed only by car payments, the grocery bill, and the mortgage), many families decide that it doesn't make economic sense for both parents to work.

Wondering what the bottom line looks like for your family? Pull out your pencil and do some number crunching for a moment.

Estimate how much you spend on the following items each month while you are working outside the home:

> Clothing (suits, dresses, shoes, purses, boots, coats)_____
> Transportation: the cost of a monthly public transit pass or of keeping a second car on the road (loan or lease payments, automobile insurance, gas, repairs) _____
> Lunches out _____
> Convenience foods (because you're too tired to cook) _____
> Miscellaneous (shower gifts and birthday cards for co-workers) _____
> Childcare _____

Total A _____

Watch Out!
Don't forget to factor in the cost of parking. In some metropolitan areas, $10–$20 per day is the norm.

Now go through those same items again, and consider how much money you would save if you didn't have to go out to work.

> Clothing (casual wear versus formal wear) _____
> Transportation (Would you need a second car if you weren't working?)_____
> Lunches out _____
> Convenience foods _____
> Miscellaneous _____
> Childcare _____

Total B _____

If the only reason people worked was sheer economics, your decision about whether to work outside the home would be pretty clear cut: If the difference between Total A and Total B is bigger than your salary, you would stay home, and vice versa.

Your reasons for working outside the home while your children are young may go far beyond economics. You may choose to continue working because you find your work personally fulfilling or because you're in a profession where it's difficult to take a couple of years off (if you're self-employed, the vice-president of a large corporation, or a doctor with a busy medical practice, for example).

In this case, you may decide it's worthwhile to continue to work outside the home, even if your childcare and other work-related expenses mean that you're working for minimum wage at best, or even losing money. After all, your years of paying for full-time childcare are relatively few.

The economics of second and subsequent children

You'll notice that whoever said two could live as cheaply as one didn't try to stretch it to three, four, or five. As you've no doubt discovered by now, having children is anything but a money-making venture.

Fortunately, it's not all bad news for parents who choose to have more than one child. Certain types of childcare are less expensive on a per-child basis once you have two or more children.

Unfortunately, you're not likely to see a lot of savings when it comes to out-of-home childcare: Most family daycare providers and daycare centers offer only a minimal discount to families with more than one child—assuming they offer any type of discount at all.

Where you can make your large family pay off is in the in-home childcare market. While you'll probably want to pay your in-home caregiver more to care for three young children rather than just one, it's unlikely you'll triple her salary. As a result, the cost of paying for her services becomes downright affordable when you consider it on a per-child basis. What's more, there are other benefits to be gained from this arrangement—the kind you can't put in the bank. I'll discuss the benefits of in-home care later in this book.

There's just one small caveat. If your number comes up in the reproductive lottery, as the McCaughey's did when they conceived their famous septuplets, you're still going to be looking at some fairly significant childcare expenses. Not only would it be cruel and unusual punishment to leave a single caregiver with seven infants, it's also downright illegal.

Bright Idea
Ask your employer if he or she would be willing to pay for a caregiver to come to your house to care for your sick child if doing so would enable you to make it in to work. A surprising number of companies are happy to fork over the big bucks to keep key employees on the job whenever possible.

What you need to know about government childcare subsidies

If the number crunching exercise that you did a little earlier made you painfully aware of how big a chunk your childcare costs are going to eat out of your family budget, you might want to investigate what childcare subsidies—if any—you might be eligible for in your state.

The truth about childcare subsidies

Childcare subsidies are funds that help families to pay at least a portion of the cost of childcare. Unfortunately, there are only enough funds to

Moneysaver
To find out what childcare subsidies might be available to you, contact either your local Child Care Resource and Referral Agency (CCRRA) or your state childcare administration. (You can find the contact information for both your local CCRRA and your state childcare authority in Appendix B or you can call Child Care Aware at 1-800-424-2246.)

provide government childcare subsidies to 10 percent of children who qualify for them. At last count, there were 100,000 children in 38 states on waiting lists for subsidized childcare.

What this means is that you might be surviving on an income below the poverty line and still not qualify for a childcare subsidy. Families who find themselves in this situation often feel like they're caught between a rock and a hard place: They're too poor to afford to pay for childcare on their own, but too well off in the eyes of some government bureaucracies.

Now that I've spilled the beans about the shortage of subsidy money, let's talk about what you have to do to be considered for the funds that are available.

Because there are so few dollars to go around, you will be asked to fill out an application to assess the extent of your need. In most cases, the following criteria are used to determine eligibility:

- income and family size (families must meet the low income guidelines established by each state)

- reason for requiring care (the parent or primary caregiver must be either working, attending an approved educational activity or job training program, seeking work, or ill or incapacitated)

- age of the child (the child requiring childcare must be six weeks to 12 years of age or, if older, either disabled or under court supervision)

To apply for a childcare subsidy, you must complete an application form and submit the appropriate documentation (typically pay stubs or your most recent tax return) to substantiate the financial information which you are providing.

Most programs operate on the basis of a sliding scale based on income and family size. As a result, you may be required to pay part of the cost.

Most programs let parents make their own out-of-home or in-home childcare arrangements. If this is the case in your state, you should expect the state subsidy-granting body to scrutinize your childcare arrangement to ensure that it is above-board (that is, that the caregiver is declaring the income) and that the provider is meeting state health and safety requirements.

If your application for a subsidy is approved, you will receive a voucher or certificate indicating that the child is eligible for a subsidized childcare payment and notifying the provider of the hours care is required and the portion of the fee (the parent co-payment) for which you are personally responsible.

Your case will be reviewed on a regular basis (typically every six months) to determine whether you still qualify for a childcare subsidy. You are required to notify the subsidy office if your situation changes at any time. For example, if you:

- stop working
- go on medical leave, maternity leave, sick leave, or personal leave
- change jobs
- change hours of employment
- return to school
- have an increase or decrease in family size
- change care providers

Government-funded early childhood education programs

Unofficially...
While there used to be a variety of federal programs designed to provide funding for childcare, all federal childcare dollars are now being channeled through a single program—under an amendment to the Childcare and Development Block Grant (CCDBG) Act of 1990. You can find more details on childcare subsidies at the Childcare Bureau Web site: www.acf.dhhs.gov/programs/ccb/policy/index.htm.

The federal government, through the states, provides funding to a series of programs designed to give low-income or otherwise disadvantaged children the best possible start in life. The best known of these programs are Head Start (for three- to five-year-olds) and Early Head Start (for younger children). You can find the contact information for Head Start and Early Head Start in Appendix B. If your family meets the income criteria and there is space available in one of these programs, you will not have to pay to have your child participate in one of these programs. Your state licensing office can tell you about the eligibility requirements in your state. (See Appendix B.)

Note: Some Head Start and Early Head Start programs are offered only on a half-day basis during the school year. If this is the case and you're relying on this type of childcare to go to work or school, you'll need to obtain a childcare subsidy to pay for the remaining hours of care that your child requires. Ask your state licensing office what subsidies are available to families requiring "wrap-around care" (the term used to describe care before or after a half-day preschool program).

What you need to know about private childcare subsidies

The government isn't the only source of childcare subsidies. There are a number of private sources of childcare dollars. Be sure to ask your local Child Care Resource and Referral Agency to let you know if you are eligible to apply for any of the following types of private funding.

Employer-run programs

A growing number of employers are getting into the childcare subsidy business. Many contribute to Dependent Care Assistance Plans (DCAPs) on their employees behalf, thereby providing a valuable non-taxable benefit.

You probably know all about DCAPs, but just in case you've forgotten a few of the details, let's quickly review how the plans work.

Section 129 of the Internal Revenue Code lets employers provide care in a company-sponsored daycare center or to pay all or a portion of the cost of a childcare arrangement chosen by the employee. To qualify under Section 129, these programs must be seen as nondiscriminatory. In other words, they must be open to all employees.

Your employer can set up a DCAP for you if you have:

- a child aged 13 or under who is listed as a dependent on your tax return

- an older child who is physically or mentally unable to care for himself/herself, regardless of age

- a child who is named as your dependent in a divorce decree

You can still take advantage of the benefits of a DCAP, even if your employer isn't prepared to kick in any money. A Salary Redirection DCAP—a plan set up on your behalf by your employer—allows you to set aside as much as $5,000 in pretax earnings in a special account that is used to cover dependent care expenses such as childcare. If you earn more than $20,000 per year, establishing a Salary Redirection DCAP could reduce the amount of tax

Watch Out!
Once the money comes off your paycheck and is deposited in your DCAP, you can't get it back. You use it or you lose it, period.

that you and your employer have to pay on your earnings.

Some companies provide other types of childcare subsidies, like childcare vouchers or reimbursements. Employees of Levi Strauss and Company, for example, receive childcare vouchers worth up to 50 percent of their childcare costs each month (to a maximum of $100 per month per child). The vouchers may be used to purchase any legal form of childcare for a child under the age of 13.

Under a voucher or reimbursement program, your employer reimburses you for all or a portion of your childcare costs. Reimbursement under such a program is typically based on a:

- percentage of the total childcare cost
- sliding scale that is linked to your income
- flat fee that is offered to all participating employees

In some cases, employers pay the provider of your choice directly rather than continuously reimbursing you for fees you have paid to her already.

Other employers subsidize childcare in less direct ways by purchasing a set number of childcare spaces at a daycare center and then making these spaces available to employees at reduced rates. It's a relatively inexpensive way for a company to show its support on the childcare front, and one that you might consider suggesting to your employer if such a program is not already in place.

Union/management-run programs

Be sure to find out if there's a union/management childcare fund in place in your workplace. Applications to such funds are reviewed by a joint management-union committee which distributes the funds, tax-free, to individuals in financial need. In New York City, for example, the 1199/Employer Child Care Fund provides funds to members of Local 1199 of the National Health and Human Services Employees Union. Over $7.9 million was contributed by the Fund's 147 member employers in 1996. A similar initiative, the New York State Labor/Management Child Care Advisory Committee, provides grants to state employees who need help paying for childcare. Both programs also invest in daycare centers and take other measures designed to improve the quality of childcare in their communities.

University or college-run programs

If you're a student, you might be able to get some help in paying your childcare fees from your college or university. In recognition of the fact that it can be very difficult to pay your way through school and cough up a significant amount of money for childcare expenses at the same time, a growing number of colleges and universities are offering childcare subsidies to needy students. The childcare subsidy program at the University of Michigan, for example, provides approximately $150,000 in subsidies each year to students with childcare expenses. The money is drawn from two sources: the school's general revenues and a special $1-per-term student fee. If you want to apply for aid under these types of programs, you are asked to complete an application, file a Free Application for Federal Student Aid (FAFSA), and submit copies of your previous year's tax return.

Charitable organizations

Certain philanthropic individuals across the country have set aside pools of money that are specifically designated to help low-income families defray at least a portion of their childcare costs.

The Child Care Scholarship Fund of the Marin Community Foundation in Marin County, California, for example, provides financial assistance to low- and moderate-income families. The fund was originally designed to help Marin families whose incomes exceeded the eligibility limits for state childcare subsidies, but who nonetheless found themselves unable to afford childcare. Over time, the program was extended to low-income families as well. At last report, the upper-income limits ranged from $35,000 for a family of two to $40,000 for a family of four or more.

Once again, the best way to get the scoop on these types of programs is to contact your local Child Care Resource and Referral Agency.

Other programs

You may be eligible for childcare subsidies or discounts by virtue of being a member of a particular group such as an alumni association. Graduates of Penn State University, for example, are entitled to a reduction in childcare fees at any of the university's onsite daycare facilities.

Child and Dependent Care Credit

Even if you're not eligible for a childcare subsidy through a federal or state government program or a private source, you may be eligible to take advantage of the Child and Dependent Care Credit on your income tax. (You can find out more at the IRS Web site: www.IRS.gov.) To be eligible for the credit, you must pay someone to care for your dependent under age 13 so that you can either work or look for work. Depending on your income level, the credit can be worth up to 30 percent of your expenses.

Are you eligible?

To be eligible to claim the credit for Child and Dependent Care expenses, you must meet all of the following tests and file either Form 1040 or Form 1040A (not Form 1040EZ):

- The care must be for one or more qualifying persons (children under the age of 13 or older children who are disabled).

- You and your spouse (if you are married) must share your home with the qualifying person or persons and be personally responsible for the costs of keeping up the home (property taxes, mortgage interest, rent utility charges, and so on). If you receive funding from the state (Aid to Families with Dependent Children) that constitutes more than half the cost of keeping up your home, you are not eligible for the Child and Dependent Care Credit. If, however, you share a home with another family, the living spaces of the two families are treated as separate households, so you only have to worry about whether you are providing half (or more) of the funds required to keep up your part of the home.

- You and your spouse (if you are married) must have earned income during the year. (There are exceptions for students and for families in which one or more of the parents was unable to care for himself/herself.)

- You must be paying childcare expenses to enable yourself (and/or your spouse, if you are married) to work or look for work.

- You must make payments for child and dependent care to someone you (or your spouse) cannot claim as a dependent. This means that

Moneysaver
Canadians are also able to deduct certain childcare-related expenses from their income. For details on the tax breaks available to Canadian parents, call Revenue Canada at 1-800-959-5525 or visit the Revenue Canada Web site at www.rc.gc.ca.

Timesaver
You can obtain the tax forms and guides you'll need to take advantage of the Child and Dependent Care Credit by calling the IRS at 1-800-424-FORM or downloading them from the IRS Web site at www.irs.ustreas.gov.

you are free to purchase childcare services from relatives who are not your dependents. Note: If you are claiming expenses paid to a daycare center, the center must meet all applicable state and local regulations.

▪ Your filing status must be one of the following: single, head of household, qualifying widow(er) with dependent child, or married filing jointly. You must file a joint return if you are married, unless you are legally separated or living apart. (It's actually a bit more complicated than that, so call your local IRS office for details if you and your spouse are living apart.)

▪ You must identify the caregiver on your tax return. You're required to provide the name, address, and taxpayer identification number for anyone who cared for your child during the year. If the caregiver is an individual, the taxpayer identification number is her social security number or individual taxpayer identification number. If the care provider is an organization, then you need to provide the employer identification number (EIN). You don't, however, have to provide the taxpayer identification number if the organization providing care is one of certain tax-exempt organizations (a church or a school). In this case, you write "tax-exempt" on the form. If you are unable to provide all of the information required about your caregiver, you must prove to the government that you exercised "due diligence" in trying to obtain the necessary information.

▪ You must exclude less than $2,400 (less than $4,800 if two or more qualifying persons were cared for) of dependent care assistance benefits provided by your employer or insurance company.

How to calculate the credit

The credit that you are eligible to receive is a percentage of your work-related expenses paid during a given tax year. Regardless of how much you paid out in expenses, however, you cannot receive more than $2,400 for one child (or $4,800 for two or more children).

To determine the amount of your credit, multiply your total eligible work-related expenses by the percentage that applies to your income bracket (see Table 3.2).

TABLE 3.2: CHILD AND DEPENDENT CARE CREDIT

$0–$10,000	30%
$10,000–$12,000	29%
$12,000–$14,000	28%
$14,000–$16,000	27%
$16,000–$18,000	26%
$18,000–$20,000	25%
$20,000–$22,000	24%
$22,000–$24,000	23%
$24,000–$26,000	22%
$26,000–$28,000	21%
$28,000–no limit	20%

How to claim the credit

To claim the Child and Dependent Care Credit, you must file a tax return by using either Form 1040 or Form 1040A. (You can't use Form 1040EZ.)

■ If you use a Form 1040, you will need to complete and attach Form 2441.

Moneysaver
If you received dependent care benefits from your employer, you may be able to use the Child and Dependent Care Credit to exclude all or part of them from your income. Dependent care benefits include:

▪ money your employer pays directly to either you or your care provider for the care of your child while you are working

▪ the fair market value of care in a daycare facility that is provided or sponsored by your employer

If you received dependent care benefits, they should be shown in box 10 of your Form W-2.

▪ If you use a Form 1040A, you must complete Schedule 2 (Form 1040A) and attach it to your form.

Before you spend an evening knocking back coffee and wading through tax forms, you should probably read the fine print on this particular credit: Your tax credit for child and dependent care expenses cannot be more than the amount of your tax liability. In other words, you cannot get a refund for any part of the credit that is more than the tax you owe to the government.

Child Tax Credit

While it's not specifically tied to childcare expenses, the new Child Tax Credit (introduced under the Taxpayer Relief Act of 1997) may help you to put a bit of extra cash in your pocket. Beginning in 1998, there will be a $400 tax credit for each child under the age of 17. The credit will increase to $500 per child in 1999. The credit is phased out at higher income levels, beginning at $75,000 for single income families and $110,000 for dual working couples. Don't miss out on the tax credit by failing to provide the IRS with all the information it needs. You must provide Social Security numbers for all dependent children who are being claimed as dependents, including those born at the end of the tax year.

Some states offer additional tax incentives as well. Because the situation is tremendously complex and constantly changing, you should consult with your local tax office to get the latest scoop on childcare related credits. If, however, you want to do a bit of homework before you pick up the phone to make that call, you can get the lowdown on childcare tax

credits for your state by surfing over to www.
pewtrusts.com/docs/childcare/child0155.html.

Now it's time to move on to the stickiest financial issue of all—paying your caregiver under the table!

"Above board" versus "under the table" childcare payments

There's no question about it: Childcare costs money—and plenty of it. Because it's a significant budget item for most families, some succumb to the temptation to pay a caregiver under the table—typically for less than minimum wage.

While this initially may seem to be a good way to cut down on your childcare expenses, it's a strategy that could end up costing you dearly in the long run.

Here are just a few of the implications worth considering:

■ You could find yourself in hot water with the IRS.

Even if you and your caregiver agree that you will not be making Social Security, Medicare, and FUTA payments (where applicable) on her behalf, you're still legally required to make them. If you have a falling out a few years down the line and she reports on you to the IRS, you could be required to make up these payments out of your own pocket.

■ You could get yourself in trouble with the INS.

The U.S. Immigration and Naturalization Service (INS) levies stiff penalties on those who employ people who aren't legally entitled to work in the United States. Perhaps the reason

Watch Out!
The Child and Dependent Care Credit can only be claimed for childcare that is employment-related. Trying to claim your babysitting expenses for a night at the movies with your partner is definitely out—unless, of course, you're both film industry moguls.

your caregiver wants to be paid under the table is because she's an illegal alien.

- You could end up shooting yourself in the foot at tax time.

You aren't eligible for the Child and Dependent Care Credit on your tax return unless you provide full information about your caregiver—something you won't be able to do if you don't have any receipts. Depending on your tax bracket, this lost credit could end up costing you a significant amount of money.

- You could end up losing everything.

If these other scenarios weren't enough to scare the dickens out of you, surely this one will. If you don't carry Workers' Compensation or appropriate automobile insurance coverage on your illegal caregiver, you could leave your family open to lawsuits from your caregiver and anyone else she happens to injure while on the job. Just think of the devastating consequences if a neighbor's child happened to drown in your swimming pool while under the supervision of your caregiver.

The bottom line? Most families feel that peace of mind alone justifies their decision to keep their childcare situation above board. So, unless you're feeling particularly lucky, you're better off not playing caregiver roulette.

Just the facts

- It's important to do some research and find out what the going rate for childcare is in your community.

- The high cost of childcare may cancel any financial advantages to having a second income.

- While in-home childcare is an expensive option if you only have one child, it becomes increasingly affordable on a per-child basis if you have two or more children.

- You can find out about government and privately funded childcare subsidies by contacting your local Childcare Resource and Referral Agency.

- Don't forget to take advantage of the Child and Dependent Care Credit—an income tax credit designed to compensate you for a portion of the money you spend on childcare—and the Child Tax Credit—an income tax credit that works on a sliding scale percentage that is tied to income.

- While you might be tempted to pay your caregiver cash under the table rather than asking for receipts, you could find yourself in trouble with the immigration and tax authorities. It's not worth the risk.

The Truth About
Out-of-Home Childcare

PART II

A Bird's-Eye View of Your Out-of-Home Childcare Options

Nearly half of American babies, toddlers, and preschoolers spend their days being cared for in a place other than their own homes. According to a recent *ABC News* report, approximately 30 percent spend their days at daycare centers and 16 percent more are cared for by family daycare providers in their own homes.

In some of these settings, children receive excellent care.

In others, care is so inadequate as to cause harm.

The majority of American children, however, receive care that falls somewhere in the middle— neither particularly good nor terribly bad, but certainly not good enough.

Unfortunately, there are no easy solutions to America's childcare crisis. Until we as a society decide to raise the childcare bar a little higher, the onus for finding suitable childcare arrangements will continue to rest on the shoulders of individual parents.

The purpose of this chapter—and the one that follows—is to arm you with all the tools you'll need to come up with the best childcare options for you and your family. You'll find updates on the latest childcare-related research, the inside scoop on what happens during a typical day at a daycare center, and a crash course in the childcare-related buzz words that every working parent needs to know.

The pros and cons of each type of out-of-home childcare

Before I get into the real nuts and bolts discussion, let's start out by quickly reviewing the basic advantages and disadvantages of the three most common types of out-of-home childcare: daycare centers, nursery schools, and family daycare settings (also referred to as family daycare homes or family daycare environments).

Just to refresh your memory: Daycare centers are facilities that offer childcare to a large number of children (usually over 20); nursery schools (or preschools) are typically half-day programs that run between September and June, and family daycare settings are home-based businesses that provide care to a relatively small number of children in the childcare provider's own home.

Daycare centers
Pros:

- Daycare centers provide reliable care. You can count on the fact that someone will be available to care for your child, even if your child's own caregiver is ill.

- They are usually regulated and inspected to ensure that basic health and safety requirements are met. Because these standards are minimal at best, you'll want to use other, more rigorous criteria when you conduct your own daycare center evaluations. See Chapter 5.

- They often employ staff who have had specialized training in child development. Because such training is not mandatory in all parts of the country, however, it's important to ask about staff credentials when you're considering a particular daycare center.

- They can offer your child a greater variety of educational materials or facilities than either an in-home caregiver or family daycare provider can offer. Once again, there's tremendous variation between daycare centers, so you'll want to consider this point as you conduct your evaluations.

Cons:

- It can be difficult to find a space in a daycare center, particularly if you're looking for care for an infant or toddler. If you live in a small or rural community, you might not have access to a daycare center.

- Your child will be exposed to more children—and consequently more illnesses—than she would encounter in either an in-home or family daycare environment.

- Staff turnover can be a particular problem in daycare centers. Your child's caregiver may move to another group within the center or leave her position at the center altogether.

Bright Idea
When you're evaluating daycare centers, be sure to inquire about each center's sick policies. You want to find a center whose policies are stringent enough to ensure that the sickest of children are cared for elsewhere, but that aren't so rigid that you're expected to take time off work each time your child has a runny nose.

- If the daycare center has especially rigid age-based groupings, your child could find herself being shuffled from caregiver to caregiver every couple of months.

- Your child may be expected to fit into the day-care center's routines rather than having her own schedule for eating, sleeping, and so on, accommodated. This will be of particular concern to you if your child is very young or has an erratic schedule. As a rule of thumb, the best daycare centers are child-driven, not teacher-driven. In other words, they allow the children in their care to set the pace, not vice versa.

- The center's hours are often inflexible. If they mesh with your working hours, terrific; if they don't, well, you're out of luck.

- Center-based care is the most expensive type of out-of-home care. If you're looking for care for more than one child, it may be out of your price range.

Nursery schools

Pros:

- Nursery schools seek to provide enriching environments that are designed to stimulate young children and provide them with opportunities for socialization. Initially designed to accommodate the children of well-to-do stay-at-home moms, they are one of the more elite (pricier on a per-hour basis) types of childcare.

- No matter what your childrearing philosophy may be, you can probably find a nursery school that accommodates it.

Moneysaver
If you like a particular daycare center but feel that its fees are out of your price range, ask if you could barter a skill or service (bookkeeping, painting, or plumbing, for example) in exchange for a portion of your child's fees.

Cons:

- Nursery school programs are almost always offered on a part-time basis—something that limits their usefulness to working parents. They also close up shop during the summer months.

- Most nursery schools are only licensed to accept children between the ages of two and five. That rules them out as a childcare option for many families.

- Many nursery schools insist that the children in their care be toilet-trained—a policy that prevents many two- and three-year-olds from attending.

- Not all nursery school programs are operated by fully trained professionals.

Family daycare settings

Pros:

- Family daycare settings offer a familylike atmosphere that many parents consider ideal for infants and toddlers.

- Because children of different ages can be accommodated in a single family daycare setting, it is possible for siblings to share the same caregiver. Some family daycare providers encourage such arrangements by offering discounts to second and subsequent children from the same family. Just don't expect these discounts to be too deep. Childcare providers make meager enough wages as it is.

- Your child's routines are more likely to be respected in a family daycare setting where the group is small, rather than in a large institutional setting. This is an important

Unofficially . . .
Studies have shown that children in small groups receive more attention from their caregivers than children in larger groups. Caregivers in smaller groups are more actively involved with the children in their care. As a result, children in smaller groups are often more verbal, more involved in activities, and less aggressive than those in larger groups. Consequently, they are able to make greater gains in standardized tests and vocabulary than children who are cared for in larger groups.

consideration if your child is very young or has yet to settle into a predictable schedule.

- There is likely to be more flexibility concerning the hours of care than you will find at a daycare center. What's more, some family daycare providers have moderately liberal policies concerning sick children, something that may be important to you if your child is prone to recurrent ear infections.

- Family daycare is the least expensive type of out-of-home care and often the easiest type of care to find.

Cons:

- You can always find "illegal" family daycare—even in states that require licensing. The onus is on you to find out whether a particular family daycare provider is in full compliance with state regulations. At the very least, you should insist on seeing a copy of the license.

- Family daycare providers are less likely to have had specialized training in child development than their center-based counterparts. This is not to say that they offer inferior care; many family daycare providers are highly experienced caregivers who have raised children of their own. Still, they may lack the background in child development that some of their more highly trained center-based counterparts may possess.

- A family daycare setting may not have as much of the costly equipment and elaborate facilities that are more commonly found in large daycare centers. This may or may not be an issue, depending on the age, interests, and abilities of your child.

- Your caregiver might not have a backup lined up to replace her in the event that she becomes ill, takes holidays, or requires time off to have a baby or deal with a family emergency. Even if she does have some sort of plan in place, you might not like her backup caregiver.

- It can be difficult to find family daycare for more than one child. State legislation limits the number and ages of children who are cared for by a single caregiver.

As you can see, there are definite advantages and disadvantages to each type of out-of-home care. The needs of your family will help you to decide which option is best for your child.

What the experts are saying about kids and out-of-home care

Now that you've taken some time to weigh the pros and cons of your various out-of-home childcare options, you're probably wondering what the experts are saying these days about out-of-home care.

It wasn't all that long ago that childcare in general got an unreservedly bad rap. Remember? Only bad mothers returned to work while their children were young. The good mothers stayed at home to bake chocolate chip cookies.

While society quietly tolerated nannies and other in-home caregivers when large numbers of women with young children began entering the workforce in the 1970s, it was much less accepting of daycare centers, painting them as cold, institutional places where children received impersonal, assembly-line care.

Watch Out!
Be sure to find out whether the number of children being cared for by your child's provider will fluctuate over the course of the day. Some caregivers attempt to pick up a little extra cash by caring for additional children after school. If this is the case with your child's caregiver, make sure that the total number of children in her care never exceeds the legal maximum.

In recent years, researchers have devoted considerable energies to investigating the long term effects of childcare—particularly out-of-home care. Time and time again they have concluded that good childcare is good for children and bad childcare is, well, bad for them.

Let's take a moment to highlight a few of the more significant findings about the effects of out-of-home childcare on children:

- **Opportunities for socialization:** Children who are cared for in out-of-home childcare arrangements are exposed to more people, experiences, and ideas than those who are cared for in their own homes. A recent study at the University of Miami concluded that children in high quality out-of-home childcare arrangements not only learn to get along with others, they also develop leadership abilities and a strong sense of their own worth.

- **Improved cognitive and language abilities:** Studies have shown that children who benefit from high quality out-of-home childcare have superior cognitive and language abilities and are more likely to stay in high school than children who have not benefited from similarly high quality childcare arrangements. A study conducted by the University of North Carolina at Chapel Hill revealed that eight-year-olds who had attended preschool scored ten points higher on standardized reading tests and about five points higher on standardized math tests as compared to children who had not benefited from this type of early childhood education experience.

■ **Maternal-infant attachments:** A recent study by the National Institute of Child Health and Human Development concluded that placing an infant in out-of-home childcare does not jeopardize the mother-child bond unless the child receives poor quality care, spends an extensive amount of time in childcare, frequently changes caregivers, and does not receive much care or attention from her parent during the parent's nonworking hours.

While these findings about the benefits of out-of-home childcare are obviously good news for working parents, there is a dark side, unfortunately. High quality childcare arrangements are in extremely short supply.

A 1995 study conducted by researchers at the University of Colorado in Denver, the University of California at Los Angeles, the University of North Carolina at Chapel Hill, and Yale University in New Haven, Connecticut, ranked just one in seven day-care centers as "good." The researchers rated the care in most of the other settings as poor to mediocre, and concluded that 40 percent of infants and toddlers were receiving inadequate care. Debbie Cryer, one of the principal investigators for the study, recently told journalist Sandi Kahn Shelton that the study's results should serve as a wake-up call for America. "The study is not saying that putting children in childcare is harmful. It's saying that parents have to become better-informed consumers, and that society has to support quality childcare more than it does now."

An earlier study by the Families and Work Institute reported similar findings. The researchers in that study concluded that 14 percent of children

Unofficially . . . Researchers at the National Institute of Child Health recently concluded that the amount of time spent in out-of-home childcare affects boys and girls differently. Spending more than 30 hours a week at childcare makes girls feel more secure but boys feel less secure. Clearly, the differences between the sexes kick in at a very early age.

in regulated family daycare settings and 50 percent of children in unregulated family daycare receive care that can best be described as inadequate. That's why you owe it to your children—and yourself—to shop around to find the best childcare arrangement possible.

Now before you allow your guilt-o-meter to go off the scale and start beating up yourself about your decision to put your child in the care of another person, here are some reassuring words. A study conducted by Massachusetts Mutual Life Insurance indicated that 80 percent of 15 to 31 year olds whose mothers worked outside the home during their growing up years approved of their mothers' decisions to work. What's more, almost all stated that they plan to continue working after they have children of their own. So, perhaps the experts protest too much.

What a typical day at a daycare center is really like

Given what you've just read about the advantages and disadvantages of out-of-home care, you're probably wondering what the out-of-home daycare experience is like for most children.

Over the next few pages, I'll give you a behind-the-scenes look at what a typical day in daycare is like for both a baby and a toddler or preschooler. Along the way, I'll point out what you might expect to encounter in both a top quality and poor quality daycare environment.

What a typical day at a daycare center is like for a baby

As you've no doubt gathered by now, the baby who sticks to a strict schedule is anything but ordinary.

The majority of babies have not yet read *What To Expect the First Year,* and so they honestly don't know how to behave. As a result, the best daycare environments are those that respect this basic fact of babyhood and work around—rather than against—each child's individual need for food, sleep, and stimulation.

A typical day at a daycare center for a baby looks something like this:

7:00 a.m. to 9:00 a.m. Drop off time. Parents and babies are greeted by each child's own caregiver at the daycare center. The caregiver takes the baby from the parent and makes an effort to engage the baby in an activity so that the parent is free to make his or her exit at the appropriate time. At better quality daycare cemters and family daycare settings, the parent and the caregiver take a few minutes to exchange important information, like how long the baby slept the night before, whether she has been more hungry or less hungry than usual, whether any new developmental milestones have been achieved, and so on. At poorer quality daycare centers and family daycare settings, the caregiver either seems rushed or distracted because she has too many children in her care.

9:00 a.m. to 5:00 p.m. The daycare program: In better quality daycare environments, babies are fed by bottle, cup, or spoon whenever they are hungry. They are never left unattended while they are eating. When they are tired, they are soothed to sleep and allowed to nap for as little or long as they need. When they are awake, their caregivers give them all the attention they deserve. Babies are given the opportunity to play in a variety of different positions (on their tummies, on their backs, and in a sitting up position) so they can develop all of their muscle groups. In poorer quality environments, babies are forced to eat and sleep at predetermined times, and are generally ignored when they are awake. They are dumped in playpens and baby swings or, even worse, left to spend the bulk of the day in their cribs.

5:00 p.m. to 6:00 p.m. Pick up time. At the end of the day, parents arrive to pick up their babies. At better quality centers and daycare homes, nursing mothers are encouraged to squeeze in an end-of-day feeding before heading home. Caregivers take this opportunity to bring the parents up to speed on the day's events, highlighting anything noteworthy that has taken place since the parents dropped their babies off in the morning. In poorer quality environments, parents and babies are rushed out the door so that the caregivers can finish their workday as soon as possible.

For a toddler or preschooler

While no two daycare programs are alike, here's what your toddler or preschooler's day might be like at a typical daycare center or family daycare setting. Once again, I've thrown in some comments designed to provide you with concrete examples of the differences between superior and substandard care.

7:00 a.m. to 9:00 a.m. Drop off time. There's a constant parade of parents and children arriving at the daycare center to begin their day of childcare. In a well-run program, the caregivers make themselves available to greet each child as he or she arrives and will manage at the same time to maintain control over the other children despite the ongoing interruptions. In a poorly run program, the caregivers will either be unavailable to greet the children as

Moneysaver
Cooperative daycare centers (sometimes called family centers) and nursery schools can offer lower-than-average fees because parents help to staff the programs. Assuming you or your partner can get time off from work to put in your "duty days" at the center or school, participating in a cooperative can help you to stretch your childcare dollars further.

they arrive or they will be so distracted by the chaos breaking out elsewhere in the room that they will only be able to give each newly arriving child a token amount of attention.

9:00 a.m. to 9:30 a.m. Morning circle time. After everyone has arrived at daycare, the providers and the children gather together to greet one another and talk about what they have planned for that particular day. In well-run programs, the children are encouraged to share and participate. In poorly run programs, their input is neither welcome nor tolerated, and circle time becomes a battle of wills between a frustrated teacher and a room full of restless preschoolers.

9:30 a.m. to 10:30 a.m. Free play time. Every daycare program should include one or more periods of "free play time" daily—a time in which children are free to move from activity center to activity center as they wish. In better-quality programs, children have the opportunity to participate in many different activities, either individually or in small groups. There are puzzles, crafts, dress-up centers, building blocks, water play centers, and other types of age-appropriate activities waiting for them to enjoy, and their caregivers are actively involved in their play as well. In poorer quality programs, children are inadequately supervised or aren't given the opportunity to choose their own activities at all.

10:30 a.m. to 11:00 a.m. Snack time. In some daycare settings, all of the children sit down together to enjoy a snack. In other settings, food is set out at a snack center that children can visit whenever they feel hungry. Both alternatives work equally well, as long as the snack center is appropriately supervised to reduce the risk of choking.

Unofficially . . .
More than half of
American women
with children
under the age of
one work outside
the home. The
majority return
to work during
their child's first
three to five
months.
Sources: Carnegie
Institute,
National
Institutes of
Health, Carnegie
Corporation

11:00 a.m. to 12:00 p.m. Outdoor play time or active indoor play. Children should be given the opportunity to play outdoors unless the weather is particularly miserable. Highly motivated caregivers will treat this as an essential part of the daycare program, making the effort required to ensure that all of the children in their care are bundled up in their outdoor clothing and taken out to play. Less motivated caregivers may decide that it's easier to let the children run around inside instead, or may discourage active play altogether.

12:00 p.m. to 1:00 p.m. Lunch time. Feeding a room full of children is a challenging task, so every available adult should be on hand to pitch in if needed. In the better-quality daycare centers, the staff eat lunch with the children in their care, thereby teaching them that mealtime is a social occasion. In poorer quality daycare programs, the staff stand apart from the children, only intervening if a particular child needs help.

1:00 p.m. to 3:00 p.m. Nap time or quiet play. Some children continue to take naps until well past their third birthday. Others give up the nap habit long before their caregivers or parents are ready. Whether they actually sleep or not, children need a quiet time to recharge their batteries. That's why most daycare programs include a quiet period after lunch when children can rest, look at books, or engage in other types of quiet activities. Younger children need a quiet place where they can sleep without being disturbed, and yet still be in eyeshot and earshot of their caregivers. In poorer quality programs which lack separate sleeping facilities for younger children, the needs of the younger children often conflict with the needs of the older children. Either the younger children miss out on badly needed sleep, or the older children are forced to be unnaturally quiet for an extended period of time.

3:00 p.m. to 5:00 p.m. Free play time. Children should once again be given the opportunity to try their hand at a number of different individual and small group activities, depending on what interests them at the time. Some teachers may want to include a group activity or two, depending on the age of the children.

5:00 p.m to 6:00 p.m. Pick up time. At the end of the day, parents arrive to pick up their children. In better-quality daycare environments, caregivers provide parents with a quick summary of the day's activities, alerting them to any areas of particular interest (for example, the fact that their child learned how to do up the buttons on his sweater) or concern (the fact that the their child seemed unusually sleepy). If parents take the time to stay for a while and chat with the caregivers and one another, you can feel confident that the families who use the daycare center or family daycare home are satisfied with the quality of care their children are receiving. In poorer quality centers, caregivers are unavailable to greet parents as they arrive because they're either too busy looking after other children or not sufficiently motivated to make the effort.

Licensed? Accredited? Nonprofit? What they really mean

Some parents feel reassured when they hear that a particular daycare center is licensed, accredited, or nonprofit but only a few actually understand what these terms really mean. Here's the scoop.

Timesaver
Buy an oversized change bag and keep it stocked with a week's worth of diapers, wipes, and clothing. That way, you won't have to restock it at the end of each working day.

Licensed daycare

To put it simply, licensed daycare means government-regulated daycare. The nature of the licensing regulations and the extent to which they are enforced varies tremendously from jurisdiction to jurisdiction. While I've reproduced the highlights of each state and province's regulations in Appendix E, I recommend that you contact your licensing authority or agency directly to request a copy of the regulations that apply in your area.

As reassuring as the term "licensed" may be, the fact that a daycare center or family daycare home is licensed is no guarantee of quality. Licensing standards are low, focusing on basic health and safety measures rather than on whether a particular daycare environment is stimulating or nurturing. To make matters worse, some states neglect to inspect daycare centers and family daycare settings to ensure that licensing requirements are met on an ongoing basis. That's why it's important for you to look beyond the license. In the world of daycare, there's no such thing as a *Good Housekeeping* stamp of approval.

That said, you can get more information on the National Health and Safety Performance Standards for daycare centers at //nrc.uchsh.edu/national/index.html.

Accreditation

A better indicator of quality than the fact that a particular daycare center is licensed is whether it has been accredited through one of the national daycare accreditation programs offered by the National Association for the Education for Young Children (NAEYC), the National Childcare Association (NCCA), and the National Association for Family

Childcare (NAFCC). The NAEYC and NCCA programs are open to daycare centers and their staff, while the NAFCC program focuses on family daycare settings. Studies have shown that caregivers who participate in voluntary accreditation programs deliver a higher standard of care than their nonaccredited counterparts.

You can find the contact information for these organizations in Appendix B.

Nonprofit versus for-profit

Another important bit of childcare lingo is the distinction between nonprofit and for-profit daycare.

Many daycare centers are operated as nonprofit programs. They are frequently sponsored by such community groups as churches, synagogues, colleges, universities, and YMCAs, which offer daycare programs as a service to parents.

Other daycare centers and most family daycare settings are in business to make a profit.

While some studies have indicated that the quality of care may be higher in nonprofit daycare centers or family daycare settings than in their for-profit counterparts, it's not a statement that can be applied across the board. The fact that a particular daycare center or family daycare setting is nonprofit is no guarantee that it will provide better care than a comparable for-profit business. This is definitely a situation in which your mileage may vary.

Just a quick word about two of the best-known nonprofit daycare programs before I move on. As you may recall from an earlier discussion, the federal government funds two programs designed to meet the needs of children who are deemed to be "at risk": Head Start and Early Start.

Unofficially . . .
According to the National Center for the Early Childhood Education Work Force, only 5,000 of the country's 97,000 childcare centers are accredited.

Head Start—which has been around since the mid-1960s—is designed to meet the needs of low-income families. It provides enriched preschool programming to three- and four-year-olds as well as comprehensive support services to their families. Traditionally a half-day program, Head Start is now being offered as a full-day program in some areas, a change that makes Head Start more suitable for parents who are working or participating in retraining or educational programs.

Early Head Start is similar to Head Start, but is aimed at children under the age of three. It was launched by the federal government in 1994.

As I mentioned back in Chapter 3, if your child qualifies for either Head Start of Early Head Start, the government will pick up the tab for your child's preschool fees. To find out more about the program and to determine if your child is eligible, call your local Head Start agency.

How out-of-home childcare can meet your child's needs

When you're evaluating your out-of-home childcare options, it's important to consider how well—or how poorly—each daycare center or family daycare setting will meet the needs of your child. Obviously, this is where such factors as age, temperament, and your child's special needs all come into play.

Your child's age

As you may recall from our detailed discussion back in Chapter 1, infants, toddlers, and preschoolers have very different needs when it comes to childcare. Not surprisingly, given the huge developmental leaps that occur in just a matter of months, the very same environment that is endlessly stimulating to an infant can bore a toddler to tears.

Let's quickly review what children need at various stages of their development and consider how these needs may influence your out-of-home childcare choices.

Infants (from birth to eighteen months) thrive in environments in which there is a low caregiver-child ratio (ideally 1:1 but no more than 1:3) and a small group size (ideally three or less but certainly no more than four). Because they need to have the opportunity to build strong attachments to their caregivers, they should be cared for by the same caregiver day after day. These caregivers should genuinely love babies and be prepared to respond to their needs as quickly and effectively as possible.

Babies need to eat and sleep when their own bodies dictate (as opposed to when the clock says they should), but at the same time they need a predictable environment in which they can feel secure. They also need a safe yet stimulating environment in which they are free to explore (as opposed to being confined to playpens or cribs for unreasonably long portions of the day).

When you're shopping for care for an infant, you'll want to pay particular attention to the caregiver-child ratio and the interaction between the caregiver and your child. Yes, it's nice if the playroom is decorated in eye-pleasing primary colors, and it's an added bonus if the toy shelves look like a store window at Christmas time, but what really matters for children of this age is the quality of the relationship they can forge with their caregivers. If your child's caregiver is too busy to cuddle him between diaper changes and feedings or seems disinterested

Bright Idea
If a space becomes available at the daycare center or family daycare home of your choice before you actually need it, consider snapping it up anyway. You could either start your child in his new care arrangement a little sooner than originally scheduled or pay for an unused childcare space while you continue to care for your baby at home—a small price to pay for long-term peace of mind.

in his day-to-day accomplishments, he won't receive the quality of care that he deserves.

Toddlers (eighteen months to three years) receive the best care when the caregiver-child ratio is relatively low (ideally 1:3 or less, but certainly no more than 1:5) and the group size is six or less (four if you can find it). They need caregivers who have the patience and energy required to contend with their ever-changing moods, and who have realistic expectations of their behavior. And they need a safe environment that encourages their natural love of physical activity and active exploration while providing them with plenty of opportunities to practice new skills, do things for themselves, and make simple choices.

When you're looking for care for your toddler, you'll want to focus on such factors as the safety of the physical environment and the way the caregiver interacts with the toddlers in her care.

Preschoolers (three to six years) do well when the caregiver-child ratio is appropriate (ideally 1:5 or less, but certainly no more than 1:8). They need caregivers who have the time and patience to field their endless questions. And they need an environment that provides them with access to age-appropriate activities and equipment as well as plenty of opportunities to build on their increasingly sophisticated language skills and to socialize with other children their own age.

When you're selecting care for your preschooler, you'll want to consider such factors as the quality and quantity of play materials and the availability of other children his own age—factors that frequently put family daycare providers at a disadvantage. Unless the caregiver in your neighborhood belongs

Unofficially . . .
Studies have shown that infants and toddlers are more likely to imitate adult gestures and speech when there are fewer children being cared for by each adult.

to the Toy of the Month Club, her house is likely to lack some of the bells and whistles that larger centers have to offer. Likewise, unless she specializes in caring for preschoolers rather than infants or toddlers, your child is less likely to enjoy the same number of interactions with children his own age as he would enjoy in a larger center.

Note: This is not meant to imply that more is necessarily better. Certain children thrive in settings with fewer children. And, what's more, a closet full of toys is no substitute for the care of a loving and committed caregiver, wherever you may find her.

And here's some more food for thought: While it's important to find an environment that meets your child's needs today, you'll want to be sure that the situation will be suited to him for the long-term. Otherwise you'll be back to square one in another year or two and actively looking for another care arrangement for your child.

Unfortunately, it's not easy to find a daycare arrangement that can grow with your child. Some centers provide excellent programming for toddlers and preschoolers, but don't have low enough caregiver-child ratios to deliver top-notch infant care. Likewise, some family daycare providers are wonderfully responsive to babies, but lack the patience required to work with toddlers and preschoolers. You should consider yourself blessed indeed if you manage to find a caregiver or facility that is capable of providing your child with an excellent standard of care from birth until the time he starts school.

Your child's temperament

Your child's temperament is every bit as important as his age in determining the suitability of a

Watch Out! If the daycare center you are evaluating groups children according to age, be sure to ask what they do about preschool-aged children who aren't toilet-trained. Some centers keep preschool-aged children in the toddler room until they are out of diapers, a situation that can lead to considerable distress if a preschool-aged child is left behind by his friends.

particular daycare arrangement. Quiet, shy children may feel more comfortable in family daycare environments than in large daycare centers. Likewise, particularly active and outgoing children may find family daycare settings too quiet for their liking (particularly if the others in care are younger children), and may prefer the buzz of activity at larger daycare centers instead.

The best way to assess the fit between your child and a particular daycare environment is to give him the opportunity to test drive it for himself. Take your child along when you visit daycare centers or family daycare providers and note how comfortable he is with the caregiver and other children.

Your child's special needs

If your child has any special needs, you'll want to scrutinize his childcare arrangements with particular care. Factors to consider in an out-of-home care arrangement include whether a particular caregiver has the experience and/or training required to deal with your child's particular needs.

You might also want to find out whether there is a resource worker available to work with your child or—at the very least—to provide his caregiver with some pointers on designing a program that will meet his needs. Your state or local childcare licensing authorities can put you in touch with the government office responsible for coordinating care for children with special needs.(See Appendix B.)

How out-of-home childcare can meet your family's needs

When you're evaluating your out-of-home childcare options, it's also important to consider how well—or how poorly—each daycare center or family daycare provider is suited to meeting the needs of your family. Obviously, this is where such factors as your work schedule, the location of the daycare center or family daycare setting, and your expectations of care come into play.

As you already know, it's a lot easier to find out-of-home care for your child if you work a standard nine-to-five work day. If you work nonstandard hours, you're most likely to find suitable care for your child in a daycare center at your workplace or in a family daycare home (especially if it's operated by a caregiver whose hours are flexible). If you manage to find an out-of-home caregiver who is willing to work around your schedule, consider yourself blessed. Such arrangements are few and far between.

Location is another important factor in evaluating your childcare options. Ideally, you want to find a daycare arrangement that's close to either your place of employment, your partners's place of employment, or your home—particularly if you rely on public transportation to travel to and from work. If you end up finding a care arrangement that's outside your desired area, be sure to test-drive the commute during rush hour so that you can get a realistic idea of how much time the trip to daycare is likely to add to your morning and evening schedules.

While work schedules and location are both important considerations, the most important issue for most families shopping for out-of-home childcare is their care expectations. Many parents have clearly defined ideas of what the ideal care arrangement for their child will be like. For some families, it will be a daycare center staffed by highly trained

Bright Idea
If possible, try to find care within your school district. While this may be the last thing on your mind when you're choosing care for your three-month-old, it's much easier to find a suitable care arrangement now than to try to find another childcare arrangement in the right part of town a few years down the road.

early childhood educators. For others, it will be a warm and friendly family daycare home operated by an experienced mother who has a genuine love of children. To avoid spinning your wheels unnecessarily, it's important to be clear from the outset about what you're looking for in an out-of-home childcare arrangement.

A word to the wise: Before you make up your mind about the suitability of center-based care versus home-based care for your child, it's important to know the facts about each option. Don't just go by the horror stories you've picked up from the media. A preliminary visit to both a daycare center and a family daycare setting can help dispel any myths you might believe about either or both of these childcare options.

Just the facts

- There are both advantages and disadvantages to each type of out-of-home childcare. The number and age of your children and your need for backup childcare arrangements will help to determine which option is best for you.

- Good quality daycare can help a child to develop strong social skills and cognitive abilities, and, in most cases, doesn't do anything to erode the maternal-child bond.

- A typical day in a quality daycare environment is light years away from what you will experience at a poor quality setting. The attitude and skills of the caregiver play a huge role in determining the overall quality of care.

- The fact that a particular daycare setting is accredited is a far better indicator of quality than the fact that it is licensed. There's also no guarantee that a nonprofit program is automatically superior to a for-profit program.

■ Consider your family's long-term needs as you shop for childcare. Neglecting to choose a caregiver within your child's school district almost guarantees that you'll be looking for a new care arrangement a few years down the road.

GET THE SCOOP ON...
Doing preliminary screening by phone ▪ What to
ask the director of a daycare center ▪
What to ask a family daycare provider ▪ How to
evaluate a daycare center in person ▪ How to
evaluate a family daycare setting (daycare
home) in person ▪ What to ask other parents ▪
How to check references

Evaluating Your Out-of-Home Childcare Options

Chapter 5

If your brain is going into overload and you feel like you know about ten times as much about childcare as the average parent does, you're doing things right. After all, there's no such thing as over-preparation when it comes to making a decision as important as this one.

Now that you've short-listed the daycare centers and family daycare settings that seem best suited to meeting your family's needs, it's time to dig a little deeper. That's what this chapter is all about.

Because you need to find out what's really going on in a particular daycare center or family daycare home, that is, what happens the moment parents walk out the door, this chapter shows you how to find out everything you could ever want to know about a particular daycare environment.

Screening by phone

If you plan to evaluate more than one childcare alternative—something I most definitely recommend—you'll probably want to take a three-pronged approach to your research by making a few preliminary phone calls, visiting a number of daycare centers and family daycare homes, and then checking each of their references.

Before you pick up the phone and start making calls, it's important to decide who the best person to talk to is; when the best time to speak to her might be; and what kinds of questions you should ask.

If you're calling a daycare center, you will want to talk to the director because she is the person responsible for setting policy for the center and therefore is the most qualified to answer your questions. She is also likely to be the person who's most available to take your call. The caregivers, after all, are busy with the children. If a caregiver is willing to chat with you on the phone for hours at a time, it can be an indication that the quality of care that the children at that center are receiving is substandard.

If you're calling a family daycare provider, there's no director to ask for, so you'll be speaking directly with the care provider.

The timing of your call is also important. A center director is busy with parents during drop off and pickup times, and a family daycare provider may be unavailable to field your call during her work day. It's not that these people are reluctant to take your call; it's just that their priorities lie with the families already in their care. As a rule of thumb, try to avoid mealtimes and drop-off and pick-up times. This means that the best time to call or visit is either mid-morning or mid-afternoon.

What to ask the director of a daycare center

After you manage to get the director on the phone, you'll want to obtain as much information as you can in as short a time as possible. It's best to use this preliminary phone call to zero in on the real nuts-and-bolts issues.

The following checklist should help you to evaluate if it's worth your while to set up an appointment to visit this daycare center in person—or if it makes more sense to scratch it off your list entirely.

Note: You can find a photocopy-ready version of this checklist in Appendix D.

About the childcare checklists:

- Each checklist is divided into two parts: the telephone portion and the in-person portion. You may decide to weed out or move some questions from one checklist to the other, depending on how much time the daycare center director or family daycare provider can devote to your call or visit.

- It is unlikely that you will have enough time to ask all of the questions in each checklist. Rather than attempting to ask all of the questions, ask only those that are relevant to your situation.

- After your visit, reread the checklist. You might be able to answer some additional questions based on your own observations.

Daycare center and nursery school telephone checklist

Location
Where is the center located?
Is it close to your home or place of work?

Bright Idea
Besides noting the specific answers to your questions, listen to the tone of the director's voice. Does she appear interested in helping you to find care for your child? Does she sound proud of her facility and staff? Some of the most valuable information you will obtain is gathered by reading between the lines.

Hours of operation

What are the hours of operation?

Is there a limit to the number of hours a child can spend at the center each day?

What are the pickup and drop-off times?

Are there any times during the year when the center is closed? If so, when?

Availability of spaces

How many children are enrolled at the center?

How many children would be in your child's group?

What would the age range be within your child's group?

Are there spaces available? If not, how long is the waiting list?

Is part-time care available?

Does the center accept children on a drop-in basis?

What would happen if you needed to increase or decrease your childcare hours because of scheduling changes at work?

Are there any special criteria for admission? If it is a workplace-based daycare center, are children of nonemployees welcome?

Fees

What fees does the center charge for infants, toddlers, preschoolers, and school-aged children?

Are receipts provided?

Are there any additional costs (for example, diapers, meals, or field trips)?

Are parents expected to participate in fund-raising activities or otherwise financially contribute to the operation of the center?

Does the center offer discounts to families with more than one child enrolled at the center?

Is subsidized care available? If so, what are the criteria and how does a parent apply?

Is there a deposit or an enrollment fee required? If so, how much is it?

When are fees due?

Is there a fee for picking up a child late? If so, how much is charged and how soon does the fee kick in?

Is there a charge for days when your child is absent for care? What about holidays?

How much notice is required to withdraw a child from the center?

Licensing and accreditation

Is the center licensed? If not, does the state or county require that it be licensed?

What ages of children is the center licensed to accept?

Is the center accredited by either the National Association for the Education of Young Children (NAEYC) or the National Childcare Association (NCCA)?

Is the center nonprofit or for-profit? If the center is for-profit, is the owner on the premises full-time? (Quality slips when the person who owns—or directs—the daycare center isn't around to monitor the situation.)

Staff training and certification

Have all staff members had appropriate training in early childhood education?

Have staff members had training in cardiopulmonary resuscitation (CPR), infant CPR, and first aid?

Are staff members assigned to the same children on a regular basis to ensure continuity of care?

Do staff members keep up-to-date on their immunizations?

Are criminal background checks conducted on all staff and volunteers?

Philosophies, goals, and policies

Bright Idea
Be sure to jot down some notes about the types of formal training that staff members have received. Studies have shown that caregivers who have had training in early childhood education are less likely to use authoritarian styles of discipline and are more likely to be actively involved with the children in their care.

Are the center's goals and philosophies stated in writing? Do you agree with these goals and philosophies?

Are the center's policies stated in writing? Do these policies seem reasonable to you?

What does the center do to encourage ongoing staff development and training?

Does the center have a written policy on discipline which states explicitly that corporal punishment is not to be used?

Does the center have a written statement outlining its behavior management policies? Is this statement consistent with your own beliefs about what is and is not appropriate when it comes to disciplining a child?

Does the center have a written policy outlining the procedures used to resolve conflicts between parents and caregivers?

What to ask a family daycare provider

Because you want to find out as much as possible about a particular family daycare provider before you actually set up a home visit, you should use this preliminary telephone call to inquire about the issues that are of the greatest importance to you.

Note: You can find a photocopy-ready version of the following checklist in Appendix D.

Family daycare provider telephone checklist

Location

Where is the family daycare setting/home located? Is it close to your home or place of work?

Hours of operation

What are the hours of operation?

Is there a limit to the number of hours a child can spend at the family daycare home each day?

What are the pickup and drop-off times?

Are there any times during the year when the family daycare home is closed? Is so, when?

Will the agency (where applicable) or your caregiver provide you with backup care while the family daycare home is closed?

Availability of spaces

How many children are enrolled at the family daycare home? What are their ages?

Are there spaces available? If not, how long is the waiting list?

Is part-time care available?

Does the family daycare provider accept children on a drop-in basis?

What would happen if you needed to increase or decrease your childcare hours because of scheduling changes at work?

Fees

What fees does the family daycare provider charge for infants, toddlers, preschoolers, and school-aged children?

If you are using an agency, are there any additional agency fees? Are receipts provided?

Are there any additional costs (for example, diapers, meals, or field trips)?

What equipment, if any, are you expected to supply (strollers, high chairs, playpens, cribs, car seats, and so on)?

Does the family daycare provider offer discounts to families with more than one child enrolled at the family daycare home?

Is subsidized care available? If so, what are the criteria and how does a parent apply?

Bright Idea
If the caregiver plans to arrange her own backup for times when she is ill or otherwise unavailable, let the caregiver know that you would like to meet the backup caregiver, too.

Is there a deposit or an enrollment fee required? If
so, how much is it?

When are fees due?

Is there a fee for picking up a child late? If so, how
much is charged and how soon does the fee kick in?

Is there a charge for days when your child is absent
for care? What about holiday times?

How much notice is required to withdraw a child
from the family daycare home?

Licensing and accreditation

Is the family daycare home licensed? If not, does the
state, city, or county require that it be licensed?

What ages of children is the family daycare home
licensed to accept?

Watch Out!
Be sure to ask a
potential family
daycare provider
if she owns her
home or rents it.
If she rents it,
be forewarned:
There's a distinct
possibility that
she may move to
a location that is
unacceptable to
you for one rea-
son or another
(for example, one
that's located on
the other side of
town or on a
busy street).

Is the state, city, or county license posted in a visible
spot? If so, is it current?

Is the family daycare home accredited by the
National Association for Family Childcare?

Is the family daycare home nonprofit or for-profit?

Caregiver training and certification

Has the caregiver had appropriate training in early
childhood education?

Has she had training in cardiopulmonary resuscitation (CPR), infant CPR, and first aid?

Is she up-to-date on her immunizations?

Have criminal background checks been conducted
on all adults who are present while your child is present (the caregiver, her partner, any adult children
or tenants, agency personnel, and so on)?

Philosophies, goals, and policies

Are the family daycare provider's goals and philosophies stated in writing? Do you agree with these
goals and philosophies?

Are the family daycare provider's policies stated in writing? Do these policies seem reasonable to you?

Does the family daycare provider have a written policy on discipline which states explicitly that corporal punishment is not to be used?

Does the family daycare provider have a written statement outlining her behavior management policies? Is this statement consistent with your own beliefs about what is appropriate when it comes to disciplining a child?

Are there any other businesses being run out of the home? If so, are they compatible with a family daycare operation?

Conducting personal visits

After you've reduced your daycare choices to a more manageable number of options, you're ready to conduct some personal visits. The purpose of the personal visit is to physically inspect the daycare environment, meet potential caregivers, and obtain detailed answers to all of your questions about the center or family daycare provider's policies and procedures. Because these visits can be time-consuming and exhausting, you'll probably want to share this responsibility with your spouse or another adult.

When to visit

Daycare centers and family daycare homes have both busy times and quieter times. While you'll have a more peaceful visit if you stick to the quieter times of day, you'll learn a lot more about the quality of care your child will receive if you schedule your visit to coincide with the morning drop-off period, lunch hour, or the afternoon pickup period. Things to note during these busier times of day include how much attention each child receives, how calm (or harried!) each caregiver is, how well the caregivers relate to the parents who use the daycare center or family daycare home, and how comfortable you would feel leaving your child in such an environment.

While it can be difficult to find the time to spend a half-day or more checking out a daycare center or family daycare setting, it's definitely time well spent. You'll have the opportunity to observe how the daycare staff organizes their day, and to see how well the children settle once the early morning chaos subsides.

Another issue that you'll have to grapple with when it comes time to make your visits is if you should drop by unannounced. The upside of dropping by without any prior notice is that you'll have the chance to see what the daycare center or family daycare home is really like. The downside is that you could make the effort to show up, only to find that no one is available to answer your questions or give you a tour. Your best bet, provided you've got the time to do it, is to make two visits: an initial scheduled visit and a follow up one that is unannounced.

Should you take your child?

The age of your child should determine whether you take her on the visit to the daycare. After all, a breastfeeding baby or highly active toddler can really slow you down.

While you might not want to take your child on every visit, it's important to give her the chance to visit the daycare center or family daycare home that is your final—or even semifinal—choice. The reason is simple: Your child is going to spend a lot of time at the daycare center or family daycare home,

Watch Out!
Be suspicious of a daycare center or family daycare home that is overly tidy. Excessive tidiness can be an indication that the caregiver is rigid and unwilling to allow the children to engage in any activities that might make a mess, regardless of how fun or educational those activities might be.

so it's important that she feel comfortable in that particular environment and that she relate well to the caregiver. Just one small caveat before I move on: Some children are often shy, standoffish, or behave a little strangely the first few times they meet someone new. If your child is like this, you might not be able to use her initial reactions as a gauge of caregiver suitability.

Evaluating a daycare center in person

The purposes of the personal visit are to physically inspect the daycare center, to meet each potential caregiver, and to obtain detailed answers to all of your questions about the center's policies and procedures. During your visit, you'll want to address such issues as child-staff ratios, safety, health and hygiene concerns, rest periods, mealtimes, diapering and toileting, transportation policies, what the program is like, and the extent of parent involvement that is expected.

The following checklist should help you gather the information you need to properly evaluate each of the centers you are considering.

Daycare center and nursery school in-person checklist

Child-staff ratio

Does the center adhere to government regulations limiting group size?

Does it meet the following guidelines, as recommended by the National Association for the Education of Young Children and the American Academy of Pediatrics?

Moneysaver
Be sure to find out whether you will be required to pay a reinstatement fee if your child stops going to care for a period of time (for example, during your maternity leave or a layoff). Some centers require that parents go through the entire application process again, even insisting that they fork over a second application fee.

Age	Ratio	Group Size
Birth to 12 months	1:3	Maximum group size of 6
12 to 24 months	1:3	Maximum group size of 8
24 to 30 months	1:4	Maximum group size of 8
30 to 36 months	1:5	Maximum group size of 10
3-year-olds	1:7	Maximum group size of 14
4-year-olds	1:8	Maximum group size of 16
5-year-olds	1:8	Maximum group size of 16
6- to 8-year-olds	1:10	Maximum group size of 20
9- to 12-year-olds	1:12	Maximum group size of 24

Is the group size small enough that children appear to be secure and comfortable rather than lost in a crowd?

Do the staff members appear to be comfortable with the number (and ages) of children in their care?

Safety

Are electrical outlets covered?

Are radiators covered and heaters kept away from the children?

Are there window guards above the first floor?

Are there safety gates at the tops and bottoms of stairs?

Is the surface of the floor safe and clean?

Are countertops and edges rounded and well-finished?

Are dangerous materials (cleaning supplies, scissors, and so on) stored out of the reach of children?

Is the center free of such hazards as radon, asbestos, and lead paint?

Is equipment well-maintained?

Are smoke detectors used?

Is there a fire extinguisher?

Is emergency lighting properly installed and checked regularly?

Are emergency evacuation plans posted?

What is the center's fire escape plan?

Does the center conduct monthly fire drills?

Is there an updated list of telephone numbers beside the phone?

Does the center maintain updated emergency contact and medical information for each child?

What are the center's policies for handling accidents and other serious occurrences?

What are the center's policies concerning the administration of medication?

Does the center have a fenced playground?

Does the playground contain safe and age-appropriate equipment?

Is the area around and under the play equipment covered with a soft material like rubber? Are there guard rails on all elevated surfaces? Are there any sharp edges or other hazards?

Is the center appropriately insured?

Are the children well-supervised?

Are children only released to persons whom their parents have authorized, in writing, to pick them up?

Health and hygiene

Is the room well-ventilated? Is it well-lit? Is it kept at a comfortable temperature?

Is there enough open space for crawling and walking?

Is the center kept clean?

Are infant and toddler toys disinfected on a regular basis?

Are garbage cans, diaper areas, and bathrooms disinfected regularly?

Bright Idea
Watch what happens when the children leave the building to play in the backyard. Are the caregivers in control of the children at all times or are the children allowed to run too far ahead?

Are hot running water (less than 120 degrees), soap, and paper towels used after toileting and before and after meals and snacks?

Is smoking permitted?

Are families required to produce proof that their children have been immunized?

Is there a clearly stated policy for isolating and caring for children who become ill?

Is there a private rest area where sick children can rest?

Under what circumstances are parents called at work and asked to pick up their children?

Is there a first aid kit?

Rest periods

Are rest periods provided for children? If a child is unable to sleep, is she permitted to engage in quiet alternatives?

Are infants' individual sleep patterns respected? Can they be seen and heard while they are sleeping?

Are infants left in cribs or playpens when awake?

Are the sleeping areas clean and appealing?

Do the cots and cribs conform to current safety standards?

Are there enough cots or cribs to allow all of the children to take naps?

If more than one child is using a cot or crib, are the sheets changed after one child is finished with it? Who is responsible for supplying and washing the sheets?

Mealtimes

Are the kitchen and food preparation areas hygienic?

Are meals varied, nutritious, and age-appropriate?

Are menus posted ahead of time?

Are you expected to supply food for your child? If so, is there refrigeration available?

To what extent is the center willing to accommodate special diets?

How will the center support your efforts to breast-feed and wean your baby?

Are infants held while they are bottle-fed?

Are infants' individual feeding patterns respected?

Are highchairs available for older babies? If so, are they safe and sturdy?

Are eating areas clean and appealing?

Is mealtime pleasant and unhurried?

Does the center use nonbreakable drinking cups or paper cups?

Is food ever withheld as a punishment?

What does the center do if a child does not like a particular type of food?

Diapering and toileting

How often are diapers changed?

Are disposable gloves used when changing diapers? If they aren't, do caregivers routinely wash their hands before changing the next child?

Are the diapering and toileting areas hygienic? Is there a sink close by?

Is there a safety belt on the change table to prevent children from rolling off?

Is the diaper-change area sanitized after each use?

Are you expected to supply diapers, lotions, and baby wipes?

Are the bathrooms safe and easy for young children to use?

Is there a potty or special toilet seat in the bathroom?

How will the staff support your efforts to toilet train your child?

Watch Out!
Be sure to note if the caregivers disinfect the change table in between diaper changes. Outbreaks of diarrhea can result from unsanitary change facilities.

Transportation policies

If children are transported to daycare by someone other than their parents, is the driver licensed, qualified, properly trained, and in good health? Has he had a criminal background check?

Are field trips a regular part of the program? If so, what mode of transportation is used? Do parents have the right to refuse to allow their children to participate in field trips that are not within walking distance?

Do the vehicles that are used to transport children have seat belts and car seats that meet safety standards? Are the drivers properly insured?

Are children always placed in safety restraints when they are in vehicles?

Caregiver

Who will be working with your child?

What are her qualifications? Does she participate in ongoing professional development and training?

How long has she been working at the center?

How long has she been working with young children?

Does she demonstrate a genuine love of children?

Is she relaxed and involved with the children?

How does she relate to your child?

Does she seem like someone with whom you and your child could develop a relationship?

What ages of children is she most comfortable with?

Does she have enough time to look after all the children in her care?

Is she experienced in working with children with special needs (if applicable)?

Does she seem to possess a solid understanding of what children can and want to do at various stages of development?

Bright Idea
Jot down some adjectives that describe your impressions of the caregiver: warm, caring, impatient, cold, and so on.

Does she encourage the children to master new skills?

Does she allow them to make choices (where appropriate)?

Does she talk to the children and encourage the children to express themselves through words and language?

Does she encourage good health habits, such as handwashing before eating?

What are her feelings about pacifiers and comfort objects?

Does she offer assistance when a child needs it?

Does she react with enthusiasm to children's discoveries and accomplishments?

Does she sit with the children as they play?

Does she offer physical and verbal reassurance if a child is unhappy?

What is the rate of turnover at the center?

Will any nonstaff members be in contact with your child (students, senior citizens)? Have background checks been conducted on these individuals?

Program

What are the center's program goals? Are they compatible with your own childrearing philosophies?

How will center staff help to ease your child into the program?

Are routines clear and predictable?

How is the day structured?

Is the room set up and ready when families arrive?

Is there a safe place for your child's belongings?

Are children given a choice of developmentally appropriate activities?

Are both group and individual activities offered?

Are there a variety of activities offered (activities that promote both gross and fine motor skills as well as ones that promote language, cognitive, social, and emotional development)?

Are there sufficient quantities of art supplies? Are they within easy reach of the children?

Are the toys and equipment in good condition and within easy reach of the children?

Are children allowed to watch if they aren't interested in participating in a particular activity?

Are infants separated from older children during active indoor and outdoor play?

Are children under six separated from older children during active indoor and outdoor play?

Do the children look happy and involved in the program?

Do the children interact comfortably with both other children and their caregivers?

Does the program appear to be both organized and busy yet warm and welcoming?

Are children encouraged to take out and put away play materials by themselves?

Is the children's artwork displayed in the center as well as sent home to parents?

Is television watching permitted? If so, under what circumstances?

Does the program take into account the varied cultural and ethnic backgrounds of the children and their families?

Do children have the opportunity to speak English as well as their native language (where applicable)?

Is the program unbiased in terms of gender, income level, and physical or mental capabilities?

Are there any special features to the program?

Is the center affiliated with any religious organization? If so, how does that influence the program?

Does the center offer a formal educational program?

> 66
> Count how many ride-on toys there are and how many kids there are waiting to use them. Ride-on toys are popular with toddlers and preschoolers, so you will want to make sure that the center has purchased a significant quantity of them to avoid unnecessary battles.
> —Ann, mother of four
> 99

Do children receive two hours of outdoor play time each day, weather and health permitting?

Are they adequately supervised?

Is there ample space for all the children and equipment?

Parent involvement

Are parents encouraged to drop by at any time? Are you welcome to phone during the day to see how your child is doing?

Are parents given opportunities to meet with other parents who use the center?

Are parents treated as partners to the caregiver?

Are parents recognized as experts when it comes to the needs of their own children?

What policies does the center have in place to promote ongoing communication between parents and center staff?

References

Is the center willing to provide you with the names and phone numbers of parents who have used the center?

Are the parents you speak with enthusiastic about the quality of care that their children have received?

Overall impression

Does the center seem warm and friendly or cold and institutional?

How does your child react to the center?

Would you feel comfortable leaving your child at the center?

Evaluating a family daycare setting in person

The purpose of the personal visit is to physically inspect the family daycare setting/daycare home, to meet each potential caregiver, and to obtain

Watch Out!
Don't just take what the center director says at face value. Conduct informal reference checks with as many parents as possible to get the most accurate impression possible of the center's strengths and weaknesses.

detailed answers to all of your questions about the caregiver's policies and procedures. During your visit, you'll want to address such issues as caregiver-child ratios, safety, health and hygiene concerns, rest periods, mealtimes, diapering and toileting, transportation policies, what the program is like, and the extent of parent involvement that is expected.

The following checklist should help you to gather the information you need to properly evaluate each of the homes you are considering.
About the childcare checklists:

- Each checklist has been divided into two parts: the telephone portion and the in-person portion. You may decide to weed out or move some questions from one checklist to the other, depending on how much time the daycare center or family daycare provider is able to devote to your call or visit.

- It is unlikely that you will have enough time to ask all of the questions in each checklist. Rather than attempting to ask all of the questions, ask only those that appear to be particularly relevant to your situation.

- After your visit, reread the checklist. You might be able to answer some additional questions based on your own observations.

Family daycare setting in-person checklist

Child-caregiver ratio
Does the family daycare setting or home adhere to government regulations limiting the numbers (and ages) of children in a family daycare home?

Does the caregiver have children of her own? If so, what are their ages and have they been included in the child-caregiver ratio?

Does the caregiver appear to be comfortable with the number (and ages) of children in her care?

What is the maximum number of children she would be willing to accept?

Safety

Are electrical outlets covered?

Are radiators covered and heaters kept away from the children?

Are there window guards above the first floor?

Are there safety gates at the tops and bottoms of stairs?

Is the surface of the floor safe and clean?

Are countertops and edges rounded and well-finished?

Are dangerous materials (for example, cleaning supplies, scissors, and so on) stored out of the reach of children?

Is the family daycare setting free of such hazards as radon, asbestos, and lead paint?

Is equipment well-maintained?

Does the caregiver have any pets? If so, where are they kept? Do they pose any risk to the children?

Are smoke detectors used?

Is there a fire extinguisher?

What is the family daycare home's fire escape plan?

Does the family daycare provider conduct monthly fire drills?

Is there an updated list of telephone numbers beside the phone?

Does the family daycare provider maintain updated emergency contact and medical information for each child?

What are the family daycare provider's policies for handling accidents and other serious occurrences?

What are its policies concerning the administration of medication?

Does the family daycare setting have a fenced playground?

Is there a playground or park nearby? If so, is it located on a quiet or busy street? Can your caregiver get the children there safely?

Does the playground contain safe and age-appropriate equipment?

Are there guard rails on all elevated surfaces? Are there any sharp edges or other hazards?

Is the family daycare provider appropriately insured?

Are the children well-supervised?

Are children only released to persons whom their parents have authorized, in writing, to pick them up?

Health and hygiene

Bright Idea
Ask the caregiver if she belongs to the local family daycare network. Such networks can be a valuable source of information and support for in-home caregivers.

What areas of the house will your child have access to? Are these areas well-ventilated, well-lit, and kept at a comfortable temperature?

Is there enough open space for crawling and walking?

Is the family daycare home kept clean?

Are infant and toddler toys disinfected on a regular basis?

Are garbage cans, diaper areas, and bathrooms disinfected regularly?

Are hot running water (less than 120 degrees), soap, and paper towels used after toileting and before and after meals and snacks?

Is smoking permitted?

Are families required to produce proof that their children have been immunized?

Is there a clearly stated policy for isolating and caring for children who become ill?

Is there a private rest area where sick children can rest?

Under what circumstances are parents called at work and asked to pick up their children?

Is there a first aid kit?

Rest periods

Are rest periods provided for children? If a child is unable to sleep, is she permitted to engage in quiet alternatives?

Are infants' individual sleep patterns respected? Can they be seen and heard while they are sleeping?

Are infants left in cribs or playpens when awake?

Are the sleeping areas clean and appealing?

Do the cots and cribs conform to current safety standards?

Are there enough cots or cribs to allow all of the children to take naps?

If more than one child is using a cot or crib, are the sheets changed after one child is finished with it?

Who is responsible for supplying and washing the sheets?

Mealtimes

Are the kitchen and food preparation areas hygienic?

Are meals varied, nutritious, and age-appropriate?

Are menus posted ahead of time?

Are you expected to supply food for your child? If so, is there adequate refrigeration available?

To what extent is the caregiver willing to accommodate special diets?

How will the caregiver support your efforts to breastfeed and wean your baby?

66
Count how many times the caregiver goes to check on sleeping children while you are visiting.
—Marie, mother of four
99

Are infants held while they are bottle-fed?

Are infants' individual feeding patterns respected?

Are there highchairs available for older babies? If so, are they safe and sturdy?

Are the eating areas clean and appealing?

Is mealtime pleasant and unhurried?

Does the family daycare home use nonbreakable drinking cups or paper cups?

Is food ever withheld as a punishment?

What does the family daycare provider do if a child does not like a particular type of food?

Diapering and toileting

How often are diapers changed?

Are disposable gloves used when changing diapers? If they aren't, do caregivers routinely wash their hands before changing the next child?

Are the diapering and toileting areas hygienic? Is there a sink close by?

Is there a safety belt on the change table to prevent children from rolling off?

Is the diaper-change area sanitized after each use?

Are you expected to supply diapers, lotions, and baby wipes or are these items supplied?

Are the bathrooms safe and easy for young children to use?

Is there a potty or special toilet seat in the bathroom?

How will the staff support your efforts to toilet-train your child?

Transportation policies

Are field trips a regular part of the program? If so, what mode of transportation is used? Do parents have the right to refuse to allow their children to participate in field trips that are not within walking distance?

Do the vehicles that are used to transport children have seat belts and car seats that meet safety standards? Are the drivers properly insured?

Are children always placed in safety restraints when they are in vehicles?

Caregiver

What are the caregiver's qualifications? Does she participate in ongoing professional development and training?

How long has she been operating a family daycare home? For how many more years does she intend to continue operating the family daycare home?

How long has she been working with young children?

Does she demonstrate a genuine love of children?

Is she relaxed and involved with the children?

How does she relate to your child?

Does she seem like someone with whom you and your child could develop a relationship?

What ages of children is she most comfortable with?

Does she have enough time to look after all the children in her care?

Is she experienced in working with children with special needs (if applicable)?

Does she seem to possess a solid understanding of what children can and want to do at various stages of development?

Does she encourage the children to master new skills?

Does she allow them to make choices (where appropriate)?

Does she talk to the children and encourage the children to express themselves through words and language?

Does she encourage good health habits, such as handwashing before eating?

Watch Out!
If the caregiver's home looks too perfect, it could be because she spends more of her day doing housework than playing with the children in her care.

What are her feelings about pacifiers and comfort objects?

Does she offer assistance when a child needs it?

Does she react with enthusiasm to children's discoveries and accomplishments?

Does she sit with the children as they play?

Does she offer physical and verbal reassurance if a child is unhappy?

What is the rate of turnover at the family daycare home?

Will any other than the caregiver be in contact with your child (others who live in the home, agency personnel, and so on)? Have background checks been conducted on these individuals?

Program

Unofficially . . .
A good family daycare provider should have a predictable daily routine for the children in her care. After all, children thrive on routine.

What are the caregiver's program goals? Are they compatible with your own childrearing philosophies?

How will the caregiver help to ease your child into her program?

Are routines clear and predictable?

How is the day structured?

Is the room set up and ready when families arrive?

Is there a safe place for your child's belongings?

Are children given a choice of developmentally appropriate activities?

Are both group and individual activities offered?

Are there a variety of activities offered (activities that promote both gross and fine motor skills as well as ones that promote language, cognitive, social, and emotional development)? Are there sufficient quantities of art supplies? Are they within easy reach of the children?

Are the toys and equipment in good condition and within easy reach of the children?

Are children allowed to watch if they aren't interested in participating in a particular activity?

Are infants separated from older children during active indoor and outdoor play?

Are children under six separated from older children during active indoor and outdoor play?

Do the children look happy and involved in the program?

Do the children interact comfortably with both other children and their caregivers?

Does the program appear to be both organized and busy yet warm and welcoming?

Are children encouraged to take out and put away play materials by themselves?

Is the children's artwork displayed in the family daycare home as well as sent home to parents?

Is television watching permitted? If so, under what circumstances?

Does the program take into account the varied cultural and ethnic backgrounds of the children and their families?

Do children have the opportunity to speak English as well as their native language (where applicable)?

Is the program unbiased in terms of gender, income level, and physical or mental capabilities?

Are there any special features to the program?

Do children receive two hours of outdoor play time each day, weather and health permitting?

Are they adequately supervised?

Is there ample space for all the children and equipment?

Parent involvement

Are parents encouraged to drop by at any time? Are you welcome to phone during the day to see how your child is doing?

Bright Idea
Try to determine how the other members of the caregiver's family feel about having a daycare business operated out of their home. Do the children resent having to share their mother with other children? Does the woman's partner seem less-than-thrilled about the whole situation?

Are parents given opportunities to meet with other parents who use the family daycare home?

Are parents treated as partners to the caregiver?

Are parents recognized as experts when it comes to the needs of their own children?

What policies does the family daycare provider have in place to promote ongoing communication between parents and family childcare staff?

References

Is the caregiver willing to provide you with the names and phone numbers of parents who have used the family daycare home? Are the parents you speak with enthusiastic about the quality of care that their children have received?

Overall impression

How does your child react to the family daycare provider?

Would you feel comfortable leaving your child at this family daycare home?

What to ask other parents

One of the best indicators of the quality of a particular daycare arrangement is the feedback that you receive from current or past users. While you will be checking out the formal references that are provided to you by the daycare center director or family daycare provider, a lot can be learned from impromptu encounters with other parents.

You will probably want to ask these parents specific questions about the childcare environment as well as number of questions about the caregiver herself:

What led you to choose this daycare center (or family daycare home?)

What other options did you consider? Why did you rule them out?

How long have your children been cared for at the center (or family daycare home?) What are their current ages?

How long did it take for them to adjust to care when they first started coming here?

To what extent has the center (or family daycare) met your expectations?

Does the caregiver appear to enjoy working with children? Explain.

Does she appear to have a solid understanding of the particular needs of children of various ages?

How does the caregiver discipline the children in her care?

What does the caregiver do to make the children feel good about themselves?

Is the caregiver always aware of where the children are and what they are doing?

In general, is the caregiver calm and in control of the situation?

Does she create an environment that is stimulating to the children?

How well does she relate to the parents of the children in her care?

What ages of children is she most comfortable with?

What ages of children is she least comfortable with?

What is her daily routine?

What are her strengths as a caregiver?

What are her weaknesses as a caregiver?

How did the caregiver handle your child's demand feeding, toilet training, temper tantrums, and so on? Were you satisfied with the way she handled these situations?

Can you give me an example of a situation which this caregiver handled particularly well?

Watch Out!
Be wary of a caregiver who only likes babies. You could find yourself looking for a new care arrangement as soon as your child becomes a toddler.

Bright Idea
You can, for example, hand-pick another family with circumstances similar to your own (for example, infant twins or a high-needs toddler) and find out how satisfied they are with the care that their children are receiving.

Can you give me an example of a situation which this caregiver didn't handle as well as you would have liked?

What is your overall impression of the daycare center or family daycare home?

What advice would you give other parents who are considering having their children cared for in this daycare center or family daycare home?

Is there anything else you think I should know before deciding to place my child at this daycare center or family daycare home?

You can learn as much about the daycare center or family daycare home from what the parents you're interviewing won't say as from what they will say. Most people are reluctant to admit that they've made a poor childcare choice. As a result, if they're dissatisfied with the care their children are receiving, they're more likely to dodge questions or answer in vague generalities than to launch into a tirade. Consequently, if the parents you speak to appear to be less than enthusiastic about the quality of care that their children are receiving, you should take that as evidence that something's amiss.

Checking references

After you've conducted your personal visits and settled on a few finalists, you're ready to check references. The purpose of these reference checks is to verify that your initial impression of each daycare center or family daycare setting is, in fact, accurate.

The daycare center director or family daycare provider will provide you with the names of parents who have used, or are currently using, their services. Because the needs of infants, toddlers, and preschoolers are radically different, you should ask for the names and numbers of families with children the same age as yours. In the case of a daycare center, you should make sure that the references can speak to the suitability of the particular caregiver who will be assigned to your child as opposed to the staff in general.

What a reference check will—and won't—tell you

Because the list of references supplied by a daycare center director or family daycare provider is hand-picked by that person, you can expect the people you call to paint the daycare center or family daycare home in the best possible light. Even if they have had an unpleasant experience (which is unlikely, given that they've agreed to act as references) the fear of litigation or other repercussions will cause most people to think twice before they say anything negative.

If the people you call give the daycare center or family daycare home a uniformly glowing recommendation, don't just rely on their experiences. After all, you're the only one who can decide whether a particular childcare setting is right for your child.

That said, you can gain some valuable information from references—provided, of course, that you're prepared to read between the lines. Besides asking the types of questions listed in the previous section, you might also want to ask those people who are no longer using the center or caregiver: Who terminated the arrangement and why?

How the pros do it

Ever wonder how human resource professionals obtain any useful information from references? Here are a few pointers on how you can make the most of your reference checks:

> **"**
> Make sure the caregiver's references are credible. Don't settle for a reference check from someone who hasn't seen the caregiver in years or from someone whose child was only cared for on a single occasion.
> —Diane, mother of three
> **"**

Bright Idea
For complete guidelines on health and safety in childcare, call the National Resource Center for Health and Safety in Child Care at 1-800-598-KIDS, http://nrc.uchsc.edu, or write to: NRC for Health and Safety in Child Care UCHSC School of Nursing C-287 4200 E. 9th Avenue Denver, CO 80262

- Start out by establishing the credibility of each person providing a reference. Obviously the comments of someone who has only known a particular caregiver for a few weeks carry less weight than those of someone who has known her for years. Likewise, the comments of a close friend or relative who may or may not have had her children cared for by this person are also of limited value.

- Ask for concrete examples whenever possible. Rather than settling for a vague comment that the caregiver in question is "good with babies," ask the person to explain how she soothes a crying baby.

- Take detailed notes so you'll have something to refer back to later. It's not good enough to simply trust your memory. If you're checking the references of more than one caregiver, the responses can start to blur together. Besides, it helps to have written notes in case you want to ask one of the references a few more questions in a week or two.

By the time you've screened by telephone, made personal visits, and checked each caregiver's references thoroughly, you should have enough information to evaluate if a particular childcare setting is suitable for your child.

Just the facts

- You can save yourself a lot of time and effort by conducting a portion of your research by phone and enlisting the help of as many family members as possible.

- Plan to bring your child along on personal visits so that you can see how well she relates to her potential caregivers.

- Try to visit the daycare center on more than one occasion. Ideally, your second visit should be unannounced.

- Make sure that references supplied by a daycare center director or family daycare provider are from credible sources.

The Lowdown on In-Home Childcare

PART III

GET THE SCOOP ON...
The pros and cons of each type of in-home care
■ What the experts say about kids and in-home
care ■ When you need an agency—and when
you don't ■ How in-home care can meet your
child's needs ■ How in-home care can meet your
family's needs ■ Creating a suitable childcare
environment in your home

A Bird's-Eye View of Your In-Home Childcare Options

Until recently, having your child cared for in your own home had a certain cachet. It was perceived as an upper-crust thing to do, like renting a summer house in the Hamptons or starting a trust fund for Baby's Ivy League education. Of course, this has not always been the case, nor is it now. Still, the fallout from the recent au pair murder trial has taken a bit of the shine off of in-home childcare. Even highly trained nannies— caregivers whose credentials are spotless, and who genuinely seem to be in their profession for all the right reasons, are being scrutinized as never before. Some parents are even rushing out to buy $650 teddy bears that are specially equipped with hidden cameras designed to record their in-home caregiver's every move. Although it is true that this sort of high-tech scrutiny has resulted in firings, many more nannies have failed to give their employers any reason to doubt their commitment or affection for the children in their care. While there's no magic formula for finding the perfect in-home caregiver, you increase your odds of finding a suitable candidate if you understand what each type of in-home care will—and won't—deliver.

The pros and cons of each type of in-home care

At its best, in-home care is every parent's dream-come-true: a way to have your child cared for in your own home while you go to work. At its worst, it can be an extremely unpleasant experience for both you and your child.

Because you're leaving your child in the care of a stranger who may be receiving little or no supervision while you're away from home, it's critically important to find a caregiver with the skills required to provide your child with the quality of care he deserves. It's one thing to find an in-home caregiver who can guarantee the physical safety of your child; it's quite another to find someone who is willing to develop a nurturing and creative in-home childcare program.

Part of the problem is that many parents have unrealistic expectations about what they can expect from in-home caregivers. They also neglect the realities of the childcare marketplace, assuming that the au pair who receives $139 per week plus room and board will deliver the same quality of care as the nanny who earns roughly five times as much or that a total stranger will be willing to shower the children in her care with as much TLC as your average doting grandmother.

Your best bet is to understand the pros and cons of each type of in-home childcare—nannies, au pairs, relative care (the trendy term for care by a relative), and other types of in-home care.

Nannies

Nannies are generally considered to be the *crème de la crème* when it comes to in-home childcare. They might be—provided you're getting the services of a bona fide nanny.

The problem is that the term "nanny" is often used to refer to any in-home caregiver, rather than just in-home caregivers who have received special training from an accredited nanny school. (In New York City, for example, many parents refer to their full-time babysitters, mature women with little or no formal childcare training, as "nannies.")

That's the catch: an accredited nanny school. The last thing you want to discover about the expensive nanny you've just hired, is that she's received her early childhood education training from a less than exceptional educational institution. It is essential for parents to check out any potential caregiver's credentials—whether she is recommended by a good friend or comes to you through an exclusive nanny service. The best way to find out if a particular post-secondary institution is an accredited nanny school is by contacting the American Council of Nanny Schools, Delta College, University Center, MI 48710 (517) 686-9417. So if you don't recognize the name of the school listed on your nanny's résumé, pick up the phone and call.

Now that you know how to tell a real nanny from a fake one, let's focus on the pros and cons of hiring a nanny.

Pros:

- Nannies have completed specialized training in early childhood education. The best of the bunch can deliver a preschool-caliber program right in your own home.

- Caring for children is a nanny's chosen profession. She's likely in it for the love of children— not money.

Cons:

- Nannies are the most expensive type of in-home caregiver. Their salaries price them out of the market for all but the most affluent of families.

- They are in short supply, so it's not always easy to find one. That's why it's important to start your search early: at least three months ahead of time for an American nanny, and even earlier than that if you're interested in hiring a nanny from another country.

- Nannies may be less willing to perform household chores than other types of in-home caregivers. If you've absolutely got your heart set on hiring someone who can cook, clean, and entertain your child, forget about hiring a nanny.

Au pairs

As you are no doubt aware, an au pair is a young person, typically from a foreign country, who exchanges childcare duties for the opportunity to live and study in the United States. The au pair program lasts for one year, and host families are carefully screened to ensure that they can fulfill their obligations under the program.

Since the au pair program began in 1986, at least 50,000 au pairs have been placed with host families

Unofficially . . .
Until recently, American nannies were considered to be second-rate as compared to their British counterparts. These days, however, the graduates of accredited United States nanny schools are considered to be every bit as qualified to care for young children as nannies from other countries.

in the United States. Approximately 80 to 85 percent of these au pairs stayed with the first family they were placed with; the rest moved on to a second or subsequent placement, or hopped the first plane for home.

In a perfect world, au pairs and host families would know exactly what to expect from one another. Unfortunately, that's not the case.

While I'm not about to make any friends with the folks at the various au pair agencies, I owe it to you and your children to be completely honest about them. Want to know what I think about au pairs? I think they're a bad idea. Period.

I'm not just bashing au pairs because they're an easy mark in the aftermath of the Louise Woodward murder trial. I'm bashing them because I can't imagine a more ridiculous idea than pairing up young children with young women from foreign countries who, more often than not, are here to party.

Just for the record, I'm not the only person who feels this way. The International Nanny Association recently launched a campaign to urge members of the House Committee on International Relations to discontinue the au pair program.

There's also been a bit of a backlash against au pairs in the media. In a recent article in *Time* magazine, writer Daniel Kadlec shared his insights on the problem: "Many au pairs are oblivious to the daily rigors that await them in tending to small children. Their main aspiration is to be far away from their own homes. To them, it's an adventure, not a job. But if it's going to work, it must be a job. Working parents of toddlers have little time or energy to indulge teenage naivete."

Bright Idea
Ask to see a copy of the brochure that the au pair agency uses to recruit au pairs. That way, you can decide whether the agency does an adequate job of informing potential au pairs of the realities of the position. If the brochure emphasizes travel and glamour rather than the day-to-day drudgery of caring for young children, you could end up with a highly disillusioned au pair.

If you're prepared to deal with some of the situations that Kadlec's family encountered—like dealing with an au pair who liked to swim topless, much to the fascination of the neighbors—read on. If you would rather go with a caregiver who's years removed from puberty, however, jump to the next section of the book.

Pros:

- It is less expensive to have your children cared for by an au pair than most other types of in-home caregivers. Once you've paid an initial agency fee (which includes your au pair's return airfare) and her tuition allowance, you're looking at a relatively low weekly childcare expense ($139 per week on average). In fact, the 11,000 au pairs who come to the U.S. each year earn no more than $7,250 during their stay.

- You and your children will have the opportunity to share your home with a young person from another part of the world. For many families, this, rather than the cost, is the key reason for participating in the au pair program.

Cons:

- Because the program is limited to young people between the ages of 18 and 26, it's possible to get an au pair who is relatively inexperienced in dealing with young children. What's more, because of their age, some au pairs find it difficult to be away from their friends and families and can become homesick.

- Au pairs are not permitted to care for infants under the age of three months unless another adult is in the house. They're also only permitted to care for children under the age of two if they've had at least six months of previous infant care experience.

- The au pair program sets out specific responsibilities for the host family, some of which you may find difficult to meet. You are, for example, required to provide the au pair with a private bedroom and a set amount of time off each week, and each adult member of your household will be required to successfully pass a background check before you will be approved as a host family. You can get the scoop on host family obligations by referring to the Visitor Exchange Program information in Appendix B or by contacting Au Pair in America, American Institute for Foreign Study, 102 Greenwich Avenue, Greenwich, CT 06830, 1-800-727-2437 or (203) 727-2437.

- While your au pair is required to be English-speaking, her mastery of the language may be less than you might desire. What's more, the cultural differences that can be so enchanting when she first arrives at your home may be downright irritating a couple of months down the road.

- Because the au pair program requires that an au pair live with her host family, you may find the loss of privacy disconcerting.

- Your toddler's fluctuating moods may seem like nothing in comparison to the raging hormones of your teenaged or twenty-something au pair. If the biggest challenge you've faced as a parent to date is potty training, the trials and tribulations of being a surrogate parent to a teenager may be more than you can handle.

Watch Out!
If you decide to go with an au pair, make sure you establish some ground rules right from day one. One family learned the hard way that their au pair was handing out their address and phone number to young men in bars—a situation that put both herself and the family's children at risk.

Relative care

A full 41 percent of American children are cared for by relatives—this is despite the fact that 72 percent of women between the ages of 45 and 54 are now holding down jobs and are therefore unavailable to care for their grandchildren. In many cases, these children are cared for in their own homes. Like any other childcare options, care by a relative has its pros and cons.

Pros:

- You will probably feel more comfortable leaving your child with a family member than with a complete stranger. After all, you've probably known this relative for years and will have had the opportunity to observe his or her capability to care for young children.

- Because you come from the same family, you are more likely to share common childrearing philosophies and values.

Cons:

- Day-to-day problems can become emotionally charged when you're dealing with a family member. Don't believe me? Just try to imagine yourself explaining to your mother why her method of toilet-training your child is wrong!

- Grandparents (one of the most popular choices for in-home caregivers) have an abundance of love for their grandchildren, but they may lack the stamina required to keep up with active toddlers and preschoolers. Both sides may feel awkward if it becomes apparent that the arrangement isn't working out after all.

- Money can be a sticky issue between family members. The very same relative who agrees to watch your child for free—or next to nothing—may assume that she now has the right to dictate how you spend your paycheck. After all, she's doing you a favor by helping you to keep your childcare costs at a minimum.

Babysitters

Now let's consider the pros and cons of using babysitters.

Pros:

■ A caregiver who has not had any formal training in child development is generally less expensive to hire than a nanny. As mentioned previously, these caregivers (usually mature women) are often referred to as "babysitters" in some parts of the country. In others, the term "babysitter" is reserved for a teenager who provides child-care on an ad hoc basis. Some people consider the term "babysitter" offensive, so don't use it to describe your caregiver unless she uses the term first!

■ It is much easier to find a babysitter than it is to find a nanny or an au pair. It's an issue of supply and demand.

■ Fancy credentials aren't everything: Some babysitters have had more "hands-on" experience with young children than even the most highly trained caregivers.

Cons:

■ If your caregiver has not received any formal training in child development, you will need to monitor her closely to ensure that the care she is providing is appropriate—particularly if she has had little, if any, experience in caring for young children.

- Many people who have not had much experience in caring for young children assume that it's an easy way to make a living. It's not. As a result, there is a high rate of turnover among childcare workers, particularly those who are new to the field. Another explanation for high turnover rates among caregivers is that compensation is often low and health and other benefits usually nonexistent.

What the experts say about kids and in-home care

Whether your child is cared for at home or in a large daycare center isn't important. What matters is the quality of the interaction between her and her caregiver.

Studies have shown that children who receive high-quality care from their caregivers have superior cognitive and language abilities and are more likely to finish high school than those children who have not benefitted from similarly high-quality childcare arrangements.

Because your child will spend the majority of her waking hours being cared for by someone other than you, it's critically important that you chose someone who is genuinely interested in young children and who is willing to provide her with ongoing opportunities to learn about the world around her. Parking a child in front of the television set isn't childcare; it's copping out.

Another area of concern to many families who have in-home caregivers is the fact that their children don't have the same opportunity to interact with other children as they would have in either a childcare center or family childcare home. If you're worried that your child may lag behind socially when the time comes for her to start school—something that may or may not be true, depending on which expert you believe—you can take some proactive steps to ensure that your child has plenty of opportunity to be with other children. Here are some ideas:

- enroll her in a part-time preschool program
- sign her up for a recreational activity that involves other children
- encourage your childcare provider to take her to the park or some other place in your neighborhood where children congregate
- let your nanny know that your child is welcome to have a friend over during the day.

Then, there's the whole issue of maternal-infant attachments—a key area of concern for many working parents. A recent study by the National Institute of Child Health and Human Development concluded that placing an infant in childcare does not jeopardize the mother-child bond unless the child receives poor-quality care, spends an extensive amount of time in childcare, frequently changes caregivers, or does not receive much care or attention from her parent during the parent's nonworking hours. The moral of the story? Choose your caregiver wisely and plan to spend as much of your nonworking time as possible with your child.

When you need an agency—and when you don't

Whether you decide to use the services of a domestic agency will be determined in large part by how much time you have to devote to your search for a caregiver and the type of worker you're hoping to hire.

There are certain situations in which you'll want to use the services of an agency. If you're anxious to hire an au pair or a nanny from overseas, for example, it's virtually impossible to do so without the help of the pros. Even if you could handle the recruiting on your own—a risky venture, to say the least—the amount of government red tape that you would have to cut through would be certain to defeat you.

While it's often not necessary to use an agency to help you in your search for an American nanny or other in-home caregiver, many families welcome the help with the tasks of sorting through mountains of résumés, checking references, and weaving through the maze of governmental red tape.

On the other hand, their fees can be quite steep. You can expect to pay as much as a full month of your caregiver's salary to the agency. What's more, some require a hefty deposit before they will put you in touch with any of the caregivers that they represent—a situation that can get quite sticky if you're less than impressed with the candidates that they send your way.

How to choose an agency

When you're shopping around for a domestic agency, be sure to look for one that complies with practices recommended by the International Nanny Association (INA)—a private nonprofit organization that serves as an advocacy organization for nannies, educators, nanny placement agencies, and parents who employ in-home caregivers. You can find out more about the INA by contacting the International Nanny Association, Station House, Suite 438, Collingswood, NJ 08108 (609) 858-0808 www.nanny.org.

While I'm on the topic of nanny agencies, another organization you should know about is The Alliance of Professional Nanny Agencies (APNA)— a nationwide association of nanny agencies that was formed to promote a high level of professionalism within the industry. Its members are required to adhere to a code of ethics. To find out whether a particular domestic agency is a member of APNA, contact The Alliance of Professional Nanny Agencies (APNA), 540 Route 10 West 337, Randolph, NJ 07869 1-800-551-2762.

The INA recommends that agencies:

■ interview candidates in person whenever possible, and advise prospective employers what alternate interviewing methods have been used (telephone interview, an interview by a third party) in the event that a face-to-face interview did not take place

■ check a minimum of two references by telephone and provide prospective employers with the opportunity to verify these references themselves

■ provide prospective employers with the results of the candidate's reference checks, Social Security verification, criminal check, and driver's license check

■ prepare a written agreement with each prospective employer that clearly outlines the agency's fees, refund/replacement policies, and the range of services that are to be provided

■ make adjustments/refunds promptly and in accordance with the written policies of the agency

When you're shopping for an agency, you should try to find one that specializes in placing the

Moneysaver
While you might be tempted to go with the domestic agency that charges the lowest fee, you could end up spending more in the long run than if you went with the more expensive firm. The more reputable (and pricier) agencies provide a guarantee with their caregivers. If either you or the caregiver you hire decide that the arrangement isn't working, the agency must find you another caregiver. Bargain basement domestic agencies are less likely to stand behind their candidates—a situation that could cost you well over a thousand dollars if the caregiver doesn't work out.

Bright Idea
Ask if the agency routinely hires private investigators to conduct its background checks. If it doesn't, make sure that the background checks that it conducts on its own are every bit as circumspect as what a private investigator can provide.

type of caregiver that you're interested in recruiting (a nanny versus an au pair versus another type of childcare provider).

If you're interested in hiring a nanny from overseas, you'll want to be sure that the agency that you select is experienced in recruiting nannies from the country of your choice. Be sure to find out how they operate. Does a representative from the U.S. office fly overseas periodically to interview potential candidates in person or do they rely on a third party to conduct these interviews on their behalf? If they rely on a third party to do this screening for them, what are that person's qualifications?

If you're interested in hiring an au pair, you'll want to find out how the agency screens its applicants and what it does to ensure that the au pair experience is accurately represented to young women abroad. You'll also want to find out what support services—if any—it provides after the au pair has arrived. One parent who dealt with a well-known au pair agency was less than impressed with the follow-up service her family received: "I expected the local coordinator to make a personal visit to the au pair and family or to take the au pair out for a social event on her arrival, but she received nothing but a welcome phone call and a letter with a list of other au pairs living in the same city."

If you're interested in hiring another type of in-home caregiver, you may end up dealing with a more mainstream type of employment agency (one that places everyone from bank tellers to office clerks to construction workers). If you find yourself in this situation, you'll want to be sure that the agency personnel understand the qualities that are required to care for young children and that their screening process is sufficiently rigorous. After all, it's one thing to refer a bad apple to a retail store; it's quite another to send that person into someone's home to care for an infant!

Regardless of the type of agency you decide to use, you will want to ask the following questions:

- How do you recruit caregivers?

- What type of screening is done?

- How many references do you check? Are these references checked by mail, by phone, or in person?

- Do your candidates go through a criminal background check?

- Do you check their driving records?

- What measures do you take to verify that each candidate is eligible to work in the U.S.?

- How long will it take for you to find a suitable candidate for this position?

- What are your fees? When are they payable?

- Is there a specific salary level expected by your candidates? If so, what is it?

- Will I hear from candidates directly or will they submit their résumés through you?

- Do I hire the person directly or will you extend the offer of employment on my behalf?

- Do you handle the employment agreement?

- Do you guarantee your placements? (This means that the agency will replace an unsuitable candidate with a more suitable one at no additional charge. If they are unable to find you a suitable candidate, they should be prepared to refund your fee. One quick word of caution:

Timesaver
You can speed up the process of finding a suitable caregiver by using both an in-town and out-of-town agency. The out-of-town agency might be able to hook you up with candidates who are interested in relocating to your part of the country.

make sure the guarantee is for a reasonable period of time—at least three months.)

- Can I have the names and phone numbers of other parents who have used your services? (Many parents insist that this is a must because not all agency reports are reliable.)

In some cases, the agency provides an initial home visit to find out about your needs, advise you of your responsibilities, and inquire about the type of accommodation, remuneration, and benefits you can offer to an in-home caregiver. During this visit, they should help you to fine-tune the job description which you've drafted. Hint: The more explicit you are about your needs, the more probable it is that the agency will be able to find you a suitable caregiver quickly.

The agency's staff can be a source of valuable information. They can tell you whether the salary you're offering is out of line for someone with the qualifications you're seeking, and they can encourage you to rethink some of the responsibilities of the position if they're concerned that the breadth of those responsibilities may discourage top caliber applicants from applying.

One thing you don't want them to do, however, is to oversell the position. Otherwise, you could end up with a rather disillusioned caregiver. To avoid this all-too-common problem, insist on being given the opportunity to sign off on the job description and make sure that the description is accurate on the following points:

- geographical location
- type of living accommodations provided
- job responsibilities

- number and ages of children
- any perks you can provide (for example, use of an automobile, a trip out-of-state each summer, and so on)

What an agency can—and can't—do for you

As much as you might be tempted to do so, it's not possible to delegate your parental responsibilities to a domestic agency, no matter how capable their staff might be.

While you can expect a reputable agency to do their best to screen applicants on your behalf, they can't supply the most important ingredient of all: your own gut instinct.

How in-home care can meet your child's needs

Earlier in this chapter, I talked about the pros and cons of various types of in-home care. Now let's consider how your child's age, temperament, and special needs may influence your in-home childcare choices.

Your child's age

As noted earlier in the book, infants, toddlers, and preschoolers have different needs when it comes to childcare.

Infants (birth to eighteen months) thrive in environments in which there is a low caregiver-child ratio (ideally 1:1 but no more than 1:3) and small group size (ideally three or less but certainly no more than four). Because they need to have the opportunity to build strong attachments to their caregivers, they should be cared for by the same caregiver day after day. These caregivers should genuinely love babies and be prepared to respond to their needs as quickly and effectively as possible.

66

Trust your gut. You can do background checks and ask questions all you want, but ultimately any parent who's in tune with their child and halfway conscious will 'feel' when something is right and know when something doesn't feel right. I interviewed more than 10 nannies and when the one I hired came for an interview, I knew the first minute she was in my house that I wanted to hire her. It just felt right.
—Suzi, mother of two

99

Babies need to eat and sleep when their own bodies dictate (as opposed to when the clock says they should!), but at the same time they need a predictable environment in which they can feel secure. They also need a safe yet stimulating environment in which they are free to explore (as opposed to being confined to playpens or cribs for unreasonably long portions of the day).

In-home care is often an ideal choice for infants. They have the opportunity to forge strong bonds with their caregivers. They are able to eat, sleep, and play on their own schedule—not somebody else's. And because they are exposed to relatively few children (if any), they are less likely to come down with as many colds and other communicable diseases than other children the same age who are being cared for in daycare centers or family daycare settings.

Babies should ideally be cared for by fully qualified nannies or other experienced caregivers. Au pairs are not considered to be suitable caregivers for very young infants, which is why the U.S. Information Agency which oversees U.S.-based au pair programs specifies that they are not to be given sole responsibility for infants under three months of age. Unless they've had a great deal of experience with infants, they're not a particularly good choice for older babies either.

Toddlers (eighteen months to three years) receive the best care when the caregiver-child ratio is relatively low (ideally 1:3 or less, but certainly no more than 1:5) and the group size is no more than six (four if you can find it). They need caregivers who have the patience and energy required to contend with their ever-changing moods, and who have realistic expectations of their behavior. And they need a safe environment that encourages their natural love of physical activity and active exploration while providing them with plenty of opportunities to practice new skills, do things for themselves, and make simple choices.

In-home care is also an excellent choice for toddlers. They benefit from being cared for by the same person day after day. They are able to play in a safe environment that has been child proofed in accordance with their own unique stage of development. And they pick up fewer cold and flu bugs than children who are cared for in group settings.

Once again, fully qualified nannies or other experienced caregivers are better suited to caring for toddlers than less skilled caregivers such as au pairs. As any veteran parent can tell you, toddlers know how to try the patience of a saint. It takes a mature and experienced caregiver to know how to contend with their tears and tantrums.

Preschoolers (three to six years) do well when the caregiver-child ratio is appropriate (ideally 1:5 or less, but certainly no more than 1:8). They need caregivers who have the time and patience to field their endless questions. And they need an environment that provides them with access to age-appropriate activities and equipment as well as plenty of opportunities to build on their increasingly sophisticated language skills and to socialize with other children their own age.

In-home care can be terrific for preschoolers—provided that they are given the opportunity to interact with other children on a regular basis and they are exposed to a variety of age-appropriate materials. Often this means taking them to swimming lessons or enrolling them in a story time program at the local library, where they can both interact with other children and explore an environment other than home.

While fully qualified nannies and other experienced caregivers are an ideal choice for preschoolers as well, most au pairs are fully capable of caring for preschoolers, too, although the quality of care will, of course, be determined by the skills and experience of the particular au pair.

Your child's temperament

Your child's temperament is every bit as important as his age in determining the suitability of a particular type of childcare arrangement.

In an in-home care arrangement, the interaction between the child and his caregiver is critical. That's why it's important to choose someone who has the patience to deal with his shyness or the energy to deal with his high activity level—whichever the case may be. Don't make your final hiring decision until you have observed your child and the caregiver together.

Your child's special needs

If your child has any special needs, you'll want to scrutinize his childcare arrangements particularly carefully. Factors to consider in an in-home care arrangement include whether a caregiver has the experience and training required to deal with your child's needs. (You'll find a more detailed discussion about finding childcare for a child who has special needs in Chapter 11.)

You might also want to find out whether there is a resource worker available to work with your child or—at the very least—to provide his caregiver with

Watch Out!
If your child is particularly shy and has a hard time bonding with strangers, you might want to think twice about hiring an au pair. Because the program only lasts for one year, you will need to find another caregiver for your child just a few months down the road.

some pointers on designing a program that will meet his needs. Your state or local childcare licensing authorities can put you in touch with the government office responsible for coordinating care for children with special needs. (Please see Appendix B for a list of state and provincial childcare licensing authorities.)

How in-home care can meet your family's needs

Your family's needs should also be taken into account when you're searching for a suitable caregiver. Two important factors for most families are the hours of care required and their expectations of the type of care that their child will receive.

Hours of care

Your schedule at work (and your partner's schedule) will help to determine the hours during which your child will need care, and whether you want a live-in or live-out caregiver.

Some families look for in-home care because they have erratic schedules. Perhaps one spouse is "on call" on a regular basis, while the other frequently has to travel out of town. If this is the case with your family, you'll want to be up-front about your needs with any potential caregiver. After all, she's likely to be less than pleased if she discovers after the fact that she's expected to be on call whenever you're on call!

While it might not be possible to pinpoint the exact hours when you'll be in need of her services, try to tell her as much as you can. Let her know the maximum number of hours she would ever be asked to work in a given week and how you intend to handle any overtime that is required. Will you be paying her at time-and-a-half for any additional hours worked or will you encourage her to take time off at a future date in lieu of payment for overtime? It's also important to discuss which holidays will be paid—and which ones won't. If you can afford it, try to err on the side of generosity.

Expectations of care

You'll also want to be clear about your expectations of care. You need to let a potential caregiver know what tasks other than childcare (if any) will be included in her job description. You'll probably find that the more skilled the worker is, the less likely she is to be willing to perform routine housekeeping tasks.

66

We pay Janine for 25 hours per week, even if she gets sent home early or we don't need her. This was our choice. We feel that perks like this will pay off because they will show her that we value her. To me, childcare is no place to cut corners.
—Jennifer, mother of one

99

Many families expect far too much from their in-home caregiver. If the caregiver's primary responsibility is to care for your child, don't expect her to cook, clean, and perform a variety of other household duties as well. Remember: The time she spends attending to other tasks is time that she could have spent playing with your child. As a rule of thumb, don't ask your caregiver to be responsible for any more tasks than you yourself could reasonably accomplish with a child underfoot.

You also need to be clear about whether you want a highly trained professional (such as a nanny who has graduated from a certified nanny school), a full-time babysitter, or a less skilled worker (such as an au pair, who has likely had limited childcare experience and little or no formal training). Some families wouldn't even consider hiring anyone other than an experienced nanny; others have had wonderful experiences with babysitters and au pairs. Only you can decide what's right for your family.

Creating a suitable childcare environment in your home

When your child is cared for in a daycare center or family daycare environment, someone else is responsible for creating a child-friendly environment. When the care is being provided in your own home, you're the one who's responsible for providing a safe yet stimulating environment.

Here are some pointers on things you can do to provide your child with the best possible in-home childcare experience.

Choosing toys and other equipment

Plan to have a variety of learning materials on hand. While you don't have to fill up a U-Haul at Toys-R-Us, you do need to be sure that you've got a variety of safe and age-appropriate materials on hand.

When you're choosing toys and books, look for materials that can grow with your child. Here are some examples:

- The pegs from a peg board can be used for dump-and-fill play (for example, dumping a bucket of toys and then picking everything up again—a popular activity for one-year-olds) and counting as the child matures.

- Basic board books can double as learn-to-read books a few years down the road, provided the subject matter is suitable for an older child.

- Plastic puzzle pieces can be used as shape cutters for modeling clay.

- Sock puppets—a popular toy for infants—can double as hand puppets for an older child.

- A plastic bathtub for a baby can evolve into a water play center for an older child.

Watch Out!
Toys that have been pulled off the market for safety reasons often show up at garage sales. A recent episode of the Canadian Broadcasting Corporation's consumer affairs show *Marketplace* pointed out that lawn darts, walkers, and other equally unsafe products are readily available at garage sales.

- An infant blanket can be strung across the lower half of a door frame to make a puppet theater for an older child.

- Play materials like clay, child-safe scissors and paste, paint brushes and paint, blocks, markers, crayons, colored pencils, chalk, and pastels are ideal for all but the youngest of babies.

Unless your toy budget rivals that of any member of the Kennedy clan, you might want to use some of these tips for stretching your dollar further:

- Hit garage sales and consignment shops and scoop up quality second-hand toys and books.

- Arrange a toy exchange with other families who have children the same age. A $300 indoor climber is much more affordable if it's shared between four families.

- Borrow materials from your library or family resource center (assuming there is one in your community). This is a budget-friendly way of ensuring that your child has access to a steady stream of high-quality books, videos, and other learning materials.

- Organize learning activities that make use of things you already have around the house: magnets, magnifying glasses, leaves, stones, feathers, plant seeds, bird feeders, and so on.

- Before you discard old clothing, consider whether it could enjoy a second life as dress-up clothing. Jackets, dresses, hats, wigs, and handbags can be combined with such props as paper money and dolls to provide a sensational dress-up center.

- Transform oversized cardboard boxes into playhouses, fire stations, schools, hospitals, and so on by using a bit of paint.

- Use old shirts as paint smocks and create an easel by hanging an oversized cardboard box over the back of a chair.

- Fill a large plastic container with sand and use it as an indoor sand box.

- Different sizes of plastic food containers can be used as nesting toys.

You can find all kinds of valuable information about choosing toys at the Child and Family Canada "Play" page: www.cfc-efc.ca/menu/eng011.htm.

There's also some great material on the National Network for Child Care Web site www.exnet.iastate.edu/pages/nncc/Curriculum/activity.page.html including a number of tip sheets on making your own toys.

Bright Idea
Use old tires to create an inexpensive outdoor play area for your child. Tires can be hung from trees (to create a swing), partially buried in the ground (to create an obstacle course), or filled with sand (to create a small sandbox).

Designing your space
After you've accumulated all of this stuff, you need to give some thought to setting up a section of your home as a playroom. Here are just a few of the factors that you should keep in mind as you go about designing this space:

- Choose wallcoverings, flooring materials, and furnishings that can be cleaned easily.

- Incorporate as many storage areas as possible to help keep clutter to a minimum. Make sure that at least some of these storage areas are easily accessible to your child so that he can pull out his favorite toys without help.

- Make sure that the change area is adjacent to the play area—particularly if you have more than one child. This way, the caregiver won't have to leave your older child unsupervised while she goes to change the baby.

- If your child is an infant, ensure that there's a spot where he can pull himself up safely and be sufficiently cushioned if he tumbles or falls.

- If he's a toddler or a preschooler, make sure that there is sufficient room for active play.

Moneysaver
Encourage your caregiver to take your child on trips to the local fire station, the library, the zoo, the playground, and so on. Not only are these outings stimulating and fun; they're often free!

- Try to provide as many of the following types of activities as possible (either on a permanent or rotating basis, depending on the size of your playroom and the age of your child): table toys (puzzles, games, peg boards, beads, and lacing toys); music (tapes and simple musical instruments); blocks made from a variety of different materials (wood, plastic, cardboard, and so on); imaginative play (dress-up center); arts and crafts (sponges, finger paints, crayons, pastels, pencils, markers, collage material such as dry pasta and fabric scraps, child-safe paste and glue, modeling clay); science and nature (pine cones, rocks, books about the outdoors); books and stories (cloth, vinyl, board or paper books, depending on the age of your child); water play (containers for pouring, no-sting shampoo to use to make bubbles); sand play (a container filled with wet or dry sand); and vigorous activities (jumping on an indoor trampoline, playing with ride-on toys, and so on).

- Don't overfill the room. Your caregiver needs to move around freely while she's carrying your child, and your child needs room to explore.

Just the facts

- Not all in-home caregivers are created equal. Make sure you understand the pros and cons of hiring a nanny versus an au pair versus a relative or other caregiver.

- Encourage your caregiver to take your child to the playground or other places where he can play with other children.

- An agency can't do your thinking for you. Your gut instinct is still your best guide to choosing a caregiver.

- If you opt for in-home care, you should make sure that you provide your child and his caregiver with a childcare environment that would do any childcare center proud.

Evaluating Your In-Home Childcare Options

Chapter 7

L ast fall, a first-time parent in New York City started looking for a part-time caregiver for her two-month-old daughter. She placed advertisements in two local newspapers: the *Village Voice* and the New York University student newspaper. The papers had no sooner hit the street when her phone began ringing off the hook. "We began getting a call every 90 seconds," she recalls. "We had to screen them through the answering machine; there was just no way to respond to each call."

As this example illustrates, looking for an in-home caregiver can be time-consuming and stressful. While it may be difficult to find the right person for your particular childcare needs, it can be done—and in this chapter I'll show you how. I'll give you some tips on conducting your search, reviewing résumés and letters of application, screening by phone, conducting personal interviews, checking references, and even hiring a private investigator—a step that a growing number of families are taking in the hope of purchasing a little peace of mind.

Evaluating potential caregivers

Whether you decide to contract the services of an agency to assist you in your search for an in-home caregiver or conduct this search yourself, your first step should be to draw up a detailed job description that contains the following information:

- the number of and ages of your children
- the nature of the job (if any housekeeping is required)
- the hours when you require care (full-time versus part-time; live-in versus live-out; daytime versus evening or if weekend work is required)
- the amount of training and experience a candidate should have (if you're only interested in hiring a graduate from a certified nanny school, then say so).
- the salary you're prepared to offer
- the starting date for the position

If you're working with an agency, the director will help you to polish your job description before sending it on to prospective applicants. If you're handling the search on your own, the staff of the classified department of the local newspaper can help you with the wording of your ad, suggesting abbreviations and acronyms that can save you money.

Reviewing resumes and letters of application

After your job description has been posted with the agency or published in the newspaper, you are likely to start receiving résumés from individuals who are interested in being considered for the position.

While the number of responses can be overwhelming (particularly if you've chosen to go with a newspaper ad), you can reduce the number of candidates under consideration by eliminating those whose résumés reveal unexplained gaps in employment, an unstable work record, a lack of related experience, or who are missing a key requirement for the position (for example, a vehicle or a valid driver's license).

Screening by phone

After you've come up with a short list of candidates, it's time to conduct some preliminary telephone interviews. The purpose of these interviews is to find out a bit more about each candidate before you decide who you should—and shouldn't—interview.

Here's a list of points you should consider covering during this initial contact with each caregiver:

- What hours and days of the week is the caregiver available?

- What are her salary expectations?

- What experience has she had in caring for young children?

- What was her most recent position? What were her responsibilities? What was her reason for leaving this position?

- Has she had any formal training in early childhood education?

- Is she certified in cardiopulmonary resuscitation (CPR) and first aid?

- Does she have any health problems?

- Does she smoke?

Timesaver
If you want to cut back on the number of responses to your ad, insist that all candidates respond in writing. If you're not comfortable having your home address published, ask that applications be directed to your workplace or to a post office box. If you don't want the expense and hassle of getting a post office box through your local post office, you can rent one from companies such as Mail Boxes Etc. for as little as $10 per month. Just one quick word of caution: You might miss out on some excellent caregivers this way— those who decide to apply for another position with a less rigorous application process.

- Does she have a valid driver's license and her own vehicle?

- Would she be prepared to undergo a background check at your expense?

If a particular candidate appears to be a good fit for your family, based on her responses to your questions, you might want to take a few minutes to tell her a bit more about the job and your family, the specific duties, the hours of work, the pay, your policies regarding holidays, vacation, and other time off, where your home is located, and so on. This will help her to assess whether the position is right for her.

Conducting personal interviews

After you've screened each of the candidates by phone, you'll be ready to schedule personal interviews with the most promising candidates. When you call to schedule each interview, be sure to remind each candidate to bring along both proof of her eligibility to work in the United States and a list of references since the penalties for hiring someone who is not legally entitled to work in the United States can be significant. Before you extend an offer of employment to a nanny, babysitter, au pair, or other caregiver, make sure you've fulfilled your responsibilities under the law. If you're not sure what you're required to do, contact the United States Immigration and Naturalization Service at 1-800-755-0777 or (202) 514-2000 for details.

Now let's talk about the ins and outs of interviewing—something you may not have had experience with on the job.

Interviewing can be exhausting—particularly because there's so much at stake. No matter how anxious you may be to wrap up the hiring process, however, it's important to resist the temptation to interview only the most promising candidate. While you might save time in the short run, you'll be back to square one if the candidate you have in mind turns out to be less than ideal. Besides, it's far better to have a pool of candidates to choose from as you go about making your final decision.

Some parents prefer to stagger interviews over a couple of days; others prefer to put on a pot of coffee and dive right into a day-long interviewing marathon. Regardless of which method you choose, be prepared for at least a few no shows—a lesson one working parent found out the hard way. She took a day's vacation to interview six potential caregivers for her twin daughters only to find herself faced with six separate excuses for missed interviews. Fortunately, she had already interviewed an excellent caregiver the weekend before. Needless to say, that's who she ended up hiring.

Because you don't have to evaluate the physical environment or get into detailed discussions about policies and procedures (as would be the case if you were checking out a daycare center or family daycare setting, you can devote the bulk of your interview to assessing the caregiver's suitability to care for your child. That's why the interview should focus on the caregiver's experience, training, and skills in caring for young children.

Rather than barraging a potential caregiver with too many questions all at once, start out with a few that are particularly relevant to your childcare needs. The main thing is to spark a conversation that will be informative for both of you. Here are a few of the the types of questions you may want to ask:

Watch Out! Make sure that your home is suitably child-proofed. A study published in the *Journal of the American Medical Association* concluded that children being cared for in their own homes were more likely to be injured than those being cared for in out-of-home childcare environments.

Bright Idea
Top caliber candidates will often bring a written statement outlining their childcare philosophies and personal goals.

- What led her to pursue a career with children?

- What does she like most about her work?

- What does she like least about her work?

- What age group is her favorite?

- What age group is her least favorite?

- What are her personal goals?

- How long does she intend to continue working in the childcare field?

- Is she prepared to make at least a one-year commitment to your family?

- Does she participate in professional development opportunities on a regular basis?

- Does she belong to the local nanny association or childcare provider's network? Why or why not?

- Does she demonstrate a genuine love of children?

- How does she relate to your child(ren)?

- Does she seem like someone with whom you and your child could develop a relationship?

- What ages of children is she most comfortable with?

- Is she experienced in working with children with special needs (if applicable)?

- Does she seem to possess a solid understanding of what children can and want to do at various stages of development?

- Could she recognize and deal with illness?

- Does she encourage the children to master new skills?

- Does she allow them to make choices (where appropriate)?

- Does she talk to the children and encourage the children to express themselves through words and language?

- Does she encourage good health habits, such as hand washing before eating?

- What are her feelings about pacifiers and comfort objects?

- Does she offer assistance when a child needs it?

- Does she have CPR and first-aid training?

- Does she react with enthusiasm to children's discoveries and accomplishments?

- Does she sit with the children as they play?

- Does she offer physical and verbal reassurance if a child is unhappy?

- What is her approach to discipline?

- How does she deal with crying?

- What activities does she like to do with babies? toddlers? preschoolers?

- Is she willing to provide you with a list of references?

- Is she prepared to sign a work agreement?

- Are the references you speak with enthusiastic about the quality of care that their children have received from this caregiver?

- How does your child react to her?

- Would you feel comfortable leaving your child with her?

Arranging for the caregiver to meet your child

As important as it is to find out about the potential caregiver's experience and training, what really matters is how she relates to your child. That's why it's important to schedule the interview at a time when

Bright Idea
Because it can be difficult to conduct an interview with a young child in the room, you might consider having someone else care for your child while you get through the first part of the interview. Then, once you've asked all your questions, you can bring in your child to meet the caregiver. If your partner entertains your child while you conduct the first part of the interview, they'll both have the chance to meet the caregiver.

your child is available to meet her—even if that means staggering the interviews over the course of a few days so that your child can be on hand for each and every one.

You can learn a lot about her skills as a caregiver by watching the way she acts as she meets your child for the first time. Here are some questions you might want to consider as you observe the way she interacts with your child:

- Does she respect his initial wariness of strangers or does she intimidate him by coming on too strong too soon?

- Does she squat down to talk to him at his level?

- Does she use voice qualities and mannerisms that are likely to engage a child?

- Does she seem to like him?

- Does he seem to like her?

Checking references

After you've conducted your personal interviews and settled on one or more candidates who seem to meet your family's needs, you're ready to check her references. The purpose of these reference checks is to verify that your initial impression of each caregiver is, in fact, accurate.

Whether or not you use the services of an agency, the responsibility for checking a particular caregiver's references ultimately rests with you. The degree to which references are scrutinized varies tremendously from agency to agency. One parent discovered to her horror that a particular agency was referring caregivers without ever seeing their résumés, let alone checking their references. The moral of the story? Don't be satisfied with anything less than a written report summarizing the agency's reference and background checks, and be prepared to verify this information yourself.

There's a very good reason, by the way, for double-checking references yourself. According to nanny agency owner Denise Collins, who was recently interviewed by *Kiplinger's Personal Finance Magazine*, you might have more luck getting the references to spill the beans than the agency: "Employers will often share something with another employer that they may be afraid to tell an agency for fear of liability."

Although you needn't ask all of them, here are some questions you might consider asking. Once again, the object of asking these questions is to initiate a useful and informative discussion, not an interrogation:

- What led you to choose this particular caregiver?

- How many other candidates did you consider? Why did you rule them out?

- What were her specific duties?

- Did she have any problems meeting those responsibilities?

- How long were your children cared for by this person? What are their current ages?

- How long did it take for your children to feel comfortable with her?

- To what extent did she met your expectations?

- Did the caregiver appear to enjoy working with children?

- Did she appear to have a solid understanding of the particular needs of children of various ages?

- How did she discipline the children in her care?

Timesaver
Rank your reference check questions in order of importance. If the potential caregiver flunks out on one of the big issues, like reliability, terminate the reference check immediately. There's no point in wasting your own or the other person's time.

- What did she do to make the children feel good about themselves?

- Was she always aware of where the children were and what they were doing?

- In general, was she calm and in control of the situation?

- Did she create an environment that was stimulating to the children?

- How well did she communicate with you?

- What ages of children is she most comfortable with?

- What ages of children is she least comfortable with?

- What is her daily routine?

- What are her strengths as a caregiver?

- What are her weaknesses as a caregiver?

- How did she handle your child's demand feeding, toilet training, temper tantrums, and so on? Were you satisfied with the way she handled these situations?

- Can you give me an example of a situation which she handled particularly well?

- Can you give me an example of a situation which she didn't handle as well as you would have liked?

- What is your overall impression of her?

- Was she punctual and reliable?

- Did she miss a lot of workdays due to illness?

- Why is she no longer working for you?

- What advice would you give other parents who are considering having their children cared for by her?

■ Is there anything else you think I should know before deciding to hire her?

You can learn as much about the caregiver from what the parents you're interviewing won't say as from what they will say. Most people are reluctant to admit that they've made a poor childcare choice. After all, it's as much as admitting that you're a bad parent. As a result, if they're dissatisfied with the care their children received from a particular caregiver, they're more likely to dodge questions or answer in vague generalities than to launch into a tirade about her shortcomings. Consequently, if the parents you speak to appear to be less than enthusiastic about the quality of care that their children received from the caregiver in question, you should consider that to be fair warning that she may not be all that she appears to be.

What a reference will—and won't—tell you

Because the list of references supplied by a particular caregiver is hand-picked by that person, you can expect the people you call to paint her in the best possible light. Even if they have had an unpleasant experience (which is unlikely, given that they've agreed to act as references on her behalf) the fear of litigation or other repercussions makes most people think twice before saying anything overly negative about a former caregiver. The best way around this particular situation is to describe your family situation—the numbers and ages of your children, your childrearing philosophies, and so on—and then ask whether the person providing the reference thinks that the caregiver in question would be a good fit for your family.

The liability issue is something you should also bear in mind if you're asked to provide a reference

Unofficially . . .
Studies have shown that 20 to 25 percent of job applicants provide false information to potential employers, and as many as 10 percent have criminal records.

for a former caregiver. While certain states have recently introduced legislation designed to protect employers who provide factual—but nonetheless damning—information in reference checks, most human resource experts recommend that employers err on the side of caution when providing less-than-enthusiastic reference checks. Increasing numbers of employees are hiring private investigators to conduct bogus reference checks to find out what their former employers are saying about them. It's a strategy that has netted some employees in excess of $1 million in damages—reason enough to be careful about what you say about a former employee. Even if the people you call do give the caregiver a uniformly glowing recommendation, be prepared to read between the lines.

How the pros do it

Ever wonder how human resource professionals obtain any useful information from references? Here are a few pointers on how you can make the most of your reference checks:

- Start out by establishing the credibility of each person providing a reference. Obviously, the comments of someone who has only known a particular caregiver for a few weeks carry considerably less weight than those of someone who has known her for years. Likewise, the comments of a close friend or relative who may or may not have had her children cared for by this particular person are of limited value.

- If the reference calls you, ask for a number where you can call her back. If the person is reluctant to provide you with her name and phone number, she could be supplying a bogus reference.

Bright Idea
The quickest way to find out if a particular reference is bogus is to deliberately make mistakes when you're asking questions. For example, slip up on the number of children that the caregiver supposedly cared for, the dates of employment, and so on. If the person providing the reference doesn't pick up on the error, don't assign much credibility to the reference.

- Ask for concrete examples whenever possible. Rather than settling for a vague comment that the caregiver in question is "good with children," ask the person to describe how the caregiver structures a typical day of care.

- Take detailed notes so you'll have something to refer to later on. It's not good enough to trust your memory. If you're checking the references of more than one caregiver, the responses can start to blur together. Besides, it helps to have written notes in case you want to ask one of the references a few more questions in a week or two.

What a private investigator can do for you

Concern about the quality of care that their child receives is leading some parents to contract the services of private investigators to conduct background checks or otherwise monitor their in-home caregivers—both before and after the hire. Criminal background checks, driver's record checks, and employment verifications are becoming more and more common as growing numbers of parents look for ways to feel more confident that their in-home caregiver is everything she claims to be. This doesn't mean that everyone is doing it, or that it's the right choice for your family. It's just one more thing to consider as you embark on the process of choosing a caregiver.

While it's fairly routine to request a background check on any new employee, it's quite another to have that person followed. Before you contract the services of a private investigator, you need to have a clear idea about the type of information you're seeking—and how far you're prepared to go to get it. On the other hand, if you suspect that there is something seriously amiss with a caregiver's backgroud, you may opt to terminate your relationship with her instead of going to the trouble and expense of confirming your worst suspicions. After all, where the care of one's children is concerned, trust is everything. If your gut feeling tells you that a caregiver is untrustworthy, you don't need any other "reason" or "evidence" not to hire her. However, if you won't rest until you've gone as far as you can go to check a caregiver's background, a private investigator can provide you with the information you want.

Criminal record checks

Criminal record checks tell you whether or not the caregiver in question has a criminal record. Contrary to popular belief, it's not possible to do a nationwide criminal record check—unless, of course, you're the F.B.I. Private investigators have to conduct record checks on a state or countywide basis, a process that can be complicated if the prospective caregiver has worked, lived, or attended school in a number of different states. Some states forbid statewide searches. Others require fingerprints to process a search request. And still others take so long to respond to criminal record requests that your child could be in college before you get the go-ahead to hire her caregiver. These are just a few of the unfortunate realities of conducting a criminal record check.

Where information is available, a private investigator can track down the following types of details about any offences that the potential caregiver has committed:

- the case number
- the charges
- the arrest date
- the file date
- the deposition date
- the verdict
- the sentence
- the names of the parties involved

This information can be made available to you within a few business days.

Court record checks

Criminal history information and civil record filings are yours for the asking. The only catch is that you have to visit the appropriate courthouse or state repository in person—no easy task if you're in New York and the caregiver's last address was in California. Because most private investigators can tap into a countrywide network of researchers, it's still possible to get your hands on this information.

What you can do with this information is an entirely different matter. If, for example, the proceedings of a particular trial violated the accused person's rights under Equal Employment Opportunity legislation, you might not be able to use that information as an excuse for not hiring the person. Bottom line? Consult with an attorney if the court record check comes back with damaging information about a potential caregiver.

Civil record searches

While it's possible to search both upper and lower courts in a given jurisdiction, to save time and money, most private investigators choose to zero in on the most serious offences only, searching the records of the upper courts. These records searches typically turn up the following type of information:

- the case number
- the case type
- the file date
- the deposition date
- the judgement
- the award
- the names of the parties involved

It's an excellent way to find out whether the prospective caregiver has sued or been sued by any former employers. In most cases, civil searches can be conducted within two to five business days.

Federal court searches

A federal court search will reveal if your caregiver has violated a federal law. Such offences might include treason or offenses that cross state lines (for example, drug smuggling).

Education verification

Education verifications confirm whether your caregiver graduated from the prestigious nanny school, as she claims, or whether she's actually a grade school dropout. Educational verifications are used to verify such facts as the degree(s) earned and the date(s) completed. In most cases, you will need to have the employee's written permission to find out more.

Social Security verification

A Social Security verification is used to confirm that the Social Security number that the caregiver has supplied has, in fact, been issued to her.

Driver's license report

A driver's license report can provide you with information on any driving-related offenses. It's an excellent way to find out whether a potential caregiver's license is suspended, restricted, or has expired; whether she has been convicted of any drug or alcohol-related offenses; whether she has paid all outstanding fines or showed up in court at the required times; and so on.

Employment verification checks

Employment verification checks are designed to uncover any inaccuracies on the potential caregiver's résumé. Past employers are contacted to verify job titles, dates of employment, the reason for leaving, and the overall job performance. A skillful private investigator can often get off-the-record interviews with individuals who wouldn't otherwise be willing to discuss the caregiver's personal and professional experiences.

Credit reports

There are two types of reports that you or a private investigator can obtain through a credit bureau: an investigative consumer report and a credit report.

An investigative consumer report provides information about the caregiver's character, general reputation, personal characteristics, and lifestyle. It is compiled by conducting interviews with the caregiver's friends, neighbors, and so on. You are required to get the caregiver's permission before ordering this type of check.

The second type of check—a credit report—contains information about court cases, judgements, bankruptcies, and liens against the caregiver; as well as information on her financial record

Bright Idea
The simplest way to access credit reports is through a private investigation firm. If you don't choose to go this route, however, you should ask the caregiver to supply you with a copy of her credit report. She can purchase a copy for less than $10 from any of the three major credit reporting agencies: Equifax (1-800-685-1111), TransUnion Corp. (1-312-408-1400), or TRW (1-800-392-1122).

(for example, if she has any outstanding loans, what her payment record is like, and so on).

You can also garner some information that the caregiver chose to omit from her résumé—such as addresses from parts of the country where she's lived and been convicted of criminal offenses!

In most cases, you'll need to have a private investigator obtain credit reports on your behalf. Most credit reporting firms only do business with organizations that are in a position to use their services on a regular basis.

Workers' compensation checks

In most states, once an employee's claim goes through the state system or the Workers' Compensation Appeals Board, the case becomes public record. This is an excellent way to find out if a potential caregiver has a history of making fraudulent workers' compensation claims. One quick word of caution: The federal Americans With Disabilities Act prevents employers from discriminating against job applicants who have filed a workers' compensation claim.

Medical records

Medical records are considered to be highly confidential information, so you'll require the applicant's permission to access this type of information.

Some families require that caregivers undergo a medical examination prior to being hired. If you decide to go this route, it's only reasonable to offer to pick up the tab for this expense. Your health care provider can provide you with a fee schedule for this type of service.

As you can see, a private investigator can take a lot of the guesswork out of hiring a caregiver—and his or her services are probably far more affordable than you think, with the tab for a comprehensive background search typically coming in at less than $100.

Preparing a work agreement

Sharing your home with another adult is never easy—something you no doubt discovered for yourself when you and your partner first began living together under one roof. While the glow of the early stages of romantic love probably made it easier for you to forgive him or her for committing such unspeakable crimes as forgetting to put the cap on the toothpaste or turning the coffee pot off before you've poured your second cup, over time these minor domestic faux pas might well have started to take their toll. Opening your home to a live-in or live-out caregiver can be a similar type of experience. During the initial honeymoon period, you and your caregiver will go out of your way to be considerate to one another. In subsequent weeks, however, as the newness of the relationship begins to wear off, there's a tendency to allow some of these niceties to go to the wayside. It's how you relate to one another during this post-honeymoon phase that will determine whether you and your caregiver are prepared to make the relationship work—for better and for worse.

One of the best ways to avoid future problems with your child's caregiver is to put as much as you can in writing right from the very beginning.

Most families that choose to go this route find that having a written work agreement with their child's caregiver enables them to prevent minor misunderstandings from becoming major problems. It's kind of like having a prenuptial agreement, but instead of focusing exclusively on the

Timesaver
Rather than asking your caregiver to come to you each time she needs money for parking or other incidentals, you might want to establish a small petty cash fund that she can access at her discretion.

Bright Idea
Because it's dif-
ficult to learn
much about one
another during
the interview
process, it's
fairly common
practice for fam-
ilies and care-
givers to agree
to a three month
probationary
period during
which time the
two parties are
free to assess
the suitability of
the arrangement
before making a
long-term com-
mitment to one
another. If either
the family or the
caregiver is dis-
satisfied with
the arrangement
within that time
period, the
arrangement can
be terminated
without any hard
feelings on
either side.

larger financial issues, work agreements focus on the minutiae of everyday life: whose job it is to bathe the children, start the dinner, or empty the diaper pail.

While some of these issues may seem almost laughably simple, it's better to err on the side of caution and discuss a particular issue in advance than it is to find yourself trying to come up with a solution that's fair to both sides in the heat of the moment.

As you might expect, the most effective work agreements tend to be fairly comprehensive, covering both basic issues such as working hours, the rate of pay, job responsibilities, and so on, as well as issues that are of particular concern to the family in question, such as policies concerning use of the telephone or the family car. (You can find a particularly comprehensive contract—written by a veteran nanny, no less—in Appendix D. Because each family's situation is unique, you'll want to modify the contract to make it fit your own needs.)

While you might find it intimidating to attempt to write your own work agreement, it's not nearly as scary as you might think. Your goal isn't to produce some encyclopedia-like document that is positively oozing with legalese; what you want is a friendly document that describes the caregiver's rights and responsibilities as thoroughly as possible while conveying your confidence in her ability to do the job.

There's a lot to be covered in a typical work agreement. Here are just a few of the elements that you might want to incorporate into yours:

- starting date
- scheduled working hours (and whether additional hours of work may be required from time to time)

- the salary agreed upon and the payment schedule (for example, weekly, biweekly, semi-monthly, or monthly)

- who is responsible for paying which taxes to which levels of government (see Chapter 8 for further details)

- what benefits are being provided (for example, health insurance, automobile insurance, a membership at the local gym, and so on)

- how the salary will be adjusted if another child is added to care (either through an addition to your family or a joint care arrangement with another family)

- policies regarding sick time, vacation time, and personal days off (both yours and hers)

- how much notice is required in the event that the caregiver decides to take another job or you decide to terminate her employment

- when the caregiver's performance will be evaluated

- when merit or cost of living increases will come into effect

- the major job responsibilities (feeding and dressing the children, teaching them about personal hygiene, engaging them in learning activities, putting them down for naps, playing with them, disciplining them, and so on)

- whether the caregiver will be required to transport the children by car (and, if so, who will be responsible for picking up the tab for the necessary automobile insurance coverage)

- what steps the caregiver should follow in the event of an emergency (fire, medical, and other)

- who the caregiver is authorized to release the children to in the event of an emergency (neighbors, grandparents, or other family members)

- under what circumstances the caregiver is authorized to administer medication

- general house rules (policies regarding visitors, the supervision of maintenance personnel, phone use, and so on)

Let's take a few moments to consider some of the more complex issues in greater detail.

Scheduled working hours

Timesaver
If you know someone else with an in-home caregiver, ask if you can use the work agreement that they've drafted as a starting point for your own. You may also want to refer to the sample work agreement that we've included in Appendix D.

There are few issues that cause as much grief between families and caregivers as that of working hours. Some families operate on the misguided assumption that an in-home caregiver is at their beck and call whenever they require her services— an attitude that doesn't sit well with most caregivers!

Your work agreement should specify both the standard hours of employment as well as under what circumstances she may be asked to work additional hours. While it's obviously impossible to predict every possible scenario beforehand, there are some circumstances you can anticipate in advance, and these are the ones that should be documented in the agreement. If both you and your partner are accountants, for example, you know only too well that you will be putting in long hours at the office during tax season. Likewise, if you're a single parent with a live-in caregiver and your job requires you to be on call one weekend per month, you might want to alert your caregiver to the fact that you will be expecting her to be on call during this time period as well.

The agreement should also include wording that indicates how the caregiver will be compensated for any additional hours that she is required to work. Will you pay her time-and-a-half (the standard going rate for overtime) for any additional hours she puts in when you're particularly busy at work? Or will you give her additional time off a few weeks or months down the road to compensate her for these extra hours? This is definitely a decision that you'll want to make with your caregiver. If she's saving to purchase a new vehicle, she may want to have her overtime hours added to her paycheck; if, on the other hand, she has friends or family in another part of the country, she may prefer to accumulate a few extra days off to add to her vacation time.

A brief aside: You are not legally required to pay overtime rates to a caregiver who is employed on a casual (as opposed to regular) basis. However, even if you're not required to do so by law, paying a caregiver fairly for the hours she's put in is clearly the right thing to do.

Benefits

Many families choose to provide their caregivers with some additional benefits. The most common types are health insurance and automobile insurance.

The rationale for providing health care coverage for your caregiver is simple: It will eliminate a lot of financial stress for her in the event that she is injured or becomes ill.

Before you start shopping for health insurance for your nanny, make sure that you understand the difference between permanent health insurance and temporary health insurance. Permanent health insurance is automatically renewable at the end of

Moneysaver
If you're looking for health insurance for your caregiver, you might consider purchasing coverage for her through a group plan. This kind of coverage is both cheaper and easier to obtain. The National Association for the Education of Young Children (NAEYC), which is open to both in-home and out-of-home caregivers, offers its members access to a number of different health insurance plans. You can find the contact information for the NAEYC in Appendix B.

each term, even if your nanny has contracted a life-threatening illness in the meantime. Short-term insurance policies, on the other hand, are written for a specific period of time (for example, six months) and are not automatically renewable at the end of each term. As you might expect, short-term health insurance is considerably less expensive than permanent health insurance, usually ringing in at just half of the cost of a comparable permanent plan. Consequently, it's the type of insurance most families choose to purchase for their caregivers.

Automobile insurance is another benefit that is offered by many families—particularly those who require their caregivers to transport their children from activity to activity. If your nanny will be using the family vehicle for family or personal business, it's important that she is fully covered under the family automobile insurance policy. In most states, an automobile insurance policy covers a particular automobile as well as any other automobile which is operated by members of the family. While your nanny is likely covered under your policy, it makes sense to phone your insurance broker to double-check.

The automobile insurance issue gets even more complicated if your nanny intends to use her own vehicle while she is working. Unless she has special business coverage, her insurance policy likely won't cover her if she has an accident while she's on the job. You—as her employer—could be held liable for any accident which occurs. To make matters worse, your insurance policy wouldn't cover this situation, so you would be personally responsible for paying for damages.

In order not to jeopardize your family's financial well-being, make sure your nanny is properly insured on the family car and/or her own vehicle.

Sick days, personal days, and vacation days

Obviously, even the most committed employee is likely to need the occasional day off to recuperate from a flu bug, or visit the dentist. That's why it's important to include some wording in your work agreement about how many sick days, personal days, and vacation days your in-home caregiver is entitled to take in a given year, and whether she will be paid for this time off.

While you aren't legally required to pay your employee for sick days or personal days, it's a good idea to do so. If you don't pay for sick days, your caregiver may feel compelled to drag herself into work when she's really too ill to be working, thereby exposing your child and the rest of the family to a cold or virus. If you don't pay for personal days off, you make it extremely difficult for your caregiver to schedule dentist appointments and attend to family responsibilities—something that could lead to a growing amount of resentment over time.

You'll also need to decide what to do about those days when you don't need your caregiver's services, either because the entire family is ill or Grandma and Grandpa are visiting from out of town. As a rule of thumb, you should plan to pay for your caregiver's services on the days and hours she is scheduled to work—whether or not you need her.

Vacation time can be an equally sticky situation for families who employ in-home caregivers. The caregiver is legally entitled to a certain amount of time off with pay. (Be sure to check with the appropriate authorities to find out what the rules are in

Bright Idea
If you're wondering how many days a year to give your caregiver for sick days, personal days, and vacation days, use your own plan at work as a guideline.

your state.) What the law doesn't dictate, however, is when that time must be taken.

Everything works out neatly for all concerned if you and the caregiver decide to take the same weeks for vacation. It can start to get messy, however, if she needs a week off to attend a family wedding out of state at a time of year when you're unable to get time off from work. In this case, you will need to find a backup caregiver—something that can be particularly difficult during the peak vacation months.

Then there's the issue of your own vacation time. Some families choose to have their in-home caregiver accompany them on holidays—something that can work well for both the family and the caregiver, provided the caregiver's willing to tag along. Au pairs and nannies from overseas, for example, often welcome the opportunity to see more of the country during these working vacations.

Moneysaver
When you're booking hotel accommodations for your family and your caregiver, remember to mention any personal or professional memberships that you hold. You could be eligible for a discount on the basic room rate.

Assuming your caregiver's willing to accompany you and your children on your vacation, you should expect to pick up the tab for her portion of the travel costs. It's a working holiday for her, after all, and it would be unreasonable for you to expect her to pay for her air fare, hotel, meals, and other own pocket expenses.

Job responsibilities

It's a good idea to include a detailed description of job responsibilities in the work agreement. That way, both you and the caregiver will know exactly what she is—and isn't—expected to accomplish during an average working day.

You'll note that I said "average working day." Anyone who cares for young children on a regular basis can tell you that there are good days and—well, not-so-good days.

Because it's impossible to tell from the outset how a particular day is going to shape up when you're caring for young children, it's important to spell out some basic priorities for your caregiver. If the baby is really fussy and only sleeps for 20 minutes all day, would you prefer that she spend that 20 minutes folding the baby's laundry or doing a puzzle with your preschooler?

General house rules

You can save both yourself and your caregiver a lot of grief by establishing some general house rules right from the very beginning. You'll want to cover both those house rules that apply to your child (for example, just how many hours per day your son is allowed to play Nintendo!) and those that apply to the caregiver (whether she's welcome to have personal visitors over when you're not at home).

Some of the topics you'll want to cover include:

- use of the telephone (especially how long-distance phone charges are to be handled!)

- use of the family vehicle (is she welcome to use it to run personal errands or only those related to the care of the children?)

- curfew (particularly important with an au pair, but also a good subject to broach with any live-in caregiver)

- privacy (which areas of the house are off limits to the caregiver and under what circumstances, if any, are you or the children welcome to enter her bedroom?)

- housekeeping (if the caregiver makes herself a bedtime snack, who's responsible for putting the dishes in the dishwasher?)

- mealtimes (which meals is the caregiver responsible for making for herself, and which ones is she welcome to enjoy with the family?)

- entertaining (under what circumstances is the caregiver welcome to entertain her own friends in your home? Would you prefer that she be out of the house when you're entertaining your own friends?)

- smoking (is smoking permitted in your home or in your car?)

Confidentiality

Rather than suing and being sued by your caregiver after the fact, you should include some language about confidentiality in your work agreement.

Getting off to a good start

While the work agreement that you and your caregiver prepare should be as comprehensive as possible, you should also plan to be on hand during her first few days on the job so that you can help her to get to know your child and familiarize her with your household routines.

If you have more than one child, you might want to arrange to introduce them to the caregiver one at a time. This will let each child spend a little one-on-one time with the caregiver—something that's beneficial to both the caregiver and the child. If, on the other hand, one of your children is particularly fearful of strangers, you might decide that she would benefit from the reassurance of having a sibling close by.

This orientation period is particularly important if your caregiver is coming from overseas or another part of the country—so important, in fact, that the United States Information Agency (USIA) insists that host families be on hand for at least three days following the au pair's arrival.

Your relationship with your child's caregiver will get off to a good start if your orientation covers each of the following elements:

- a review of the contents of the work agreement

- a discussion about what types of discipline you do and do not consider appropriate to your child's stage of development

- a tour of your home to familiarize the caregiver with the location and functioning of household equipment (for example, the dishwasher, the microwave, and so on) and to indicate which areas of the home she is welcome to be in (the kitchen and livingroom, but not your bedroom)

- a discussion of safety procedures in the home (fire evacuation procedures, where toxic substances and any other harmful materials are stored, procedures for answering the door, guidelines for bathtub and swimming pool safety; and so on)

- a tour of the neighborhood to familiarize her with the location of your child's friends' homes, the local playground, the doctor's office, the hospital, and so on

- an overview of daily routines (when your child wakes up in the morning, what he has for breakfast, how much help he needs with tooth brushing and other personal hygiene tasks, and so on)

- a discussion about how she can go about contacting you and your partner while you're at work (should she have you paged whenever she has a question or only in emergency situations?)

66

I did not leave our au pair alone with the children for a full two weeks after her arrival. I spent every minute helping her adjust to this country, our family, the language, and the unique traits of each of my children.
— Pat, mother of three, explaining what she did to get her relationship with her au pair off to a good start

99

Bright Idea
You might want to ask your caregiver to keep a daily log book describing your child's activities for the day— what she ate, how long she napped, and so on. In addition to providing you with valuable feedback about how well your child is adjusting to the new care arrangement, it can become a precious keepsake that records your child's growth and development over time.

Because you will be covering a great deal of information in a very short time, you might want to provide your caregiver with some written notes summarizing the material you cover during the orientation. You should also plan to schedule a series of follow up meetings so she can obtain answers to any questions that arise once she actually gets into the job.

Establishing boundaries

Earlier in this chapter, I talked about how difficult it can be to open up your home to someone who is, for all intents and purposes, a stranger.

Sure you had the chance to size her up during the initial job interview. You know that her personal hygiene habits are good (or at least they were on this one occasion!) and that she's articulate and well-mannered. What you have no way of knowing, however, is what it will be like to actually share a home with this person. Is she messy? Does she like to spend endless hours talking on the phone? Is she a night owl? These are things you're bound to discover during the early weeks of the new arrangement. While it's unlikely that you'll find someone who's a perfect fit for you and your family—someone who shares your love of old *M*A*S*H* reruns and believes that civilized people should refrain from speaking to one another until they've all had their morning coffee—you're likely to experience fewer conflicts if you take the time to establish some clearly defined boundaries right from the very beginning.

Then there's the financial issue to consider. If the caregiver takes your child on an outing to the zoo, who should be responsible for paying the admission fee for the two of them? What if she treats your child to an ice cream cone or takes him out to lunch afterwards? Assuming you're picking up the tab for these incidental costs, do you want her to clear these expenditures with you ahead of time?

There's also the curfew issue—something that isn't likely to be as much of an issue with a live-in nanny, but can be a bit of a problem if you're a combined employer and surrogate parent to a teenaged au pair. If you're unable to go to sleep at night until the au pair (and your car) are home safe and sound, it's quite reasonable for you to insist that she be home at a decent hour. While the au pair program coordinator may be able to provide you with some insight into how other families are tackling this particular issue, in the end, it's something you and your au pair will have to resolve for yourselves.

Building trust

It isn't easy leaving your child in the hands of another person—no matter how wonderful or capable she may be. Most parents still wrestle with issues of trust from time to time.

While parents who have their children cared for at daycare centers might worry about the quality of care their child is receiving from his or her individual caregiver, they may be reassured by the fact that there are other staff members, parents, and children around. Parents with in-home caregivers, on the other hand, must assume responsibility for supervising the caregiver themselves—a situation that frequently raises issues of trust.

In the aftermath of the high-profile murder trial of British au pair Louise Woodward, parents with in-home caregivers are even more aware of how important it is to monitor the quality of care their children are receiving. In addition to making

Unofficially . . .
According to a recent article in *Time* magazine, approximately 70 percent of parents who use surveillance cameras end up dismissing the caregiver for some major faux pas—like chatting too long on the phone or watching her soap operas.

impromptu visits to ensure that everything's going well on the home front, some parents are choosing more high tech solutions to find out what goes on in their absence.

There are a number of products on the market that are designed to let parents secretly monitor their nanny's activities. These "nanny cams" are marketed under a number of different brand names and come in many shapes and sizes, but all are basically hidden cameras that record (or transmit) the activities taking place in your home.

While you may be tempted to purchase such a product to monitor the way your in-home caregiver treats your child, the products aren't nearly as foolproof as they appear to be. First of all, most only record video (not audio), so it can be difficult to figure out exactly what's going on between your child and the caregiver. Secondly, you are only able to monitor what's going on while your child and the caregiver are within camera range. Therefore, what you see may not be a representative sample of what goes on during the rest of the day. Thirdly, if your caregiver finds out that you have been monitoring her activities via a hidden camera, she's likely to feel hurt and betrayed—a situation that can seriously damage your relationship. Nanny cams should only be used as a last resort. You'll find it virtually impossible to look your nanny in the eye in the morning if you know in your heart that you'll be spying on her on and off during the day. A far better strategy is to hire wisely in the first place rather than to rely on some electronic gizmo to do the work for you after the fact. If you're this concerned about the quality of care your child is receiving, you might want to give serious consideration to the idea of terminating the care arrangement altogether.

Just the facts

- Screening by phone will let you save time by eliminating the least qualified candidates immediately.

- Check references yourself, even if you're working with an agency.

- Hiring a private investigator lets you obtain detailed information on a potential caregiver. A typical background check costs under $100.

- A work agreement should contain a summary of important house rules like curfews, use of the family vehicle, policies regarding visitors, and so on.

- Spend as much time as you can with your caregiver during her first few days on the job. This period of orientation can help the two of you to avoid future conflicts and misunderstandings.

GET THE SCOOP ON...
Employment taxes ▪ Withholding federal income
tax ▪ The Earned Income Credit (EIC) ▪ Making
tax payments ▪ What forms you need to file ▪
Labor practices ▪ Workers' Compensation
Insurance ▪ New hire reporting

The Fine Print: Your Responsibilities as an Employer

While having an in-home caregiver may be the ideal solution to your childcare woes, there's one aspect of the situation that may leave you feeling rather uncomfortable: the business of being an employer.

Not only can it be awkward to attempt to have an employee-employer relationship with a member of your household, it can also be very time consuming. Whether you like it or not, you could end up devoting a fair chunk of your so-called leisure time to a less-than-exciting hobby: cutting your way through the endless quantities of red tape that the government sets out for those who choose to have household employees.

Chapter 8

Unofficially...
According to the IRS, up to 75 percent of household employers fail to pay the required taxes on the wages of their household employees.

Employer Obligations

While you might think of your in-home caregiver as another member of the family, in the eyes of the Internal Revenue Service (IRS), she's your employee.

Because you set the rules concerning the employment arrangement between your nanny and yourself (number of hours worked, rate of pay, job responsibilities, and so on), your nanny or in-home caregiver is considered to be an employee rather than an independent business person who offers childcare services. It doesn't matter if you employ your in-home caregiver on a full-time or part-time basis, whether you found her through an agency or from a list provided by that agency, or whether you pay her by the hour, the day, the week, or by the job—you're still considered to be her employer.

If, on the other hand, if you use a placement agency that exercises control over what work your caregiver does and how it is done, the caregiver is not considered to be your employee. This control might consist of providing rules of conduct and appearance and requiring her to submit reports on a regular basis. In this case, the agency would also be responsible for issuing her paychecks.

If your caregiver is considered an employee, you are responsible for meeting the obligations that the government sets out for all employers: that is, paying Social Security tax, Medicare tax, federal (and, where applicable, state) unemployment tax, and (if you and your employee agree on this arrangement) withholding federal income tax for your in-home caregiver.

The following brief checklist summarizes your key obligations as an employer—at least as far as the

IRS is concerned! Don't worry if you don't understand all of the terminology right away; I'll cover it in greater detail later in this chapter.

While this chapter focuses exclusively on the United States tax situation, Canadians who employ in-home caregivers can obtain detailed information about their rights and responsibilities as employers at the Revenue Canada Web site http://www.rc. gc.ca/~paulb/smallbus/employer.htm or by calling Revenue Canada at 1-800-959-5525.

When you hire a caregiver, you need to:

- find out if she is legally entitled to work in the United States
- withhold Social Security and Medicare taxes
- withhold the Federal Unemployment Tax (FUTA) from her wages
- find out if you need to pay state taxes (unemployment insurance) on her wages
- withhold federal income tax (but only if you and she agree that this tax will be withheld at source)
- make advance payments of the Earned Income Credit
- decide how you will make tax payments
- keep detailed tax records
- obtain an employer identification number (by the end of the subsequent January)
- provide your employee with copies B, C, and 2 of Form W-2 (Wage and Tax Statement) by the end of the subsequent January
- send Copy A of Form W-2 to the Social Security Administration by the end of the subsequent February

Timesaver
You can obtain
the tax forms
and guides you'll
need by calling
the IRS at
1-800-424-FORM
or downloading
them from the
IRS Web site
at www.irs.
ustreas.gov.

- file Schedule H (Form 1040—Household Employment Taxes) with your federal income tax return (Form 1040 or 1040A) by the subsequent April 15

Here's a list of publications to request from the IRS:

- Publication 15, Circular E—Employer's Tax Guide

- Publication 503—Child and Dependent Care Expenses

- Publication 550—Tax Withholding and Estimated Tax

- Publication 926—Household Employer's Tax Guide

- Form 2441—Child and Dependent Care Expenses

- Form 6251—Alternative Minimum Tax—Individuals

- Schedule 2 (Form 1040A)—Child and Dependent Care Expenses for Form 1040A Filers

- Schedule H (Form 1040)—Household Employment Taxes

- Form W-10—Dependent Care Provider's Identification and Certification.

If your head is spinning and you think it would be a heck of a lot easier to just quit your job and abandon the whole idea of hiring a caregiver than to sort your way through all this governmental red tape, get yourself a good tax accountant and stop reading now.

If, on the other hand, you're one of the brave souls who chooses to handle the paperwork yourself, pour yourself another cup of coffee and read on. I'll walk you through the ins and outs of being an employer and tell you what you need to do to stay on the good side of the IRS.

Your first responsibility as an employer is to ensure that the person that you have hired is, in fact, legally entitled to work in the United States. Because many illegal aliens attempt seek employment as domestic workers, you've got to be especially vigilant.

If your caregiver cannot produce the necessary documents to prove that she is entitled to work in the United States, do not hire her. The penalties that you could face for hiring an illegal alien don't justify the risk.

To meet your legal obligations, you will have to ensure that your caregiver completes the employee portion of the Immigration and Naturalization Service (INS) form I-9, Employment Eligibility Verification. (You can obtain a copy of the form by calling the INS at 1-800-755-0777.) You must then fill out the employer portion of the form and keep the completed form in your records for at least three years (or one year after your caregiver's employment ends, whichever is greater).

Employment taxes

Employment taxes are the bane of any employer's existence. They're a pain to calculate, a pain to collect, and a pain to remit. Unfortunately, you don't have a lot of choice in the matter.

There are a number of different types of taxes that you might be required to pay on your employee's behalf. These include Social Security, Medicare, Federal Unemployment Tax (FUTA), and state employment taxes (where applicable).

Bright Idea
Find out what you can expect to pay in nanny taxes by using the online payroll calculator at www.nannynetwork.com/nanitax.htm.

Social Security and Medicare

Social Security and Medicare taxes pay for benefits that workers and their families receive under the Federal Insurance Contributions Act (FICA). Social Security tax pays for benefits received under the old-age, survivors, and disability programs of FICA, whereas Medicare tax pays for benefits under the hospital insurance program.

You are required to pay Social Security and Medicare taxes on your employee's wages if:

- her wages exceed $1,000 per calendar year
- the total wages that you pay to all household employees is $1,000 or more in any calendar quarter
- the caregiver is someone other than your spouse, your child (age 21 or younger), or your parent
- she is over the age of eighteen (or, if she's under the age of eighteen, childcare is her full-time occupation)

The tax rate for Social Security and Medicare taxes is 15.3 percent of wages paid. You and your caregiver are responsible for splitting these taxes, that is, you pay 7.65 percent and she pays 7.65 percent. (Of this 7.65 percent, 6.2 percent is allocated to Social Security and 1.45 percent to Medicare.)

Note: You only have to pay Social Security and Medicare taxes on wages that you pay to your parent, if you are divorced and have not remarried, are a widow or widower, or are married to and living with a person whose physical or mental condition prevents him or her from caring for your child for at least four continuous weeks in a calendar quarter; and if your child is eighteen years of age or younger or has a physical or mental condition that requires the personal care of an adult for at least four continuous weeks in a calendar quarter.

You are responsible for payment of your caregiver's share of the taxes as well as your own. You can either withhold her share from her wages or pay it from your own funds. If you choose to pay the Social Security and Medicare taxes from your own funds, you must include these amounts in her taxable income. They are not, however, counted as Social Security and Medicare wages or FUTA wages.

If you pay your caregiver more than $1,000 per year, all wages that you pay to that employee during that year (regardless of when the wages were earned) are subject to Social Security and Medicare tax.

Because it's difficult to calculate in advance how much a particular employee will earn during a given tax year, it's easy to make mistakes when you're deciding whether to withhold these types of taxes. If you find out that you've made some errors when calculating these taxes, you need to make the appropriate adjustments. If you've withheld too little Social Security and Medicare tax, you should withhold additional taxes from a later paycheck. If you've withheld too much, you should repay the employee.

Federal Unemployment Tax (FUTA)

The Federal Unemployment Tax is part of the federal and state program under the Federal Unemployment Tax Act (FUTA) that pays unemployment compensation to workers who lose their jobs. Like most employers, you may owe both the Federal Unemployment Tax and a state unemployment tax. Or you may owe only the FUTA tax or

Watch Out!
The value of food, lodging, clothing, and other noncash items that you give to your caregiver are not subject to Social Security and Medicare taxes, but cash that you give her in place of these items is.

only the state unemployment tax. To find out about your obligations, contact your state's unemployment agency. (You can find a list of state unemployment agencies in IRS Publication 926—Household Employer's Tax Guide.)

Because the nature of the program varies from state to state, FUTA can get a bit complicated. The basic FUTA tax rate is 6.2 percent of your caregiver's FUTA wages, but it is reduced to 0.8 percent if the FUTA wages you pay are not more than the wages that are subject to state unemployment tax, and you pay all the required contributions for the year to your state unemployment fund by April 15 of the following year.

Before you can pull out your calculator, however, you need to understand what a FUTA wage is—at least in the eyes of the IRS. If you pay cash wages to household employees that total $1,000 or more per calendar quarter (January through March, April through June, July through September, or October through December), the first $7,000 you pay to each employee is considered to be FUTA wages. Note: if your employee's cash wages reach $7,000 during the year, you don't calculate the FUTA tax on any wages you pay her for the remainder of the year.

If you pay less than $1,000 in cash wages in each calendar quarter but had a household employee last year, the cash wages you pay this year may be considered FUTA wages if the cash wages you paid to household employees in any calendar quarter last year totaled $1,000 or more.

You don't, however, count wages that you paid to your spouse, a child under the age of 21, or your parent.

Moneysaver
You may be able to take a credit of up to 5.4 percent against the FUTA tax, resulting in a net tax rate of 0.8 percent, but to do so you must pay all your required contributions for the previous tax year by April 15. Fiscal year filers must pay all required contributions by the due date of their federal income tax returns.

Withholding federal income tax

You are not required to withhold federal income tax from the wages you pay your caregiver, but you are allowed to do so if your caregiver requests it and you agree. In this case, the caregiver must give you a completed Form W-4 (Employee's Withholding Allowance Certificate). Obviously, if you agree to withhold federal tax from your caregiver's paychecks, you are responsible for paying it to the IRS.

You can calculate the amount owed by using the income tax withholding tables in Publication 15, Circular E (Employer's Tax Guide). Be sure to calculate any federal tax owed before you deduct any amounts for other withheld taxes.

Federal income tax is calculated on both cash and noncash wages that are paid to your caregiver. You should not, however, include the following types of items when you're calculating her wages:

- meals that are provided at your home for your convenience

- lodging that is provided at your home for your convenience and as a condition of employment

- up to $65 per month for bus or train tokens that you give to your caregiver (or for any cash reimbursement you make to her to cover her public transit expenses)

- up to $170 per month for the value of parking that you provide to your employee at or near your home or at or near a location from which your employee commutes to your home

If you pay income tax for your employee without withholding it from her paycheck, you must report this amount as part of her income. It's also counted when Social Security, Medicare, and FUTA taxes are calculated.

Watch Out!
Make sure you pay attention to the filing status and exemptions shown on your caregiver's Form W-4 when you calculate the amount of federal income tax to withhold from her paycheck. Otherwise, she could end up with a nasty tax bill at the end of the year.

You can find out more about nanny taxes at www.nannytax.com.

The Earned Income Credit (EIC)

Your caregiver may be eligible to take advantage of the Earned Income Credit (EIC) on her federal income tax return—a credit that reduces her tax or enables her receive a payment from the IRS if she doesn't actually owe any tax.

As her employer, you may be required to either make advance payments of part of her EIC along with her wages or provide her with a notice about the EIC.

Advance EIC payments

If your caregiver gives you a properly completed Form W-5 (Earned Income Credit Advance Payment Certificate), you must make advance EIC payments to her. Any advance EIC payments you make reduce the amount of Social Security and Medicare taxes and withheld federal income tax you are required to pay to the IRS.

Use the advance EIC payment tables in Publication 15, Circular E (Employer's Tax Guide), to find out how much you need to pay your employee.

Note: Don't pay your employee more than the amount of Social Security and Medicare taxes and withheld federal income tax you would otherwise need to pay to the IRS.

Notice about the EIC

The employee copy (Copy C) of the IRS 1997 Form W-2 (Wage and Tax Statement) contains a statement about the EIC on the back. As long as you give your caregiver her copy by the end of January, you do not have to give her any other information about the

EIC. Otherwise, you must give your caregiver a notice about the EIC only if you agree to withhold federal income tax from the employee's wages, but the income tax withholding tables show that no tax should be withheld.

If your caregiver's wages will be below $29,290, you are encouraged to give her a notice about the EIC, even if you're not legally required to do so.

The following documents are considered suitable for the purposes of notifying your caregiver about the EIC:

- Copy C of the W-2 Form
- Notice 797 (Possible Federal Tax Refund Due to the Earned Income Credit)
- your own written statement with the same wording as Notice 797

How to make tax payments

So you've been merrily deducting this smorgasbord of taxes from your caregiver's paychecks. You know you're not allowed to keep the money, but you're not quite sure exactly who you're supposed to send it to—or when.

Fortunately, this part of the process is surprisingly simple—as it should be, considering all the hoops you've had to jump through to get this far.

When you file your personal income tax form, you adjust the amount of money you owe the government by adding the federal employment taxes on your caregiver's wages and subtracting any advance EIC payments you made to the employee. The amount you owe must be paid to the IRS by April 15.

You can avoid owing tax with your return by asking your own employer to withhold additional

Moneysaver
Prior to 1998, the penalty for not having enough federal income tax withheld or paying enough estimated tax did not apply to employment taxes for household employees. Starting in 1998, however, it will. If you find yourself owing more than $500 when your return comes due, you could face a penalty.

income tax from your wages or making additional payments directly to the IRS yourself.

If you would like your employer to withhold additional tax, you will need to give him a new Form W-4 (Employee's Withholding Allowance Certificate). Complete it as before, but show the additional amount you want withheld from each paycheck.

If you want to make estimated tax payments to cover the employment taxes for your caregiver, get Form 1040-ES (Estimated Tax for Individuals) from the IRS.

One word of caution before I move on. While some American families have managed to get away with ignoring their obligations to pay taxes on their caregivers' income, the IRS has upped the penalties for noncompliance. In the past, you simply risked having to pay back taxes with penalties and interest. Now you could be charged with filing a fraudulent return—something that could cost you a penalty of 75 percent of the tax you should have paid but didn't. You could also spend up to three years in jail.

If you are the sole proprietor of a small business or your home is on a farm operated for profit, you also have the option of including the federal employment taxes for your caregiver in your federal employment tax deposits or other payments for your business or farm employees.

What forms do you need to file?

If you pay Social Security and Medicare wages, FUTA wages, or wages from which you withhold federal income tax, you will need to file specific forms to the IRS.

You must include your Employer Identification Number (EIN) on the forms you file for your caregiver. An EIN is a nine-digit number issued by the

IRS. It is not the same thing as a Social Security number.

If you don't already have an EIN, you will need to obtain Form SS-4 (Application for Employer Identification Number) from the IRS. You can obtain your number immediately if you apply by phone or in about four weeks if you apply by mail.

Form W-2

You must issue a separate Form W-2 for each household employee to whom you pay Social Security and Medicare wages or wages from which you withheld federal income tax.

You are required by law to complete each W-2 and give copies B, C, and 2 to your employee by the end of January. (The actual date varies with each calendar year.) You must send Copy A along with Form W-3 (Transmittal of Wage and Tax Statements), to the Social Security Administration by March 2, 1998.

If a caregiver leaves your employment during the year, you can file a Form W-2 and provide copies to your employee as soon as you have made your final payment of wages. If the employee asks you for Form W-2, you must give it to her within 30 days of her request or of the last wage payment, whichever is later.

Schedule H

If you pay your caregiver Social Security or Medicare wages, FUTA wages, or wages from which you deduct income tax, you are required to submit Schedule H (Form 1040—Household Employment Taxes) to report the federal employment taxes which you have paid on her behalf. Schedule H is filed along with your income tax return. (If you

Timesaver
Companies such as Home/Work Solutions (1-800-626-4829) specialize in handling tax matters for families that have domestic employees. For $150, the company registers you with state and federal agencies, provides you with the necessary tax and immigration forms, and tells you how much tax to withhold from your caregiver's paycheck.

don't have a federal income tax to file, Schedule H must be filed by itself.)

If you need additional tax information, call the IRS at 1-800-829-1040.

Business employment tax returns

If you choose to pay the employment taxes for your caregiver along with your business or farm employment taxes, you need to use Form 941 (Employer's Quarterly Federal Tax Return) or Form 943 (Employer's Annual Tax Return for Agricultural Employees). Include the FUTA tax for the employee on your form 940 (or 940-EZ—Employer's Annual Federal Unemployment Tax Return).

If you report the unemployment taxes for your household employee on Form 941 or Form 943, be sure to file Form W-2 for the employee with forms W-2 and W-3 for your business or farm employees.

What records do you need to keep?

Like any employer in the United States, you are required to keep your copies of Schedule H and other employment-related tax forms as well as records that support the information contained on those forms.

If you are required to file Form W-2, you will need to keep a record of your employee's name, address, and Social Security number.

You will also need to record the following information on each payday:

- your employee's cash and noncash wages
- any employee Social Security tax you withhold or agree to pay for your employee
- any employee Medicare tax you withhold or agree to pay for your employee

- any federal income tax you withhold
- any advance EIC payments you make
- any state employment taxes you withhold

You must also keep a record of your employee's name and Social Security number exactly as they appear on her Social Security card if you pay the employee either Social Security and Medicare wages or wages from which you withhold federal tax.

You are required to keep your tax records for at least four years after the due date of the return on which you report the taxes or the date the taxes were paid, whichever is later.

Labor practices

Domestic service workers—including full-time care-givers—are covered by the provisions of the Fair Labor Standards Act (FLSA) provided that they earn at least $1,000 in cash wages from a single employer in a calendar year or work more than eight hours per week for one or more employers.

The Act establishes the minimum wage that can be paid to such workers as well as rates of overtime pay.

Minimum wage

Under the terms of the Fair Labor Standards Act (FLSA), employees are entitled to be paid a minimum wage of not less than $5.15 per hour, effective September 1, 1997.

The only caregiver who isn't entitled to receive minimum wage (or overtime pay, for that matter) is a casual babysitter—someone who works for you on an irregular basis and whose primary occupation is not caring for young children.

A word to the wise: When in doubt, err on the side of caution. A caregiver who is entitled to receive

Watch Out!
You must ask for your employee's Social Security number no later than the first day on which you pay the wages. It's a good idea to ask for it at the time of hiring.

minimum wage but who does not receive it can file a grievance with the Department of Labor during the time that she is employed by you—or up to two years after leaving your employ. If the grievance is found to be justified, you could be found liable for the difference in wages.

Hours worked and overtime pay

The Fair Labor Standards Act does not limit the number of hours in a day or days in a week an employee may be required to work, but it does stipulate that those employees are to be paid not less than one and one-half times their regular rates of pay for all hours worked in excess of forty in a work week.

Record keeping

Bright Idea
You can find detailed information about your responsibilities as an employer in the Department of Labor's Small Business Handbook, available online at http://www.dol.gov/dol/asp/public/programs/handbook/overview.htm.

The Act requires that you, like any employer, keep detailed records covering the wages and hours worked by your caregiver. It's in your best interest to keep your records up-to-date as they are your only defense against any complaints filed by officials from the Department of Labor and your caregiver.

Workers' Compensation Insurance

Some states require that families that employ in-home caregivers carry Workers' Compensation Insurance. According to a recent article in *U.S.A. Today*, the states that require such coverage for full-time domestic employees are Colorado, Illinois, Kentucky, Michigan, New Jersey, New York, Utah, and Washington, while those that require it for both full-time and part-time domestic workers are Alaska, California, Connecticut, Delaware, District of Columbia, Hawaii, Iowa, Kansas, Maryland, Massachusetts, Minnesota, New Hampshire, Ohio, Oklahoma, and South Dakota.

If you don't have such coverage and it is mandated by law in your state, you could find yourself liable for your caregiver's medical expenses and lost wages if she has a work-related accident—even if the accident was in no way your fault.

Even if your state doesn't require that you carry this type of insurance for your caregiver, it's certainly a good idea.

New hire reporting

Federal legislation has mandated that all states implement New Hire Registration Programs to track individual employment data. Each state has its own procedures for collecting this data. You can find out about the specific policies in effect in your state at www.4nannytaxes.com/newhire.htm or by calling your local employment office.

Just the facts

- In most cases, your in-home caregiver is considered to be your employee, whether she works part- or full-time.

- As her employer, you are responsible for verifying that she is legally entitled to work in the United States, collecting employment taxes (Social Security, Medicare, Federal Unemployment Tax, and, where applicable, state unemployment taxes); informing her about the Earned Income Credit (EIC); making tax payments; complying with labor regulations (for example, minimum wage and overtime rates; obtaining Workers' Compensation Insurance coverage for her (where required by law); and reporting her hire to the appropriate state agency).

- While you are not legally required to withhold federal income taxes from her paycheck, you may agree to do so if she asks you to perform this service.

Sticky Situations and How to Handle Them

GET THE SCOOP ON...
Settling your child into care ▪ Establishing a
good relationship with your child's caregiver ▪
Keeping a good nanny (or full-time
babysitter) ▪ Preparing your children for your
au pair's departure ▪ Avoiding conflicts with a
relative who is caring for your child ▪ Feeling
like a part of your child's "other" family ▪
Protecting yourself against allegations of sexual
harassment ▪ Protecting yourself against allegations of child abuse ▪ Developing a good
backup plan

PART IV

An Ounce of Prevention

Turnover in the childcare profession is alarm-
ingly high—as much as 30 percent per year,
according to some reports.

Because it's hard on your child and stressful to
have to look for a new childcare arrangement, you
will want to do whatever you can to ensure that the
childcare arrangement that you've set up for your
child works for everyone involved: your child, his
caregiver, and yourself.

Your first priority is to ensure that the arrangement is right for your child. That means taking the
time to settle him into care, and seeing that he
forms a healthy attachment to his caregiver.

Your next obligation is to his caregiver. You want
to make sure that you keep the lines of communication open so that you can troubleshoot any

problems before they arise, and that you make a point of letting her know how much you value the service she provides your family.

Your final obligation is to yourself. You want to take steps to prevent yourself from feeling cut off from your child's daycare arrangements, to protect yourself against false accusations of sexual harassment and/or child abuse, and you need to come up with a backup plan that enables you to get to work on days when your child or his caregiver is ill.

That, in a nutshell, is the focus of this chapter: providing you with a smorgasbord of solutions designed to help you avoid some of the common difficulties caregivers and families face.

Settling your child into daycare

Let's start out by talking about one of the biggest problems that working parents face—settling a child into a new daycare arrangement.

Because children go through developmental stages in rapid succession during their first few years of life, there are different challenges involved in helping an infant to adjust to daycare than a toddler or a preschooler. Here are some tips on dealing with children in each of these three age groups.

Infants

Because babies cannot communicate their needs verbally, parents have to play an active role in helping them to adjust to daycare. If your child is an infant, you may want to try some of the following strategies for making his transition from home to daycare as stress-free as possible for all concerned—yourself, your child, and your caregiver:

■ Describe your child's daily routine, his likes and dislikes, his food preferences, his sleeping habits, and your family situation (for example, names and ages of siblings) to his caregiver in as much detail as possible. Ideally, you should provide this information in writing—either on a form supplied by the caregiver (a common practice for daycare centers and family daycare homes) or in a letter from yourself to his caregiver. You might want to use the Family Profile Worksheet provided in Appendix D as a guide.

- Arrange to take a few days off work, if possible, so that you can be on hand to help your caregiver and your baby get used to one another. You might want to use this time to demonstrate his favorite position for being held when he is drinking his bottle and your tried-and-true methods for getting him to fall asleep.

- Resist the temptation to sneak out while your child isn't looking. You'll only create more problems for yourself in the long run, as your child may be constantly fearful—even when he's at home—that you're about to abandon him again.

- When it's time to say your goodbyes, hand your child to the caregiver rather than letting her take him from you. It may seem like a minor detail, but it's a nonverbal way of conveying to your child that you trust this person and that he will be safe with her. You will also want to reinforce this message with words, regardless of the age of your child: "Jane will take care of you while I'm at work." Your tone of voice and body language can be used to reassure even the youngest of infants: Your baby won't understand your words, but he will pick up the fact

Bright Idea
If your child is having a particularly difficult time settling into his new routine, you might want to give him something of yours to take with him—perhaps a photo of yourself or an item of your clothing that smells like you. Many children find this reassuring, and it may give your child the boost he needs to feel comfortable while he's away from you.

that you feel calm and confident about the whole arrangement.

■ Say goodbye and mean it. Don't hang around for an extended period of time or keep picking him up. If you seem hesitant about leaving him, you're conveying to him that you don't feel good about leaving him with his caregiver. If you are worried about whether he's going to settle, exit stage left and then call the caregiver as soon as you get to work.

■ Be prepared for some more tears when you come to pick him up. Researchers at Boston Children's Hospital have discovered that babies are fussier when their parents return than they are while their parents are at work. The researchers explain that babies express their strongest emotions when they're in the company of those they feel most strongly about.

■ Remind yourself that it takes time for an infant to adjust to a new routine. To feel safe, he needs to form an attachment to his new caregiver—something that can take anywhere from a few days to a month to occur.

Toddlers and preschoolers

Because toddlers and preschoolers can understand better what's going on around them, there are some additional strategies that you can use to help them to adjust to daycare. Here are a few ideas you might want to try:

■ Make sure that your child understands what daycare is all about. It's particularly important that he realizes that you will be coming back for him at the end of the day—something that may seem obvious to you, but that is typically anything but obvious to your average two-year-old.

- Try a few dry runs. Don't let your child's first day at daycare be the first time in his life he has ever been away from you. Leave him in the care of his ever-loving Grandma from time to time while you run a few errands.

- Visit the daycare center or family daycare provider together on a few occasions before his first day. Take him on the grand tour, pointing out both the highlights (where the trucks are kept) and the necessities (the quickest route to the bathroom).

- Try to get your child engaged in an activity with his caregiver before you have to leave. He's less likely to protest your departure if he's having fun working on a puzzle or playing with his blocks.

- Say goodbye to your child and tell him exactly when he can expect you to return. Be sure to do so in a way that he can understand. Tell him you'll be back after he has his lunch, has his nap, and finishes playing outside.

- If your child is more attached to one parent than another, try having the other parent take him to daycare. The very same child who sobs and clings to his mother's leg might be able to say a calm goodbye to his father without so much as a single tear.

- Don't be surprised if your child has a particularly difficult time settling into daycare after a long weekend or a week of holidays. He may need the chance to readjust following this change to his normal routine.

Timesaver
Throw a meal into the crockpot before you head to work in the morning so that you don't have to worry about making dinner the moment you walk in the door. This will free you up to give your child what he really needs after a day away from you: your time and attention.

- Try not to be hurt if your child doesn't seem particularly thrilled to see you at the end of the day. He's likely to be experiencing a smorgasbord of emotions—anger that you left him, joy at seeing you, and relief that it's time to go home—and may express these conflicting emotions in behavior that is anything but pleasant.

- Be prepared for similar outbursts at home. Some parents say that it's almost as if their children have used up all their emotional reserves trying to cope during the day, and have nothing left by the time they get home.

- Smile through your tears. No matter how hard you may be finding it to start him in daycare, try not to let your child see how upsetting it is for you to be apart from him. Otherwise, he may begin to wonder if there's a reason for your tears. Even the most confident preschooler may second-guess his confidence in his new arrangement: After all, if you're this upset, maybe daycare is far worse than he ever imagined.

- Mark the occasion. Treat his start at daycare as you would any other milestone in his life: as an event that is worthy of celebration. If you're finding it a bit difficult to get too enthusiastic about the whole thing, given your own wildly fluctuating emotions, see if you can get Grandma and Grandpa in on the act. He could take them for a visit to his daycare center, or invite them to be on hand for a special celebration following his first day at daycare.

- Avoid major changes to his routine. Starting daycare is a big adjustment for most children, so it's best to avoid making any other changes (for example, toilet training, weaning, or moving him from a crib to a bed) until he's well settled into his new environment.

■ Do what you can to make the last part of the day as pleasant as possible. Give your child enough time to wrap up his day as he sees fit and then help him to get ready to go home. If it'll be a while before dinner is ready, bring some juice and a snack for him to enjoy on the way home in the car.

■ Remind yourself that this too shall pass—like the sleepless nights and infant colic that preceded it. While it's anything but fun to start your day by trying to peel a screaming toddler off your leg, it won't always be this difficult for the two of you to say your goodbyes.

Establishing a good relationship with your child's caregiver

Like any important relationship, your relationship with your child's caregiver requires mutual respect and a lot of give and take. To get your relationship off on the best possible footing, the two of you should plan to sit down to clarify your respective responsibilities.

Your responsibilities

As the child's parent, you should expect to be responsible for

■ respecting the daycare provider's rules and the terms of the work agreement you and your caregiver have signed

■ paying the daycare provider or your caregiver on time

66

I recognized how difficult it would be for my au pair to be alone with my three young children all day long, so I made arrangements for my oldest child to spend half-days at daycare and arranged for the au pair to attend classes at the local university and visit with some of her friends each day. It was tough on me having someone using my vehicle at times when I needed it, but I knew this was a small trade-off for what she was doing for my children and my family.
—Pat, mother of three

99

- providing agreed-upon items such as extra clothing, diapers, and food, and replacing these items as needed

- dropping off and picking up your child on time

- calling ahead if you are going to be more than 15 minutes late

- providing adequate notice if your child is going to be absent from daycare or if you need to withdraw him from the program

- providing the daycare center or caregiver with up-to-date medical information and emergency phone numbers

- notifying your caregiver of any changes to your schedule, your work location or phone numbers, your child's behavior, or your family situation

- communicating with your caregiver on a regular basis

- keeping your child at home when he is sick and picking him up as promptly as possible if he becomes ill while he is at daycare

- providing your caregiver with written notification if your child is going to be picked up by someone other than yourself

Your caregiver's responsibilities

You should expect your child's caregiver to be responsible for

- ensuring that the daycare environment is as safe and child-friendly as possible

- respecting the confidentiality of all information about your child and your family

- providing you with daily reports (written or oral) about your child

- respecting your wishes concerning childrearing practices

- notifying you immediately if your child is ill so that you can arrange to pick him up

- administering medication only when written consent has been given

- providing you with adequate notice if she is going to be late or absent from work, taking holidays in the near future, or resigning from her position

- providing you with adequate notice of any fee increases

- providing you with receipts (if it's an out-of-home care arrangement)

- providing you with advance notice of any outings

- informing you of any changes to the daycare environment (for example, whether there are any new children or new staff members)

The key to a successful parent-caregiver relationship is ongoing communication. You can prevent unnecessary misunderstandings and ensure that your caregiver feels valued by giving her plenty of opportunity to communicate with you about your child's day.

The most convenient method of communication for both you and your caregiver will be the discussions that you have at the start and end of each day. These daily contacts—rushed as they may be—provide an ideal opportunity for sharing information about your child and touching base about any concerns either of you might have about the way your child is adjusting to daycare.

Timesaver
Use a "fill-in-the-blanks" format in your child's log book to save both yourself and your child's caregiver time.

If your child's caregiver is less than forthcoming about what has happened over the course of the day, you will have to ask the types of questions that elicit detailed answers. Here are some examples of questions that are likely to produce more than a simple "yes" or a "no":

- How long did my child cry after I left? What did you do to settle him?

- What activities did he seem to particularly enjoy today?

- What did he eat for lunch?

- How many bowel movements did he have?

- How long was his nap? What kind of mood was he in when he woke up?

While you will probably do the bulk of your communicating while you are picking up or dropping off your child, it's also a good idea to schedule the occasional face-to-face meeting with your child's caregiver. These lengthier discussions provide an ideal opportunity to discuss any problems the two of you may be having, review your child's development, and express your appreciation for the quality of care the caregiver is providing to your child.

This last point cannot be emphasized too heavily. Because financial compensation is absurdly low in the childcare profession, the rate of turnover is high. You increase your chances of keeping a good caregiver if you continually look for opportunities to express your appreciation for the excellent job she does in caring for your child.

Many daycare centers use log books to communicate information about a child's day. Both the parent and the caregiver use the log books to exchange information about the child's sleep patterns, food

Bright Idea
Express your appreciation whenever the caregiver does something above and beyond the call of duty, like keeping him for an extra half hour so you can attend an important meeting at work or organizing a picnic for all the children in her care. Buy her a can of gourmet coffee, prepare a craft activity that the children in her care can do the next day, or tuck a thank you card into your child's change bag.

consumption, toileting habits, as well as any additional comments about the way the day has been progressing. It's helpful, for example, for the caregiver to know that the child she is caring for was up for a good part of the night. It's equally useful for his mother to find out from the caregiver that the baby refused to try the green beans that she packed in his lunch—if only to help explain why he insisted on eating a bowlful of mashed banana the moment he arrived home.

This form of communication works well in any daycare setting, be it a daycare center, a family daycare home, or your own home.

Keeping a good nanny

Because there is a shortage of experienced full-time babysitters and highly trained nannies—whose services are in especially high demand—one of the biggest challenges you may face is keeping her.

If you find a good nanny or full-time babysitter, you should do whatever you can to ensure that she will stay with your family for a long time. While it's important to compensate her appropriately, money is not the only issue. Most nannies and babysitters are reluctant to stay in a position in which they feel unappreciated. You can show your appreciation for your nanny or babysitter in a number of ways, including the following:

- Compensate her fairly by offering a decent salary and a comprehensive benefits package

- Offer her a bonus or merit increase at the end of each year of service

- Meet with her regularly to discuss your child's progress, and be sure to praise her for the quality of care she is providing to your child. If you have criticisms to make, present them in a constructive and diplomatic manner.

- Give your nanny or babysitter an opportunity to express any concerns that she may have, and do whatever you can to come up with mutually-acceptable solutions.

Moneysaver
Keep the first year's bonus relatively small so that you can increase it over time. The bonus your nanny receives after three years of service should be higher than the one she received at the end of the first year.

- Provide her with plenty of time away from work so that she can avoid the two occupational hazards of her chosen profession: isolation and burnout.

- Recognize the importance of her profession by encouraging her to take advantage of professional development opportunities on an ongoing basis—and at your expense, if at all possible.

- Do whatever else you can think of to ensure that she feels like an important and highly valued member of your household.

- Compare notes with other families in your area to ensure that the salary that you are paying your nanny or babysitter continues to be competitive. If you don't have anyone to compare notes with, a quick call to a local nanny agency should provide you with the salary information that you need.

While there's no easy way to ensure that your nanny or babysitter will stick around for as long as you need her, following these steps increase your odds of making the relationship work.

Preparing your child for your au pair's departure

One of the chief drawbacks to the au pair program, at least so far as the families involved are concerned, is the fact that it lasts for only one year. No matter how well the arrangement is working and how much your children like the au pair, at the end of the year, she's gone.

The short duration of the au pair program can be difficult for children who are slow to form attachments. If you do decide to hire an au pair—knowing full well that you'll be looking for another caregiver in a year's time—it's important to prepare your children for the loss of the au pair before it's actually time for her to return home. Here are some tips on making her departure as painless as possible for your children:

- Make sure that your children understand right from day one that your au pair is a temporary visitor rather than a permanent member of the household.

- Plan a going-away party for the au pair, and encourage your children to make going-away cards for her. The more they participate in the ritual of saying goodbye, the easier it will be for them to come to terms with their feelings.

- Recognize that your children may experience real feelings of grief about losing the au pair, and be prepared to help them work through these emotions.

- Talk about ways that your children and the au pair can keep in touch after she returns home: by phone, by mail, by e-mail, and—assuming either you or her can afford it—in a follow-up visit a few months or years from now. Just make sure that the au pair is prepared to honor her promises once she's back in her home country.

Bright Idea
If your child is too young to express in words how he's feeling about the au pair's departure, provide him with crayons, paints, or other art materials so that he can express his feelings in another way.

Avoiding conflicts with caregivers who are relatives

Families who rely on relatives for childcare services face two key difficulties: figuring out how to handle disagreements and resolving the issue of payment.

While there are a lot of advantages to having a relative care for your child, one of the biggest disadvantages to this type of care is that it can be extremely awkward to handle if any disagreements arise concerning the care of your child.

If, for example, the methods your sister-in-law uses to toilet train your child aren't in keeping with your own child-rearing ideas, you need to consider how you will handle the situation.

As with any type of conflict, your best bet is to be direct. Explain what it is that bothers you about her techniques, but do so in a way that is constructive rather than merely critical: "Stephen's pediatrician doesn't think he's ready to be toilet-trained yet because his diaper is still wet most of the time. I'd feel better if we put the toilet-training on the back burner for a couple of months at least."

If your child is being cared for by an older relative—perhaps your own mother—try not to be intimidated by the fact that she has more years of childrearing experience than you do. You and your partner are the only ones with hands-on experience in raising your child so you are uniquely qualified to make decisions about the way he is raised.

That said, you may find that it's too difficult to work with a relative. If, for example, every discussion you have about your child with your mother dissolves into a shouting match that is reminiscent of your hormonally challenged teen years, it's probably best to rethink your childcare arrangements.

The payment issue can also be a sticky one. Many people feel awkward about accepting money from other family members. Even if your mother-in-law is willing to take care of her grandchild for free, it's probably not a good idea to take her up on the offer. You could end up feeling guilty about the arrangement and she could come to regret her decision to care for your child—something that might explain why so many relative care arrangements last for less than a year. You can avoid a lot of grief by insisting that your relative accept some form of compensation for providing this valuable service, even if it's at a rate below market value.

Feeling like a part of your child's other "family"

After weeks of trying every trick in the book to encourage your child to feel at home with his caregiver, you may find that the tide may suddenly shift. Instead of crying when it's time for you to leave in the morning, he may cry when it's time to come home!

Around the same time, it may suddenly dawn on you that you don't know a lot about what happens in his life while you're at work. You don't know the words to the new song that he's been humming at dinnertime, and you've never even met his new best friend.

It's not unusual to feel a bit cut off from your child's other "family"—the people he spends his days with. The best way to overcome this feeling is to communicate as much as possible with his caregiver and to familiarize yourself with his daily routine. Here are some strategies to help yourself feel more connected with the other people in your child's life:

Watch Out!
Resist the temptation to provide an out-of-town relative with room and board—and nothing else—in exchange for childcare services. Everyone needs a certain amount of pocket money, and your relative is likely to begin to resent the arrangement over time if she has to come to you to ask for $10 each time she wants to go out for coffee with her friends. A better solution is to agree on a weekly salary that she will receive in addition to her room and board.

- Talk to him about his experiences at daycare. Ask him which toys he played with, what friend he sat beside at snacktime, and what story the caregiver read to the children during quiet time.

- Learn the names of his friends—and greet those friends when you come to pick up your child.

- Invite his friends to your child's birthday, or have them over just for fun.

- If your child is being cared for at a daycare center, make a point of scanning the bulletin board and reading the center's newsletter.

- Find out how a typical childcare day is structured: when the children eat, when they play outside, and so on. This will help you to feel more tuned into what's happening in your child's life.

- Attend open houses or parent get-togethers at the daycare center or family daycare home so that you'll have the chance to meet the other children's parents. If you're really energetic, organize a potluck dinner or other social event.

- Take a half-day off work and spend some time observing your child. He'll welcome the chance to show you around, and you'll have the chance to get to know his caregiver and his playmates. What's more, the more you get to know about your child's daycare situation, the better you'll feel about sending him there each day.

Proctecting yourself against allegations of sexual harassment

Protecting yourself against allegations of sexual harassment may seem like an unnecessary exercise, but if you're sharing your home with a nanny, au pair, or other type of caregiver, you and your partner need to take precautionary measures. The best way to protect yourself is to understand what is considered sexual harassment under the law, and to ensure that your relationship with your child's caregiver is completely above board.

As you probably know, the United States Supreme Court has ruled that sexual harassment occurs in two ways: when an employer insists on receiving sexual favors as a condition of employment, and when he or she creates a working environment that would be considered "hostile or offensive" to any "reasonable person."

Here are some examples of behaviors that would be considered sexual harassment in the eyes of the law:

- repeated sexual flirtations, advances, or propositions that are offensive in nature

- subtle pressure for sexual activity

- continued or repeated verbal abuse

- innuendos of a sexual nature

- uninvited physical contact such as touching, hugging, patting, groping, or pinching

- comments of a sexual nature about an individual's body

- the display of sexually suggestive objects or pictures

- making jokes or remarks of a sexual nature

- asking questions about a person's personal life

- prolonged staring or leering

- making obscene gestures, or suggestive or insulting sounds

Because the judgements being handed down by the courts are massive—$250,000 seems to be the norm—it's important to ensure that your relationship with your child's caregiver is above reproach.

Protecting yourself against allegations of child abuse

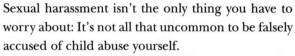

Sexual harassment isn't the only thing you have to worry about: It's not all that uncommon to be falsely accused of child abuse yourself.

Because childcare providers in many states are legally required to report instances of child abuse, parents who use their services are at risk of being falsely accused of this horrendous crime.

Here are some steps you can follow to protect yourself against false allegations of child abuse:

- If your child receives a bruise, burn, or cut, point out the injury to your child's caregiver and explain the circumstances surrounding the incident to her.

- Keep a written log at home that includes the date, the nature of the injury, the circumstances under which it occurred, and who was with the child at the time. You might even consider taking photos to support your written documentation.

- Some caregivers may suspect abuse if your child appears to be malnourished or consistently overtired. If there are medical reasons which would explain why your child is underweight or lacking in energy, be sure to share this information with the caregiver.

- Keep the caregiver informed about any occurrences on the homefront that could result in a sudden change in your child's behavior. The caregiver may suspect abuse if your child is unnaturally quiet or timid, overly active and aggressive, extremely afraid of strangers or looking to strangers for affection, too eager to please, extremely manipulative, or constantly craving attention.

While there's no guarantee that taking these types of actions will protect you against false accusations of child abuse, they could save your skin if you find yourself being charged with this type of crime.

Developing a good backup plan

No matter how much time and energy you put into choosing the right person to care for your child, there will be days when your childcare plans fall apart because either your child or his caregiver is ill. That's why it's so important to have a detailed backup plan in place that will allow you to make it into work.

When your child is ill

All children suffer from colds and flu bugs from time to time, but those who are cared for in group settings (daycare centers or family daycare settings) are particularly susceptible to illness. It's not that these types of care are necessarily inferior to in-home care; it's simply that if you throw a large number of runny-nosed kids together under one roof, viruses are bound to get passed around.

Sick kids are the wildcards in the lives of working parents. You never know when your child is going to come down with the latest flu bug, but you do know what you're expected to do when the dreaded phone call reaches you at work: Drop everything and go pick up your child.

I remember one instance when I received such a call at work. I had to cancel the class I was teaching and head for my son's family daycare home immediately. When I got there, it turned out that what ailed him wasn't anything even mildly life-threatening: his stomach had simply rejected the yellow crayon that he had eaten instead of his lunch! While my child didn't really need me, the caregiver was certainly grateful to see me. Not only had she been splattered while my son emptied the contents of his stomach, she had also been spewed on by the other child she was caring for—a sympathetic vomiter.

Part of the art of being a working parent is knowing when your child's well enough to go to daycare—and when he's not. While it's generally okay to send your child to daycare if he has a case of the sniffles, there will be times when your child is too ill to be anywhere but in bed—either because he's too ill to participate in activities or he's at risk of infecting the other children.

As a rule of thumb, you should be prepared to keep your child home from daycare if he has

- a fever (for some kids even a low fever can mean real trouble)
- repeated diarrhea or vomiting (more than two bouts in a 24 hour period)
- a contagious disease such as chicken pox, measles, mumps, or an unexplained rash
- strep throat
- head lice
- pink eye with yellow or white discharge
- impetigo
- ringworm
- scabies

Other factors to consider when you're trying to decide whether to send him to daycare or keep him home are as follows:

- Is he well enough to participate fully in the program?

- Will his caregiver be able to give him the attention he needs?

- How important is it that you make it to work today?

- How many days of work have you missed recently due to your child's illnesses?

- What guidelines did your child's pediatrician provide? (Many illnesses—like strep throat, pink eye, ear infections, ringworm, and head lice—are no longer contagious after treatment has been started.)

There may also be occasions when the daycare center or family daycare home has to be closed due to an outbreak of a contagious disease—a situation a Canadian publishing executive encountered when a measles epidemic went through the infant room at her daughter's daycare center. Because her daughter hadn't been immunized against measles, the woman had to keep her at home until the health unit gave the daycare center the okay to reopen its infant room.

When your caregiver is ill

Your child's health isn't the only wildcard in your life. If you rely on the services of a family daycare provider who doesn't have a backup arrangement with another caregiver or you use the services of an in-home caregiver, you will have to make alternative arrangements for your child whenever your

Unofficially...
According to a recent report in the *Journal of the American Medical Association*, children who are cared for outside of their own homes are two to four times more likely to contract infectious diseases than those who are cared for in their own homes.

Watch Out!
Don't send your child's medications in his lunch box. Another child might mistake a bottle of brightly colored, fruit-scented antibiotics as a special drink. Instead, transport the medication in a separate bag and hand it to his caregiver directly, along with an authorization to administer medication and a copy of the doctor's instructions.

caregiver is ill or otherwise unavailable. Your caregiver might, for example, come down with the chicken pox—an occupational hazard for any caregiver who wasn't lucky enough to break out in spots as a child—or be called out of town on a family emergency.

Because these types of curve balls almost always arise when you have a critically important report to finish up at work, it's essential to have a backup plan in place.

Here are just a few options you might want to consider as you go about trying to arrange backup care for your child:

- Telecommute for the day. As long as your job is suited to this type of arrangement and you're realistic about what you can reasonably expect to accomplish with one or more young children underfoot, this can be an ideal solution to your childcare crisis. If you get some advance warning that you're likely to be away for a day or two, bring a laptop computer and a briefcase full of work home from the office, and make arrangements to touch base with your colleagues on a regular basis.

- Use some banked overtime and take the day off entirely. Remember the long hours you put in while the company was finishing up its year end? Now's the time to draw on all those hours of overtime you banked. Even if your company doesn't have a formal flex-time program, you should keep a written log of any overtime you put in so that you can convince your boss that he's getting his money's worth out of you, even if you do miss the occasional day when your child is ill.

- Take a personal day. Most employers recognize that there will be days when a particular employee is unable to make it to the office. That's why many firms allocate a certain number of so-called personal days to their employees. This is what personal days are designed for, so use them.

- See if your partner can take a day off work. Perhaps he or she is able to telecommute, draw on banked time, or take a personal day.

If you absolutely have to make it into the office, here are some other strategies you might want to try:

- If you recruited your caregiver through an agency, find out whether the agency provides access to a backup caregiver as a service to the families they deal with. If they do, you should ideally try to meet the caregiver or caregivers who provide this service before you actually need them—something that may or may not be possible. Obviously, this strategy, like the one that follows, won't work particularly well if it's your child who is ill.

- Look for another family in your neighborhood who would be willing to share their in-home caregiver. If you also have an in-home caregiver, the two caregivers could agree to act as backups for one another in the event that either of them is ill.

- Find out if there is an organization in your community that provides care to sick children in their homes. Some health-care agencies, for example, can provide you with the services of a registered nursing assistant. Of course, this type of care is best reserved for days when you absolutely have to make it to the office: It is, after all, anything but cheap. Still, a growing number of companies are picking up the tab for sick child services in recognition of the fact that it's far cheaper to pay for a day of nursing care than to lose the services of a key employee.

- Find out if there's a childcare facility in town that accepts children who are too sick to go to their regular care arrangements. This type of care is extremely rare, but can be a lifesaver if you find yourself with no other backup plan. Your local health unit should be able to tell you if such a facility exists in your community.

- See if there's a family member who would be willing to help you out. While Grandma and Grandpa might be reluctant to provide childcare services on a regular basis, they might be willing to pinch-hit from time to time.

- Call the local community college or university and find out if there are any student nurses available to provide sick childcare to families in need, or ask your clergyman if he knows of someone who might be available to care for your child. Obviously, you will want to make arrangements to meet these individuals before you leave your child with them. This is something you should ideally do before your child gets sick.

If your child seems to be getting sick on a regular basis, you may want to do a little digging to find out what seems to be causing the problem. Take a critical look at his childcare environment and see if you can spot any of the following problems:

Bright Idea
If your child picks up every bug that's going around his day-care center, you might consider pulling his from group care for a couple of weeks to give his immune system a chance to get back up to speed. Obviously, either you or your spouse will need to have a flexible type of job arrange-ment—or access to a particularly doting rela-tive!—in order to try out this particular strategy.

- How often does the caregiver wash her hands?

- Does she wash them each time she changes a diaper or wipes a child's runny nose?

- Does she wash them before handling food? How clean is the sink that she uses to wash her hands?

- Is the bed or crib where your child naps changed before and after he uses it?

- Is the bed at least three feet away from the other children's beds?

- Where does the caregiver put sick children who are waiting for their parents to arrive?

If you are not satisfied with the caregiver's hygiene practices, you should plan to either speak to her directly or ask another person to intervene on your behalf (for example, the director of the daycare center or the local public health inspector).

While it isn't easy to come up with a childcare backup plan that covers all possible situations, you need one that's comprehensive enough to enable you to meet your obligations to your employer. Obviously, this is definitely one of those situations in life when creativity counts.

Just the facts

- There are a number of strategies you can use to smooth your child's transition to daycare.

- To ensure that your relationship with your child's caregiver gets off to the best possible start, be clear about your responsibilities to one another and make a point of communicating in person, by phone, and in writing.

- To prevent yourself from feeling cut off from your child's "other" family, plan to spend time

Watch Out!
Make sure that your child's caregiver knows how to spot the symptoms of an allergic reaction: swollen eyes, swollen lips, rashes, eczema, hives, nose and lung congestion, mucus, muscle spasm, vomiting, diarrhea, nausea, and cramps. A child who is having a severe allergic reaction requires medical attention immediately.

with him and his caregiver whenever you can get some time off work.

■ Because you may find yourself without childcare if either your child or your caregiver is ill, you need to have a comprehensive backup plan in place that will enable you to make it to work as often as possible.

GET THE SCOOP ON...
Why childcare arrangements break down ▪
What to do if your childcare arrangement isn't
working ▪ Coping with suspected abuse ▪
Finding a new childcare arrangement ▪
Helping your child to make the transition

A Pound of Cure

You did everything by the book: assessed your family's needs, evaluated your various childcare options, and—after a few sleepless nights—finally zeroed in on an arrangement that you thought would solve your family's childcare woes for the next year at least. So how on earth did you end up back at square one?

If you didn't already know it before, you just discovered one of the ugly truths about being a working parent: There's no such thing as a sure bet when it comes to childcare. Just when you think you can lean back in your office chair, put your feet up, and breathe a sigh of relief, you find out that your childcare arrangements have fallen apart.

It's practically a universal experience—one that most working parents have to face eventually. One childcare study found that 30 percent of parents find themselves looking for a new childcare arrangement within the first six months, and a full 50 percent find themselves in a similar boat within the first year. It doesn't take a genius to realize how many

245

lives are thrown in turmoil when the next round of childcare musical chairs starts up.

While there are no easy solutions to the childcare problem, this chapter will provide you with the information you need to make the best possible choices for your child. We'll discuss the reasons why childcare arrangements break down, talk about the factors that may influence whether you decide to work things out and move on, tell you what to do if you suspect that your child is being abused, give you some tips on finding a new childcare arrangement, and offer some advice on helping your child to make the transition.

Why childcare arrangements break down

While there are almost as many reasons for terminating a childcare arrangement as there are caregivers and families, let's take a few moments to run through a few of the most common reasons for moving on.

Caregiver unreliability

A few years ago, our family had a caregiver who was wonderful in every respect—except for one. We couldn't bank on the fact that she'd be available to care for our children on the days when we needed her. Some days she couldn't care for our children because she was ill; other days she was unavailable because of family emergencies. And each time she was unable to take our children, I had to cancel everything on my calendar for the day.

As much as I liked this caregiver—and she really was a lovely person—we felt that for the sake of our careers and our sanity, we needed to find someone who was a bit more reliable. It was simply too stressful to hop out of the shower first thing in the

Unofficially...
In Italy, young children stay with the same caregiver until they are at least three years old.

morning, only to find a message on the answering machine saying that our care arrangements for the day had fallen through.

Poor quality care

Another reason for terminating a care arrangement is dissatisfaction with the quality of care that your child is receiving. One working mother pulled her six-month-old son from a particular family daycare setting when she discovered that the caregiver put all the children down for naps right after lunch—whether they were ready to sleep or not. Another removed her eight-year-old daughter from a different family daycare home when she found out that the caregiver was permitting her child to watch *The Young and the Restless*—steamy bedroom scenes and all! While it's impossible to monitor your child's care situation every moment of every day, you can watch for signs that something's not quite right. You have every right to be concerned if your child's caregiver

- won't allow you to enter the house when you drop by unexpectedly

- becomes angry or defensive when you raise concerns about your child

- implies that a problem that she is having with your child is all your fault

- complains about the other children or parents or shares personal information about them that you really have no right to know

- refuses to give you feedback on your child's day

- allows the children to watch excessive amounts of television

- spends an inappropriate amount of time on the telephone, ignoring the children in her care

> **66**
>
> I learned very quickly that the family childcare provider who had seemed so competent at first was totally overwhelmed by the task of caring for two infants at the same time. She called me often and I could hear my daughters crying in the background. Then I'd arrive to find them with formula stains down to their navels.
> —Katie, mother of twins
>
> **99**

- allows the quality of food she is providing to deteriorate
- forces the children to play outside regardless of the weather or how they are feeling
- fails to greet your child with a touch or a smile
- seems to lose interest in caregiving
- complains about being lonely, isolated, and/or burdened with responsibilities
- looks physically drained and unhappy
- is overwhelmed by personal problems
- takes on more children then she can reasonably handle

You should consider terminating the childcare arrangement if you

- are constantly worried about your child while you're at work
- feel that the relationship between your child's caregiver and yourself is becoming more and more strained
- feel that the caregiver's values and child rearing practices are incompatible with your own
- do not feel welcome or accepted in the child-care environment
- feel intimidated by the caregiver or have difficulty communicating with her
- feel that the caregiver has unrealistic expectations of your child and suspect that she doesn't particularly like her
- do not trust the caregiver or have reason to believe that she is not carrying out your instructions

Personality conflicts

Personality conflicts can also be a major source of problems between parents and caregivers. Sometimes they have incompatible child rearing styles—something that may or may not be obvious until the "honeymoon period" of childcare is over.

Let's assume for the moment that your family childcare provider is an experienced mother of four and this is your first baby. You might resent it if she has a tendency to imply that you don't know as much about caring for your baby as she does, or if she insinuates from time to time that if you loved your baby as much as she loves her kids, you'd find a way to be at home with your child.

If your caregiver has a tendency to rub you the wrong way, but she's wonderful with your baby, you might decide to grit your teeth and bear it.

If, however, you're less than impressed with the overall quality of care that she is providing, you just might decide that the time has come to move on.

Change in caregiver circumstances

Because caring for young children is a stressful and poorly paid profession, rates of turnover among family daycare providers and other childcare workers tend to be quite high. It's not unusual to go through a series of caregivers between the time that your child is born and when she starts school.

Your caregiver may also decide to close up shop if her family situation changes dramatically—for example, if she decides to have another baby or her youngest child starts school. You might also lose her services if you employ her on a part-time basis and a full-time employment opportunity comes along.

Unofficially...
A 1988 study by childcare consultant Ellen Galinksy revealed that many caregivers have negative feelings about the parents of the children in their care.

Change in family circumstances

Your caregiver isn't the only one whose life can be thrown into turmoil. Much as you might hate to even consider the possibility, yours could be plunged into chaos as well—with little or no notice.

If you're a natural-born optimist who has not yet mastered the art of pessimism, try this little exercise: Just think of your life as a game of Snakes and Ladders in which any bit of bad luck could cause you to slide right back to start.

Just imagine how your childcare needs might change if:

- you lost your job
- your hours were cut at work
- your partner's salary was chopped in half
- your working hours changed dramatically (i.e. from day shift to night shift)
- one of you came down with a serious illness
- an aging relative moved in with you
- you unexpectedly gave birth to triplets

If even one of these events happened, you might find yourself looking for an alternative form of care—assuming, of course, that you could afford any amount of childcare at all. And even if your situation reversed itself in the near future (i.e. you were called back to work after a layoff or recovered from a serious illness), you could very well find that your caregiver had already taken a position elsewhere, sending you right back to square one in your search for childcare.

Suspected abuse

And last, but not least, we come to every working parent's nightmare: finding out that your caregiver has been abusing your child. If this is the case, you have no choice but to move on. We'll discuss this issue in great depth later on in this chapter.

What to do if your childcare arrangement isn't working

If you are dissatisfied with the quality of care that your child is receiving from his caregiver, but the problems with your child's caregiver are not in any way threatening to your child's well-being, you will have to decide whether you want to attempt to resolve the situation or whether it would be best for all concerned if you simply parted ways.

Because caregiver consistency is important for very young children, the ideal situation is to try to work out the problems between yourself and your child's caregiver. Sometimes, that's simply not an option. If your child is being abused, you have no choice but to look for another care arrangement immediately.

Attempting to resolve the situation

In some cases, it's possible to resolve the problems that have arisen between your child's caregiver and yourself. If you intend to go this route, you should schedule a face-to-face meeting at a mutually convenient time. Don't try to address complex issues while you're picking up or dropping off your child: It's not fair to your caregiver or the children in her care.

Here are some tips on handling this meeting:

- Express your concerns in a calm, sensitive manner and listen patiently as the caregiver expresses her concerns as well. Rather than trying to assign blame for the problems you are experiencing, focus on finding solutions together.

- Try to focus on one or two areas of particular concern. Set up a second meeting to tackle some of the less pressing matters.

- Deal with issues as they arise rather than postponing your discussion indefinitely. Otherwise, you're likely to blow a gasket over some inconsequential matter.

- Be assertive, but not aggressive. The fact that you are acting as an advocate on behalf of your child is no excuse for being rude or dismissive.

- Document the key points of your discussion by writing her a letter outlining the solutions that the two of you have agreed upon.

- Plan to touch base on a regular basis so you can compare notes on how well things are going and identify other areas for improvement.

Deciding to go your separate ways

If you don't feel good about leaving your child with her caregiver or your gut feeling is telling you that you aren't going to be able to resolve the situation, perhaps it's time to move on.

While you may be eager to part company as soon as possible so that your child won't become any more attached to the caregiver than she has already become, you will likely have to provide your caregiver with a certain amount of notice (typically two weeks) before you can terminate the childcare relationship. If you provide less than the agreed upon amount of notice, you should expect to fork over that many weeks' worth of wages or daycare fees instead. Regardless of which route you decide to go, make sure that you keep your thoughts to yourself until you're ready to inform your caregiver of your decision. Otherwise, your three-year-old might spill the beans prematurely.

Moneysaver
You can protect yourself against a wrongful dismissal lawsuit by providing your in-home caregiver with written notice of any problems with her job performance. If you do end up firing her, you'll be able to prove that you gave her every opportunity to improve her performance, but she chose not to do so.

While it's relatively easy to terminate a relationship with a caregiver in a daycare center or family daycare home, it's much more complicated to part ways with an in-home caregiver with whom you have an employee-employer relationship. Because the caregiver is legally your employee, you must fulfil certain legal obligations before you can terminate the relationship. That's the subject we're going to tackle about next.

The do's and don'ts of firing

There are entire books written about how to protect yourself against a wrongful dismissal lawsuit, so I won't attempt to replicate them here. However, I will provide you with a few basic "do's" and "don'ts" of firing.

Do

- Obtain legal advice before you fire your caregiver if you think there is even the slightest possibility that she may attempt to sue you for wrongful dismissal.

- Take things one step at a time. Unless there is misconduct or incompetence involved, you are required to provide your caregiver with a reasonable amount of notice prior to dismissing her. What is considered reasonable notice depends on such factors as her age, the nature of her position, her length of service, the chances of her obtaining similar employment elsewhere, and whether or not she was induced to leave a secure position elsewhere in order to accept your offer.

- Ensure that you have generated an adequate paper trail to substantiate your claims that the caregiver was given every opportunity to improve her performance, but didn't.

Watch Out!
An employee may have grounds for a lawsuit if she is unjustly dismissed or demoted, has her salary reduced, or experiences any other significant change to the fundamental terms of her employment (i.e. her job description).

- Plan the exit interview carefully. Who will deliver the message? When it will be delivered? What will you or your partner say to the caregiver? If you recruited your caregiver through an agency, the director of the agency may wish to participate, too.

- Present the facts as they are. Don't gloss over the truth or give a false excuse for termination. Your words could come back to haunt you. If you felt that she wasn't sufficiently experienced in caring for young children, state it in black and white.

- Be prepared for your caregiver to react with anger or even tears. The key is to empathize with how she is feeling, but to stand by your decision to fire her. Handling this part of the exit interview well may help to diffuse her anger, therefore reducing the chances of her launching a wrongful dismissal lawsuit.

Don't

- Fire your caregiver on a Friday afternoon. Scheduling a termination meeting early in the day and early in the week will allow your caregiver to set up an appointment with a domestic agency, meet with her financial planner, and do whatever else she needs to do to get her life in order.

- Expect her to function as usual. Have a backup childcare arrangement in place in case she's too upset or distracted to care for your child.

- Offer to provide her with a glowing letter of reference in order to ease any guilt you may feel about firing her. If someone else hired her on the basis of your recommendation and she proved to be grossly underqualified for the position, you could be sued for misrepresenting her abilities.

Finding a new childcare arrangement

Before you end one childcare arrangement and plunge into another, it makes sense to re-evaluate your childcare priorities. After all, your situation may have changed significantly since the last time you took time to assess your needs. A change in your situation at work, for example, might lead you to conclude that in-home care is better suited to your needs than out-of-home care, or that you would rather go with part-time care than full-time care.

If you've had a particularly bad experience with one particular type of care, you might be wary of going the same route again. This might lead you to abandon center-based daycare in favor of a family daycare situation—or vice versa.

First things first

Before you start looking for a new childcare arrangement, take a few moments to figure out what went wrong with your previous arrangement. Here are some questions you might want to ask yourself:

- Was the arrangement no longer meeting my child's needs? If not, what do I need to look for in a new arrangement?

- Was the arrangement no longer meeting the family's needs? If not, what do I need to look for in a new arrangement?

- Have my expectations of care changed since the last time I was looking for childcare? If so, how will this affect my new search?

Timesaver
If your caregiver and you are parting on good terms, ask her if she can recommend another caregiver who may be a good fit for your children.

- Did I run into conflicts with my caregiver? If so, what were the sources of those conflicts? What could I do to avoid running into similar problems in my next childcare arrangement?

- What have I learned from this experience and from my relationship with my child's caregiver?

How you may be feeling

Don't be surprised if you find yourself feeling angry and frustrated about having to look for childcare again, even if you know in your heart that it's time to move on. Now that you've played childcare roulette once—and lost—you're probably far less likely to want to play again. You may also be feeling guilty about having placed your child in a poor childcare arrangement in the past, or worried that you won't be able to find anything better this time around.

Coping with suspected abuse

Shortly after the birth of my first child, I happened to be channel surfing during a particularly gut-wrenching episode of *Geraldo!* The subject that was being discussed was one that I would have preferred to avoid: caregivers abusing the children in their care.

While it's been nearly a decade since I chanced upon that TV program, I've never forgotten one particular segment of video footage that showed a caregiver slapping a six-month-old baby across the face. Each time I look for a caregiver, I think of that baby and remind myself of the importance of choosing a caregiver wisely.

That's not to say that children are abused because their parents have made poor childcare choices, or that your child won't be abused just because you've exercised considerable care in choosing a caregiver. I wish the issue of child abuse was that simple, but it's not. Good judgement isn't enough. You also need good luck.

What you can do to reduce the chances of abuse

While there are no guarantees that your child won't be harmed, there are some steps you can take to reduce the likelihood that your child will be abused while she is in daycare. When you're considering a particular daycare arrangement, you should

- find out how the daycare center, family daycare provider, or domestic agency recruits and hires its caregivers and whether it routinely conducts reference and background checks

- note the quality of the interactions between the children and their caregivers (i.e. whether the children appear to be happy and comfortable or nervous and fearful)

- monitor your child's childcare arrangement on an ongoing basis

You should also watch for the following "red flags" that may indicate that something isn't quite right about a particular childcare environment:

- The daycare center or family daycare setting has a policy requiring parents to phone before they drop by.

- You find unexplained bumps and bruises on your child's body, and you're unable to get a satisfactory explanation about what caused them.

- The caregiver uses inappropriate methods of discipline (i.e., hitting, bullying, or threatening).

- The caregiver takes children off the premises without their parents' permission.

Watch Out!
Be sure to find out who will be interacting with your child other than the caregiver and other staff members. Much of the sexual and physical abuse of children occurs at the hands of individuals who are not directly responsible for their care: i.e. the caregivers' relatives, other children's parents, bus drivers, janitors, and so on.

- The caregiver provides inadequate supervision during naptimes or when the children are using the bathroom—a situation which could leave the children vulnerable to abuse.

The warning signs of abuse

You should consider the possibility that your child is being physically or sexually abused if she has

- bite marks

- unusual bruises, lacerations, and burns

- a high incidence of accidents or frequent injuries

- fractures in unusual places

- welts, especially to the back of her body

- dislocated hips or shoulders

- scars in a regular pattern

- injuries or swelling to her face and/or extremities

- skin discoloration

- torn clothing

- difficulty in walking, sitting, going to the bathroom, or swallowing

- pain, itching, bleeding, and bruises in the genital or anal area or in the throat

- stained or bloody diapers or underwear

- vaginal odor or discharge

Sudden changes in your child's behavior can also be an indication that something is very wrong. You should consider the possibility that your child has been abused if she

- is suddenly reluctant to go to daycare or to be with her caregiver

- is uncharacteristically fearful of adults and/or closed spaces

- is suddenly unwilling to have anyone dress her or change her diaper

- develops nervous mannerisms (i.e., thumb sucking, hair pulling) or seems more dependent than usual on comfort objects (i.e., blanket or pacifier)

- plays aggressively to the extent that she injures her playmates or exhibits uncharacteristically hyperactive behavior

- gives inconsistent explanations about the occurrence of any injuries that she has received

- shows inappropriate displays of affection or engages in sexual acting out (i.e., excessive masturbation or seductive behavior)

- expresses unusual knowledge or sophistication in describing sexual behavior

- doesn't want other people to touch her

- develops sleep problems such as insomnia, nightmares, a refusal to sleep alone, or an insistence on having the light left on all night

- reports instances of abuse

You should be concerned about the quality of care that your baby is receiving if she

- cries much more or less than usual

- seems indifferent to your words and smiles

- is agitated and jumpy

If your baby exhibits these signs of depression, it could be because she is being dumped in a crib or playpen all day and ignored by her caregiver.

This type of neglect can be literally life-threatening. A severely depressed infant can lose the ability to process her food—a condition that can lead her compromised immune system vulnerable to disease and possibly even lead to death. This tragic situation—one that medical professionals call "failure to thrive"—tends to occur when an infant who is being severely neglected decides that there's no point in crying out or asking for help because no one will help her, and simply loses her will to live.

You should be concerned about the quality of care that your toddler or preschooler is receiving if she

- no longer wants to go to daycare
- can't sleep at night or has nightmares
- stops eating
- starts wetting the bed at night or begins having accidents during the day again
- refuses to have a bowel movement
- either cries and clings or avoids you altogether
- seems more fearful or anxious than usual
- stops caring about how you react to her behavior—either positively or negatively
- suddenly becomes unhappy when she has always been a happy child

If your child is old enough to talk and reports an instance of child abuse to you, it is very important that you reassure her that she has done the right thing. Tell her that

- you believe her and you're glad that she told you about the abuse
- she didn't do anything wrong

- you will do your best to see that she is not hurt again

What to do if you suspect abuse

If you suspect that your child has been abused, you should

- remove your child from the childcare situation immediately

- call the appropriate authorities (i.e., the police or your local child protection agency) and allow them to handle the investigation (as opposed to confronting the daycare director or caregiver yourself)

- ensure that your child is examined by a medical doctor

- consult with a doctor, social worker, or law enforcement official to find out what counseling services may be available to your child

Note: The best strategy for dealing with child abuse is to prevent it from happening in the first place. If you have a gut feeling that there's something wrong with a particular daycare arrangement, do not send your child there.

Helping your child to make the transition

More often than not, it's usually something far less worrisome than child abuse that causes you causes you to change caregivers—perhaps something as harmless as a simple personality conflict. If this is the case, it's important to realize that you and your child may be feeling quite differently about the whole situation. While you may heave a huge sigh of relief as your nanny loads up her suitcases and

Watch Out!
If your child tells you an elaborate story about a cruel giant who comes to daycare and hurts the children, listen up. Many children who have been abused tell stories involving monsters, animals, and non-human characters to explain what has happened to them.

heads down the driveway for the very last time, your child might not share your feelings. In fact, she may be downright grief stricken.

You can conclude that your child is having difficulty coping with the loss of her caregiver if she begins to exhibit some of the classic symptoms of grief:

- insomnia
- frequent illness
- restlessness and irritability
- excessive or diminished appetite
- poor concentration
- increased crying
- nightmares

While it's a lot easier to empathize with your child if you're also feeling sad about bidding goodbye to her caregiver, it's important to acknowledge her feelings of grief and loss—even if you don't exactly share them.

Many children find it difficult to understand why they are losing their caregiver. Your child may wonder if she did something bad enough to make the caregiver go away, or if the caregiver simply decided that she didn't like her after all.

Most child development experts feel that it's important that children be given the chance to say goodbye when they change caregivers, even if the care they received was less than adequate. You can explain to your child that she will be going to a new daycare center where the people will take better care of her, and then ask her if she wants to say goodbye to her caregiver and the children at her former daycare center. She may very well decline your offer, but it's important to give her the opportunity to close the door on this particular chapter in her life by allowing her to say goodbye.

Some children have a harder time saying goodbye to their caregivers than others. You can expect your child to have a particularly difficult time with the transition if

- she is very young and therefore unable to understand why she is having to bid farewell to her caregiver

- she has had the same caregiver for a very long time and has grown quite attached to her

- she is also coping with another type of loss (i.e., the death of a grandparent or a pet)

- she is inadequately prepared for the loss (i.e., you tell her about it after the fact)

You can help your child to work through her feelings of loss by encouraging her to express her feelings, giving her extra love and attention, and assuring her that you aren't about to disappear, too. You might also look for opportunities for her to participate in the process of saying goodbye to her caregiver. Depending on her age and the circumstances surrounding the caregiver's departure, you might encourage your child to bake the caregiver a cake or make her a card.

You should also make an effort to provide her with as much information about the situation as possible—and as soon as possible:

- Share the news about the caregiver's departure as soon as you can so that she'll have time to get used to the idea that the caregiver is leaving before it's actually time to say goodbye.

Bright Idea
If you and your child's caregiver are parting on good terms, you might want to ask her if she would be willing to stay in touch with your child, at least over the short term. Having a phone call, postcard, or visit from the caregiver during the early weeks may help to ease the pangs of separation for your child.

- Tell her where the caregiver will be going and when she can expect to see or hear from her again.

- If your child is old enough to understand the reasons for the caregiver's departure, provide her with a reasonable explanation of the circumstances leading to the change. Be as honest as possible, but don't be afraid to indulge in a few euphemisms if doing so allows you to avoid bashing her beloved caregiver.

- Involve her in the process of finding a new caregiver—but don't be surprised if she claims to hate every potential caregiver who walks through your front door. It's her way of being loyal to the caregiver she has grown to love so dearly.

Changing care arrangements is stressful for the entire family, and something you'll want to avoid as much as possible. Families whose childcare arrangements keep falling apart need to re-evaluate their policies toward the caregivers they employ. Lack of consideration, failure to pay for overtime and unreasonable expectations are usually at the top of most caregivers' list of reasons for leaving a job. By taking the time to choose your child's new caregiver wisely, and making a point of treating her as well as you expect her to treat your child, you'll reduce the chances of having to hop on this merry-go-round again—at least for the foreseeable future.

Just the facts

- Childcare arrangements break down for a number of reasons, including caregiver unreliability, poor quality care, personality conflicts, a change in your caregiver's or your own circumstances, and suspected abuse.

- Depending on the nature of the problems which you are experiencing with your child's caregiver, you may decide to either work things out or seek another childcare arrangement.

- If you suspect that your child is being abused by her caregiver, remove her from the childcare situation immediately and report the suspected abuse to the appropriate authorities.

- Before you plunge into a new childcare arrangement, you should take some time to re-evaluate the needs of your child and your family.

- Changing childcare arrangements isn't easy for young children. It's important to recognize that your child may experience feelings of grief at the idea of saying goodbye to her caregiver, and to help her to work through her feelings.

Solutions Unlimited

GET THE SCOOP ON...
Your child's needs ▪ Your family's needs ▪ Out-
of-home versus in-home care ▪ The advantages
and disadvantages of out-of-home care ▪ The
advantages and disadvantages of in-home care
▪ What to look for in an out-of-home arrangement ▪ How to find a good in-home caregiver

Finding Care For Your Special Needs Child

Chapter 11

While finding childcare is difficult at the best of times, finding childcare for a child who has special needs can be even more challenging—especially if you live in a community which is chronically short of childcare spaces for children with physical or emotional challenges.

The key to finding a suitable arrangement is to have a clear idea of what you're looking for and to start your search as early as possible.

In this chapter, I will give you the tools you need to find the best possible childcare arrangement for a child who has special needs. I'll talk about the merits of out-of-home and in-home childcare arrangements and pass along some tips on finding a caregiver who's right for your child and your family.

Your child's needs

When you're evaluating your out-of-home and in-home childcare options, it's important to consider how well—or how poorly—each daycare, family daycare setting, or in-home caregiver is equipped to meet the needs of your child. Obviously, this is where such factors as your child's developmental stage and temperament come into play.

Because your child may be experiencing developmental delays, it's not particularly helpful to consider his needs solely in terms of his chronological age. In most cases, it makes more sense to consider the suitability of a particular childcare setting by considering how well it meets his overall needs.

If your child's physical, emotional, and social skills are such that he is more like an infant than an older child, you will want him to benefit from a low caregiver-child ratio (ideally 1:1 but no more than 1:3) and a small group size (ideally three or less but certainly no more than four) and that he is cared for by the same caregiver on an ongoing basis. The caregiver should be a person who genuinely loves young children and who is either experienced in dealing with your child's particular types of needs or prepared to learn about them by taking courses, reading up on his specific disorder, and so on.

If your child is mobile and yet is experiencing other types of developmental delays, you will probably want to seek out an environment in which there is a relatively low caregiver-child ratio (ideally 1:3 or less, but certainly no more than 1:5) and a small group size (ideally four or less but certainly no more than six). You will also want to examine the physical environment carefully to identify any potential hazards and to point these out to your child's caregiver.

While the childcare environment may be perfectly safe for other children, it may pose unique risks to your child because of his particular needs.

If you would like to find out more about developmental issues, you might want to check out the following Web sites: Internet Resources for Special Children (IRSC) at www.irsc.org, the American Academy of Pediatrics (AAP) at www.aap.org, the Sesame Street Parents Resource Links at www.ctw.org/parents/links/index.htm, the National Academy for Child Development at www.nacd.org/articles.html and www.earlychildhood.com. You might also want to call Woodbine House, a book publisher in Bethesda, Maryland, that specializes in books and resources for families of individuals who have special needs. The company's number is 1-800-843-7323.

Here's one last resource you need to know about before we move on: The Child Care Law Center, 973 Market Street, Suite 550, San Francisco, CA 94103 (415)495-5498 has a series of low-cost publications for parents and childcare providers concerning children with disabilities in childcare.

Your child's temperament is every bit as important as his developmental stage in determining the suitability of a particular childcare arrangement. Quiet, shy children may feel more comfortable in family daycare environments than in large daycare centers. Likewise, particularly active and outgoing children may find family daycare too quiet for their liking (particularly if the others in care are younger children), and may prefer the buzz of activity at larger daycare centers instead. You can find out more about how your child's temperament affects his capability to learn and to relate to his caregiver

Bright Idea
Be sure to ask if there is a resource worker available to work with your child or—at the very least—to provide his caregiver with some pointers on designing a program that will meet his needs. Your state or local childcare licensing authorities can put you in touch with the government office responsible for coordinating care for children with special needs.

by visiting www.temperament.com—a Web site that's packed with information on how temperament affects infants, children, and adults.

The best way to assess the fit between your child and a childcare environment is to give him the opportunity to test drive it for himself. Take your child along when you visit daycare centers or family daycare homes and note how comfortable he is with the caregiver and other children.

Your family's needs

When you're evaluating your out-of-home childcare options, it's also important to consider how well—or how poorly—each out-of-home or in-home childcare arrangement is suited to meeting the needs of your family.

In addition to considering such factors as your working schedule, the location of the daycare center or family daycare home (assuming you choose out-of-home care), you will also want to consider your expectations of care—a key consideration for any family, but especially important for families with children who have special needs.

As we mentioned earlier in this book, it's a lot easier to find out-of-home care for your child if you work a standard nine-to-five work day. If you work non-standard hours, you're most likely to find suitable care for your child in a daycare center at your workplace or in a family daycare setting (especially if it's operated by a caregiver whose hours are similar to your own). If you manage to find a caregiver who is willing to work around your schedule, consider yourself blessed. Such arrangements are few and far between.

Location is another important factor in evaluating your childcare options. Ideally, you want to find a childcare arrangement that's close to either your place of employment, your partner's place of employment, or your home—particularly if you rely on public transportation to travel to and from work. If you end up finding a care arrangement that's outside your desired area, be sure to make the trip to the caregiver's home during rush hour so that you can get a realistic idea of how much time the trip to childcare is likely to add to your morning and evening schedules.

While work schedules and location are both important considerations, the most important issue for most families shopping for childcare is their care expectations. Many parents have clearly defined ideas of what the ideal care arrangement for their child will be like. For some families, it will be a daycare center staffed by highly trained early childhood educators. For others, it will be a warm and friendly family daycare environment operated by an experienced mother who has a genuine love of children. To avoid spinning your wheels unnecessarily, it's important to be clear from the outset about what you're looking for in an out-of-home childcare arrangement. For most families, this goes far beyond sheer physical care. It also encompasses the caregiver's philosophy.

While your search for childcare is likely to be anything but easy, there is some light at the end of the tunnel. The Individuals with Disabilities Education Act (IDEA) guarantees a free, publicly funded education to children between the ages of three and twenty-one who have disabilities. You can find out more about IDEA at http://TheArc.org/faqs/pl94142.html, by contacting the Americans with Disabilities (ADA) Information Line at 1-800-514-0301 or your state protection and advocacy

Timesaver
If your child needs to be driven to medical appointments on a regular basis, you might want to choose a daycare center or family daycare environment that is situated reasonably close to his doctors' offices.

association. You can obtain the contact information for your local protection and advocacy organization by contacting National Association of Protection and Advocacy Systems (NAPAS) 220 I Street N.E., Suite 150, Washington, D.C. 20002 (202)546-8202.

Out-of-home care versus in-home care

After you have clearly defined your child's and your family's needs, it's time to consider whether you want to find an out-of-home or in-home care arrangement for your child. Obviously, there are both advantages and disadvantages to out-of-home and in-home care arrangements in general as well as each type of out-of-home and in-home care in particular (daycare center, family daycare, nanny, full-time babysitter, au pair, and so on). That's why it's important to consider how each option measures up when it comes to caring for a child who has special needs.

Note: You can find additional information about out-of-home care in Chapter 4 and in-home care in Chapter 6. The discussion in this chapter is limited to pros and cons that relate specifically to children with special needs.

The advantages and disadvantages of out-of-home care

Pros:

- You don't have to share your home with a stranger—something that simply goes with the territory if you opt for an in-home caregiver.

- You don't have to spend a fortune to pay someone to care for your child. If your budget is already stretched to the max because of your child's medical bills, in-home care may be out of the question. While you can still pay a great deal for out-of-home care, you are more likely to find an arrangement that suits both your needs and your budget.

▪ Your child will have the opportunity to be with other children his own age—an important consideration for most families with children with special needs.

Cons:

▪ Taking your child to a daycare center or family daycare home is not nearly as convenient as having someone come into your home. You won't have to take your child and all his assorted paraphernalia off to childcare in the wee hours of the morning.

▪ Your child is more likely to be exposed to illness if he's in an out-of-home care arrangement. This may be a major issue for you if your child has a compromised immune system, chronic respiratory problems, and so on.

▪ Caregiver consistency can be a problem due to high levels of turnover in the childcare profession. Your child's caregiver may decide to leave the daycare center or close up her family daycare business after your child has become attached to her—and after you've integrated her into your child's routine.

▪ Out-of-home care becomes expensive if you're purchasing services for more than one child.

▪ You will still need a backup plan in case your child becomes ill—a real issue for many families who have children with special needs. Vomiting, feverish, and otherwise seriously ill children should recuperate at home, not at daycare.

> 66
> I look for evidence that the caregiver will be able to relate to Laura and find ways to help her do things that are important to her, like going bowling, having her school friends over, and so on. These elements of Laura's care are so important to me that I actually write them into the caregiver's job description.
> —Linda, mother of a developmentally delayed teenager
> 99

Unofficially . . .
An Individualized
Family Service
Plan (IFSP) is
developed by a
child's parents
and the members
of his medical
team once the
child has been
diagnosed with a
particular dis-
ability. His care-
giver should also
be a member of
this team.
Wherever possi-
ble, the IFSP
should specify
that the resource
workers assigned
to work with the
child should pro-
vide service to
him in his regu-
lar childcare
setting.

There are also some specific advantages and disadvantages to each particular type of out-of-home childcare. Let's consider each of the three basic types in turn and consider their suitability for a child with special needs.

Daycare centers

Pros:

- Daycare centers provide reliable care. You can count on the fact that someone will be available to care for your child, even if your child's own caregiver is ill. Because caregiver consistency is critical to families who have children with special needs, this may be reason enough for you to go this route.

- They often employ staff who have had specialized training in child development. Because such training is not always mandatory, however, it's important to ask about staff credentials when you're considering a particular daycare center. You may want to find out, for example, if anyone on staff has been trained to care for a child with a feeding tube or change an IV.

- They might be able to offer your child a greater variety of educational materials and facilities than either an in-home caregiver or family daycare provider can offer—something that may appeal to you, depending on the type and extent of your child's needs. Once again, there's tremendous variation between daycare centers, so you'll want to consider this point as you conduct your evaluations.

Cons:

- Your child will be exposed to more children—and therefore more illnesses—than he would encounter in either an in-home or family day-care environment—something that may be an important consideration for you, depending on the medical status of your child.

- Staff turnover can be a particular problem in daycare centers. Your child's caregiver may move to another group within the center or leave her position at the center altogether. Because routine is important for many children with special needs, this particular turn of events could represent a major disruption to your entire family.

- Your child may be expected to fit into childcare routines rather than being cared for by some-one who is willing to accommodate her own schedule for eating, sleeping, and so on. This may pose a problem for you, depending on the nature of your child's special needs.

- It can be difficult to find a space in a daycare center, particularly if you're looking for a space for a child who has special needs. If you live in a small or rural community, you might not have access to a daycare center at all.

Nursery schools

Pros:

- Nursery schools seek to provide enriching environments that are designed to stimulate young children and provide them with opportunities for socialization. They can be an ideal part-time childcare arrangement for a child with special needs.

Cons:

- Nursery school programs usually are part-time—something that limits their usefulness to

Moneysaver
If you like a particular childcare center but feel that its fees are out of your price range, be sure to inquire if there are any subsidies available to help offset the cost of care.

working parents. They also close up shop during the summer months—something that might be difficult for your child to adjust to, once he gets into a regular weekday routine.

- Most nursery schools are only licensed to accept children between the ages of two and five. What's more, a fair number of schools insist that the children in their care be toilet-trained— something that rules them out as care alternatives for many children with special needs.

Note: if you're wondering what a typical day at nursery school is really like, check out "A Day in the Life of a Preschooler" by Sharlene Johnson. The article is posted on the Sesame Street Parents Web site. You can find it at www.ctw.org/parents/weekly/ 2796/279601t1.htm.

Family daycare
Pros:

- Family daycare offers a familylike atmosphere that many parents consider ideal.

- Because children of different ages can be accommodated, family daycare makes it possible for siblings to share a single caregiver.

- Your child's routines are more likely to be respected in a small group setting like a family daycare home than in a large institutional setting.

Cons:

- Family daycare providers are less likely to have had specialized training in child development than their center-based counterparts. You may not feel comfortable leaving your child with someone who has not received specialized training in coping with his particular needs.

- A family daycare home may lack some of the costly equipment and elaborate facilities that are more commonly found in large daycare centers. This may or may not be an issue, depending on the age, interests, and abilities of your child.

- Your caregiver might not have a backup lined up to replace her in the event that she becomes ill, takes holidays, or requires time off to have a baby or deal with a family emergency. Even if she does have some sort of plan in place, the backup caregiver may not be suitably trained to care for your child or you may not feel comfortable subjecting your child to this type of disruption to his usual routine.

As you can see, there are definite advantages and disadvantages to choosing each type of out-of-home care. The needs of your family will help you to decide which option is best for your child.

The advantages and disadvantages of in-home care
Pros:

- The same person will care for your child day after day. Because caregiver consistency is so important for children with special needs, in-home care may be the ideal form of childcare for your family.

- Your child will receive one-on-one care (unless, of course, he has siblings, in which case he'll have to share her caregiver with her brothers and sisters!). While the staffs of daycare centers and family daycare providers do their best to keep ratios low, most operate on staff-child ratios that start at 1:3 and work their way up.

Moneysaver
Your local Child Care Resource and Referral Agency can inform you about childcare subsidies designed to help families who have children with special needs.

- You can start your day in a relatively sane fashion because your childcare provider is coming to you. There's no need to get your child out of bed before he's ready or to load up the van with all his assorted paraphernalia before you take him to a daycare center or family daycare home. If your child relies on a large number of assistive devices (for example, a nebulizer, an IV, a wheelchair, and so on), the convenience of having in-home care can be particularly compelling.

- Your child can stick to his own schedule when it comes to eating, sleeping, and playing. This type of flexibility is much harder to find in a large group setting.

- An in-home caregiver can accommodate your erratic work schedule better than the staff of either a daycare center or family daycare provider. If you have to work into the evening hours to meet a pressing deadline, your in-home caregiver may be willing to assume responsibility for caring for your child until you can come home. This may be an important consideration for you if you wouldn't be comfortable having a second caregiver caring for your child on evenings or weekends—even if your work schedule required it.

- Your child won't pick up as many illnesses as he would if he were being cared for in a large group setting—a key consideration if your child has any type of immune disorder.

Cons:

- In-home care is the most expensive type of childcare. Many families don't have the incomes required to hire caregivers to come into their own homes. If a good portion of your monthly budget goes toward your child's medical bills, you might not be able to afford the services of an in-home caregiver.

- The stress of caring for young children in relative isolation leads to high levels of burnout among in-home caregivers. As a result, turnover can be a problem. You could find yourself investing a lot of time and energy into familiarizing a particular caregiver with your child's routines, only to lose her a few months down the line.

- Your home may not be large enough to provide adequate privacy for an in-home caregiver—particularly if you've had to modify it to make it wheelchair accessible.

- If your child is home alone with your caregiver, she may miss out on the chance to interact with other children her own age—something that is particularly important during the preschool years.

- It's hard enough to share your child with a caregiver without having to share your home with that person as well. Jealousy of the caregiver's relationship with your child can be a major issue for many working parents (especially mothers).

- The government doesn't license in-home care arrangements, so you're on your own when it comes to supervising the quality of care that your child is receiving. If your child is nonverbal and therefore more vulnerable to abuse, you may have concerns about shouldering this responsibility on your own.

Bright Idea
Because it's easy to become isolated when you're caring for a special needs child, you'll want to make a particular point of finding ways to help your caregiver get out and about with your child. If there's a local parent-child drop in center, purchase a membership for your caregiver. If there isn't one up and going, encourage her to start a playgroup with other nannies and caregivers who are at home with young children.

- Your home is likely to lack some of the specialized equipment that your child would have access to in a well-equipped daycare center. If your child's medical team feels that it would be advantageous for him to have access to some of this equipment, you may want to consider an out-of-home childcare arrangement.

Just as there are advantages and disadvantages to in-home care in general, there are advantages and disadvantages to each type of in-home care in particular: nannies, au pairs, and other types of in-home caregivers.

Nannies

Pros:

- Nannies have completed specialized training in early childhood education. Some have taken additional training to prepare themselves to work with children who have special needs.

Cons:

- Nannies are the most expensive type of in-home caregiver. Their salaries price them out of the market for all but the most affluent of families. Because families who have children with special needs typically have a large number of medical expenses to contend with, hiring a nanny may not be an option for you.

Au pairs

Pros:

- There really aren't any particular advantages to having a child with special needs cared for by an au pair.

Cons:

- Because the program is limited to young people between the ages of 18 and 26, it's possible to get an au pair who is relatively inexperienced in dealing with young children. You might not feel comfortable leaving your child with a young person who has had little exposure to children period, let alone a child with special needs.

- The au pair program sets out specific responsibilities for the host family, some of which you may find difficult to meet—particularly if a large portion of your time is taken up with medical appointments, and so on.

Family members
Pros:

- You will probably feel more comfortable leaving your child with a family member than with a complete stranger—particularly if this family member is acquainted with your child's routines and knows how to meet his medical needs.

Cons:

- Grandparents (one of the most popular choices for in-home caregivers) have an abundance of love for their grandchildren, but they may lack the stamina required to cope with a child with special needs. Both sides may feel awkward if it becomes apparent that the arrangement isn't working out after all.

Other types of caregivers
Pros:

- A caregiver who has not had any formal training in child development is generally less expensive to hire than a nanny—savings you may welcome if you are contending with a large number of medical bills.

Timesaver
If your child is prone to asthma attacks, allergic reactions, or other medical emergencies, tape the details about your child's medical conditions above each phone. This will enable your caregiver to convey the important information to medical personnel in case of an emergency.

Cons:

- Because your caregiver has not received any formal training in child development, you will need to monitor her closely to ensure that the care she is providing is appropriate—particularly if she has had little, if any, experience in caring for young children. You may not feel comfortable leaving your child with someone who has not had any specialized training in dealing with his needs.

- Many people who have not had much experience in caring for young children assume that it's an easy way to make a living. It's not. As a result, there is a high rate of turnover among childcare workers, particularly those who are new to the field. If your child has an especially difficult time coping with disruptions to his usual routine, you may wish to consider an alternative form of care.

Evaluating out-of-home care arrangements

Once you've pulled together a list of daycare centers and family daycare homes that meet the needs of your family, it's time to evaluate your various options. You'll want to take a three-pronged approach to evaluating your options: making some preliminary phone calls, visiting some centers and family childcares in person, and then checking references.

You can find more detailed information about evaluating your out-of-home childcare arrangements in Chapter 5, but I'll briefly consider how each of these steps relates to a search for care for a child who has special needs before I move on to the discussion about finding out-of-home care.

Unofficially . . .
Children with diabetes cannot be refused a space in either a childcare center or family childcare home, according to a recent federal court ruling. "Children with diabetes shouldn't be left on the sidelines," said Attorney General Janet Reno when she was asked to comment on the ruling. The ruling follows other similar cases in the past that have upheld the rights of children with disabilities.

Screening by phone

The purpose of preliminary telephone interviews is to save yourself some legwork by eliminating some childcare options immediately. These interviews focus on the real meat and potatoes issues: the ages of children the center or family daycare home is licensed to accept, whether they have any openings at this time, what you could expect to pay for care, and so on.

The out-of-home childcare checklist in Appendix D will provide you with some guidelines about what to ask as you make these initial phone calls, but you will probably want to ask some additional questions related to your child's special needs. Here are some questions you might consider adding to your list:

- Is the center equipped to care for children with special needs? Is the center physically accessible to your child? Are the doors wide enough for his wheelchair to fit through? Is the bathroom sink low enough for him to reach? Are there wheelchair ramps or an elevator that he can use if he needs to access other areas of the building?

- Are the director and staff experienced in caring for children with special needs? (Look for evidence that the director or caregiver understands the unique challenges of caring for a child with special needs, but also recognizes the joys that can accompany such an experience.)

- How comfortable does the center feel about caring for someone with your child's particular types of special needs? (Be sure to explain the nature of your child's needs in sufficient detail so that the center director or family childcare provider will have an accurate idea of what is

Watch Out!
Be wary of a caregiver who seems to imply that she knows more about caring for your child than you do. While she may have taken a few courses in child development, you've had months—if not years—of on-the-job training.

involved in caring for him. While you might not get the answer you want, it's important to find out at the outset if the caregiver is less than enthusiastic about caring for your child. Otherwise, you could find yourself embarking on another search for childcare in the very near future.)

Conducting personal visits

After you've reduced your childcare choices to a more manageable number of options, you're ready to conduct some personal visits. Because these visits can be time-consuming and exhausting, you'll probably want to share this responsibility with your partner.

As you can see from the out-of-home childcare checklist in Appendix D, the purpose of the personal visit is to physically inspect each childcare environment, meet each potential caregiver, and obtain detailed answers to all of your questions about the center or family daycare provider's policies and procedures.

Checking references

After you've conducted your personal visits and settled on a few finalists, you're ready to check references. The purpose of these reference checks is to verify that your initial impression of each daycare center or family daycare setting is, in fact, accurate.

The daycare center director or family daycare provider will provide you with the names of parents who have used or are currently using their services. If possible, you should ask for the names and numbers of families with children who have special needs so that you can find out how happy they've been with the care their child has received. In the case of a daycare center, you should ensure that the references are able to speak to the suitability of the particular caregiver who will be assigned to your child as opposed to the staff in general.

You can find more detailed information on checking references in Chapter 5.

Evaluating in-home care arrangements

Whether you decide to contract the services of an agency to assist you in your search for an in-home caregiver or conduct this search yourself, your first step should be to draw up a detailed job description which contains the following type of information:

- the number of and ages of your children
- the nature of the job (feeding, toileting, escorting your child to medical appointments, and so on.)
- the hours when you will require care (full-time versus part-time; live-in versus live-out; daytime versus evening; whether weekend work is required)
- the amount of training and experience a candidate should have (CPR, first aid, training in administering medications, and so on)
- the salary you're prepared to offer
- the starting date for the position

If you're working with an agency, the director will help you to polish your job description before sending it on to prospective applicants. If you're handling the search on your own, the staff of the classified department of the local newspaper may be able to help you with the wording of your ad, suggesting abbreviations and acronyms that can save you money.

Timesaver
Make sure that your newspaper advertisement specifies that your child has special needs. There's no point in fielding dozens of calls from candidates who lack the skills and experience required to care for your child.

Reviewing resumes and letters of application

After your job description has been posted with the agency or published in the newspaper, you are likely to start receiving resumes from individuals who are interested in being considered for the position.

While the number of responses can be overwhelming (particularly if you've chosen to go with a newspaper ad), you can reduce the number of candidates under consideration by eliminating those whose resumes reveal unexplained gaps in employment, an unstable work record, a lack of related experience, or who are missing key requirements for the position (a vehicle and a valid driver's license or CPR training).

Preliminary telephone interviews

After you've come up with a short list of candidates, it's time to conduct some preliminary telephone interviews. The purpose of these interviews is to find out more about each candidate before you decide who you should—and shouldn't—interview.

Here's a list of points you should consider covering during this initial contact with each caregiver:

- What hours and days of the week is the caregiver available?

- What are her salary expectations?

- What experience has she had in caring for children who have special needs?

- What was her most recent position? What were her responsibilities? What was her reason for leaving this position?

- Has she had any formal training in early childhood education?

- Is she certified in cardiopulmonary resuscitation (CPR) and first aid?

- What other types of training has she taken that might help her in this position?
- Does she have any health problems?
- Does she smoke?
- Does she have a valid driver's license and her own vehicle?
- Would she be prepared to undergo a background check at your expense?

If a candidate appears to be a good fit for your family, based on her responses to your questions, you might want to take a few minutes to tell her a bit more about the job: the specific duties; the ages and sexes of your children; the hours of work; the pay; your policies re: holidays, vacation, and other time off; where your home is located; and so on. This will help her to assess whether the position is right for her.

Conducting personal interviews

After you've interviewed each of the candidates by phone, you'll be ready to schedule personal interviews with the most promising ones of the bunch. You can find a detailed list of suggested interview questions in Appendix D.

As important as it is to find out about the potential caregiver's experience and training, what really matters is how she relates to your child. That's why it's important to schedule the interview at a time when your child is available to meet her.

You can learn a lot about her skills as a caregiver by watching the way she acts as she meets your child for the first time.

In addition to asking the types of interview questions that you can find in Chapter 5, you'll also want to consider how the caregiver relates to your child as

Bright Idea
If your child's needs are complex, you might want to provide the applicant with more detailed information about his exceptionalities as well as the specific job requirements. Some families find it helpful to prepare a family profile that contains information about each family member, including the child with special needs. You can find a sample family profile in Appendix D.

a person. Does she, for example, seem to be more concerned with his disability than what he is like as a person?

Checking references

After you've conducted your personal interviews and settled on one or more candidates who seem to meet your family's needs, you're ready to check references. The purpose of these reference checks is to verify that your initial impression of each caregiver is, in fact, accurate.

In addition to the questions listed in Chapter 5, you might consider asking the following questions:

- How long were your children cared for by this person? What are their current ages? Did any of them have special needs?

- Does she appear to have a solid understanding of the particular needs of children at various developmental stages?

- Is there anything else you think I should know before deciding to hire her, given the special needs of my child?

Getting off to a good start

You can get your relationship with your child's caregiver off to the best possible start by preparing a work agreement, providing an orientation period, and laying the groundwork for regular communication.

Preparing a work agreement

One of the best ways to avoid future problems with your child's caregiver is to put everything in writing right from the very beginning.

Most families that choose to go this route find that having a written work agreement with their child's caregiver enables them to prevent minor misunderstandings from becoming major problems.

As you might expect, the most effective work agreements are comprehensive. These agreements cover basic issues such as working hours, the rate of pay, job responsibilities, as well as issues that are of particular concern to the family in question, such as policies regarding use of the telephone or the family car. (You can find a particularly comprehensive contract—written by a veteran nanny—in Appendix D. Because each family's situation is unique, you'll want to modify the contract to make it fit your own needs.)

Note: Try to make arrangements for your caregiver to have a day off from time to time. Many health care agencies provide respite workers who are available to fill in when a child's regular caregiver is unavailable. This service may be covered by your health insurance and/or employee benefits package.

If possible, include some information in the contract about how the caregiver's job performance will be evaluated. The criteria that you might want to include might be as follows:

- whether your child's Individualized Education Plan (IEP) or Individualized Program Plan (IPP) has been implemented

- whether the terms of the work agreement have been met

- whether the caregiver and the child have a positive relationship

- whether the child has shown any progress

- whether the caregiver has been reliable and shown initiative

Moneysaver
It's not usual for a family to pay the caregiver one rate for her programming time (the time she spends developing an Individualized Program Plan for the child in her care) and another for basic caretaking duties (feeding, toileting, and so on). If you will be paying your caregiver different rates for different types of work, make sure that your agreement specifies the number of hours at each rate of pay that she is being contracted to deliver.

- whether the caregiver has attempted to use community resources (books, courses, workshops, and so on) to improve her skills in caring for your child

It's important to provide her with this information if you have hired her on a probationary basis.

Getting off to a good start

While the work agreement that you and your caregiver prepare should be as comprehensive as possible, you should also plan to be on hand during her first few days on the job so that you can give her the opportunity to get to know your child and familiarize her with your household routines.

You should ensure that your orientation covers each of the following elements:

- a review of the contents of the work agreement

- a discussion about what types of discipline you consider appropriate to your child's stage of development

- a tour of your home to familiarize the caregiver with the location and functioning of household equipment (for example, the dishwasher, the microwave, and so on) and to indicate which areas of the home she is welcome to be in (the kitchen and livingroom, but not your bedroom)

- a discussion of safety procedures in the home (fire evacuation procedures, where toxic substances and any other harmful materials are stored, procedures for answering the door, guidelines for bathtub and swimming pool safety, and so on)

- a tour of the neighborhood to familiarize her with the location of your child's friends' homes,

Bright Idea
Ask the potential caregiver to demonstrate her capability to change a g-tube, switch an IV, and so on. That way, you'll feel confident that she's fully capable of meeting your child's medical needs.

the local playground, the doctor's office, the hospital, and so on

- an overview of daily routines (when your child wakes up in the morning, what he has for breakfast, how much help he needs with toothbrushing and other personal hygiene tasks)

- details about any charting programs that you have in place for your child (for example, recording seizures or the results of behavior management strategies)

- a review of safe procedures for lifting your child (if lifting is required)

- a discussion of the goals that you, your partner, and your child's doctor have set for him, and details about the strategies that you would like her to use to help him to achieve those goals

- a discussion about how she can contact you and your partner while you're at work (for example, should she have you paged whenever she has a question or only in emergency situations?)

You should also plan to have a frank talk about your child's special needs. You should provide the caregiver with as much information as possible about your child's particular challenges and explain the specifics of administering medication, changing g-tubes, and so on. You might want to refer her to the IRSC web site's disability links (www.irsc.org/disability.htm) where she can find detailed information on a variety of different types of disabilities. Because the information you are providing may seem overwhelming to her—particularly if this is her first experience in caring for a child who has special needs—be sure to reassure her that you're confident in her capability to care for your child.

Bright Idea
Provide your caregiver with guidelines about what she is at liberty to say to other people about your child's special needs. Caregivers are often faced with awkward questions about the children in their care, and she will appreciate having some guidelines about what you consider to be private (rather than public) information about your child.

Laying the groundwork for ongoing communication

Because you will be covering a great deal of information in a short time, you might find it worthwhile to provide your caregiver with some written notes summarizing the material you have covered during the orientation. You should also plan to schedule a series of follow up meetings so she can obtain answers to any questions that arise after she actually gets into the job. Communicating with your caregiver on an ongoing basis will allow you to monitor the quality of care your child is receiving and resolve any problems as they arise.

During the orientation period, look for evidence that the caregiver has a positive attitude. Instead of focusing on what your child can't do ("He can't draw"), she should be focusing on what he can do ("We can draw together using hand-over-hand").

Encourage your caregiver to become an advocate on behalf of your child when dealing with his health care team. If you or she need additional information on advocating on behalf of a special needs child, you'll find plenty of food for thought at www.irsc.org/parents.htm.

Just the facts

- It's important to keep both your child's needs and your family's needs in mind as you search for a suitable care arrangement for your child.

- There are both advantages and disadvantages to in-home and out-of-home care.

- To make the best possible use of your time, you should plan to screen both in-home and out-of-home care arrangements by using a combination of telephone calls and in-person meetings.

■ To get your relationship with your child's caregiver off to the best possible start, prepare a work agreement, provide an orientation period, and take some time to lay the groundwork for regular communication.

GET THE SCOOP ON...
Restarting care after your maternity leave or
layoff ▪ What to do with your older child during
your maternity leave ▪ What to do with your
two children when you return to work ▪
Finding childcare for multiples ▪ Childcare and
the single parent family ▪ Childcare and the
work-at-home parent ▪ The joys and challenges
of combining care

Other Special Circumstances

Chapter 12

You would think by this point in the book that I would have covered every childcare situation imaginable. After all, I've talked about in-home care, out-of-home care, finding childcare for a child with special needs, and so on.

Believe it or not, I still have a few areas left to cover, such as restarting care after your maternity leave or layoff; finding childcare for twins, triplets, or other multiples; how to handle the special concerns that single parents face when looking for childcare; what to do about the challenges that work-at-home parents face in finding childcare; and the joys and challenges of combining two or more part-time childcare arrangements. These are the issues I'll discuss in this chapter.

Restarting care after your maternity leave or layoff

Just when you finally start to get the hang of being a working parent, baby number two comes along. While the search for childcare is considerably easier to handle the second time around, it's still no piece of cake—and this time you'll have the needs of two children to consider as you go about evaluating your various options.

Watch Out!
Don't sign up your second child for care at the childcare center that your older child attended five years earlier without taking the time to reevaluate it first. A change in directors or care-givers at the center can dra-matically affect the quality of care.

The birth of a second or subsequent child justi-fies a reevaluation of your childcare needs. This is definitely one of those situations in which one plus one doesn't always equal two. What I mean is that the best solution for your family once baby number two comes along may not necessarily be purchasing a second childcare space in the daycare center that your older child has been attending up until now. The preferred solution might, in fact, be something entirely different.

Let me explain.

Even if you've been completely satisfied with the quality of care that your older child has received in a particular daycare center or family daycare home, it might not be the solution to your baby's childcare needs. You might find, for example, that your older child's family daycare provider is more comfortable dealing with toddlers and preschoolers than she is with infants or that the childcare center that your older child attends isn't licensed to accept infants. You can find out more about these types of issues by reading "Wanted: Babysitter for Two" by Antonia Van Der Meer at www.ctw.org/parents/weekly/3696/369603t1.htm.

More often than not, the decision to change your older child's childcare arrangement comes down to sheer economics. Whoever said that two could live as cheaply as one certainly hadn't priced out childcare arrangements! The monthly childcare fee that seemed so reasonable for one child can be outright horrifying if you have to pay that amount for each of your two children—something one publishing executive discovered shortly before the birth of her second child. Her solution was to hire an in-home caregiver to care for her two children—a form of care that proved to be less expensive overall than having her two children cared for at the same daycare center that her older son had previously attended.

I'll discuss a number of possible childcare scenarios a little later in this chapter, but for now I'm going talk about an issue that's a little more pressing: what to do with your older child during your maternity leave.

What to do with your older child during your maternity leave

You have three basic choices when it comes to deciding what to do with your older child during your maternity leave: You can keep her at home with you and the baby, continue to send her to daycare as usual, or reduce the number of hours she spends at daycare so that she can spend part of her week at home with you and the baby.

If you decide to keep your child home during your maternity leave, you risk losing her daycare space—unless, of course, you're willing to continue to pay for it even though she won't be using it. What's more, when it's time to restart daycare, you could be in for another round of that most heart-wrenching of childhood afflictions: separation anxiety.

Bright Idea
Licensed child-care spaces for infants are in chronically short supply. Alert your older child's caregiver to the fact that you will need an infant space a few months down the road as soon as your pregnancy is confirmed. While doing so doesn't necessarily guarantee that you can obtain a spot in the childcare center or family childcare home of your choice, it will certainly help to put the odds in your favor.

If you continue to send her to daycare as always (that is, on her usual full-time basis), you could find yourself dealing with an angry toddler or preschooler who resents the fact that the baby gets to stay home with you, but she doesn't.

A solution that worked well for one consulting engineer when her second son arrived was to continue to send her older child to daycare while she was at home with his baby brother. The older child enjoyed the best of both worlds: He could play with his friends from childcare certain days of the week and enjoy spending time at home with his mother and baby brother on other days of the week. The mother also benefited from the arrangement: She used the days when her older child was in day-care to take the baby to bed and catch up on some much-needed sleep—a major achievement for a woman who found herself at home with a newborn and a seventeen-month-old!

What to do with your two children when you return to work

You have four options when it comes to arranging childcare for your two children when you return to work. You can:

- send them both to a daycare center
- send them both to a family daycare home
- hire an in-home caregiver to take care of them
- have them cared for in separate childcare environments

As you might have gathered, there's no perfect solution to this childcare problem. Rather, there are advantages and disadvantages to each of these potential solutions. Let's take a moment to consider the pros and cons of each option.

Sending them both to a daycare center

Pros:

- If your older child is already being cared for at a center and you're happy with the quality of care that she has been receiving, you may feel comfortable sending her baby brother or sister there, too. After all, you already know the staff and are familiar with the center's policies and procedures.

- You can avoid disruptions to your older child's routine by keeping her in the same childcare environment, something that can be particularly beneficial when she's already coping with a major adjustment on the homefront—the arrival of her new baby brother or sister.

- You're likely to be given first crack at any infant spaces that become available at your older child's daycare center. Most centers have a policy of giving existing families priority when vacancies arise.

- Having both children cared for at the same location can eliminate the need to make multiple pit-stops before and after work, something that not only simplifies your own weekday routine but also helps to minimize the amount of time that your two children spend in daycare.

- Your baby may feel reassured by the fact that your older child is nearby—and vice versa.

Cons:

- Paying for two childcare spaces can be extremely expensive. You might have to eliminate this particular possibility for reasons of sheer economics.

Watch Out!
The fact that you are satisfied with the quality of care that your older child receives from a daycare center or family daycare home is no guarantee that it's the ideal situation for your younger child. Your second child might be much quieter or more outgoing than your first child and consequently better suited to a different type of childcare environment.

Bright Idea
If you know in advance that you will be moving your child to a new care arrangement after her younger sister or brother arrives, try to make the switch a few months before the baby is born. That way, your child will not blame the new baby for this disruption to her routine. Besides, switching childcare arrangements is stressful at the best of times and should ideally be done when a child is experiencing no other major changes to her routine. You may be asking too much of your child if you expect her to welcome the new baby and say good-bye to her beloved caregiver at the same time.

- Being in the same daycare center doesn't guarantee that your two children will be together often—or even at all. Make sure that you understand the center's policies about caring for children from the same family: Do they deliberately separate them or place them in the same group?

- Your older child might not want to share "her" caregiver with the baby—something that's likely to be a particular concern if the two children end up in the same mixed age group.

- There are two sets of caregivers to communicate with and possibly two log books to review at the start and end of each day.

- The sheer logistics of getting a baby and toddler dressed and undressed simultaneously is enough to leave your average parent gasping for air. Do you put the baby in her car seat before or after you start wrestling the toddler into her coat and boots? How do you entertain a restless preschooler if the baby wants to nurse before you head home? Inquiring minds need to know!

Sending them both to a family daycare home
Pros:

- If your older child is already being cared for in a family daycare home and you're happy with the quality of care that she is receiving, you may feel comfortable sending her baby brother or sister there, too. After all, you already know the caregiver and are likely comfortable with her modus operandi.

- You can avoid disruptions to your older child's routine by keeping her in the same childcare

environment, something that can be particularly beneficial when she's already trying to
come to terms with the arrival of her new baby
brother or sister.

■ You're likely to be given first crack at any infant
spaces that open up in the family daycare home.

■ You can avoid making multiple pit-stops in the
morning and afternoon, something that not
only simplifies your own weekday routine but
also helps to minimize the amount of time that
your two children spend in daycare.

■ Your baby may feel reassured by the fact that
your older child is nearby—and vice versa.

Cons:

■ Paying for two daycare spaces can be extremely
expensive (although it is still likely to be less
expensive than paying for two spaces in a childcare center).

■ Your older child might not want to share "her"
caregiver with the baby.

■ Your older child's caregiver might not have an
infant space available in her home. Even if she
does, she might be reluctant to take on the care
of a baby. This is likely to be a particular problem for you if the caregiver has an admitted
preference for preschoolers or toddlers who are
fully toilet-trained.

Hiring an in-home caregiver to take care of them

Pros:

■ Hiring an in-home caregiver may actually be
cheaper than paying for two spaces in a daycare
center or family daycare home.

Unofficially . . .
Studies have
shown that low-
income families
are hardest hit
when it comes to
paying for day-
care. According
to the U.S.
Census Bureau,
families earning
$14,999 or less
typically spend
25 percent of
their annual
income on day-
care as compared
to the 6 percent
spent by families
earning $54,000
or more.

- An in-home caregiver may be willing to assume responsibility for some light housekeeping tasks—something that can help to reduce the overall stress of being a working parent.

- You wouldn't have to drag two kids and their assorted paraphernalia to and from childcare each day.

- Your in-home caregiver might be willing to care for your children when they're ill, something that can prevent you from missing a significant numbers of days off work when one or the other is ill.

Cons:

- It can be difficult to find an in-home caregiver who's willing to take care of an infant as well as an older child. Some may not feel up to the task of juggling the demands of a baby with the needs of an older child. Even the wonderful in-home caregiver who's been caring for your older child up until now may balk at the idea of caring for her baby brother or sister.

Having them cared for in two separate arrangements

Some parents make a conscious effort to place their children in two separate childcare arrangements so that they can choose the type of situation that's best for each child. Others end up doing so as an interim measure while they wait for an infant space to open up at their older child's daycare center or family daycare home.

Pros:

- You can take into account the unique needs of each child. Rather than sending a shy child to the noisy daycare center that her two-year-old brother adores, you could find her a space in a quiet family daycare environment instead.

Cons:

- It can be expensive to pay for two separate childcare arrangements. You won't be able to take advantage of any sibling discounts, however small, that might otherwise be available to you.

- If you find it exhausting enough to drop one child off at one daycare center, just imagine what it would be like to try to drop two children off at separate locations before heading in to work.

- Your children would be apart for the majority of their waking hours—a situation that many families understandably want to avoid.

Finding childcare for multiples

Some families with multiples want their babies to be cared for by the same caregiver. Others prefer to have each baby cared for separately so that their babies can make their own friends and get a sense of being separated from one another.

What you want and what's out there can be two entirely different matters. As you know, in most parts of the country, licensed daycare for infants is in extremely short supply. As a result, it can be next to impossible to find two infant daycare spaces in the same daycare center or family daycare home.

But that's not the only difficulty that parents are likely to face when they are looking for childcare for more than one baby. Here are a few more important issues.

Moneysaver
The birth of your second child might change your financial situation enough to make you eligible for a daycare center. Contact your state or local licensing authority to get the scoop. (You can find the contact information in Appendix B.)

Cost

Because infant care is the most expensive type of childcare, you can expect to pay a small fortune if you require childcare for more than one baby. While some daycare centers and family daycare homes offer discounts to families with more than one child, you're not likely to be able to take advantage of the break, given the chronic shortage of infant spaces.

Not surprisingly, in-home care is a popular choice for families with multiples. It's more convenient to have your caregiver come to you than to try to drop off two or more babies at a daycare center or family daycare home on your way to work. Besides, in-home care is typically a more affordable option than purchasing out-of-home childcare spaces for three or more children.

Equipment

If you want your family daycare provider to be able to take your twins or triplets for a walk, she's going to need a specialized tandem stroller. If she doesn't already own one, you might have to supply it, and as any parent of multiples would be only too happy to tell you, specialized equipment such as this doesn't come cheap.

She's also unlikely to have two highchairs, two cribs, and two baby swings, so you might be expected to supply some of this equipment as well. (For most families, this involves loading an extra highchair or baby swing into the car at the start and end of each childcare day.)

Not surprisingly, many families decide it's simpler to have their babies cared for in their own homes where they already have double—or triple—the baby gear on hand.

A suitable caregiver

Then there's the business of finding a caregiver. Not everyone is up to the challenge of caring for twins. Once you've found someone who's up to the task of caring for your babies, be sure to establish effective methods of communication right from the start.

It's not realistic to expect to be able to carry on a detailed conversation with your babies' caregiver at the start and end of each day—unless, of course, you don't mind communicating via megaphone! That's why some families find it helpful to provide the caregiver with a log book so that she can record such information as which baby finished her mid-morning bottle—and which one didn't.

Childcare and the single parent

Now I come to the third set of special circumstances to be covered in this chapter: the childcare-related concerns you may experience if you are a single parent.

Here are just a few of the issues that you may be thinking about:

Cost

Single-income households typically have less disposable income than dual-income households do, so cost may be a major concern as you begin searching for childcare and may significantly limit your childcare choices.

Caregiver compatibility

While it's always important to have a good rapport with your child's caregiver, you may be particularly anxious to find someone to whom you can turn for a second opinion on such issues as weaning, toilet-training, and discipline—particularly if this is your first child.

Bright Idea
If there's a book that expresses your parenting philosophies particularly well, purchase a copy for your child's caregiver.

Caregiver availability

Rather than introducing more than one caregiver into your child's life, you might prefer to find a caregiver who is available to work evenings and/or weekends on occasion. (The need for evening or weekend care is less likely to be an issue for you if you have a shared custody arrangement with your child's other parent that covers the hours when care is needed.)

Caregiver reliability

Timesaver
If you're concerned that your childcare plans might fall apart on occasion and you can't afford the cost of emergency childcare, you might want to ask your employer if you can come up with some mutually agreeable solutions. Your employer might, for example, be willing to allow you to work from home if your child or your caregiver is ill.

Because you don't have a second parent to turn to if your childcare arrangement falls apart, caregiver reliability is a major issue for you. Regardless of how reliable your caregiver is, however, there will be times when she's not available. That's why it's important to have a watertight backup plan.

Convenience

Convenience is likely to be another major factor, because you're probably the only one doing the childcare drop off and pickup. For sanity's sake, you'll want to be sure to choose a childcare arrangement that is situated close to your home or workplace.

If you're interested in finding out how other single parents manage to juggle their families with their careers, you'll find food for thought at the National Organization of Single Mothers (NOSM) Web site: www.parentsplacecom/readroom/nosm.

Childcare and the work-at-home parent

Whether you run a business out of your home or telecommute on a regular basis, it's important to avoid making one of the biggest mistakes that work-at-home parents make: assuming that you can care for your children and do your job at the same time.

Here are some pointers on preventing your family from taking over your business—and vice versa:

- Find a caregiver who's willing to work around your schedule. Most self-employed people find that their businesses go through cycles. Either they're working like crazy or fretting that they'll never have another day's work in their life. If this is what your working life is like, you'll want to find a caregiver who's willing to work five days one week and one day the next. You'll probably have to guarantee her a minimum number of hours each week to make it worth her while to work around your schedule, and you might want to offer a higher-than-average hourly rate in recognition of her flexibility.

- Set aside a particular room in your house for your office. Ideally you should pick a room that is far removed from the room where your child will be. That way, he'll get used to the idea that he's with his caregiver while you're "at work," and you won't be tempted to rush in and help every time he seems to need something.

- Establish some ground rules with the caregiver so that she'll know when it's okay to bring your child to you and when it's not. You might want to tend to him if he's hurt or upset or feed him if he's still nursing, but you might not appreciate being interrupted every half an hour to see his latest work of art.

- If it's been a few weeks or months since you started working from home and your child still can't seem to accept the fact that you're at home and yet unavailable to him, consider either taking your office elsewhere or sending him to an out-of-home childcare arrangement.

Bright Idea
Come up with some type of signal to let your child know when it's okay to pop into your home office for a cuddle—and when it's not. Some work-at-home parents leave the office door open; others hang up color-coded signs (green, yellow, and red). It doesn't matter what type of signal you choose as long as you and your children are clear about its meaning.

The joys and challenges of combining care

Some parents make a conscious effort to choose two part-time rather than one full-time childcare arrangement. Others are forced into this position because they can't find suitable full-time childcare. Regardless of how you end up in this situation, you need to be aware of both the pros and cons of combining two or more childcare arrangements.

Pros:

- You can take advantage of an attractive childcare option that might only be available to you on a part-time basis, like a half-day nursery school program or the chance to have your child cared for by his grandmother on a part-time basis.

- Your child might enjoy the variety that comes from being in more than one childcare setting.

Cons:

- It's usually far more expensive to pay for two part-time childcare arrangements than it is to pay for one full-time arrangement.

- Scheduling can be a nightmare. What do you do if nursery school ends at 12:00 p.m., but the university student you've hired to care for your child in the afternoon can't get to your house until 1:00 p.m.?

- Some children find it difficult to adjust to more than one childcare situation. While you might consider it a bit of an adventure—"This is Tuesday, so it must be daycare!"—your child may be upset by the lack of consistency in her childcare environment.

- One plus one sometimes equals three. What I mean by this is that splicing together two half-day programs doesn't necessarily produce the same results as enrolling your child in a full-day program. If, for example, your child goes to a daycare center in the morning and then a half-day kindergarten program in the afternoon, she could find herself doing arts and crafts twice in the same day and missing out on outdoor play time altogether. The only way to avoid this situation is to ensure that the caregiver at the daycare center is aware of what the kindergarten teacher is planning for the day, and vice versa—a situation that can only realistically be arranged if a large number of children in the kindergarten class happen to go to the same daycare center.

While there are no easy solutions to the challenges facing today's families, a little creativity can take you a long way. Whether you're trying to decide what to do with your children after your maternity or deal with any other childcare-related challenge, trust your instincts and you'll be well on your way to coming up with a solution that's right for you and your family.

Just the facts

- You should plan to reevaluate your childcare needs when baby number two comes along. You may decide to keep your older child in an existing arrangement or move her to a new arrangement that is better suited to the needs of both of your children.

- You will also need to consider what to do with your older child while you are at home on your maternity leave with the new baby. Will you continue to send her to daycare on a full-time basis, withdraw her from daycare altogether, or send her to daycare on a part-time basis?

- Finding childcare for multiples can be a challenge, especially while they're infants. Many families find that in-home care is a more convenient and affordable solution than out-of-home care.

- Some of the issues you may be concerned about if you're a single parent looking for childcare include cost; caregiver compatibility, availability, and reliability; and the convenience of the childcare arrangement.

- Don't assume that you don't need childcare just because you're working from home. If you're working, you need childcare—period.

- There are both advantages and disadvantages to combining two or more part-time childcare arrangements. If your child finds it upsetting to have to adjust to two or more environments, you might want to seek out a full-time arrangement instead.

GET THE SCOOP ON...
Planning ahead ▪ Choosing a breast pump ▪
Pumping tips ▪ Dressing for breastfeeding
success ▪ Storing breast milk ▪ Introducing
a bottle ▪ What your schedule may be like

Breastfeeding and Working

In the mid-1980s, La Leche League International conducted a comprehensive study of breastfeeding in the workplace. The organization interviewed over 500 nursing mothers to find out what factors seemed to have the most positive affect on breastfeeding success.

The researchers found that women who rejoined the workforce when their babies were at least sixteen weeks old, who worked part-time rather than full-time hours, and who expressed breast milk for their babies rather than leaving bottles of formula nursed longer than other working mothers. The study also revealed that women who combined breastfeeding and working were overwhelmingly satisfied with their decision to do so. A full 82 percent of the mothers surveyed said that they would make the same decison again.

Although it takes both planning and perseverance, the benefits of continuing to breastfeed after you return to work are undeniable:

Chapter 13

Unofficially...
A 1987 survey of the hundred most profitable companies in the United States revealed a shortage of workplace policies designed to support breastfeeding. Since that time, the tide has started to shift. Corporate America is beginning to realize that breastfeeding isn't just good for moms and babies; it's good for business.

- Your baby may be sick less often than a formula-fed baby because you can pass immunities to him through your breast milk.

- You reduce your chances of developing certain life-threatening illnesses.

- Breastfeeding enables you to bond with your baby in a very special way—something that you will both find comforting if you're finding it difficult to be apart.

- Breastfeeding is budget-friendly—an important consideration because you're likely to be faced with hefty childcare bills when you return to work.

If you're thinking about continuing to breastfeed your baby after you return to work, read on. This chapter is jam-packed with practical tips on making breastfeeding go smoothly for yourself and your baby during the weeks and months ahead.

Planning ahead

Your work situation plays a major role in determining how easy it will be for you to continue breastfeeding your baby after you return to work.

Some situations are ideal. If, for example, you have access to onsite childcare in your workplace or have a caregiver who is willing to bring your baby to you for feedings, you can integrate your baby's feedings into your working day with minimal disruption.

If, however, you work irregular hours and cannot predict your schedule on a minute-to-minute basis, you may find it a bit more challenging to continue breastfeeding.

If your situation is less than ideal and you don't think you can pump and store breast milk during your working day, you might want to consider breastfeeding on a part-time basis only. You might, for example, nurse your baby in the morning and the evening, but have his caregiver offer him bottles of formula during the day. Breastfeeding isn't an all or nothing proposition: Any amount of breastfeeding is beneficial to both you and your baby.

Whether you intend to breastfeed on a part-time or full-time basis, you should lay as much groundwork as possible before you head off on maternity leave. Attend a La Leche League meeting or take a course in breastfeeding while you're still pregnant. (Your hospital, county health department, or local Women, Infants, and Children program may offer some sort of breastfeeding support program.) The second and third trimesters of your pregnancy are an ideal time to get your employer on board and to find a caregiver who will support your decision to continue to breastfeed your baby.

Investigating your company policies

As soon as the pregnancy test comes back positive, you should begin investigating what policies are in place in your workplace to support women who choose to breastfeed their babies after their return to work.

Find out what your company's maternity leave policy is like. Some companies offer generous leave packages, while others stick to the letter of the law.

It's in your best interest to take as long a maternity leave as you possibly can. Taking an extended maternity enables you to ensure that your milk supply is fully established before you attempt to return to work. It also enables you to troubleshoot any difficulties that you and your baby may be experiencing (poor positioning, incorrect latch, and so on) and to fully recover from the rigors of childbirth.

Bright Idea
If you feel awkward discussing your breastfeeding plans with your employer, write him or her a memo instead. An added advantage to putting everything in writing is that you may help to pave the way for other nursing moms seeking similar workplace policies in the future.

Be sure to find out whether you're covered by the provisions of the Family and Medical Leave Act (FMLA) of 1993. The Act requires that employers provide eligible employees with up to 12 weeks of unpaid, job-protected leave following the birth of a baby. To be eligible for this type of leave, you must

- be employed by an employer who is covered by the Act (a public agency, local educational agency, or private sector employers with 50 or more employees)
- have worked at least 12 months (not necessarily consecutively) for the employer
- have worked at least 1,250 hours during the 12 months immediately preceding the date of commencement of FMLA leave

To find out more about the FMLA, contact your nearest office of the Wage and Hour Division of the Department of Labor or visit the Department of Labor Web site at http://dol.gov/dol/asp/public/programs/handbook/fmla.htm.

While you're looking into your company's maternity leave policies, you'll also want to find out if the company is open to any alternative working arrangements such as telecommuting (working from home a percentage of the time), job sharing (splitting a full-time job with another person), or flex-time (setting your own hours of work). I'll be talking about these alternative working arrangements in greater detail in Chapter 16, so stay tuned!

If you are the first woman in your workplace to continue breastfeeding after returning to work, you may need to spend time educating your employer about what he or she can do to help you—and why it's in the company's best interests to do so.

Many women have found that it works best to spell out exactly what you would like your employer to do for you. You may want to ask for some or all of the following:

- an extended period of maternity leave (four to six months or longer)

- flexible work arrangements (telecommuting, job sharing, and flex-time)

- a private place to use your breast pump or nurse your baby (for example, your office, an empty conference room, or the company nurse's office would all be ideal)

- access to a hospital-grade electric breast pump and a refrigerator in the workplace. Note: Don't panic if your employer is unwilling to provide onsite refrigeration. A cooler with a few plastic ice packs will also do the trick

Medela, Inc., a manufacturer of breast pumps, offers a program designed to support breastfeeding among working mothers. The Sanvita Corporate Lactation™ Program consists of prenatal education about the benefits of breastfeeding, support during the working mother's maternity leave, and access to breast pumps and breastfeeding advice after she returns to work. To find out what's involved in getting this program up and running at your workplace, call or write to Sanvita Programs, P.O. Box 660, McHenry, IL. 60051-0660 (1-800-435-5557).

Getting your employer on board

If your employer seems reluctant to support you in your breastfeeding efforts, be sure to point out that it's in the company's best interests to do so. Here are just a few of the many arguments you can make in favor of continuing to breastfeed your baby after you return to work:

Unofficially...
According to a study conducted by Kaiser Permanente, breastfeeding for just six months can reduce health care claims by over $1,400 per family per year. You can read more about the results of this study at http://www.greatstar.com/lois/bfh.html.

- Because breastfed infants typically are ill only half as often as their bottlefed counterparts, you're less likely to have to take time off work to care for a sick baby. You'll also be doing your bit to keep health care costs down, something that your employer will appreciate when it's time to renew the company benefits package.

- Here's a bit more ammunition—just in case your boss is a real stickler for detail. According to James P. Grant, executive director of UNICEF, "Study after study now shows . . . that babies who are not breastfed have higher rates of death, meningitis, childhood leukemia and other cancers, diabetes, respiratory illnesses, bacterial and viral infections, diarrhoeal diseases, otitis media allergies, obesity, and developmental delays. Women who do not breastfeed demonstrate a higher risk for breast and ovarian cancers."

- Employers with family-friendly work policies can attract and retain the best employees—something that could help to give your company the competitive edge in the marketplace. Who knows? It might even help to lure the best employees away from your company's biggest competitors!

- There are considerable public relations benefits to being a family-friendly workplace. If you don't mind going public with your story, you might consider offering to share your experience with the local media to help position your firm as a company that cares about its employees.

When you're making your case to your employer, be sure to demonstrate that you have thought the situation through completely, and that you can continue to meet your responsibilities to the company. You might, for example, explain that you will be coming in earlier and leaving later to make up for the extra time you will be taking at lunch to feed your baby.

Finding a breastfeeding-friendly caregiver

If you intend to continue breastfeeding after you return to work, you should make a point of seeking out a caregiver who will support your decision. A caregiver who is lukewarm about the whole idea may inadvertently sabotage your efforts to continue to breastfeed by offering your baby ill-timed bottles of formula.

When you're interviewing a potential caregiver, look for evidence that she is genuinely supportive of breastfeeding and that she understands what is involved in caring for a nursing baby.

Here are some questions you might want to ask:

- Did you breastfeed your own baby? If so, how old was your child when you weaned him?

- How many breastfed babies have you cared for over the past two years? How many are you currently caring for?

- What do you consider to be the biggest challenges of caring for a breastfed baby? What do you do to meet these challenges?

- What techniques do you use to comfort breastfeeding babies who are used to nursing when they are in need of soothing?

- Would you feel comfortable if I dropped by at lunchtime to feed my baby?

Bright Idea
Be sure to ask your employer if you can stagger your return to work. You might, for example, want to start back to work on a Thursday or Friday so you don't have to work a full week, and then take the subsequent two Wednesdays off so you won't have to work more than two days in a row. It's an ideal strategy for easing your baby into childcare and ensuring that you get the rest you need to keep up your milk supply.

- What feeding methods would you use if my baby refused to take a bottle?

Some caregivers are willing to go to extraordinary lengths to help breastfeeding moms and babies. You might find someone who will cook you a hot lunch to enjoy while you drop by for a midday nursing session or who is willing to bring the baby to you to nurse whenever he is hungry.

Choosing a breast pump

There are almost as many breast pumps on the market as there are automobiles and—as is the case with cars—there's a model designed to suit every price range. If you will only need to use your pump occasionally, you can probably get away with purchasing a Chevrolet-type product. If, however, you are going to be using your pump on a daily basis and you want the best product on the market, you're best to invest in the Cadillac of breast pumps: a hospital-grade machine.

When you're shopping for a breast pump, you should keep your needs in mind:

- How often will you be pumping? Will you be pumping many times each day or just occasionally?

- Where will you be pumping? Will you have access to an electrical outlet? What about a sink for rinsing the various pump components?

- How much time will you have to devote to each pump session? If you're likely to be pressed for time, should you consider renting or purchasing a double-horned unit that will enable you to pump both breasts at once?

- Will you be taking the pump back and forth to work each day? If so, how portable is the unit?

Watch Out!
If a potential caregiver suggests that you might feel more comfortable nursing your baby in the washroom or some other area removed from the main play area, you might think twice about using her services because she is clearly uncomfortable with the whole idea of breastfeeding and is unlikely to know what to do to promote a successful breastfeeding relationship between you and your baby.

- Does the pump have continuous or intermittent pressure? (Intermittent pressure is best because it more closely imitates the suck-release pattern used by nursing babies and because it is less likely to injure your breast.)

- How easy is the unit to clean?

- What is the cost of the pump? If it's a less expensive machine, how well will it stand up to all the wear and tear?

As you might expect, there are advantages and disadvantages to each of the various types of pumps. Let's take a quick run-through of types that you can expect to find at your local drugstore or medical supply store:

- Bicycle horn-style manual breast pumps. These contraptions look a lot like the bicycle horn you had as a kid. You squeeze the big bulb to get the milk flowing from your breasts. Not surprisingly, this type of breast pump is no longer recommended by lactation experts. Not only are the pumps difficult to clean (and therefore quickly transformed into bacterial breeding grounds), they don't work well and can cause trauma to the breast or nipple.

- Syringe-style manual breast pumps. These pumps rely on the suction produced by two cylinders that fit inside one another. They're portable, easy-to-use, easy-to-clean, and affordable. They're just not quite as efficient as some of the more powerful electrical models.

- Convertible manual breast pumps. As you can gather from the name, these pumps offer the best of both worlds: the convenience of a manual pump combined with the added power of

Moneysaver
Some hospitals provide nursing mothers with a free horn, bottle, and tubing for use with a particular brand of electric breast pump. Be sure to find out if any such freebie is likely to come your way.

an electric. Many women consider them to be the next best thing to hospital-grade electric breast pumps.

■ Small battery-operated breast pumps. These pumps are convenient to use (for example, you can use them in your car or in a washroom stall at the mall), but they don't have as much get up and go as their electrically powered counterparts. You'll also need to ensure that you tote around spare batteries—or risk looking like a lop-sided Chesty Morgan for the rest of your working day.

■ Small electric breast pumps. This type of pump generally works better than a comparable battery-operated unit, but requires access to an electrical outlet and may burn out if you're using it a lot—a major consideration if you're pumping for twins.

■ Hospital-grade electric breast pumps. These types of pumps most closely resemble the sucking action of breastfed babies, cycling about 40 times per minute. Because they use a pumping action and level of suction similar to that of your own baby, you're likely to experience an efficient let-down and minimal breast soreness. Most units come with optional double-pump kits, a feature that can be a real timesaver for a busy working mom. The only problem with these units is that they're less portable than smaller pumps and can be expensive to buy or rent.

If all this talk about pumps has got your head spinning or left you feeling about as attractive and desirable as Bessie the Cow, take heart. If you're not comfortable with the idea of hooking up an intimate part of your body to a device that seems to have as much suction power as your vacuum cleaner, you can always fall back on the tried-and-true technique of hand-expressing. While it takes a little practice to master this low-tech technique, it's convenient, portable, and incredibly cost efficient. You can learn the art of hand-expression from a lactation consultant or your local chapter of La Leche League, or you can follow the step-by-step instructions provided by most books about breastfeeding. You can also find a wealth of information about breastfeeding at the La Leche League Web site: www.lalecheleague.org.

Pumping tips

One of the first things you're learn about pumping is that it's not quite as easy as it looks. While some women can fill eight-ounce bottles in a matter of minutes, they are the exception rather than the rule. Most of us mere mortals are happy when a pumping session results in the collection of two to three ounces of milk.

You might find it reassuring to learn that the amount of milk that you can extract from your breast using a breast pump doesn't necessarily reflect the amount of milk that your body is capable of producing. Some women have better results pumping than others. It's more a reflection of your relationship with the breast pump than any indication of your ability to produce ample quantities of milk for your baby. So don't sweat it if the other moms from your prenatal class seem to be capable of getting a much larger yield from their pumping sessions than you can. It could be that their breasts

Bright Idea
Before you purchase a breast pump or sign a rental contract for an extended period of time, see if you can test-drive the particular unit first. There's no point in forking over a wallet full of cash only to discover that a particular model isn't going to do the job for you.

respond better to pumping. Or it could be that they're exaggerating their results a little, just as men do when they get together to swap fish stories! Either way, don't sweat it. Your body is fully capable of producing the quantity of milk that your baby needs.

That said, there are some techniques you can use to maximize the amount of milk you can obtain by pumping.

Timing is everything

You will probably obtain the greatest quantity of milk if you pump first thing in the morning, when your breasts are particularly full. You're also likely to get more milk early in the week, when you're more rested, than toward the end of the week.

The numbers game

Increase the frequency of pumping sessions rather than the duration of each session. It's better to pump four times per day for five minutes a session than to settle in for a single twenty-minute marathon.

The more the merrier

You can increase the amount of breast stimulation (and hence the amount of milk) by either double-pumping or nursing your baby on one side while you pump on the other. Pumping both of your breasts at the same time can help to boost your milk supply by convincing your body that it needs to produce enough milk for two babies. While this second maneuver may sound like something that is best left to the more coordinated folks among us, it's actually not as difficult as it sounds. If your baby is a world-class wiggler and likes to let go of the breast a few times until your milk really gets flowing, you might find it easiest to get him latched on first and then put the pump to the other breast.

Different strokes for different folks

Some women find it helpful to spend a few minutes massaging their breasts before they try to pump. Basically, it's a matter of using the same techniques that you use when you conduct your monthly breast-self examination.

Here's how to get started:

- Sit in a comfortable position, ideally with your feet up.

- Place a warm towel across one breast (or both breasts, if you're double-pumping) for a minute or two and then massage your breast(s), using a circular motion. (For best results, start at the top and move around the sides and the bottom.)

- When you're finished massaging your breast(s), lean over and shake your breasts gently. This should encourage the milk to start flowing.

- Relax while you pump. This is an ideal time to catch up on some leisure reading, so be sure to keep the latest issue of your favorite magazine handy.

- If the flow of milk seems to be slowing down, try massaging your breasts again.

A bit of inspiration

If you're pumping on one breast while you nurse you're baby on the other, you've already got all the inspiration you need. But during those times when you're pumping while you're away from your baby, you may find it helpful to keep a snapshot of your baby (or you nursing your baby) in front of you while you pump.

Switching sides

To maximize the amount of milk you obtain, switch breasts at least once per session (preferably twice). You'll be surprised how much more milk is left in a breast that initially appears to be empty.

Helping nature along

Bright Idea
If you're concerned that your milk supply is beginning to dip, take a "milk holiday" on the weekend. Live in your pajamas, nurse and nap a lot, eat well, drink plenty of fluids, and rest. You'll be surprised how much you can boost your milk supply by just taking it easy for a day or two.

If you're still finding it difficult to get the milk flowing initially, ask your doctor for a prescription to an oxytocin spray that you can use temporarily until you get into the whole pumping routine. Oxytocin is the hormone in your body that is responsible for causing your milk to let down. It's also responsible for the so-called nursing high that many nursing mothers experience. Bet you didn't realize that breastfeeding could be so addictive!

If pumping is becoming a chore and you're still not collecting enough milk to leave with your baby's caregiver, you might want to consider supplementing with formula. Any amount of breast milk is beneficial to your baby (although, naturally, more is better). If you do decide to introduce formula to your baby's diet, don't try to force him to change his eating habits cold turkey. Mix breast milk with formula, gradually reducing the amount of breast milk over time as you ensure that your baby can tolerate the particular brand of formula you've selected. By proceeding slowly, you can prevent your baby from becoming unduly constipated—an all too common problem when breastfed babies are suddenly switched to formula.

Dressing for success

If you're going to be pumping at work, it makes sense to dress for the occasion. Here are a few wardrobe tips for working women who choose to breastfeed:

- Dress in pump-friendly clothing. Look for shirts and blouses that button up the front or pull up easily, or purchase special nursing garments that enable easy access to your breasts.

- Avoid light colors. Brightly patterned or dark colors help to hide breast pads and will actually help to mask any evidence of leakage.

- Choose cottons and synthetics rather than silks and linens. If it needs to be dry-cleaned, it's not worth the hassle.

- Wear breast pads for at least the first few weeks—longer if you tend to leak milk on a regular basis. Even after you stop wearing them, you should keep a box in your drawer at work for a day when your baby decides to skip a feeding unexpectedly. If you find yourself caught without any breast pads, you can resort to a sanitary napkin cut in half. Just be prepared for the less-than-runway-caliber square-breasted look!

- Keep a spare shirt or blouse at work for those days when even the most absorbent breast pad isn't enough. There's nothing worse than trying to wash your blouse in the bathroom sink and blow dry it under the hand dryer before heading into an important meeting!

Storing breast milk

To minimize the chances of contamination, you need to know as much as possible about storing breast milk.

How long breast milk keeps

Breast milk can be stored at

- 59–60°F (15°C) for up to 24 hours

- 66–72°F (19–22°C) for up to 10 hours

Moneysaver
Reusable cotton breast pads are considerably cheaper than disposable paper pads. They're also a lot more comfortable. Just be careful to avoid the waterproof type. They increase your chances of developing a breast infection.

- 79°F (25°C) for four to eight hours
- 32–39°F (0–4°C) for five to eight days
- 0°F (–19°C) for six months or longer

Note: If you are freezing breast milk, be sure to date each container of milk so you can make a point of using the oldest milk first.

Other tips on storing breast milk

Here are some additional pointers on storing breast milk:

- Breast milk should be refrigerated or frozen until use. Because freezing kills some of the antibodies in breast milk, it's best to refrigerate rather than freeze as much as possible.

- Breast milk should be frozen in heavy plastic or glass containers or specially designed freezer bags. Disposable bottle liners aren't designed to tolerate the extreme change in temperature. If you freeze your breast milk in freezer bags, double bag them or keep them in a larger container to protect them from punctures.

- Freeze the milk in two- or three-ounce portions. If you fill an eight-ounce bottle with breast milk, you run the risk of having to throw it away if your baby only drinks a portion of it.

- Refrigerate freshly pumped breast milk before adding it to frozen breast milk. This prevents the warm milk from defrosting the top layer of frozen milk.

- Breast milk often turns yellow when it has been frozen. This does not mean that the milk has spoiled.

- Once breast milk has been thawed, it should not be refrozen. It can, however, be safely kept in the refrigerator for up to nine hours—perhaps even longer.

■ It's not unusual for breast milk to separate. If this occurs, shake your baby's bottle for a moment or two until the breast milk reconstitutes.

■ Breast milk should be thawed in running water. Don't heat it in the microwave or on the stovetop. Not only do you run the risk of overheating the breast milk; you may also destroy some valuable nutrients.

Introducing a bottle

So now that I've talked about how to collect and store breast milk, it makes sense to talk about what you need to do to get the milk into the baby.

If you're lucky, your baby will accept a bottle willingly. If you're not so lucky, you may have to enroll him in Bottlefeeding 101 and hope against hope that he passes the course before you have to return to work. If the fateful day rolls around and your beloved offspring is still boycotting rubber nipples, you'll have no choice but to accommodate his wishes—a subject I'll talk more about a little later on.

While there's no guarantee that you can convince your breastfed baby to accept a bottle, there are some strategies you can use to put the odds in your favor.

Start early—but not too early

If you want to teach your baby how to take a bottle, don't wait until the week before you have to return to work. The best time to introduce a bottle is after breastfeeding is well-established (around the six week mark) but before the baby gets old enough to

Bright Idea
A few weeks before you have to go back to work, purchase a brightly colored bottle and add it to your baby's toy collection. When he is awake, but not hungry, put an ounce of breast milk in it and have someone other than you show him how this exciting new "toy" works.

be picky about where his food is coming from (something that typically happens when a baby is three to four months old).

The problem with introducing the bottle too early is that your baby may develop "nipple confusion"—a problem that occurs because the sucking action that a baby uses when breastfeeding is radically different than the one used to drink from a bottle. That's why the breastfeeding experts recommend that you wait until your baby is an experienced nurser before you ask him to master the bottle.

Once you've introduced the bottle, continue to offer it to your baby on a regular basis (for example, one to two times per week). After all, you don't want him to forget his newly mastered skill.

Have someone else offer the bottle

Breastfeeding babies are creatures of habit. They quickly learn to associate a certain person and a certain way of being held with nursing. You've no doubt noticed that breastfeeding babies root frantically for the breast whenever they're held in the cradle position.

Because most of them learn very early on to associate their mothers with food, it's often easier to have another family member give them their first bottle—perhaps Dad, Grandma or Grandpa, or an older sibling. Just don't make the mistake of having a family member offer the baby his bottle in your favorite nursing chair!

You might also get better results if the baby is held in a position other than the traditional cradle hold. You might try walking with your baby while he eats or giving him his bottle while he's still half asleep (and therefore less likely to protest).

Choose the right moment

Don't try to introduce the bottle when your baby is frantically hungry. He might not have the patience to try to figure out how it works. You're best to introduce the bottle in the middle of a feeding—perhaps after the baby has emptied the first breast but before he starts in on the second.

When you do find the right moment to offer the bottle, don't shove the bottle in your baby's mouth. Brush his mouth with the nipple and let him open his mouth to accept it when he's ready. This way, you're taking advantage of one of your baby's most instinctive reflexes, the rooting reflex.

Try offering breast milk, not formula

If your baby rejects the bottle of formula you offer him, you won't have any way of knowing whether it's the formula or the bottle he's rejecting. Instead, take things one step at a time. Offer him a bottle of breast milk first.

If you do end up offering formula to your breast-fed baby, don't be surprised if he turns his nose up at it at first. Formula has a different taste than breast milk. It's not nearly as sweet. You may have to experiment with a few different brands of formula before you find one that your milk connoisseur is willing to try.

If at first you don't succeed . . .

Try joining the Nipple of the Month Club. As any self-respecting baby can tell you, all nipples were not created equal. There are rubber ones and silicon ones. There are small ones, medium-sized ones, and oversized monstrosities that seem large enough to gag your average five-year-old! One real estate agent was so desperate to convince her daughter to take a bottle that she purchased every nipple on the market. She even imported some from Britain. She's so proud of her nipple collection that she eagerly offers it to any new mother who's faced with a bottle-challenged baby.

Don't panic

The techniques used to extract milk from a bottle are radically different from those used to extract milk from a breast. Your baby may become frustrated if he can't get the milk flowing right, or he may choke if it starts flowing too quickly. If your baby refuses to take a bottle at first, wait a day or two and try again.

If he still refuses to take one, you might consider using one of the following alternatives to a bottle:

- a small cup: even a very young infant can be taught to sip from a small cup (for example, a paper cup or medicine cup)

- a spoon, medicine dropper, or oral syringe: You can use these devices to control the amount of liquid entering your baby's mouth so that he won't choke

A day in the life

While you'll likely find the first few weeks back at work to be more than a little exhausting, it won't be long before you and your baby have established your own routine.

Weekdays

If you decide to continue breastfeeding after you return to work, the days when you go to work will probably end up looking something like this:

6:00 a.m.—Nurse baby.
6:30 a.m.—Hop in the shower, get dressed, and eat your breakfast.

> **"**
> It takes a breast-feeding baby longer to extract milk from a breast than from a bottle. Scott still wanted to suck for comfort long after his stomach was full. To give him more sucking time—but not more milk—we used a bottle nipple with a smaller opening.
> —Marie, mother of five-month-old Scott
> **"**

7:30 a.m.—Drive your baby to the caregiver's house and settle in for the second feeding of the day.

8:30 a.m.—9:00 a.m.—Arrive at work.

10:30 a.m.—Pump milk while you drink some juice and enjoy a healthy snack during your mid-morning break. If you want to avoid using formula, you will need to use the breast pump at least two to three times during your working day. As a rule of thumb, you should plan to pump milk at least as often as your baby will be receiving a bottle from the caregiver. Even if you intend to supplement with formula, you will want to pump at least once during the day to avoid feeling uncomfortable and to reduce your chances of ending up with a clogged milk duct or a breast infection.

12:30 p.m.—Either drive to the caregiver's to feed your baby or use the breast pump again. Be sure to allocate enough time to enjoy a healthy drink and a nutritious, well-balanced lunch.

2:30 p.m.—Pump milk while you drink some juice and enjoy a healthy snack during your mid-afternoon break.

4:30 p.m.–5:30 p.m.—Wrap up your working day.

5:00 p.m.–5:30 p.m.—Arrive at the daycare center or family daycare home (or back at home, if you have an in-home caregiver), and nurse your baby. As soon as you get home, transfer the milk you pumped during the day into the next day's bottles.

6:00 p.m. to 6:00 a.m.—Demand feed your baby throughout the evening and night. Head to bed as soon as you can, but by 10:00 p.m. if at all possible.

You may find that your baby starts "reverse cycling" after you return to work, for example, he nurses more often in the evening and night than during the daytime. It's a common coping mechanism for breastfed babies who would rather hold out for the real thing (Mom, that is!) than accept any unreasonable facsimile.

Weekends

It isn't easy juggling the needs of your baby with the demands of your job. That's why you should resist the temptation to fill your weekend with chores and social engagements. Instead, use your time off to rest up for the week ahead of you.

To give your milk supply a bit of a boost, nurse your baby as much as possible on the weekend, keep your fluid intake up, and eat plenty of nutritious food. You might also try mixing a tablespoon of brewer's yeast into your orange juice. It isn't particularly tasty, but some nursing mothers find that it gives them a badly needed energy boost and helps them to increase their milk supply.

Just the facts

- Continuing to breastfeed after you return to work can be beneficial to both you and your baby.

- If you plan to continue breastfeeding after you return to work, try to get your employer on board right away and to find a breastfeeding-friendly caregiver as soon as possible.

- There are pros and cons to each type of breast pump. Make sure you understand what you're looking for before you buy.

- There are a variety of different techniques you can use to boost your milk supply, like double-pumping to trick your body into producing enough milk for twins.

- Make sure that your back-to-work wardrobe includes plenty of breastfeeding-friendly garments.

Timesaver
Continue to pump on the weekend when you're less pressed for time. Doing so will enable you to build up a surplus of breast milk—something that will enable you to leave some extra breast milk with your caregiver for those occasions when you are unexpectedly delayed in traffic and your baby is due for a feeding.

- To reduce the chances of contamination, take time to learn about the ins and outs of storing breast milk.

- Be sure to introduce a bottle to your baby early enough so that he'll still accept it—but not so early that he could develop nipple confusion.

- Because your weekdays are bound to be hectic after you return to work, it's important to reserve your weekends for rest.

The Perils of
Part-Time Childcare

Chapter 14

GET THE SCOOP ON...
Regular versus occasional part-time
childcare arrangements ▪ Drop-in childcare
arrangements ▪ Hiring a teenager ▪
Babysitting co-ops

Finding Part-Time Childcare

Part-time childcare is a bit of a catch-all term. It refers to both part-time childcare arrangements that you use on a regular basis (for example, sending your child to a daycare center one or more days per week while you go to work) and childcare arrangements that you use on an occasional or one-time basis (hiring a teenager to care for your children while you and your partner enjoy an occasional dinner out on your own). Some of these arrangements occur in formal, licensed settings and involve trained caregivers. Others occur in unlicensed settings and involve teenagers, volunteers, and others.

If you're like most parents, you will require part-time childcare on at least an occasional basis, even if you have a full-time childcare arrangement in place. The reason is obvious: Part-time childcare arrangements have saved the skin of many a working parent by serving as a stop-gap measure for parents whose regular childcare arrangements have temporarily fallen apart. Besides, unless you have a live-in caregiver who is prepared to provide childcare services whenever you need them, you are still likely to need the services of a teenager or other after-hours caregiver from time to time. There are, of course, regional differences, which explains, for example, why parents in New York City extend the hours of their regular caregivers—typically a professional babysitter or a nanny— whenever extra childcare is needed (rather than hire a teenager or use a babysitting co-op).

As you can see, there's a lot of material to cover in this chapter: everything from finding part-time childcare to evaluating your various options. This chapter focuses on three of the most popular types of part-time childcare options: drop-in childcare arrangements (health clubs, morning out programs, and more), teenaged babysitters, and babysitting co-ops. (Once again, there are regional preferences for caregivers. In New York City, for example, professional babysitting agencies are the preferred option when childcare is only occasionally needed.)

Regular versus occasional part-time childcare arrangements

Because the term "part-time childcare" is a bit too broad, I've decided to divide it into two categories: "regular part-time childcare" (part-time childcare that you use on a recurring, week-to-week basis) and "occasional part-time childcare" (childcare you use from time to time or on a one-time basis).

A regular part-time childcare arrangement might include a space in a daycare center, family daycare home, nursery school, or care in your own home by a nanny, professional babysitter, au pair, relative, or other type of caregiver.

Moneysaver
Make sure you understand the vacation policies for part-timers before you choose a daycare center or family daycare provider. Some centers prorate the number of "free" vacation days (the ones you don't have to pay for when your child is away) based on the number of days of care you use on a regular basis. If, for example, full-timers are entitled to ten working days per year as vacation time and your child attends daycare three days per week, you could expect to be given six vacation days per year.

Out-of-home childcare

Many daycare centers and family daycare homes are willing to accept children on a permanent part-time basis. Some require you to fit into their schedule (for example, Monday-Wednesday-Friday versus Tuesday-Thursday), while others are willing to work around yours. Regardless of how flexible the daycare center's policies are, in most cases, you will be expected to commit to certain days of the week. In other words, they don't want you showing up on a Tuesday one week and on a Thursday the next. The reason for this is simple: They want to find another family with a child who needs care on the days when you don't. Otherwise, they lose money on the days when your child isn't using her space.

What's more, as is the case with most full-time daycare arrangements, if your child misses her regularly scheduled day for whatever reason, you will still be expected to pay for her space. The fact that you are part-time doesn't mean that you can come and go as you please. That said, some daycare centers and family daycare homes are willing to accept children on an occasional part-time (drop-in) basis, space permitting. I'll discuss the pros and cons of this type of arrangement later on in this chapter.

Nursery school is another regular part-time option you might want to consider—provided the school's hours mesh well with your work schedule or other commitments, of course. Because most nursery school programs operate on a half-day basis, this type of childcare is best suited to a stay-at-home parent who wants a break or a parent who runs a home-based business or who has similarly flexible hours.

In-home childcare

If you're not wild about the idea of out-of-home childcare, you can, of course, arrange for regular part-time childcare to take place in your own home. Rather than repeat the material that I covered in Chapters 6 and 7—the chapters that deal with the ins and outs of hiring an in-home caregiver—I'm going to touch on a few specifics about arranging for part-time in-home care.

The first thing you need to know is that it's often more difficult to find a part-time caregiver than it is to find a full-time caregiver. The reason is simple. Most people can't afford to live on part-time wages.

That's why you'll need to start your search as early as possible and leave no stone unturned. Activate your network of family and friends and let everyone know the specifics of the arrangement you are seeking (which days you need care, the numbers and ages of your children, and so on).

As with most other types of childcare searches, you need to be as thorough as possible. Here are some tips on finding part-time in-home care:

- If you know a family with a part-time in-home caregiver, ask if it would be possible to share their caregiver. She might work at their home three days a week and your home the other two days a week, for example.

- Offer a college or university student free room and board in exchange for a certain number of hours per week of childcare.

- Find out if the teacher who runs the local half-day nursery school program is interested in caring for your children when she's not at the school. You may have similar luck with educational assistants, childcare workers, and others who only work part-time hours.

- Ask a friend who is at home with her children if she would be willing to bring her children to your home and care for your children on a part-time basis.

Now that I've covered the basics of finding regular part-time childcare, let's move on to the discussion of the three most popular types of occasional part-time childcare: drop-in care, care by a teenage babysitter, and babysitting co-ops.

The pros and cons of drop-in childcare arrangements

The term "drop-in childcare" refers to situations in which childcare is provided to an ever-changing group of children. Some drop-in centers specialize in caring for sick children—a topic discussed in greater detail in Chapter 16—but most only provide care to healthy children. Some are licensed and fully regulated, but others are not. Some require parents to stay on the premises. As you can see, there's no such thing as a typical drop-in childcare program, so you'll want to investigate any such programs thoroughly so that you'll know exactly what you and your child are getting into.

If you're interested in locating drop-in childcare programs in your community, here are some examples of where you may find them.

Daycare centers and family daycare homes

Some daycare centers and family daycare homes are set up to accept children on a drop-in basis. You call the center to book a space for your child and then drop her off at the appropriate time.

Moneysaver
Watch the timing of your getaways if you're planning to hire a caregiver through a domestic agency. Most agencies charge higher-than-ordinary rates on long weekends and other holidays.

While these types of arrangements look good on paper, there is a catch. Centers that agree to accept children on a drop-in basis while attempting to deliver a quality program to their regular group of children often fail to meet the needs of any of the children in their care. That's why it's important to find a center that specializes in providing drop-in rather than regular care and consequently understands the challenges of dealing with an ever-changing population of children. Parachuting your child into a regular daycare center where she's literally "the new kid on the block" can be, but isn't always, a disaster, especially if your child can handle relatively frequent changes in her childcare arrangements.

Churches and synagogues

Many churches and synagogues offer some type of "Mom's Morning Out" program as a service to their communities. Typically, parents can drop their children off for a couple of hours for a small fee or for no fee at all. These programs are most popular in the South, but they can be found in other parts of the country as well.

Recreation facilities

Some health clubs provide on-site daycare as a service to their members. For a nominal hourly charge, you can drop off your child while you workout.

Shopping centers

A growing number of shopping centers are beginning to offer drop-in care in recognition of the fact that Mom and Dad can spend money more efficiently if they don't have three kids in tow.

As you might expect, there are both advantages and disadvantages to drop-in arrangements. Let's run through the pros and cons.

Pros:

- Many of these programs—particularly those offered by shopping centers, recreation facilities, and church groups—charge fees at or below market value.

- You only pay for childcare when you need it— once a week, once a month, or whatever the case may be.

Cons:

- You probably won't know ahead of time who will be responsible for caring for your child.

- You might not know ahead of time if there will be a spot for your child when she needs it.

- Drop-in childcare is more expensive on a per hour basis than regular part-time childcare.

- Even if you do know the caregiver, she probably doesn't know your child as well as she would if your child attended childcare on a more regular basis.

- Your child doesn't have the same opportunity to get to know the other children as she would if she attended childcare on a daily or weekly basis.

- The caregiver has to attend to the needs of an ever-changing group of children.

If you decide to use a drop-in childcare arrangement, you will want to:

- evaluate it out ahead of time using the same criteria that you would use to evaluate a regular out-of-home childcare arrangement

- find out exactly what you need to do to reserve a space for your child, and how much notice the caregiver or childcare center typically requires

- be sure that you provide the caregivers with emergency contact information, an authorization to administer medication, and other important health and safety-related information (see Appendix D)

- arrive early enough to give the caregiver and your child the chance to get used to one another before you have to leave

While drop-in care is an ideal solution for many families, it's not for everyone. If your child finds it difficult to cope with change or is slow to warm up to strangers, drop-in care probably isn't right for your family.

The pros and cons of hiring a teenager

Babysitting is a rite of passage for many teenagers—a stepping stone to the world of work. You probably babysat at least once or twice when you were a teenager—a life experience that has no doubt made you acutely aware of the pros and cons of hiring a teenager.

Just in case you didn't babysit in your younger years or you've long since repressed those memories, let's take a moment to run through the pros and cons:

Pros:

- Teenagers typically demand a lower hourly rate than adult babysitters.

Cons:

- Some teenagers lack good judgement. Others are unreliable. It's important that the teenager you hire is up to the task.

- Some teenagers are in it for the love of money, not children.

Watch Out!
Drop-in childcare is not a good choice for children who are having difficulty with separation anxiety (those who are between eight to fourteen months of age). It's too difficult for children this age to adjust to an ever-changing parade of caregivers and children.

- There are many conflicting demands for a teenager's time. Unless you pay top dollar and treat your teenaged babysitters especially well, you might not have much luck in finding any to care for your children.

Where the teens are

In a recent article in *The Christian Science Monitor*, Abe McLaughlin described a dilemma that all too many parents find themselves facing: the shortage of teenage babysitters.

"As parents desperate for a night out can attest, there just aren't enough people willing to look after America's children," he writes. "Causes range from a demographic dip in the number of teens to a boom in the number of girls playing sports—which leaves them less time to babysit."

The article goes on to describe the lengths one mother went to in an effort to track down an available teenager—a process that included hanging out at the swimming pool in her community and approaching wholesome-looking teens. "Fifteen years ago I was trying to meet guys at the pool," she quipped. "Now I'm trying to meet babysitters."

A recent story at *GazetteNet* (www.gazettenet. com/valleylife/1217_stories/BABYSIT.VAL.html) tells a similar tale. "We've pretty much given up on high-school kids. They're more tightly scheduled than CEOs of major corporations," says Christine Stevens, a mother of two.

Is the situation really as bad as McLaughlin and Stevens would have you believe?

Unfortunately, yes.

According to the U.S. Census Bureau, there are 13 million teenagers in America—down significantly from 16 million in 1980. You don't have to be an economist to figure out what this shortage means to parents who are desperate for an evening out on their own—or what it does to the hourly rate a teenage babysitter can demand.

Does this mean that it's impossible to find a teenage babysitter? Hardly. It just means that you're going to have to start your search a little earlier and be prepared to pay a little more.

Searching for Mary Poppins, Jr.

While you'll want to start your search by relying on family members, friends, and others whose judgement you trust, you may have to cast your net a little wider to find a suitable candidate.

Here are some folks you'll definitely want to talk to in your quest for referrals:

- the instructor of the local babysitting or teen first-aid course
- teachers, coaches of sports teams, and others who work with teenagers
- members of the clergy
- the career counseling department of your local high school
- the early childhood education department of your local college or university

What to ask a teenager

Bright Idea
Offer to type a teenager's essay in exchange for a couple of hours of childcare services.

Once you've found a teenager, you'll need to assess her suitability. While you obviously don't expect her to show up for a formal interview wearing a three-piece suit complete with attache case, you should plan on having some sort of interview, however informal. Here are some questions you should consider asking her, either when you initially contact her by phone or at the actual interview:

- How old are you?

- Have you taken a babysitting or first-aid course? If so, did the course include training in infant resuscitation or CPR?

- Do you have any younger brothers or sisters? If so, how old are they and how often do you babysit them?

- Have you ever babysit anyone else's children? If so, how old were those children and how often did you babysit them?

- What would you do to keep my child safe and happy while I'm away?

- What would you do if my child threw a temper tantrum or refused to do what you told her to do?

- What is the most difficult situation you've ever encountered while babysitting? How did you handle it?

- Can you provide me with the name of at least one person who can comment on your ability to care for young children?

Wrap up the interview by giving the teenager the opportunity to meet your children. Take careful note of how she relates to them: whether she gets down on the floor to play with them and whether she actually seems to like them. After she has left, ask your children what they think of the babysitter—how they would feel about being left with her, and so on. If your children are absolutely ruthless in their assessment of the babysitter ("She's no fun at all. She just wanted to talk to her friends on the phone."), pay attention to what they have to say.

What to tell the babysitter

After you've found the right babysitter, your next task is to familiarize her with your household routines. Before you walk out the door, make sure that she knows

Unofficially...
Some movie theatres will flash a message on the screen if your babysitter needs to reach you in an emergency. Even better, many parents are now carrying beepers on their evenings out so that childcare providers can reach them in an emergency.

- where your emergency contact information is posted
- where the telephone is and how to use it
- where the exits are located
- how to activate and disarm the security system
- where the first-aid kit, fire extinguisher, flashlight, and spare house keys are kept
- where the water shutoff valve and fuse box are located
- how to administer any medication that your child may require
- where your child is free to play and what areas of the house are off limits to her
- where your child's bedroom is and what techniques, if any, you use to get her to sleep
- where the kitchen is and what foods she is welcome to eat
- what foods are safe for young children and which ones aren't (grapes, nuts, whole carrots, and hot dogs are unsafe, due to the risk of choking)
- which household appliances she is welcome to use, and how they work
- what you would want her to do if the smoke detector or carbon monoxide detector went off
- what would happen in the event that you were unable to make it home on time as planned,

due to a flat tire or other emergency. It's important to make sure that she understands the importance of staying with the children until you or a designated adult makes it home.

- a little about your child's likes and dislikes (food, clothing, activities, and so on)

- rules about having friends over while you're out (both her friends and your children's friends)

- policies about talking on the phone

- the rules about using the computer (for both her and the children)

- guidelines regarding watching TV (what the kids are allowed to watch, and what they're not, and how much they're allowed to watch)

- how long your children are allowed to play Nintendo, etc.

- what time the children should be in bed

It's always a good idea to review these rules in the presence of your children so that they won't try to con the babysitter!

If your child is an infant, you may also want to go over some of the basics of babycare, including

- feeding procedures (for example, why it's not safe to prop a bottle or to allow a baby to take food of any type to bed)

- diapering procedures (where your baby's change supplies are kept, how they are used, where you want the dirty diaper to be put, and where the babysitter can wash her hands)

- health and safety concerns (which areas of the house are babyproofed—and to what extent; how much supervision young babies need; what to do if a baby is choking; and so on).

Watch Out!
Make sure the babysitter understands the importance of supervising young children while they are eating to prevent choking. According to the National Safe Kids Campaign, the leading cause of accidental death in one- to ten-year-olds is unintentional injuries like choking. Find out more at www.safekids.org.

You can find a comprehensive checklist of these types of items at http://childcare.primelist.com/sitter.htm.

You might also want to run through some basic health and safety rules. You can find some useful information at the Fullerton (California) Police Department web site at www.ci.fullerton.ca.us/noframes/police/babysit.shm

The babysitter binder

Unofficially...
Twelve- to fifteen-year-olds often make the best babysitters. They're old enough to have the maturity and judgement required to care for young children, and yet their social lives have not yet kicked into over-drive.

Be sure to leave the babysitter with written instructions that contain emergency contacts and other important information. Rather than recording this information on a scrap of paper that might easily be misplaced, create a babysitter binder that contains both permanent pages (sheets protected with plastic page protectors) and temporary pages (sheets that can be filled out at the start of each evening out).

Your permanent pages should include the following information:

- your street address (and basic directions on how to get there, if you live in a rural area)

- emergency contact numbers (ambulance, fire department, police, poison control, and so on)

- the name and phone number of a trusted neighbor or other responsible adult who would be prepared to lend a hand in the event of an emergency

- details about any allergies or medical problems that your child has, and a list of any medications that she is currently taking

- a signed consent form authorizing the babysitter to obtain emergency medical assistance on behalf of your child if you are not available (see Appendix D)

- the name and phone number of your family doctor

- the full names of each member of your family

- medical insurance number(s)

The temporary pages should include the following types of information

- the name (restaurant name, theater name, or your host and hostesses' names), address, and phone number of the place where you will be spending the evening, and the time you will be arriving home

- details about any medications your child may be taking on a short-term (that is, nonpermanent) basis

- details about any visitors, telephone calls, and/or deliveries you are expecting

- details about any special arrangements the babysitter needs to know about (for example, "Jenny will be getting dropped off from gymnastics at 7:00 p.m. The Smiths are driving her home. Their phone number is 555-5555.")

Be sure to include some blank sheets of paper where the babysitter can record any phone messages and note any nonurgent questions or concerns that arise over the course of the evening.

If you're really creative and energetic, you might want also want to include miniprofiles of each child (i.e., a list of their likes and dislikes, a brief description of bedtime rituals, and so on) so that your babysitter will have an "owner's manual" to fall back on in your absence.

Some families also like to include a small amount of cash in the binder—enough for emergency cab fare in the event that the babysitter needed to transport a child somewhere because of an emergency.

"I don't need a babysitter."

After children reach about ten years of age, they may resent the fact that they are being babysat by someone who may be only a few years older than they are. They believe that they are old enough to care for themselves and decide to give the babysitter a run for her money.

The best way to avoid this situation is to hire a teenager who is willing to take your children places and do things with them. Look for someone who has a driver's license or who will feel confident taking your children to local attractions by bus.

Provide her with a list of activities that your children would enjoy, and look for ways that you can help make them possible (i.e., offer to drop everyone off at the local museum and then pick them up later), and encourage her to approach you with ideas of her own. Most important of all, try to find someone who your children will like so much that they'll almost forget she's their babysitter.

How to keep a good babysitter

Now that you've found a good babysitter, you're probably wondering what you can do to keep her.

While teenage babysitters are definitely a time-limited commodity—most move on to boys or jobs within a two-to-four year period—some will stick with your family for the long haul if you treat them well enough. Here are some pointers on keeping her:

- Treat your babysitter with respect. Pick her up on time and get her back home on time. If you book her services and have to cancel at the last minute, pay her anyway.

Bright Idea
Have the teenager come over an hour or two before you actually need to walk out the door so that you can observe her with the children and answer any questions she might have. You might even want to pay her to come over for an entire evening of training before you leave her alone with your children.

■ Pay her at the end of the evening—and in cash. Don't assume that she's willing to take a check or that it's okay to pay her the next day unless you ask her first.

■ Pay her well. Find out from other parents what the going rate for childcare is in your community and offer a little more. You should expect to pay $5–$7 per hour for a teenager and $7 or more per hour for a college or university student—more if you live in a community with a high cost of living or in which there's a chronic shortage of teenage babysitters.

■ Work around your babysitter's schedule. Don't expect your babysitter to choose between her basketball team's playoff game or the chance to babysit for you. Because some 80 to 90 percent of 12-year-old girls are now playing on athletic teams, you shouldn't be surprised if your own plans get pre-empted from time to time.

■ Give her a raise from time to time. The more the babysitter knows about your family's routines, the more valuable she is to you. Reward her with a series of small increases as she progresses through your in-home professional development program.

■ Use her services often. The teenager that you've come to rely on for childcare is less likely to take a job at the local convenience store if she's got a steady stream of income from you. This is definitely a case of "use it or lose it."

Babysitting co-ops

If you don't feel comfortable leaving your children in the care of a teenager but don't have the funds to

66

Every session, I get appeals from 10-year-olds. They want to make some money and have their skills validated. Meanwhile, almost no 14-year-olds are taking the course anymore.
—Babysitting course instructor Nora Holland, quoted in a story at www. gazettenet.com/ valleylife/ 1217_stories/ BABYSIT.VAL.html

99

pay what mature babysitters typically demand, you might want to join a babysitting co-op.

Babysitting co-ops function a lot like other types of bartering systems. A group of people agree to trade babysitting services on a noncash basis. What makes a co-op work better than a situation in which you swap babysitting hours with a neighbor or friend is the fact that you have a larger pool of potential caregivers to draw on, thereby increasing your chances of finding a caregiver when you need one.

The pros and cons

Before I get into a nuts and bolts discussion of how co-ops work, let's quickly run through the pros and cons.

Pros:

- Babysitting co-ops make it affordable for you and your partner to escape for an evening or even an entire weekend. Rather than forking out $6 or more per hour in babysitting fees, you agree to return the favor a few weeks or months down the line.

- The other members are experienced Moms and Dads. Consequently, you worry less about how they would handle an emergency situation than you would if you left your children in the care of a teenager.

- Participating in a babysitting co-op is a wonderful way for you and your children to make friends with other families in your community.

Cons:

- There's no formal screening process to ensure that the caregiver is suitable. You'll have no way of knowing, for example, whether she spanks her children unless you decide to do a little digging on your own.

- You have to be prepared to care for other people's children on a regular basis. Most babysitting co-ops will only let you to be so many hours in debt to the system before they'll expect you to live up to your end of the bargain.

- Personality conflicts are common, as are disputes about members who either don't use the system often enough or don't babysit other people's children often enough. If you don't need these kinds of hassles in your life, look for an alternative childcare solution.

Checking out the other members' homes

Because there's no formal screening process in a typical babysitting co-op, the onus is on you to make sure that a particular childcare home is up to scratch. Here are a few of the things you'll want to watch for:

- cigarette smoke (important because second-hand smoke has been linked to a host of childhood diseases including respiratory illnesses and ear infections)

- a lingering odor of dirty diapers (an indicator that the potential babysitter's sanitation standards are less than adequate)

- an environment that is so cluttered that it is actually hazardous to young children

- obvious dirt and dust which could trigger an asthmatic or allergic reaction

- pets like iguanas or turtles which can spread salmonella to young children

Watch Out!
The Internal Revenue Service expects you to declare the value of any income you have received by bartering services—even if that income is in the form of points or coupons. Because there's no line for "babysitting coupons" on the tax form, you need to calculate the cash value of the services you have provided by using the going rate for childcare in your community.

- a family that already has its own hands full just caring for its own children or that has children who are either much younger or much older than your own

These are just a few of the most obvious red flags. If you want to be a bit more discerning in your evaluation, you might want to refer to the family childcare home checklists in Appendix D. Just one word of caution: Your chances of finding a home that complies with all of the standards set out on our checklist are probably slim to none. In fact, your own home probably wouldn't even make the grade!

Starting your own

If you are interested in joining a babysitting co-op but there doesn't seem to be one up and running in your neighborhood, you might want to start one yourself. Here are a few tips:

- Start with your own circle of friends. That way, you can pick and choose who will be caring for your children. Just make sure that everyone you invite to join the co-op is located within a short drive of one another's homes. Otherwise, you'll be reluctant to accept a babysitting job that requires an hour's commute each way.

- Don't get too big too fast. The ideal number of families for a babysitting co-op is somewhere between 10 and 20. If you have too few families, people have a difficult time finding a caregiver when they need one. If you have too many, families don't have the same opportunity to get to know one another well.

- Decide how the system will work. Most co-ops work on either a point basis or a coupon basis. If the system operates on a point basis, members

Timesaver
Make four servings of your favorite casserole, stew, or other entree and swap them with other members of the co-op. It's far simpler to make four servings of stew in one sitting than it is to make four separate dinners.

purchasing childcare services are required to notify the co-op's treasurer of the details of the transaction. He or she then records the transactions in a manual or computerized record-keeping system and provides members with a monthly or quarterly statement detailing their credit or debit transactions. If the system operates on a coupon basis, members typically use coupons like money, "paying" one another for babysitting services as they are rendered. Most members receive a set number of coupons—typically 20 to 30 hours worth—when they first join the co-op.

■ Keep the rates as simple as possible and be clear about what families with more than one child are expected to pay to the system. Should a family with four children expect to pay four times the basic rate, or is there some kind of discount for a second or subsequent child? Obviously, point systems are better suited to handling these more complex types of transactions.

■ Plan to charge an annual membership fee to cover such incidentals as envelopes, postage, and other costs of running the co-op. Something in the neighborhood of $10 to $40 per year should do the trick.

■ Have members contact one another directly to arrange childcare services. It's too complicated and time-consuming for a third party to organize these transactions on their behalf.

■ Develop a clear set of rules that everyone can agree on. Most co-ops have a policy stating that people who move away from the area or who have to leave the co-op for other reasons are required to settle any indebtedness to the system first. If they cannot make up the hours by babysitting for other members, they are generally required to make a cash payment to the system instead.

- Have each family prepare an information sheet about each child, and insist that they bring this information with them to the other member's house. In addition to covering such essentials as food allergies, health information, emergency contacts, and so on, the form should also include some information about the child's likes and dislikes, sleep rituals, food preferences, and so on.

- Insist that parents leave a signed medical consent form with the member who is caring for their child and (where required) a health insurance card.

- Set limits on the number of children a particular babysitter can reasonably be expected to care for, and find out whether members are willing to provide care to other members' children in their own homes or the children's own home.

- Organize some social events for both parents and kids. Some co-ops host "date nights" or "errand days" in which a large number of children are cared for by a group of caregivers. Others plan family picnics, potluck dinners, and parent-and-kids outings to area attractions. You can find out more about these types of events at www.coincide.com/mdmc/babycoop.htm. Note: if you plan your parents-and-kids outing enough in advance, you may even be able to take advantage of group rates at local zoos, amusement parks, and museums.

Bright Idea
To increase your chances of having someone volunteer for the position of treasurer, either rotate the position throughout the membership on a month-to-month basis or "pay" the treasurer for her time by providing her with extra babysitting points.

■ Once your co-op is up and running, see if members would be willing to exchange other types of services—like cooking, cleaning, grocery shopping, and so on. In some communities, food co-ops, in which families pool their grocery dollars and then buy grocery products directly from wholesalers, have enabled some families to save as much as 30 percent on their grocery bill.

■ Find out whether local children's clothing stores, family restaurants, and other companies providing services to families would be willing to offer members of your co-op a discount. You may have a better chance of negotiating with these companies if you hook up with members of other babysitting co-ops in your community. After all, there's strength in numbers.

Just the facts

■ If you need childcare on a regular part-time basis, you might want to find a space in a daycare center or family daycare home, send your child to a nursery school program, or hire a nanny, professional babysitter, or other caregiver to provide care in your own home.

■ If you need childcare only on an occasional basis, you may prefer to use a drop-in service offered through a local daycare center or community organization—or, if you live in a large town or city, the services of a professional babysitting agency.

■ Teenagers are in short supply, but you can find and keep one by offering top dollar and using her services regularly.

- Participating in a babysitting co-op is a great way to keep your childcare costs down and meet other families. The key disadvantage is the fact that it's entirely up to you to decide if a particular caregiver is suitable.

Finding Care for Your School-Aged Child

Thirty years ago, after-school childcare programs were virtually nonexistent. Today, we live in an entirely different world: one in which the vast majority of married women with young children—77 percent to be exact—are either in the workforce or actively looking for work.

While American society has changed dramatically over the past two decades—it wasn't until the 1970s that large numbers of married women with young children re-entered the workforce—for the most part, society has chosen to ignore the needs of these working families. The standard school day doesn't mesh with the typical nine-to-five work day and after-school childcare programs are in chronically short supply—a situation which forces the majority of working parents to scramble to find someone to take care of their children while they're at work.

Chapter 15

Unofficially...
A recent study conducted on behalf of the California Center for Health Improvement (CCHI) revealed that 77 percent of voters in the state were willing to pay higher taxes to fund after-school childcare programs—a clear indication of growing concern about the high number of juvenile crimes that are committed between 3:00 p.m. and 6:00 p.m.

While the situation continues to be dismal, there is good news for working parents. After years of neglect, the childcare issue is finally making its way on to the public agenda. In his recent State of the Union Address, President Clinton announced his intention to introduce a series of childcare-related reforms, the most noteworthy of which was a $60 million investment in after-school programs.

While this is good news to parents who are desperate to find after-school childcare for their children, these childcare spaces won't be available during this school year or possibly even the next—nor will there be as many spaces as there are kids who need them.

Clearly the onus for finding suitable after-school childcare arrangements will rest with parents for at least the foreseeable future. That, in a nutshell, is the focus of this chapter: equipping you with strategies designed to eliminate some of the worry of being a working parent.

Why it's so difficult to find after-school childcare

According to the U.S. Census Bureau, less than 15 percent of American children live in a household with a "working father" and a "stay-at-home" mother. This means that the majority of American children are in need of some form of after-school care. Some go to after-school programs at local schools or community centers. Others are cared for by family daycare providers. Still others are greeted by a parent who is wrapping up a few loose ends in the home office before switching back into parent mode. And then there are the so-called latchkey kids who are responsible for taking care of themselves—and possibly a younger sibling as well—until their parents walk through the front door.

Most American families use strategies like these to piece together some sort of after-school childcare arrangement. A large number of families rely on more than one type of childcare arrangement. The person responsible for caring for their children may vary from day to day, sometimes even hour to hour. Some days, Mom or Dad is on hand to meet the children as they get off the bus. Other days, the children head directly to a family daycare home or sports activity.

This is one of those situations when the numbers speak for themselves. The National Child Care Survey (1990) revealed that a full 76 percent of school-aged children who have a mother who works outside the home spend time in at least two childcare arrangements during a typical week, in addition to the time they spend in school.

There are three drawbacks to having more than one childcare arrangement:

- It can be difficult to make a series of part-time arrangements mesh together neatly enough to cover a full week's worth of care. What will you do if you're stuck with no one to care for your child on a Friday afternoon, period?

- Some children find it disruptive to be sent to different places on various days of the week. If you're relying on your child to transport himself there by school bus, mass-transporation (such as the subway or a city bus), taxi, or on foot, there's obviously an element of risk involved in having overly complicated arrangements. What will happen, for example, if your child gets off the school bus at the wrong place on the wrong day or can't figure out how to get home because his regular subway train has been rerouted?

- It's typically more expensive to piece together a variety of childcare arrangements than it is to find one that will cover the bulk of your childcare needs. You may pay a premium because you will be using less than five days of before- or after-school care per week.

While you might have a clear idea about what you're looking for in an after-school program, you might have difficulty finding anything suitable, particularly if you live in a small community or rural area. Despite the fact that there are an estimated 17 million American parents in need of after-school childcare, the chronic shortage of space continues. It's almost as if American society has not yet clued into the fact that the same children who require childcare spaces when they're infants, toddlers, and preschoolers don't instantly become capable of taking care of themselves the moment they enter kindergarten.

What the experts are saying about after-school childcare programs and latchkey kids

Given society's tendency to ignore the fact that there's a chronic shortage of childcare for school-aged children, you might mistakenly assume that older children don't require childcare the same way that younger children do.

Nothing could be further from the truth.

Study after study has shown that children who are left unsupervised when they are not in school are at significantly greater risk of skipping school, doing poorly on tests and assignments, and engaging in substance abuse and other risky

Moneysaver
Rather than paying for a formal after-school childcare arrangement, share childcare responsibilities with another family in your neighborhood. Shift your working hours so that one family is responsible for getting the children on the school bus in the morning and the other is responsible for meeting the bus at the end of the day.

behaviors. On the other hand, children who attend high-quality after-school programs have better relationships with their peers and to enjoy greater success at school.

Wondering what the after-school childcare market is really like and where—if at all—quality comes into play? Here are some basic facts drawn from the National Study of Before and After School Programs sponsored by the U.S. Department of Education, a survey of the operators of 1,300 after-school childcare programs nationwide:

■ In 1991, approximately 1.7 million school-aged children were enrolled in 49,500 formal before- and after-school programs. Seventy-one percent of these children attended programs that operated both before and after school.

■ Almost 80 percent of the costs of school-aged programs were paid by the parents themselves, with the remainder of the costs being picked up by various levels of government.

■ Two-thirds of after-school programs in the survey were nonprofit, and one-third were for-profit. Here's a breakdown of the numbers: 29 percent were operated by private daycare corporations; 19 percent by private, nonprofit organizations; 18 percent by public schools; 7 percent by private, nonprofit social service or youth service agencies; 6 percent by church or religious groups; 5 percent by state, county, or local government agencies; 3 percent by private schools; and 2 percent by other types of nonprofit organizations.

■ The average fee paid by parents was $2.89 per hour for before-school care and $1.96 per hour for after-school care.

- 80 percent of the programs offered such activities as socializing, free time, board or card games, reading, block building, physical play, and time for homework.

- Despite the fact that child development experts stress the importance of having separate programming for older and younger children, less than half of the facilities surveyed offered different programs to children in the two age groups.

- Only 25 percent of the programs reported having access to a playground or park on a regular basis.

You can read more about this important study at www.exnet.iastate.edu/Pages/nncc/SACC/sac34_nat.stud.sac1.html.

What children do during their nonschool hours has a tremendous impact on their personal and academic achievements over the long run. Studies have shown that children who are left unsupervised park themselves in front of the television set for hours at a time—a less than ideal use of their time during their formative years.

Unofficially...
According to the Carnegie Corporation of New York, one in four nine-year-olds watches television for five or more hours per day.

While most children watch some TV, television watching becomes a problem if a child is watching a large amount of TV each day (three hours per day or more). Research has shown that children who spend this much time watching TV are at increased risk of experiencing behavioral problems, exhibiting increased aggression, and having difficulty in learning to read.

Quantity isn't the only problem with television watching, however. There's also the issue of the quality of the programming that they're watching. Some of the shows that air in the late afternoon are anything but suitable for young children. In addition to watching reruns of sitcoms that were originally intended for an adult audience, your child, if left unsupervised, might tune in to shows that contain graphic scenes of violence—a situation that could lead to his becoming desensitized to violence over time or fearful about the world around him. You can find out more about the issue of children and TV violence—an important issue for any parent considering leaving children in their own care—at the American Academy of Child and Adolescent Psychiatry web site: http://www.aacap.org/web/aacap/factsFam/violence.htm.

Where to find after-school programs in your community

Although the research comes out strongly in favor of after-school programs, it can be anything but easy to find such an arrangement for your child.

You might have to do a bit of digging to find out what's available in your community and then be prepared to put your name on a waiting list for a space in one of the more popular programs.

Here are some places where you might find after-school childcare

- daycare centers
- family daycare homes
- public and private schools
- community centers
- recreational facilities (the YMCA)
- park and recreation departments
- religious institutions
- youth groups (Boys and Girls Clubs)
- tutoring services

- sports clubs
- theaters, art galleries, and other arts-related organizations

Watch Out!
Don't assume that the school-aged childcare program you're considering operates year-round or you could be in for a surprise. Some only operate during the school year while others are only offered during spring break or the summer months.

What to look for in an after-school childcare program

As with any type of childcare, there are good and not-so-good programs for school-aged children. Your job as a parent is to sidestep the poorer quality alternatives and zero in on the best possible after-school childcare arrangement for your child. The secret, as with anything else, is to know what to look for. Here are some more tips from the experts.

Survey says . . .

A study conducted in the early 1980s by researchers R. Baden, A. Genser, J. Levine, and M. Seligson concluded that the best childcare programs for school-aged children share certain characteristics. According to these researchers, you should look for a program that

- offers a safe environment that encourages optimal development
- employs a sufficient number of qualified, well-trained staff
- is administered effectively
- encourages staff-parent interaction
- balances activities to include structured and unstructured time, teacher-directed and child-initiated experiences, and a range of activities
- capitalizes on the interests of the children and provides opportunities for informal play
- uses community resources as much as possible (recreation facilities, libraries, and so on)

- communicates clear, consistent expectations and limits to children
- provides indoor and outdoor spaces for active play as well as places for socialization and private time

Evaluating your options

You should plan to visit as many after-school childcare programs as possible in an effort to find one that's just right for your child. Here are some points you might want to consider as you go about evaluating your various options:

- What ages of children is the program designed for? Is your child at the upper or lower end of this age range or somewhere in the middle? Is this a problem?
- Are children of different ages divided into separate groups?
- How many children are in each group?
- What are the program's hours of operation? How do the hours compare to your working hours? Does the program run all day on days when your child's school is closed? Does it operate during the summer months?
- How will your child get to the program? Is it within walking distance of his home or school or will transportation be required? Is the school bus driver willing to drop him off at the program, or is that against the bus company's policy?
- If transportation will be required, does the childcare program provide it? If so, is the transportation arrangement acceptable to you?

Bright Idea
Some food for thought as you're evaluating a particular after-school childcare arrangement: Children spend less than 20 percent of their waking hours in school. This is because schools are typically open less than half the days of the year and, even when they are open, they are open only until mid-afternoon.

Bright Idea
You can find out more about "out-of-school time" (the academic world's term for the care that school-aged children receive during their non-school hours) by contacting the National Institute on Out-of-School Time, Center for Research on Women, 106 Central Street, Wellesley, MA 02181-8259 (781) 283-2547 Web site: http://www. wellesley.edu/ WCW/CRW/SAC/

- Is there an additional fee for transportation or is it included in the basic program fee?

- What types of qualifications do staff members have? Are they highly trained early childhood education professionals? College students? High school students?

- Are the staff actively involved with the children in their care?

- Do they treat the children with respect?

- Do they help the children without taking control?

- Do they have realistic expectations of the children in their care?

- Do they enjoy their work?

- Do they understand the unique challenges of caring for school-aged children?

- Do the staff-child ratios and group sizes allow staff members to meet the children's needs?

- Would the staffing levels be adequate in the event of an emergency?

- Do the staff work with the families in their care to make the transition from home to school to childcare go as smoothly as possible?

- Do they make the parents and children feel welcome?

- Have they been trained to handle a variety of different types of emergency situations?

- Is the rate of staff turnover high or low?

- Is the space large enough to allow children to enjoy a range of different activities?

- Are different types of activities offered or are all of the activities of the same basic type (i.e., active play vs. quiet play)?

- Is there a quiet place where older children can do their homework?

- Are there activities suited to children at varying skill levels and ages?

- Are there adequate quantities of play materials?

- Can the children get the materials out and put them away by themselves?

- Are there comfortable spaces where children who have been in large group settings all day can relax and enjoy a few moments of privacy?

- Is the room comfortable? Is it kept at an appropriate temperature? Is it well ventilated? Is the lighting suitable?

- Is the room accessible to children with disabilities?

- Is there an outdoor play area? If so, is it large enough to accommodate the number of children in the program? Is it suitable for the ages of children being cared for in the program? Does it include safe challenges for those with special needs?

- Is the daily schedule flexible? Does it give children the opportunity to relax and let off steam after a busy day at school?

- Is the emphasis on playing or learning? How do you and your child feel about this emphasis?

- Can children move from one activity to another at their own pace?

- Are the children encouraged to plan their own activities?

- Are there any observable health or safety hazards?

Bright Idea
Some of the most effective programs encourage the children to plan menus, organize games and other activities, and set their own rules.

- Does the program serve healthy foods?
- Is food served at times when the children are hungry?
- How are food allergies handled?
- Are the program fees affordable?
- How long has the program been running?
- Is it licensed and accredited?

You can learn a lot about the challenges of programming for school-aged children by reading "Programming Tips for School-Age Children" at www.exnet.iastate.edu/Pages/nncc/SACC/sac41_program.tip.sac.html.

While the article is written for caregivers, you can get a sense of what a top-quality after-school program should be like.

"Home alone" (a.k.a. "self-care")

If you don't decide to seek out formal after-school care (or if your search for such an arrangement is unsuccessful), you might consider either having your child take care of herself or having her older sibling take care of her until you get home from work. Obviously, this arrangement won't work if your child is very young (i.e., under the age of 12) or if your older child is incapable of handing the responsibility of caring for herself.

If you decide to go this route, you'll certainly find yourself in good company. A recent study by the National Institute on Out-of-School Time indicated that 35 percent of 12-year-olds are responsible for caring for themselves after school, as compared to less than five percent of eight year olds.

That said, before you decide to allow your child to take care of himself after school, you should

Bright Idea
The National Association for the Education of Young Children (NAEYC) operates an accreditation program for childcare centers that care for children up to the age of eight. You can find out more about the NAEYC accreditation program by contacting National Association for the Education of Young Children (NAEYC) 1509 16th Street, NW Washington, DC 20036-1426 (800) 424-2460 or (202) 232-8777 Web site: http://www.naeyc.org/naeyc/

assess his readiness by considering the following questions:

- Does your child know his full name, address, and phone number (including area code)? Can he provide this information to rescue personnel in the event of an emergency?

- Does he know what number(s) to call in the event of an emergency? Are these numbers both programmed into and posted by the phone?

- Is he mature enough to carry his house key discreetly (in his pocket or on a chain under his shirt)? Does he understand the importance of keeping the key with him at all times and never lending it to anyone?

- Does he know how to answer the telephone and door appropriately?

- Will he remember to keep the doors locked at all times?

- Does he know how to disarm and reactivate the security system? Does he understand the importance of not sharing the code with anyone other than family members?

- Does he know how to use a fire extinguisher?

- Does he understand the importance of not letting others know that he is home alone?

- Can he be trusted to follow some basic ground rules when you're not there to supervise him (checking in with a neighbor at the same time each day to report that he has arrived home safely)?

- How well as he coped when he has been left alone for short periods of time? Was he scared or relatively comfortable?

- Is there a neighbor nearby who is always at home during the hours when your child is alone? If so, would he or she be willing to help your child in the case of an emergency? Would your child feel comfortable asking this person for help?

The ground rules

Bright Idea
Conduct a safety check of your home before you leave your child home alone. Make sure that

- the furnace, hot water heater, and major appliances are in good working order

- there is a flashlight and spare batteries

- the locks on all doors and windows work properly

- medications have been locked away

- guns and ammunition are stored separately and kept under lock and key

If your child ends up spending part of his day caring for himself, you will need to establish some ground rules for him to follow. Make sure you spell out clear policies about

- visits from friends

- watching television

- homework

- answering the door or phone

- playing outside or at friends' houses

- using appliances (particularly the stove or microwave)

- dealing with disputes with his brothers and sisters

You might also want to find out if there are any telephone reassurance lines (special hotlines that children can call if they need reassurance or advice while they are at home alone) or Block Association Parent programs (a network of trained volunteers who make their homes available to children in the event of an emergency) in your community. Knowing that there are other people whom your child can turn to for assistance might make you feel more comfortable about allowing him to be at home alone.

Want to find out more? Read "At Home, Alone" on the Child and Family Web site: www.cfc-efc/

docs/00000366.htm. Visit "The ABCs of Self-Care" on the Whirlpool HomeLife Network web site (www. WhirlpoolCorp.com/family/self.html), and read a seven-part series called "The Hours We Can't Be Home" on the School-Age Child Care page of the National Network for Child Care: www.exnet.iastate. edu/Pages/nncc/SACC/sacc.page.html.

Brotherly love?

An alternative to formal after-school childcare programs for families with more than one child is to have the older child take care of the younger child.

While this arrangement works well for some families, it's nothing short of disastrous for others. In some instances, children have been arrested for assaulting or—in a few rare cases—even killing their siblings while their parents were at work.

Before you decide to leave your child in the care of his older brother or sister, you need to consider

- whether the older child is actually interested in taking on the job of caring for the younger child

- whether the two of them tend to get along relatively well

- whether the younger child would be willing to be supervised by the older child

- whether you are willing to pay the older child for this service (the going rate for babysitters her age) or offer her some other form of compensation for taking on this added duty

- whether your older child is reliable enough to be entrusted with this responsibility

- how much the arrangement would cut into the older child's social life, homework time, and so on

Timesaver
Here's a quick and easy way to get the lowdown on leaving your child on his own. Write to the Whirlpool HomeLife Network to request these three free brochures: "Assessing Your Child's Readiness for Self-Care," "Preparing Your Child For Self-Care," and "Finding Quality After-School Care for Your Child." The address is Whirlpool HomeLife Network, Project Home Safe Brochures, P.O. Box 405, St. Joseph, MI 49085. Send a business-sized, self-addressed, stamped envelope.

- what ground rules you would need to establish to make the arrangement work (whether the children would be allowed to have friends over or play outside while they are home alone)

One quick note before I move on: Your older child is more likely to be willing to care for his younger brother or sister if it's only a part-time arrangement. It's one thing to agree to care for him one or two afternoons a week. It's quite another to be saddled with that responsibility day after day.

Other solutions

If you're feeling a little discouraged by the limited number of options out there, you're certainly not alone. According to the National Institute on Out-of-School Time, an estimated five million school-aged children in America spend time without adult supervision during a typical week. What's more, those families that do manage to find after-school childcare often have to settle for less than the ideal.

Unfortunately, with the number of two-income families increasing at a far faster rate than the number of childcare spaces being made available for school-aged children, it's a situation that's likely to get worse before it gets better. In fact, the U.S. General Accounting Office estimates that by the year 2002, there will only be enough childcare spaces for school-aged children in certain urban areas to meet 25 percent of the demand.

This is one area where parents need to band together to work on finding ways to give their children adequate care while they're at work. Here are some practical steps you can take to help address the shortage of after-school childcare spaces in your community:

- Volunteer to survey parents at your child's school to determine whether there's sufficient interest in an onsite after-school childcare program. A growing number of schools are deciding to go this route. You can find both practical advice and a detailed needs-assessment form that you can modify to fit your own needs at www.exnet.iastate.edu/Pages/nncc/SACC/hours1.html.

- Compare notes with other parents and see if they would be willing to share the cost of hiring a permanent part-time caregiver. Because domestic agencies typically charge $10 to $15 per hour for the services of a qualified part-time caregiver, it makes sense to share this expense with other families on your street if they're in similar need of after-school childcare.

- Find out if your employer would let you to shift your hours or work from home for a portion of the day in order to eliminate your need for after-school care. If he agrees to this type of solution even one or two days each week, that's that many days less that you have to scramble for care.

- Contact Child Care Aware at 1-800-424-2246 or your local Child Care Resource and Referral Agency to find out more about the state of childcare in your community. If you're dissatisfied with what you discover, write letters to local and state politicians and call the local media to alert them to the problem.

- Drop by the Thomas Web site to find out what the federal government is doing about the entire childcare issue. Thomas—named in honor of Thomas Jefferson—is located at http://thomas.loc.gov. You can find out what bills are on the floor, how various representatives have voted, and what bills have received or are expected to receive action in the next week. You can even check up on the track record of your member of Congress when it comes to childcare or inquire about the status of a particular childcare bill by visiting http://thomas.loc.gov/home/r105query.html and using the online search engine.

Just the facts

- There is a chronic shortage of childcare for school-aged children, particularly in rural areas.

- Studies have shown that children who have the opportunity to participate in high-quality after-school programs experience a number of social and academic benefits. Latchkey children, on the other hand, are thought to be at increased risk of experiencing social and academic difficulties.

- Childcare programs for school-aged children are offered by a variety of different community organizations, but the demand continues to exceed the supply.

- Because childcare programs for school-aged children tend to be in short supply, some children are responsible for caring for themselves, while others are responsible for caring for a younger sibling.

- Parents need to band together to work on finding ways of ensuring that their children receive adequate care while they're at work.

Happily Ever After?

PART VII

GET THE SCOOP ON...
What work and family programs are ▪ Job
sharing ▪ Flextime ▪ Telecommuting ▪ Childcare-
related benefits ▪ Family leave packages ▪
Other work and family programs ▪ Why work and
family programs benefit everyone ▪ How to
approach your employer ▪ Other ways to reduce
the stress of being a working parent

Reducing the Stress of Being a Working Parent

A recent study by the Family and Work Institute of New York revealed that 87 per-cent of the 3,381 U.S. workers surveyed had some type of family responsibility that occa-sionally interfered with work.

Another study by the Work/Life Group, a national consulting firm that specializes in work and family issues, found that one-third of worker absences are caused by the need to care for sick chil-dren.

The results of these two studies hammer home what any working parent can tell you: There's a con-stant tug of war between work and family.

In recent years, forward-thinking companies have started to recognize that helping employees balance the conflicting demands of work and family is good for the bottom line. These types of policies help to increase productivity and reduce turnover. They also help to attract a better caliber of applicant, according to Rosanna Z. Milley, a principal at the Apex Management Group in Princeton, New Jersey. "The hot benefits area is work/family opportunities," she recently told Worth Online. (You can read the rest of the article at www.worth.com/articles/Z9403A08.html.)

With turnover rates on the increase—they jumped to 1.2 percent per month from 0.9 percent between 1996 and 1997, according to a recent report by the Bureau of National Affairs—work-and-family benefits are expected to become one of the most valuable tools for retaining workers.

Bright Idea
If your company is too small to offer work-and-family benefits, such as onsite childcare, see if your employer would be willing to team up with other area employers to underwrite the costs of a shared childcare facility. According to Ellen Bankert, director of corporate partners with the Center for Work and Family at Boston College, these types of partnerships are becoming increasingly more common.

What work and family programs are

Some human resource consultants call them work and family programs. Others prefer trendier terms, like worklife or lifecycle programs. Regardless of what they call them in your particular workplace, everyone's talking about the same thing: programs that make it a little easier for employees to juggle the competing demands of work and family.

While the specifics of work and family programs vary from workplace to workplace, for the most part, these programs can be classified into five types:

- job sharing
- flextime
- telecommuting
- childcare programs
- other types of work and family programs

If you've read about these programs in the newspaper or seen them profiled on evening newsmagazines, you might very well conclude that work and family programs are the best thing to hit the modern-day workplace since the office coffee pot. While there's a lot of good to be said about many of these programs, they also have their downsides as well. Let's look at the pros and cons of each of these programs.

Job sharing

Job sharing enables two or more part-time employees to share one full-time position. It's particularly popular with women with young children who are seeking an alternative to working full-time or giving up their jobs entirely.

While some job-sharing employees prefer to split each working day in half (each partner works a half day), a more common way to divide up the work week is to either split the work week down the middle (one partner works Monday, Tuesday, and half-day Wednesday, and the other partner works the remaining days of the week) or to work some sort of alternate day schedule (the first partner works Monday-Wednesday-Friday one week and then Tuesday-Thursday the next, and the other partner works the opposite hours).

While the advantages of job sharing are obvious, there are also some important disadvantages. Let's consider each in turn:

Pros:

- You have more time to spend with your child.

- You can use some of your nonworking hours to take care of household tasks that might otherwise get crammed into the evenings, thereby reducing your overall stress level.

Cons:

- You might have a hard time finding childcare because it's much more difficult to find

Watch Out!
Choose your job-sharing partner with care. Look for someone who is good at her job, hard-working, and likely to pull her weight. After all, the last thing you want is to get stuck trying to pick up the pieces for someone who is disorganized, error-prone, or just plain lazy.

part-time childcare than full-time childcare—particularly if your working hours fluctuate from week to week.

Bright Idea
Create a log book that can be passed back and forth between you and your job-sharing partner. Use it to record information about policy changes, customer or supplier problems, and other important issues that arise at work so that neither of you will be left out of the loop.

- Your paycheck will be chopped in half and your benefits package may either be trimmed or eliminated altogether—something that you need to give some serious thought to before deciding to job share.

- You could be forced to work full-time again—or change jobs—if your job-sharing partner quits and a suitable replacement can't be found. You could be thrown for a similar loop if she were off work having a baby, so make sure you know if she's planning to add to her family in the near future.

- You could be left out of the loop when it comes to important developments at work.

- Your employer may expect you to fill in at the last minute if your job-sharing partner is ill. Unless you have an incredibly flexible caregiver, you're unlikely to be able to make it into the office with little or no notice.

- Job-sharing could be a career-limiter, particularly if part-time employers in your workplace are perceived as being less committed than their full-time counterparts. This was more of a concern five to ten years ago than it is today, but it can still be an issue in some workplaces.

Flextime

Flextime is just what it sounds like: a flexible working arrangement. Rather than working from 9:00 a.m. to 5:00 p.m., you might work from 7:00 a.m. to 3:00 p.m. or 10:00 a.m. to 6:00 p.m.—whatever best suits your schedule.

According to a recent study by Catalyst—a New York-based research institute—flextime tops the wish list for most American workers.

Here are the pros and cons:

Pros:

- You can adjust your hours to better fit the needs of your family. You might, for example, choose to start work early or late so that you can split before- and after-school childcare duties with either your partner or a neighbor.

- If you put in more than your standard eight hour shift on a given day, your employer might allow you to bank additional hours and use them at some future date. Banked time comes in handy if your child is ill, you need to take him to the doctor, and so on.

Cons:

- Flextime isn't always totally flexible. There may be certain core hours when you're required to be in the office (for example, 10:00 a.m. to 2:00 p.m., for example). Make sure you understand these rules upfront. Otherwise, they could become a source of conflict between you and your employer.

- Your customers, suppliers, and colleagues may become frustrated if they don't have a clear idea of when you'll be in the office next. While your schedule may seem logical to you, don't expect others to remember it. Instead, record the details of your schedule in your voice mail system so that this information can be accessed quickly and easily by others.

Telecommuting

Telecommuting means staying in touch with your office by phone, fax, and e-mail while you work from home. The majority of companies that permit employees to telecommute require them to travel to the office from time to time (once every week or so seems to be the norm), but these employees work from the comforts of their own home offices the majority of the time.

Pros:

- Telecommuting helps to reduce your travel time and expenses (unless, of course, you have to drive your child to a daycare center on the other side of town).

- It can help you to solve some of your family's childcare problems by ensuring that you're available when your children need you (for example, when they get off the school bus).

Cons:

- You will still need childcare. Don't make the mistake of assuming that you can care for your children while you work. You can't be a good parent and a good employee at the same time. As I mentioned back in Chapter 14, if you try to work and care for your child at the same time, something (or someone) will suffer.

- Telecommuting is a downright bad idea if you've got workaholic tendencies. While you might only plan to spend a few minutes working on a client's file while you enjoy your after-dinner coffee, you could very well look up three hours later and realize you never did get around to helping your partner with the dinner dishes.

Watch Out!
Accidents can and do happen when there are children around, so make sure you set up your home office in a spot that's safely removed from the day-to-day chaos of over-turned juice bottles, half-eaten jelly sandwiches, and so on. Otherwise, you could find yourself in the rather embarrassing situation of trying to explain how the financial statements for one of your biggest clients were transformed into paper dolls by the budding artist at your house.

- It's easy to miss out on important developments at work—everything from important policy changes and office politics to news and gossip about your co-workers.

- You might be expected to buy some of your own office equipment in exchange for the opportunity to work at home. Make sure you understand these expectations upfront. Otherwise, you could find yourself scrambling to purchase a fax machine, new software, a new computer, filing cabinets, and other expensive office paraphernalia.

- Your customers, suppliers, and co-workers might find your telecommuting arrangement disruptive. This is probably the largest hurdle you'll have to overcome in making the arrangement work for you and your company. In fact, your boss is unlikely to be willing to let you try telecommuting unless you can convince him that you've managed to come up with some workable solutions to this particular problem.

Childcare-related benefits

One of the most common reasons for employees being absent from work is a breakdown in childcare arrangements. Because childcare is a major problem for many employees, most work and family programs attempt to address the childcare issue.

There are four types of childcare-related programs:

- onsite daycare services
- emergency daycare services
- childcare subsidy programs
- daycare referral programs.

Unofficially...
According to a recent report in *Fortune* magazine, 25 percent of employees with children under the age of 12 reported experiencing breakdowns in childcare two to five times in a three-month period.

Because there are advantages and disadvantages to each of these types of programs, let's consider each in turn, starting with the best of all childcare programs, onsite daycare services.

Onsite daycare services

According to a recent article in the *New York Times*, there are about 8,000 onsite daycare centers in the U.S., up from 200 in 1982.

Some of these daycare centers are operated by a single employer for the exclusive use of its employees—as is the case with the Northern Trust Company in Chicago. According to Women's Wire (www.womenswire.com), the company runs shuttle buses every fifteen minutes between its accredited daycare center and its corporate headquarters.

Others are operated by one or more companies, as is the case with The Kid Company, a daycare center in Tupelo, Mississippi that is cooperatively operated for the benefit of employees of a local newspaper, manufacturer, trust company, and bank.

These are the key advantages and disadvantages of using onsite daycare services:

Pros:

- The biggest argument in favor of onsite daycare arrangements is sheer convenience. Rather than making a pit-stop at a daycare center or family daycare home on your way to work, you and your child head to the office together.

- It can be reassuring to have your children close by—particularly if you're a first-time parent. If your baby needs to be breastfed or your toddler comes down with a fever, you're only a few steps away.

- Because your children and your co-workers' children are likely to be cared for together, the daycare center may take on a warm, family atmosphere.

- It's typically easier to find a childcare space in a daycare center operated by your employer than in any other type of daycare center because your employer has a vested interest in finding care for your child. In most cases, employees get first dibs on any spots that open up.

- You're less likely to pay full market value for a spot in an onsite daycare center than in a daycare center that is located somewhere else other than your workplace. Most employers pick up part or all of the childcare tab for their employees.

- Onsite daycare is of higher-than-average quality because your employer's reputation in on the line.

Cons:

- You might lose your space in an onsite daycare center if you decided to seek employment elsewhere. Some onsite daycare centers are operated exclusively for the use of employees and their families; others, however, accept children whose parents are employed elsewhere if and when spaces become available.

Emergency childcare services

Because it is expensive to offer onsite daycare services, many employers look for other less costly ways of assisting their employees with the issue of childcare. One common solution is to provide in-home care services for employees who have children who are too sick to go to daycare or whose childcare arrangements have fallen through because their caregivers are ill.

Watch Out!
If your employer pays childcare expenses on your behalf or provides you with a space in an onsite daycare center, be sure to declare the value of this benefit on your income tax return. Otherwise, you could find yourself in hot water with the IRS.

Here are some examples of innovative emergency childcare programs:

- Employees of Eddie Bauer in Redmond, Washington, have access to emergency childcare services through two local nursing agencies.

- Penn State University staff are able to take advantage of "snowcare" in the event that their children's schools are closed because of inclement weather. Parents can call ahead to reserve one of 60 subsidized spaces for children from birth to twelve years of age.

- Hewitt Associates, a Dallas-based consulting firm, reimburses employees for childcare required when they are away overnight on business.

Pros:

- Emergency childcare services enable you to go to the office if your childcare arrangement falls apart at the last minute.

- Because these services are typically provided at your employer's expense, you're not forced to pay for childcare twice to make it to the office. (As you may recall, most daycare centers and family daycare homes require that you pay for days when your child is ill. If you then have to pay for backup care, you are, in effect, paying for two childcare spaces for that day, even though you can only use one.)

Cons:

- You're unlikely to know the emergency childcare provider and may feel uncomfortable about leaving your child with a complete stranger.

- You may feel guilty about not being there when your child is not feeling well.

- You may feel pressured to take advantage of your employer's emergency childcare services, even if you would rather stay home to attend to your child.

Childcare subsidy programs

Another childcare-related benefit offered by some companies is childcare subsidies. Rather than getting into the childcare business themselves, many corporations prefer to either reimburse their employees for a portion of their childcare expenses or reserve a block of childcare spaces at an area childcare center and then subsidize the cost of these spaces so that they can make them available to their employees for less than market value. (Sometimes the company can obtain a discount on the cost of each childcare space by "buying in bulk"—and then can pass this savings along to its employees.)

Pros:

- Childcare subsidies reduce the amount of money you are required to pay out of your own pocket for childcare.

Cons:

- You might be required to enroll your child in a particular daycare center to take advantage of your employer's childcare subsidy program.

- There may be a limit to the amount of childcare subsidy available to you. In other words, your employer might be willing to subsidize the cost of care for one or two of your children, but not three or four.

- If your employer offers a cafeteria-style benefits package (one that allows you to pick and choose which types of benefits you would like to have), you may lose out on another type of benefit by choosing to take advantage of your employer's childcare subsidy program.

Childcare referral services

Perhaps the most cost-effective childcare-related benefit involves offering childcare referral services. Typically, a company will contract the services of a work and family company consultant who will assist employees in researching their childcare options. Eldercare referral services are frequently offered as well.

Pros:

- It can be a relief to have someone share the stressful and time-consuming task of finding childcare for your child.

Cons:

- You need to be explicit about your family's wants and needs when it comes to childcare—something that can be time-consuming in and of itself.

- There's no guarantee that the consultant can find a suitable childcare arrangement for your child. That will be determined by supply, demand, and the types of arrangements you're willing to consider.

- You can't delegate responsibility for making the final decision about childcare, even if you wanted to do so.

Family leave packages

A study conducted by the Families and Work Institute in the early 1990s indicated that women are far more likely to return to their jobs after childbirth

Unofficially...
Toy manufacturer Mattel Inc. added emergency care to its daycare center after a survey found that breakdowns in childcare were costing the company the equivalent of two working years— 568 lost days— annually for its workforce of 1,200. Source: Work and Family Connection, Inc.

if they have parental leave. The study found that while 94 percent of women with parental leave returned to their company after childbirth, only 43 percent of women without parental leave benefits did so.

This helps to explain why a growing number of companies are choosing to offer this type of benefit to their employees.

The Family Medical Leave Act, incidentally, applies to fathers as well as mothers, which means that parents can take family leave at different times. The beauty of this arrangement is that a child gets all the advantages of spending time with both Mom and Dad during his or her first year of life. (The Family Medical Leave Act also applies to adoption.) Here are the pros and cons of family leave packages from an employee's perspective:

Pros:

- An extended family leave package lets you to recover from childbirth and, should you decide to breastfeed your baby, ensures that breast-feeding is well-established before you have to return to work.

- It also gives you the opportunity to enjoy your baby before returning to the chaos of everyday living.

Cons:

- You might not qualify for your employer's extended family leave package, something that's likely to be a problem if you've only been with the company for a short period of time or you work part-time hours.

- Your leave might be unpaid—something that might prevent you from taking advantage of the opportunity to be at home with your baby for an extended period of time.

Other work and family programs

There are also a variety of other types of work and family programs that are designed to take some of the stress of juggling your conflicting responsibilities. Some of these are fairly expensive (for example, offering an onsite fitness facility so that you can work off some of your stress over your lunch hours), but programs don't have to be expensive to be effective.

Here are some types of programs that could be introduced in your workplace for little or no cost at all:

- Your employer might make a certain room available to nursing mothers who need to pump breastmilk for their babies. The room doesn't have to be like the Taj Mahal; it simply needs to be clean and private.

- Your employer might decide to designate one or more parking spaces near the front door for women in their third trimester of pregnancy—a much-appreciated perk if it's 90°F outside and you're eight-and-a-half-months pregnant.

- Your employer might invite a public health nurse in to offer seminars on such parenting-related issues as breastfeeding and discipline.

- Your employer might offer other types of general wellness programs. According to Work and Family Connections Inc., one U.S. corporation brings a chef into the workplace every other month to teach employees how to prepare delicious and easy meals for their families. Employees at Cigna Corporation pay a small fee

Moneysaver
If you're planning to have another child in another year or two, start saving a percentage of your salary now so that you will have some funds to draw on while you're on unpaid or partially paid leave.

to participate in classes on such topics as "Healthy Barbecuing" and "Heart Smart Cuisine."

■ Your employer might start an onsite lending library full of parenting-related materials: everything from childbirth videos to books on coping with your teen. Some of these materials could be acquired through donations (from employees who no longer need them), while others could be purchased by the employer or through the fundraising efforts of employees.

Why work and family programs benefit everyone

Up until now, I've been focusing on what you can expect to gain from various work and family programs. But that's only part of the picture. Study after study has shown that work and family programs aren't just good for employees, they're also good for business.

Here are just a few of the benefits that companies experience after introducing work and family programs:

Reduced turnover
Research has shown that employees stick with companies that offer work and family programs.

Reducing turnover can save a company a considerable amount of money because training is often one of a company's most significant expenses. Studies have shown that it's not unusual to spend $50,000 or more training a replacement for a middle manager who's moved on to another position.

Reduced absenteeism
Employees in workplaces with comprehensive work and family programs make it to work more often

> 66
>
> We used to think you could separate the soft stuff from the hard stuff. The soft stuff was our commitment to the workforce and the hard stuff—what really mattered—was getting pants out the door. No more. Now we know that you can't get stuff out the door unless your employees are 100% committed and free of home life distractions. And the way you get them there is simple. You do everything you can to help them handle those home life issues. So work and family can co-exist, successfully.
> —Levi Strauss Chairman Robert Haas, quoted in *Work and Family Policies: A Win-Win Formula for Business and Society,* a report by Robert MacGregor of the Minnesota Center for Corporate Responsibility
>
> 99

than employees in workplaces that lack these programs.

Certain work and family programs (for example, job sharing, flextime, and extended family leave programs) make it easier for women to breastfeed their babies. Because breastfed babies are less likely to become ill than bottlefed babies, offering breast-feeding-friendly policies helps to reduce the number of days that employees are away from work.

Other work and family programs (emergency childcare services and flextime) make it easier for employees to meet their responsibilities to their employers while simultaneously coping with problems that have arisen on the home front. They can, for example, arrange to have a sick child cared for by an emergency childcare service provider so that they can make it into the office, or they can choose to stay home with that child, drawing on the hours they have banked under the company's flextime program.

Reduced health-care costs

Certain work and family programs have been linked to a reduction in health-care claims. According to a recent article in *Parenting* magazine, after Sunbeam Oster Household Products began paying pregnant workers at its Coushatta, Louisiana plant to attend maternity classes twice a week, the self-insured plant's average medical costs per birth dropped from $27,000 in 1984 to $3,500 in 1990, and there were no more premature births.

Reduced office costs

Some work and family programs, like telecommuting, help to reduce a company's overall operating expenses by reducing the amount of space it needs to provide to its employees. If a high percentage of employees work from home on a regular basis, there are that many fewer square feet of office space required to house them.

Improved morale and productivity

Work and family programs can also help to boost employee morale. Employees feel valued and have the sense that their employer cares about them and their families. Not surprisingly, they're more likely to want to work hard for an employer who seems to care about their overall well-being.

Productivity also gets a boost for a second reason: Employees have less to worry about. Rather than spending time on the phone trying to find a suitable childcare arrangement for their preschooler or monitoring the goings-on at home when their older children arrive home from school, employees can focus on their jobs because they know that everything's fine on the homefront.

How to approach your employer

If you would like to see some family-friendly policies introduced in your workplace, here are some tips on approaching your employer:

- Do your homework first. Figure out what concerns your boss may have about implementing various types of programs and find a way to address those concerns

- Convince him that introducing these types of programs will enable employees to fulfil their job responsibilities as well as ever—if not better. Show him how working from home will eliminate the countless impromptu meetings that take place at the office, thereby boosting your work group's overall productivity.

Unofficially...
According to the American Management Association, companies that have introduced flexible scheduling options have seen rates of absenteeism cut by as much as 50 percent.
Cited in *Work and Family Policies: A Win-Win Formula for Business and Society,* a report by Robert MacGregor of the Minnesota Center for Corporate Responsibility.

Bright Idea
Suggest some ways that your boss can monitor your performance while you are working from home. Offer to submit a daily activity log or to write up a short report at the end of each week indicating how you've used your time.

- Ensure that implementing your ideas won't add to his workload. Do what you can to make the entire process hassle-free for him. Ask him if he would like you to research what's involved in implementing certain types of work and family programs—and offer to do this on your own time.

- Tackle the cost factor head-on. Instead of trying to pretend that work and family programs don't cost much to operate, acknowledge that they can be expensive to establish, but they're likely to result in considerable savings over the long run. If you need some ammunition to bolster your case, send him over to www.childrennow. org/action/busienss.html. The article at this address not only makes a good moral case for introducing work and family programs; it also makes a good economic case as well.

- Show that your co-workers support the idea. You might want to conduct a workplace survey to find out how many people support the idea of introducing a program such as flextime or job sharing. If you go this route, you'll want to measure both the percentage of people who would like to participate in such a program themselves as well as the number of people who support the idea of having this option available to others in the workplace.

- Demonstrate that introducing a particular program won't prevent the company from meeting its customers' needs. That, for many managers, is the most important issue.

- Ask your employer if it would be possible to introduce a particular program on a trial basis. While it's obviously not possible to temporarily start an onsite childcare center, other work and family programs can be piloted initially to ensure that they meet the needs of all concerned. Your boss may be more willing to agree to a six month trial run of a flextime program than to give his consent to having it introduced on a permanent basis.

Other ways to reduce the stress of being a working parent

If you can't get your employer to buy into the idea of introducing work and family programs, you can either decide to accept the status quo or exit stage left.

Working within the status quo

If you decide to remain in your current position, you'll want to look for ways that you can reduce your overall stress level—with or without your boss' co-operation.

Here are a few tried-and-true strategies that have worked for other families:

- Re-evaluate your career strategy. It's difficult to make great strides up the corporate ladder and raise three young children at the same time. Try to map out a career strategy that takes into account your responsibilities on both the home and work front. For some women, this means turning down promotions that would massively add to their stress level while their children are very young. For others, it means postponing the decision to have children until their careers are well-established. Only you can come up with a strategy that takes into account your personal and professional needs.

> 66
> When we talk about childcare, we're talking about someone's heart and soul. Industries have to find a way to convince working women to come back into the workforce. The only way is to take care of their needs, and that's good quality childcare for many.
> —Rachel Gill of Corporate Child Care Inc., quoted in a recent article in the *Mississippi Business Journal*
> 99

- Prioritize. You can't do everything for everyone, so chop a few items off your to do list at home. Give up your Martha Stewart-like housekeeping standards. Learn to live with the guilt that comes from buying store-bought cookies. Refuse to coordinate the local animal shelter fundraiser until your children get a little older. Do whatever it takes to bring your stress level back down into the sanity zone.

Timesaver
Too busy to socialize with your friends? Start a collective kitchen. By getting together to cook large batches of such staples as spaghetti sauce and chili, you can stock your freezer with nutritious and easily prepared meals while enjoying time together.

- Delegate. If a job's worth doing, it's worth getting someone else to do it. While there are certain jobs you wouldn't dream of delegating (like throwing around a football with your partner and child), there are some you could probably learn to live without. Unless you derive a great deal of pleasure and emotional satisfaction from house-cleaning or cutting the grass, hire someone else to do these jobs for you. If anything, you'll get the satisfaction of knowing that you're doing what you can to keep a neighborhood teenager gainfully employed.

- Plan ahead. Most parents agree that the worst part of the day is the period between the time you arrrive home from work and the time when you sit down to dinner. It's when your children are most in need of your attention—and when you're least able to give it. Not only are you tired after spending a harried day at the office, or doing the late-afternoon childcare run; you're also trying to whip together a semi-nutritious dinner. You can reduce the stress level in your household by having a stockpile of frozen entrées on hand that can be whipped into the microwave at the last minute.

■ To thine own self be true. You can't give to other people unless you're taking good care of yourself. Make sure that you set aside a few moments each day for yourself—even if that means ignoring the six loads of laundry that are competing for your attention.

Exiting stage left

If your employer won't budge on the work and family issue and you're at your wit's end, perhaps the time has come to move on. If this is the situation in which you find yourself, you have three choices:

■ finding another job

■ starting your own business

■ deciding to leave the paid work force altogether

Finding another job is never easy, particularly if you have to squeeze in job interviews over your lunch hour or make excuses to your employer about those mysterious phone calls you keep getting from prospective employers. But if it means reducing your stress level, it's certainly worth the effort. Just make sure that your new employer will be more willing to accommodate the needs of your family than your present employer has proven to be. Otherwise, you could find yourself trading one set of problems for another.

Working from home is another possible solution—provided you know what you're getting yourself into. Being self-employed is an entirely different ball game than working for someone else: You may not be up to the task. Because it can take months—even years—for a new business to start turning a profit, you could find yourself working without a pay check for at least the foreseeable future. What's more, your childcare problems won't just go away: If anything, they might get worse since you'll likely be searching for that rarest of options—a quality part-time childcare arrangement. You can get the low-down on self-employment by checking out the huge selection of links on Village's Work From Home page: www.ivillage.com/work/.

And then there's the final option: deciding to leave the paid labor force altogether. If you feel that your life is spinning out of control because it's too much to cope with the competing demands of work and family, this might look like the best solution of all—assuming, of course, that your family can afford to lose your income. Before you decide to go this route, read what marriage and family therapist Dr. Gayle Peterson has to say on the subject: http://www.parentsplace.com/cgi-bin/objects/family/family98.data.

Bright Idea
Seek out a mentor who can provide you with practical advice on balancing the needs of your family with the demands of your career.

Whatever you decide to do, make sure that the decisions you make are ones that you can live with for at least the foreseeable future. There's no point, after all, of quitting a full-time job in favor of a part-time one if you need full-time wages to pay your mortgage. Nor is it advisable to decide to stay at home full-time with your children if you're likely to be bored and resentful the moment the novelty wears off. You owe it to yourself and your family to make a decision that will be right for all of you over the long term.

Good luck!

Just the facts

- Work and family programs are designed to take some of the stress out of being a working parent. They include job sharing, flextime, telecommuting, a range of childcare-related benefits, and other types of programs.

- Work and family programs don't have to be expensive to be effective.

- Work and family programs aren't just good for employees; they're also good for business. They've been proven to reduce turnover and absenteeism, to cut health-care and office costs, and to boost employee morale and productivity.

- You need to do your homework before you approach your boss to ask that work and family programs be introduced in your workplace. Try to address as many of his concerns as possible before you ask for his approval.

- Other ways to reduce the stress of being a working parent include making changes to your lifestyle, changing jobs, starting your own business, or deciding to leave the workforce altogether. Whatever choice you decide to make should be one that you're prepared to live with for at least the foreseeable future.

Glossary

Accredited: A daycare center or family daycare home that has met standards for quality as established by the National Association for the Education of Young Children (NAEYC), the National Child Care Association (NCCA), or the National Association of Family Child Care (NAFCC).

After-school childcare programs: Childcare programs designed to meet the needs of school-aged children. While the term specifically refers to programs that are offered at the end of the school day, it is often used to describe programs that are offered on in-service or professional development days or during school breaks as well.

Age groupings: Childcare groups that are segregated on the basis of age.

Au pair: A young person between the ages of 18 and 26, typically from a foreign country, who provides childcare services in exchange for the opportunity to work and study in the United States.

Banked overtime: Hours of overtime that are accumulated for use at a later time.

Block Parent program: A program designed to offer a safe haven for children who need emergency assistance. Block Parents are screened by police and receive special signs to hang in their windows to indicate that children are welcome to come into their homes in the event of an emergency.

Caregiver: A person who cares for young children. Sometimes called a childcare provider (in the case of a family daycare setting), a preschool teacher (in a daycare center), or a babysitter.

Caregiver-child ratio: The number of children who are being cared for by a single caregiver.

Child and Dependent Care Credit: A tax break for families who have childcare expenses.

Child with special needs: A child whose disabilities result in physical or behavioral challenges. Terms that were formerly used to describe such children but that are no longer widely accepted include handicapped and disabled.

Childcare resource and referral agency (CCRA): An organization that assists parents in finding out what childcare options are available to them in their communities.

Childcare subsidies: Funds designed to low-income families in purchasing childcare services.

Comfort object: Objects such as stuffed toys or blankets that help a child to feel secure in an unfamiliar environment. Also called *transitional objects.*

Cooperative nursery schools: Nursery schools that are owned and operated by a group of parent volunteers. Parents are typically required to work a certain number of duty days per month to help keep childcare costs down.

Daycare: Care that a child or adult receives during the day. The term childcare is generally used to describe the type of care that children receive, while the term daycare is increasingly being used to describe the care given to adults with special needs.

Daycare center: A setting in which children are cared for in groups by one or more caregivers.

Domestic: Anyone who works in another person's home for a salary or wage. This is the term that the IRS uses to describe nannies, au pairs, and other in-home caregivers.

Domestic agency: An agency that is in the business of matching up nannies, au pairs, and other caregivers with families in need of their services.

Early childhood educator (ECE): Someone who has been specially trained to care for young children.

Emergency care: Short-term childcare services provided either in a specialized facility or daycare center or the child's own home in the event that a child is too sick to go to his regular childcare arrangement or his caregiver is unexpectedly unavailable.

Exceptionalities: Another term for special needs.

Family childcare network: A network of homes in which family childcare services are provided.

Family daycare home: A home in which a caregiver operates a childcare business. Also called a home daycare or family daycare.

Flextime: A workplace policy that enables employees to work flexible hours.

For-profit: Organizations that are in business to make money.

Group size: The number of children being cared for in a single group.

IEP/IPP: An individualized education plan or individualized program plan that sets out specific goals for a child who has special needs.

Infant: A child between the ages of birth and eighteen months.

In-home childcare: Childcare that is provided in your own home by a nanny, au pair, or other type of caregiver.

Job sharing: Sharing a full-time job with another person so that you are can work part-time hours.

Latchkey kids: Children who are responsible for caring for themselves from the time school finishes until their parents arrive home from work.

Licensed: A daycare center or family daycare home that has met minimal government standards for health and safety.

Licensing authority: The state or provincial government department responsible for issuing childcare licenses.

Mixed groupings: Childcare groups that include children of all ages.

Mother's helper: A young person who cares for young children while the children's parents are at home.

Multiples: Twins, triplets, quadruplets, quintuplets, sextuplets, or septuplets.

Nanny: A person who has been specially trained to care for young children.

Nonprofit: Organizations that are designed to break even rather than make money.

Nursery school: A childcare program that is offered to three- and four-year-olds on a part-time basis.

Out-of-home childcare: Childcare that is provided outside of your home in either a daycare center or family daycare home.

Out-of-school time: The hours that school-aged children spend out of school during the evening, on weekends, and during school breaks. Often used interchangeably with the term after-school care.

Preschooler: A child between the ages of three and six years.

Primary caregiver: The person who is primarily responsible for caring for a particular child.

Relative care: Care by a relative.

Resource worker: An individual who has received special training in working with children who have special needs, and who works with caregivers to establish developmentally appropriate programs for the special needs children in their care.

Respite care: Short-term childcare that is provided to the family of a child who has special needs to give the parents a break from the demands of providing twenty-four-hour-a-day care.

School-aged child: A child who is old enough to attend school.

Self-care: Leaving an older child to care for himself.

Telecommuting: A workplace policy that enables employees to work from home.

Telephone reassurance line: A telephone line that children can call after school if they need advice or reassurance while they are caring for themselves.

Toddler: A child between the ages of eighteen months and three years.

Transitional objects: Objects such as stuffed toys or blankets that help a child to feel secure in an unfamiliar environment. Also called *comfort objects.*

Work and family programs: Programs that are designed to take some of the stress out of being a working parent (telecommuting, flextime, job-sharing, and so on).

Wrongful dismissal: Firing someone without having a valid reason.

Resource Guide

Appendix B

State Childcare Licensing Authorities

Alabama
Department of Human Resources
Office of Day Care and Child Development
Family and Children's Services
50 Ripley Street
Montgomery, AL 36130
(334) 242-1425

Alaska
Department of Health and Social Services
Division of Family and Youth Services
P.O. Box 110630
Juneau, AK 99811-0630
(907) 465-3207

Arizona
Department of Health Services
Office of Child Care Licensure
1647 East Morten, Suite 230
Phoenix, AZ 85020
(602) 255-1272
5+ children

Department of Economic Security
Child Care Administration
Site Code 801A
P.O. Box 6213
Phoenix, AZ 85005
(602) 542-4248
1–4 children

Arkansas

Division of Children and Family Services
Child Care Licensing
P.O. Box 1437, Slot 720
Little Rock, AR 72203-1437
(501) 682-8590

California

Central Operations Branch
Department of Social Services
Community Care Licensing Division
744 P Street, Mail Stop 19-50
Sacramento, CA 95814
(916) 324-4031

Colorado

Department of Human Services
Division of Child Care Services
1575 Sherman Street
Denver, CO 80203-1714
(303) 866-5958

Connecticut

Connecticut Department of Public Health
Child Day Care Licensing
410 Capital Avenue
Mail Station 12 DAC
P.O. Box 340308
Hartford, CT 06134-0308
(860) 509-8045

Delaware
Department of Services for Children, Youth and
Families
Office of Child Care Licensing
1825 Faulkland Road
Wilmington, DE 19805
(302) 892-5800

District Of Columbia
Department of Consumer and Regulatory Affairs
Service Facility Regulation Administration
Child Care Branch
614 H Street, NW, Room 1035
Washington, DC 20001
(202) 727-7226

Florida
Department of Children and Families
Family Safety and Preservation
Child Care Services
2811-A Industrial Plaza Drive
Tallahassee, FL 32301
(904) 488-4900

Georgia
Department of Human Resources
Office of Regulatory Services
Child Care Licensing Section
2 Peachtree Street, NW, 32nd Floor
Atlanta, GA 30303-3167
(404) 657-5562

Hawaii
Department of Human Services
Self-Sufficiency and Support Services Division
1001 Bishop Street - P.O. Box 339
Pacific Tower, Suite 900
Honolulu, HI 96813
(808) 586-5770

Idaho

Department of Health and Welfare
Bureau of Family and Children's Services
450 West State Street
P.O. Box 83720
Boise, ID 83720-0036
(208) 334-5691

Illinois

Department of Children and Family Services
Bureau of Licensure and Certification
406 East Monroe Street - Station 60
Springfield, IL 62701-1498
(217) 785-2688

Indiana

Department of Family and Social Services
Division of Family and Children
Day Care Licensing Unit
402 West Washington Street, Rm W-364
Indianapolis, IN 46204
(317) 232-4442

Iowa

Department of Human Services
Adult, Children and Family Services
Child Care Licensing
Hoover State Office Building, 5th Floor
Des Moines, IA 50319
(515) 281-6074

Kansas

Department of Health and Environment
Child Care Licensing and Registration
109 SW 9th Street
Mills Building, 400-C
Topeka, KS 66612-2218
(913) 296-1272

Kentucky

Cabinet for Health Services
Cabinet for Human Resources Building
OIG - Division of Licensing and Regulation
275 East Main Street, 4th Floor East - A
Frankfort, KY 40621
(502) 564-2800

Louisiana

Department of Social Services
Bureau of Licensing
P.O. Box 3078
Baton Rouge, LA 70821
(504) 922-0015

Maine

Bureau of Child and Family Services
Maine Department of Human Services
Division of Licensing, ACL
221 State Street
State House, Station 11
Augusta, ME 04333
(207) 287-5060

Maryland

Maryland Department of Human Resources
Child Care Administration
311 W. Saratoga Street, lst Floor
Baltimore, MD 21201
(410) 767-7798

Massachusetts

Office for Children
One Ashburton Place, Room 111
Boston, MA 02108
(617) 727-8900

Michigan

Department of Consumer and Industry Services
Bureau of Regulatory Services
Division of Child Day Care Licensing
7109 W. Saginaw, 2nd Floor
P.O. Box 30650
Lansing, MI 48909-8150
(517) 373-8300

Minnesota

Department of Human Services
Division of Licensing
444 Lafayette Road
St. Paul, MN 55155-3842
(612) 296-3971

Mississippi

Department of Health
Division of Child Care
P.O. Box 1700
Jackson, MS 39215-1700
(601) 960-7613

Missouri

Department of Health
Bureau of Child Care, Safety and Licensure
P.O. Box 570
Jefferson City, MO 65102
(573) 751-2450

Montana

Montana Department of Public Health and
Human Services
Child Care
P.O. Box 8005
Helena, MT 59604
(406) 444-5900

Nebraska

Health and Human Services Agency
Resource Development and Support Unit
P.O. Box 95044
Lincoln, NE 68509-5026
(402) 471-9431

New Hampshire

Division of Public Health Services
Bureau of Child Care Licensing
Health and Human Services Building
6 Hazen Drive
Concord, NH 03301
(603) 271-4624

New Jersey

New Jersey Department of Human Services
Division of Youth and Family Services
Bureau of Licensing
P.O. Box 717
Trenton, NJ 08625-0717
(609) 292-1018

New Mexico

Children, Youth and Families Department
Licensing and Certification Bureau
PERA Building, Room 121
P.O. Box 5160
Santa Fe, NM 87502-5160
(505) 827-4118 or (505) 827-4185

New York

New York State Department of Social Services
Bureau of Early Childhood Services
40 North Pearl Street, ll-B
Albany, NY 12243
(518) 474-9454

North Carolina

Division of Child Development
Child Day Care Section
P.O. Box 29553
Raleigh, NC 27626-0553
(919) 662-4499
Child Care Resource Center Hotline
(800) CHOOSE-1

North Dakota

North Dakota Department of Human Services
Children and Family Services
600 East Boulevard Avenue
State Capitol Building
Bismarck, ND 58505-0250
(701) 328-4809

Ohio

Ohio Department of Human Services
Bureau of Child Care Services
Child Day Care Licensing Section
65 East State Street, 5th Floor
Columbus, OH 43215
(614) 466-3822

Oklahoma

Oklahoma Department of Human Services
Office of Child Care
4545 N. Lincoln, Suite 100
P.O. Box 25352
Oklahoma City, OK 73105
(405) 521-3561

Oregon

Employment Department
Child Care Divison
875 Union Street, NE
Salem, OR 97311
(503) 378-3178

Pennsylvania
Pennsylvania Department of Public Welfare
Bureau of Child Day Care Services
Office of Children, Youth and Families
Complex 3, 4th Floor
P.O. Box 2675
Harrisburg, PA 17105
(717) 787-8691

Rhode Island
Department of Children, Youth and Families
Day Care Licensing, Bldg. 3
610 Mount Pleasant Avenue
Providence, RI 02908
(401) 277-4741

South Carolina
Department of Social Services
Division of Child Day Care Licensing and
Regulatory Services
P.O. Box 1520
Columbia, SC 29202
(803) 734-5740

South Dakota
South Dakota Department of Social Services
Child Care Services
Kneip Building
700 Governors Drive
Pierre, SD 57501-2291
(605) 773-4766

Tennessee
Tennessee Department of Human Services
Day Care Licensing Unit
Citizens Plaza
400 Deaderick Street
Nashville, TN 37248-9800
(615) 313-4778

Texas
Department of Protective and Regulatory
Services
Child Care Licensing
P.O. Box 149030, M.C. E-550
Austin, TX 78714-9030
(512) 438-3269

Utah
Bureau of Licensing
Child Care Unit
P.O. Box 142853
Salt Lake City, UT 84114-2853
(801) 538-6152

Vermont
Vermont Department of Social and
Rehabilitation Services
Child Care Services Division
Child Care Licensing Unit
103 S. Main Street
Waterbury, VT 05671-2901
(802) 241-2158

Virginia
Virginia Department of Social Services
Division of Licensing Programs
730 East Broad Street
Theater Row Building
Richmond, VA 23219
(804) 692-1787

Washington
Washington Department of Social and Health
Services
Office of Child Care Policy
P.O. Box 45700
Olympia, WA 98504-5710
(360) 902-8038

West Virginia
West Virginia Department of Health and Human
Resources
Day Care Licensing
1900 Washington Street
East Capitol Complex, Bldg. 6, Room 850-B
Charleston, WV 25305
(304) 558-7980

Wisconsin
Department of Health and Social Services
Division of Children and Family Services
Bureau of Regulation and Licensing
1 West Wilson Street
P.O. Box 8916
Madison, WI 53708-8916
(608) 266-9314

Wyoming
Wyoming Department of Family Services
Division of Juvenile Services
Hathaway Bldg., Room 323
2300 Capitol Avenue
Cheyenne, WY 82002
(307) 777-6285

PROVINCIAL CHILDCARE LICENSING AUTHORITIES

Alberta
Family and Social Services
Day Care Programs
11th Floor, 7th St. Plaza
10030-107th St.
Edmonton, Alberta
T5J 3E4
(403) 427-4477

British Columbia
Community Care Facilities Branch
Ministry of Health
7th Floor, 1515 Blanshard St.
Victoria, B.C.
V8W 3C8
(604) 387-2659

Manitoba
Department of Family Services
Child Day Care
114 Garry Street, 2nd Floor
Winnipeg, Manitoba
R3C 1G1
(204) 945-2197
(204) 945-0776 (outside Winnipeg)
Toll Free 1-800-282-8069

New Brunswick
Office for Childhood Services
Department of Health and Community Services
P.O. Box 5100
Fredericton, NB
E3B 5G8
(506) 453-2950

Newfoundland
Day Care and Homemaker Services
Department of Social Services
Confederation Building
P.O. Box 8700
St. John's, Newfoundland
A1B 4J6
(709) 576-3590

Nova Scotia
Day Care Services
Department of Community Services
Family and Children's Services Division
P.O. Box 696
Halifax, N.S.
B3J 2T7
(902) 424-3204

Northwest Territories
Child Day Care Section
Family and Child Service Division
Department of Social Services
P.O. Box 1320
Yellowknife, N.W.T.
X1A 2L9
(403) 920-8920

Ontario
Child Care Branch
Ministry of Community and Social Services
2 Bloor Street West, 30th Floor
Toronto, Ontario
M7A 1E9
(416) 327-4870

Prince Edward Island
Early Childhood Services
Corporate Services Division
Department of Health and Social Services
P.O. Box 2000
Charlottetown, Prince Edward Island
C1A 7N8
(902) 368-4957

Quebec

Office des Services de Garde à l'Enfance
100, rue Sherbrooke est
Montreal, Quebec
H2X 1C3
(514) 873-2323

Saskatchewan

Child Care Branch
Department of Social Services
1920 Broad Street
Regina, Saskatchewan
S4P 3V6
(306) 787-7467
Toll free 1-800-667-7155

Yukon

Child Care Services Unit
Department of Health and Social Services
Yukon Territorial Government
P.O. Box 2703
Whitehorse, Yukon
Y1A 2C6
(403) 667-3002
Toll free 1-800-661-0408

AMERICAN CHILDCARE-RELATED ORGANIZATIONS

Au Pairs

Au Pair in America
American Institute for Foreign Study
102 Greenwich Avenue
Greenwich, CT 06830
(800) 727-2437
(203) 727-2437

Childcare International Ltd.
Trafalgar House
Grenville Place
London NW7 3SA
Great Britain
E-mail: office@childint.demon.co.uk

International Au Pair Association (IAPA)
Secretariat
Bredgade 25 H
DK - 1260 Copenhagen K
Denmark
Phone: (+45) 3333 9600
E-mail: mailbox@iapa.org

Childcare In General

American Business Collaboration for Quality Dependent Care
930 Commonwealth Ave. West
Boston, MA 02215-1274
(800) 253-5264 ext.4283

American Montessori Society
150 Fifth Avenue, Suite 203
New York, NY 10011
(212) 924-3209

Association Montessori International (AMI)
170 W. Scholfield Road
Rochester, NY 14617
(800) 872-2643
(716) 544-6709
E-mail: usaami3@aol.com

Center for Career Development in Early Care and Education
Wheelock College
200 The Riverway
Boston, MA 02215
(617) 734-5200
Web: http://ericps.crc.uiuc.edu/ccdece/ccdece.html

Child Care Action Campaign
330 7th Avenue, 17th Floor
New York, NY 10001
(212) 239-0138
E-mail: HN5746@handsnet.org
Web: http://www.usakids.org./sites/ccac.html

Child Care Institute of America
3612 Bent Branch Court
Falls Church, VA 22041
(703) 941-4329

Child Care Law Center
22 Second Street, 5th Floor
San Francisco, CA 94105
(415) 495-5498
E-mail: cclc@childcarelaw.com

Ecumenical Child Care Network
8765 West Higgins Road
Suite 405
Chicago, IL 60631
(312) 693-4040

Educational Resources Information Center's Clearinghouse on Elementary and Early Childhood Education

ERIC/EECE

University of Illinois at Urbana-Champaign

Children's Research Center

51 Gerty Drive

Champaign, IL 61820-7469

(800) 583-4135 or (217) 333-1386

Web: http://ericps.crc.uiuc.edu/ericeece.html

KCMC Child Development Corporation

2104 E. 18th

Kansas City, MO 64127

(816) 474-0434

E-mail usaccare@aol.com

National Association for the Education of Young Children (NAEYC)

1509 16th Street, NW

Washington, DC 20036-1426

(800) 424-2460 or (202) 232-8777

Web: http://www.naeyc.org/naeyc/

National Association of Family Child Care (NAFCC)

1331-A Pennsylvania Avenue NW

Suite 348

Washington, DC 20004

(800) 359-3817

E-mail: nafcc@nafcc.org

Web: http://www.nafcc.org

National Association of Child Care Professionals (NACCP)

304-A Roanoke Street

Christiansburg, VA 24063

(800) 537-1118

E-mail: admin@naccp.org

National Association of Child Care Resource and Referral Agencies (NACCRRA)
2116 Campus Drive SE
Rochester, MN 55904
(507) 287-2220
Web: http://www.childcare-experts.org/ccx2.html

National Center for the Early Childhood Work Force
733 15th Street NW, Suite 800
Washington, DC 20005-2112
(202) 737-7700

National Child Care Association (NCCA)
1029 Railroad Street
Conyers, GA 30207
(770) 922-8198
(800) 543-7161
Web: http://www.nccanet.org/
E-mail: nccallw@mindspring.com

National Child Care Information Center (NCCIC)
301 Maple Ave. West,
Suite 602
Vienna, VA 22180
(800) 616-2242
E-mail: agoldstein@acf.dhhs.gov
Web: http://ericps.ed.uiuc.edu/nccic/
nccichome.html

National Head Start Association
1309 King Street, Suite 200
Alexandria, VA 22314
(703) 739-0875
Web: http://www.nhsa.org

National Indian Child Care Association
279 East 137th Street
Glenpool, OK 74033
(918) 756-2112

National Institute on Out-of-School Time Center for Research on Women
106 Central Street
Wellesley, MA 02181-8259
(781) 283-2547
Web: http://www.wellesley.edu/WCW/CRW/SAC/

National Resource Center for Health and Safety in Child Care
University of Colorado Health Sciences Center
School of Nursing
4200 E. Ninth Avenue
Campus Box C287
Denver, CO 80262
(800) 598-KIDS (5437)
Web: http://nrc.uchsc.edu

National School-Age Care Alliance
4720 North Park
Indianapolis, IN 46205
(317) 283-3817

Program for Infant/Toddler Caregivers
Far West Laboratory and California
Department of Education
180 Harbor Drive, Suite 112
Sausalito, California 94965
(451) 331-5277

Resource for Infant Educators (RIE)
8233 West Third Street
Los Angeles, CA
90048
(213) 651-0022

School-Age Child Care Project
Wellesley College Center for Research on Women
Wellesley, MA 02181
(617) 283-2547
Web: http://www.wellesley.edu/WCW/CRW/SAC/

**To Learn and Grow Corporation
for National Service**
1201 New York Avenue, NW
Washington, DC 20525
(202) 606-5000 ext. 280
Web: http://www.nationalservice.org

USA Child Care

Waldorf School Association of North America
3911 Bannister Road
Fair Oaks, CA 95628
(916) 961- 0927

Child Development and Child Welfare

Administration on Children, Youth and Families
(Mailing address)
Head Start Bureau
P.O. Box 1182
Washington, DC 20013
(Office location)
Mary E. Switzer Building
330C Street, SW
Room 2050
Washington, DC 20201

The American Academy of Pediatrics
141 Northwest Point Boulevard
Elk Grove Village, IL 60007-1098
(847) 228-5005
(800) 433-9016
Fax: (847) 228-5097
E-mail: kidsdocs@aap.org
Web: www.aap.org

American Public Welfare Association
810 First Street NE, Suite 500
Washington, DC 20002-4267
(202) 682-0100
Web: http://www.apwa.org/

Child Welfare League of America, Inc.
440 First Street NW, Suite 310
Washington, DC 20001-2085
(202) 942-0265
(202) 638-2952
E-mail: hn3898@handsnet.org
Web: http://www.cwla.org

Children's Defense Fund
25 E Street NW
Washington, DC 20001
(202) 628-8787
Web: http://www.childrensdefense.org

The Children's Foundation
725 15th Street NW #505
Washington, DC 20005
(202) 347-3300

Council of Chief State School Officers
One Massachusetts Avenue NW #700
Washington, DC 20001-1431
(202) 336-7033
E-mail: info@ccsso.org
Web: http://www.ccsso.org

Family Resource Coalition
200 South Michigan Avenue
16th Floor
Chicago, IL 60604
(312) 341-9000

National Association of Child Advocates
1625 K Street NW, Suite 510
Washington, DC 20006
(202) 828-6950

National Association of Protection and Advocacy Systems (NAPAS)
220 I Street NE, Suite 150
Washington, DC 20002
(202)546-8202

National Association of Regulatory Agencies
P.O. Box 70612
Washington, DC 20024

National Black Child Development
1023 Fifteenth Street NW, Suite 600
Washington, DC 20005
(202) 398-1281
(202) 387-1281
E-mail: moreinfo@nbcdi.org
Web: http://www.nbcdi.org

National Center for Children in Poverty
Columbia University School of Public Health
154 Haven Avenue
New York, NY 10032
(212) 304-7100
(212) 927-8793
Web: http://cpmcnet.columbia.edu/dept/nccp/

National Center for Education in Maternal and Child Health
2000 15th Street, North Suite 701
Arlington, VA 22201-2617
(703) 524-7802
E-mail: ncemch01@gumed lib.dml.georgetown.edu

National Clearinghouse on Child Abuse and Neglect Information

P.O. Box 1182

Washington, DC 20013-1182

800-FYI-3366 or (703) 385-7565

E-mail: nccanch@calib.com

Web: http://www.calib.com/nccanch/

National Clearinghouse on Families and Youth

P.O. Box 13505

Silver Spring, MD 20911-3505

(301) 608-8098

National Information Center for Children and Youth with Disabilites

P.O. Box 1492

Washington, DC 20013-1492

(800) 695-0285

E-mail: nichcy@aed.org

Web: http://nichey.org

National Information Clearinghouse for Infants with Disabilities and Life Threatening Conditions

University of Sourth Carolina

Benson Building, First Floor

Columbia, SC 29208

(800) 922-9234 ext.201

(803) 777-4435

National Resource Center for Health and Safety in Child Care

UCHSC School of Nursing

C-287

4200 E. 9th Avenue

Denver, CO 80262

National Resource Center on Child Abuse and Neglect
63 Inverness Drive East
Englewood, CO 80112-5117
(800) 227-5242

Sanvita Programs
P.O. Box 660
McHenry, IL 60051-0660
(800) 435-5557

Zero to Three: National Center for Infants, Toddlers, and Families
2000 14th St. N. Suite 380
Arlington, VA 22201-2500
(800) 899-4301
Web: http://www.zerotothree.org

Electronic Monitoring Equipment and Surveillance

American International Security Corporation
10805 Main Street #600
Fairfax, VA 22030
(703) 691-1110

Watch Me
4851 Keller Springs Road
Dallax, TX 75248
(972) 818-1828
E-mail: info@watch-me.com

Nannies

Alliance of Professional Nanny Agencies (APNA)
540 Route 10 West 337
Randolph, NJ 07869
(800) 551-2762

American Council of Nanny Schools
Delta College
University Center, MI 48710
(517) 686-9417

Childcare International Ltd.
Trafalgar House
Grenville Place
London NW7 3SA
Great Britain
E-mail: office@childint.demon.co.uk

I Love My Nanny, Inc.
41 Crossroads Plaza
Suite 265
West Hartford, CT 06117
(860) 243-2222
E-mail: nannyluvsu@aol.com
Web: http://www.ilovemynanny.com

International Nanny Association
900 Haddon Avenue
Station House, Suite 438
Collingswood, NJ 08108
(609) 858-0808
E-mail: director@nanny.org
Web: http://www.nanny.org

National Association of Nannies
7413 Six Forks Road, Suite 317
Raleigh, NC 27615
(800) 344-6266
E-mail: NAN@Webriggers.com
Web: http://www.webriggers.com/NAN/

Work and Family Issues

Families and Work Institute
330 Seventh Avenue, 14th Floor
New York, NY 10001
(212) 465-2044
Web: http://www.familiesandworkinst.org

Home/Work Solutions, Inc.
2 Pidgeon Hill Drive, Suite 210
Sterling, VA 20165
(703) 404-8151

Women's Bureau, U.S. Department of Labor
Work and Family Clearinghouse
200 Constitution Avenue NW, Room 3317
Washington, DC 20210-0002
(202) 219-4486
Web: http://gatekeeper.dol.gov/dol/wb/

Work and Family Connection, Inc.
5197 Beachside Drive
Minnetonka, MN 55343
(800) 487-7898
(612) 936-7898
E-mail: info@workfamily.com
Web: http://www.workfamily.com

Work/Family Directions
930 Commonwealth Ave. West
Boston, MA 02215-1274
(617) 278-4000

Canadian Childcare-Related Organizations

Association of Canadian Child Care Co-Operatives (ACCC)
24 Soho Crescent
Nepean, Ontario
K2J 2W1
(613) 825-1233

Canadian Association for Young Children (CAYC)
612 West 23rd Street
North Vancouver, B.C.
V7M 2C3
(604) 984-2361

Canadian Association of Family Resource Programs
30 Rosemont Ave.
Suite 101
Ottawa, Ontario
K1Y 1P4
(613) 728-3307

Canadian Association of Toy Libraries and Parent Resource Centres
(TLRC Canada)
Suite 205-120 Holland Avenue
Ottawa, Ontario
K1Y 0X6
(613) 728-3307

The Canadian Child Day Care Federation
Suite 401-120 Holland Avenue
Ottawa, Ontario
K1Y 0X6
(613) 729-5289

Canadian Council of Social Development (CCSD)
441 MacLaren
4th Floor
Ottawa, Ontario
K2P 2H3
(613) 236-8977

The Canadian Day Care Advocacy Association
323 Chapel Street
Ottawa, Ontario
K1N 7Z2
(613) 594-3196

Canadian Institute of Child Health
885 Meadowlands Dr. East
Suite 512
Ottawa, Ontario
K2C 3N2
(613) 224-4144

Canadian Mothercraft Society
32 Heath Street West
Toronto, Ontario
M4V 1T3
(416) 920-3515

Child Care Advocacy Association of Canada
323 Chapel Street
Ottawa, Ontario
K1N 7Z2
(613) 594-3196

Child Welfare League of Canada
180 Argyle Avenue
Suite 312
Ottawa, Ontario
K2P 1B7
(613) 235-4412

Childcare Resource and Research Unit (CRRU)
Center for Urban and Community Studies
University of Toronto
455 Spadina Avenue
Suite 305
Toronto, Ontario
M5S 2G8
(416) 978-6895

Family Service Canada
220 Laurier Avenue West
Suite 600
Ottawa, Ontario
K1P 5Z9
(613) 722-8610

Learning Disabilities Association of Canada (LCAC)
323 Chapel Street
Suite 200
Ottawa, Ontario
K1N 7Z2
(613) 238-5721

The National Action Committee on the Status of Women
323 Chapel Street
Ottawa, Ontario
K1N 7Z2
(613) 234-7062

Parent Cooperative Preschool International (PCPI)
86 George Street
London, Ontario
N6A 2Z7
(519) 673-4070

Unit for Child Care Research
School of Child and Youth Care
University of Victoria
Victoria, B.C.
V8W 2Y2
(250) 721-7979

Vanier Institute of the Family
94 Centrepointe Drive
Nepean, Ontario
K2G 6B1
(613) 228-8500

**World Organization for Early Childhood
Education—Canada (OMEP)**
Faculty of Education
Laval University
Quebec City, Quebec
G1K 7P4
(418) 656-7891

YMCA Canada (National Council)
180 Argyle Avenue
Suite 309
Ottawa, Ontario
K2P 1B7
(613) 233-5647

Internet Resources
Au Pairs

Au Pair Program USA/Childcrest

www.childcrest.com

This site provides information on Au Pair Programme USA/Childcrest, an agency that provides American families with international au pairs and British nursery nurses (NNEBs). The site also contains information on the benefits of hiring a nanny or au pair.

Childcare International Ltd.

www.childint.demon.co.uk/

This page contains the contact information for Childcare International Ltd., a U.K.-based placement agency that specializes in the recruitment of nannies, mother's helpers, and au pairs.

International Au Pair Association (IAPA)

www.iapa.org/

This page contains information about the International Au Pair Association, an organization made up of au pair agencies in 26 different countries. There's detailed information about the host family and au pair's responsibilities as well as a copy of the IAPA's code of ethics.

JCR Au Pairs-R-Us

www.jcr.co.za

This page contains information about the services offered by JCR, a South Africa-based au pair agency.

Babysitting Co-Ops

Co-op America

www.coopamerica.org/immmcoop.htm

This page contains detailed information on babysitting co-ops, a cost-effective means of meeting your need for part-time childcare.

What You Can Do For Childcare

www.kidscampaigns.org/start/101childcare35.html

This is where to find the inside scoop on babysitting co-ops: how to start one, common problems to avoid, and so on.

Breastfeeding and Working

La Leche League

www.lalecheleague.org

The mother of all breastfeeding Web sites, the La Leche League Web site contains pages of information on every breastfeeding question imaginable. The information on breastfeeding after you return to work is particularly comprehensive and is filled with valuable tips from experienced nursing mothers.

L.A. Publishing's Information Center—Working and Breastfeeding

www.bookzone.com/breastfeeding/la3.html

This excerpt from the book *Breastfeeding: A Mother's Gift* contains valuable tips on breastfeeing after your return to work.

Women's Link—Breastfeeding and the Working Mother

www.womenslink.com/momness/pamphlets/working1.html

This page provides valuable tips on breastfeeding after you return to work. Topics covered include the benefits of breastfeeding and how alternate work arrangements (i.e. flextime and/or telecommuting) can help to accommodate the needs of a nursing mother.

Child Abuse

SafeChild Handbook

www.kidsuccess.com/safechld.htm

The Center for Children and Families in New York has prepared a detailed online handbook designed to make parents aware of the signs of child abuse and provide them with guidelines on how to handle the situation if they suspect that their child has been abused.

Childcare Information

American Childcare Solutions

www.parentsplace.com/readroom/ACS/

American Childcare Solutions is part of ParentsPlace.com, one of the most popular parenting Web sites on the Internet. The page is packed with information about au pairs, nannies, and other types of caregivers, and there are numerous links to other online childcare resources as well.

American Montessori Society

www.careguide.net/ams/home.html

This page contains information about the American Montessori Society, an organization that is made up of preschools that offer programs that use the methods developed by early 20th century physician-turned-educator Maria Montessori.

Child and Family Canada's Child Care Page

http://www.cfc-efc.ca/startup/child_care.htm

This site—which is maintained by the Canadian government—contains links to national, provincial, and territorial childcare organizations and other childcare-related resources. There's an entire page devoted to play-related resources www.cfc-efc.ca/menu/eng011.htm which is a must see for in-home caregivers and the families that employ them.

Child Care Experts: Child Care Resource & Referral

www.childcare-experts.org/ccx2.html

This Web site contains detailed information about childcare resource and referral (CCR&R) services, including links to various CCR&Rs in operation across the country.

Child Care Resource and Referral Agencies

http://ericps.crc.uiuc.edu/eece/pubs/digests/1991/bellm91.html

This page contains detailed information about childcare resource and referral agencies.

ERIC Clearinghouse on Elementary and Early Childhood Education

http://ericps.ed.uiuc.edu/

This site is packed with useful information on a variety of parenting-related topics. There are articles galore on choosing childcare, settling your child into care, and so on.

Facts About Child Care in America

www.childrensdefense.org/cc_facts.html

This page provides a bird's eye view of childcare in America: who's using it, what it costs, and why the system needs fixing.

Family Child Care Accreditation Project

www.earlychildhood.com/articles/artfccap.html

This page contains details about the Family Child Care Accreditation Project—a new accreditation system for the National Assocation for Family Child Care (NAFCC).

Finding and Choosing Childcare

http://ericps.ed.uiuc.edu/nccic/findcare.html

This page contains information about the National Association of Child Care Resource and Referral Agencies (NACCRRA) and other childcare-related organizations.

HomeArts and Care Guide Present Child and Elder Care

www.careguide.net/careguide.cgi/branding/home-arts/home.htm!

This Web site is packed with useful information about finding care for your child or aging relative. There is a national directory of childcare centers, preschools, and home childcare providers; a list of frequently asked questions about childcare; and an online chat and forum site that lets you to discuss your childcare-related concerns with other parents.

Misc.kids

www.cis.ohio-state.edu/hypertext/faq/usenet/misc-kids/faq/part2/faq.html

This Web site consists of postings to the misc.kids.daycare newsgroup. It's full of detailed information about a variety of childcare-related issues. Because the majority of the postings are from parents and are based on their first-hand experiences, you can pick up a lot of valuable advice on everything from choosing childcare to helping your child to adjust to his new care arrangement.

National Association for the Education of Young Children (NAEYC)

www.naeyc.org/naeyc/

This Web site provides information about the National Association for the Education of Young Children's childcare accreditation program, something that every parent who's looking for out-of-home care should know about.

National Child Care Association—NCCANet
www.nccanet.org/
NCCANet is operated by the National Child Care Association (NCCA), a professional trade association made up of individuals working in private child-care and education programs. NCCANet can assist you to in your search for childcare by making you aware of any NCCA member centers operating in your community.

National Child Care Information Center (NCCIC)
http://ericps.ed.uiuc.edu/nccic/abtnccic.html
This site contains information on the activities of the National Child Care Information Center (NCCIC) as well as links to clearinghouses and national organizations related to childcare.

National Institute on Out-of-School Time
www.wellesley.edu/WCW/CRW/SAC/
You can find information about the National Institute on Out-of-School Time, an organization that focuses on the unique childcare needs of school-aged children.

National Network for Child Care
http://www.exnet.iastate.edu/Pages/families/nncc/Choose.Quality.Care/qual.care.page.html
This page contains links to articles on a variety of childcare-related topics. There's even a link to the proceedings of the first-ever White House Conference on Child Care. Another page on the same site, www.exnet.iastate.edu/pages/nncc/homepage.html, lets you to access information on a variety of childcare-related topics, including child development, program evaluation, diversity, and employer options.

Questions to Ask

www.daycaredailies.com/questions.html

As the name suggests, this page contains a list of questions that you might want to ask a potential daycare provider.

Searching For Poppins.com

www.searchingforpoppins.com/excerpts.htm

This Web site was launched as this book was going to press. While there wasn't much there when I checked it out, it looks like it could evolve into a useful forum for parents to swap childcare-related horror stories and tips on finding Ms. Right.

State Child Care Profiles

http://ericps.ed.uiuc.edu/nccic/statepro.html

This Web site contains detailed profiles of the childcare situation in each state. You'll find demographic information (i.e. 1995 the number of children under 18 with working parents), detailed information about child-staff ratios, and contact information for various childcare-related government departments.

Child Safety

How Can We Provide Safe Playgrounds?

http://ericps.crc.uiuc.edu/npin/respar/texts/chldcare/playgrou.html

This article from the ERIC database includes detailed information on what makes—and doesn't make—a safe playground environment.

National Health and Safety Performance Standards

http://nrc.uchsc.edu/national/index.html

This Web site contains the entire text of a comprehensive document entitled *Guidelines for Out-of-Home Childcare Programs*. The document contains detailed guidelines on such issues as staffing, programs, nutrition and food services, supplies and equipment, the management of infectious diseases, and children with special needs.

National Resource Center for Health and Safety in Child Care

http://nrc.uchsc.edu

This page contains links to online material on every child safety-related topic imaginable: everything from bicycle safety to immunizations to water safety. There are a number of links on choosing childcare.

Electronic Surveillance and Monitoring Equipment

A Very Private Eye

www.orlandoonline.com/pi4.htm

This page provides details about the "Check-A-Nanny" service offered by A Very Private Eye Inc., a private investigation agency. The "Check-A-Nanny" service enables concerned parents to find out how their children are being treated by their caregiver.

American International Security Corporation

www.nannynetwork.com/agencies/aminternatl.htm

This page contains details about the nanny background checks and surveillance services available through this private investigation company.

The Integrity Center Inc.

www.integctr.com/Nanny/delivery.html

This page allows you to print out the forms required to order a background investigation on your in-home caregiver.

Intellichoice Inc. Background Verification Services

www.atlantadirectory.com/findout/

This page contains details about Intellichoice Inc.,

a company that offers background verification services.

KinderCam

www.kindercam.com

This site contains information about KinderCam, a surveillance system that lets parents monitor their children's childcare environment via the Internet. Parents can access up-to-date still photos of their child by using password codes and any standard Internet browser. Snapshots are fed into the system at the rate of six pictures per second.

Private Eye Enterprises Inc.

www.pidallas.com

This page contains information on a range of security products, including taping equipment, recoders, hidden cameras, night vision equipment, and investigation books. If you really get into this whole Sherlock Holmes thing, you can even pick up a Private Eye T-shirt!

SitterWatch.com

www.sitterwatch.com

This page contains information about SitterWatch, an electronic surveillance system.

Watch Me!

www.watch-me.com/aboutus.htm

This page contains information about Watch Me!, a surveillance system that lets parents monitor their children's childcare environment via the Internet. Parents can access up-to-date still photos of their child by using password codes and any standard Internet browser.

Employment-Related Issues

A NaniNet—Reading Room
www.nannynetwork.com/read.htm
This Web site contains articles on such topics as writing an effective work agreement, your obligations as an employer, keys to making the relationship with your nanny work, nanny insurance issues, and more.

Calculate Nanny Taxes
www.nannynetwork.com/nanitax.htm
The first time you try to calculate your nanny's pay check, you might be in for a bit of a shock. The employer's portion of the various taxes that you're required to remit on her behalf can really add to the cost of having an in-home caregiver. This helpful Web site includes a "nanny tax calculator" that lets you estimate payroll taxes for your household budget and calculate your nanny's take-home pay based on the regulations that apply to your particular state.

Department of Labor's Small Business Handbook
www.dol.gov/dol/asp/public/programs/handbook/overview.htm
You can find detailed information about your responsibilities as an employer of an in-home caregiver at the Department of Labor Web site.

Home/Work Solutions Inc.: The Nanny Tax Experts
www.4nannytaxes.com
This site contains answers to frequently asked questions about the tax implications of hiring an in-home caregiver as well as a description of the nanny tax preparation services offered by Home/Work Solutions Inc. The site also contains detailed information on your obligation to report new hires to

your state government (www.4nannytaxes.com/newhire.htm), including the name and contact information for the agency where you must report new hires in your state, the types of forms that you are required to submit, and the length of time you have to report a new hire.

Internal Revenue Service

www.irs.ustreas.gov

What better place could there be to look for tax-related information than at the IRS Web site? You can obtain detailed information about claiming your childcare expenses on your tax return and find out what you have to do to meet your obligations as the employer of an in-home caregiver. You can also download all the forms you will need to file your personal tax return.

Nannies Revisited: What You Still Have to Do or Don't Do to Keep it Legal

www.womenconnect.com/info/finance/dec1896a_fin.htm

This article discusses your legal obligations in the event that you decide to hire a nanny or other in-home caregiver.

Revenue Canada

www.rc.gc.ca/~paulb/smallbus/employer.htm

Canadian parents who employ in-home caregivers can find out about their responsibilities as employers at this federal government Web site.

Small Business Handbook—Employment Eligibility of Workers

www.dol.gov/dol/asp/public/programs/handbook/immigrat.htm

This page explains the provisions of the Immigration Reform and Control Act of 1986

(IRCA) and what they mean to you as the employer of an in-home caregiver.

TaxLogic—Child Tax Credit
www.taxlogic.com/t2bin/page/+/1997/child.html
This page provides details on what the new Child Tax Credit means to American families.

Nannies

Alliance of Professional Nanny Agencies (APNA)
www.nannynetwork.com/nannyassociation.htm
This page contains details about the Alliance of Professional Nanny Agencies (APNA), a nationwide association of nanny placement agencies, as well as the International Nanny Association (INA), a non-profit professional organization made up of nannies, nanny placement agency staff and owners, and nanny educators.

Childcare International Ltd.
www.childint.demon.co.uk/
This page contains the contact information for Childcare International Ltd., a U.K.-based placement agency that specializes in the recruitment of nannies, mother's helpers, and au pairs.

I Love My Nanny.com
www.ilovemynanny.com
This site contains information about I Love My Nanny Inc., an online nanny recruitment and placement agency. The site is packed with information on the ins and outs of finding a nanny. There's information on taxes, insurance, nanny support groups, a job board, and a weekly chat forum for nannies and nanny candidates.

International Nanny Association

www.nanny.org/

This page contains information about the International Nanny Association (INA), a private nonprofit organization that serves as an advocacy organization and information clearinghouse for nannies, educators, nanny placement agencies, and parents who employ in-home caregivers.

Learn2 Find and Hire a Nanny

http://learn2.com/08/0819/0819.html

This page contains step-by-step instructions on hiring a nanny: for example, advertising for a caregiver, checking references, drafting a work agreement, and so on.

Life With Nanny

www.atmavidya.com/lifewithnanny/

Life With Nanny is the brainchild of a real-life nanny who wanted to share her knowledge and experience with both nannies and parents. The site is packed with useful information, including safety tips, craft ideas, links galore (including a terrific list of links for kids), and an extremely comprehensive work agreement written by a real-life nanny. (I liked the work agreement so much that I've included it in this book. You can find it in Appendix D.)

National Association of Nannies (NAN)

www.webriggers.com/NAN/

This page provides information about the National Association of Nannies (NAN), an organization of nannies that seeks to improve conditions in the profession. The page also includes a list of nanny support organizations—a valuable resource for parents who are attempting to find nannies who may be looking for work in their community.

Six Tips for Hiring a Nanny

www.nannynetwork.com/tips.htm

This page is full of helpful advice on the ins and outs of hiring a nanny, for example, assessing your needs, planning the interview, checking references, and so on.

Parenting Websites

Baby Center

www.babycenter.com/refcap/Working_parents.html

Baby Center contains information on a variety of parenting-related topics. There are a number of helpful articles on working during pregnancy, choosing childcare, and so on.

Beatrice's Web Guide

www.bguide.com

Beatrice's Web Guide is a funny, informative spot to look for any issues of interest to women, and childcare is no exception. You'll find links to what the folks behind the guide consider to be the five hottest childcare-related sites.

Canadian Parents Online

www.canadianparents.com

Canadian Parents Online provides a variety of information that will be of interest to Canadian parents. There are articles on a range of parenting topics plus links to other parenting sites. There are even chat rooms where you can swap experiences or pick up helpful hints from other parents.

Family.com

http://family.disney.com

This site is overflowing with useful information on childcare. In addition to an extensive collection of columns by parenting guru Penelope Leach, you'll find hundreds of other childcare-related articles.

National Parent Information Network (NPIN)

http://ericps.ed.uiuc.edu/npin/npinhome.html
There are few sites on the Internet as packed with useful parenting information as the National Parent Information Network (NPIN). The site contains countless articles on childcare-related topics: everything from helping your child to settle into childcare to establishing a good relationship with your child's caregiver.

Parent Soup

www.parentsoup.com
Another popular online parenting site, Parent Soup features chat groups, message boards, and information on a variety of parenting-related topics.

ParentsPlace.com

www.parentsplace.com
Perhaps the best-known parenting site on the Internet, ParentsPlace.com features articles and chat groups devoted to every parenting-related topic imaginable. The site—which is operated by two parents—contains a wealth of information about childcare. You can find this material in the American Childcare Solutions portion of the Web site.

ParentTime

www.pathfinder.com/@@zevLmAcAFFT87E2S/ParentTime/Experts/childsub.html
ParentTime is another excellent source of online parenting information. The childcare page is particularly useful, containing both links and detailed

information about a number of childcare-related organizations.

Sesame Street Parents
www.ctw.org
Sesame Street Parents is another must-see site for parents. There are dozens of well-researched articles on childcare-related topics and an extremely comprehensive set of resource links www.ctw.org/parents/links/index.htm.

Stork Site
www.storksite.com
As the name suggests, Stork Site contains information of interest to new and expectant parents. There's an online magazine (*Storkzine*), a library full of pregnancy and parenting-related material, and chat forums devoted to every parenting issue imaginable.

Special Needs

Individuals With Disabilities Education Act (IDEA)
http://TheArc.org/faqs/pl94142.html
This site contains detailed information on P.L. 94-142, a federal law passed in 1975 and reauthorized in 1990 mandating that all children receive a free, publicly funded education regardless of the type or severity of their disability. The Act provides funds to assist state governments in ensuring that all disabled students benefit from an individualized education program based on their unique needs and abilities.

Internet Resources for Special Children (IRSC)
www.irsc.org
This site is packed with links and resource material on children with special needs. You'll find information on everything from adaptive clothing to

adaptive hardware and software computer aids to parenting and support resources. There's also detailed information on a variety of different disorders and syndromes, including autism, cerebral palsy, Down syndrome, Rett syndrome, and more.

Teenage Babysitters

Babysitter Basics
http://pw2.netcom.com/~cristiw/babysit.html
Written by a real-life mom, this page contains practical tips on hiring teenage babysitters.

Babysitter Checklists
www.mayohealth.org/mayo/9803/htm/baby.htm
This site contains babysitter checklists and other useful information for parents who will be leaving their children in the care of a babysitter.

Primelist—Childcare
http://childcare.primelist.com/sitter.htm
This page contains a detailed checklist of all the items you should discuss with a new babysitter before you walk out the door.

Work and Family Programs

Austin Employers' Collaborative Initiatives on Employer-Supported Dependent Care Options
www.ci.austin.tx.us/childcare/
This site contains detailed information on a variety of work and family programs including school-aged childcare, onsite childcare, voucher reimbursement programs, sick/emergency childcare, and so on. If you're looking for a clear analysis of the advantages and disadvantages of each of these types of programs, from an employer's perspective, this is where you'll find it.

Business Action for Children

www.childrennow.org/action/business.html

This site is packed with useful ideas about what businesses can do to make life easier for employers who are juggling work and family commitments.

Children Youth and Family Consortium Electronic Clearinghouse—Current Research

http://www.cyfc.umn.edu/Work/current.html

This page contains the text of a speech presented by Susan Seitel of Work and Family Connection Inc. on the research supporting the benefits of work and family programs.

Making Flextime Work

www.fastcompany.com/07/140flex.html

This article discusses ways to get your employer and colleagues to support your decision to work flexible hours.

More Working Together Stats

http://www.west.net/~bpbooks/qwsidx.html

This site contains all kinds of interesting tidbits about the workplace, including reports of some studies that substantiate the frequently made argument that work and family programs are good for business.

Work and Family Connection Inc.

www.workfamily.com

This Web site is full of valuable information about work and family programs. You'll learn about the latest research on the benefits of work and family programs and find out what types of programs the country's most forward-thinking employers are offering their employees. Contains links to information about work-life programs, policies, and practices. There are plenty of resources of interest to working parents.

Work and Family Policies: A "Win-Win" Formula for Business and Society

www.cyfc.umn.edu/Work/familypolicies.html#over
Need some ammunition to convince your boss that family-friendly work policies are good for business? This Web site is crammed with all the data you'll need to argue your case.

Your Rights Under the Family and Medical Leave Act of 1993

http://hr.gmu.edu/benefits/fmla.html
This page contains detailed information about the provisions of the Family and Medical Leave Act of 1993.

Recommended Reading List

Books for Parents

Berezin, Judith. *The Complete Guide to Choosing Child Care*. New York: Random House Inc., 1990.

Brazelton, T.B. *Working and Caring*. Reading, MA: Addison-Wesley, 1983.

Buhler, Danalee. *The Very Best Child Care and How to Find It*. Rocklin, CA: Prima Publishing and Communications, 1989.

Carnegie Task Force on Meeting the Needs of Young Children. New York: Carnegie Corporation of New York, 1994.

Darragh, Colleen. *The Perfect Nanny*. Toronto: Window Editions, 1988.

Eiger, Marvis S., M.D., and Sally Wendkos Olds. *The Complete Book of Breastfeeding*. New York: Workman Publishing Company Inc., 1987.

Eisenberg, Arlene, Heidi E. Murkoff, and Sandee E. Hathaway, B.S.N. *What to Expect the First Year.* New York: Workman Publishing Company, 1989.

Elliott, Ruth S. and Jim Savage. *Minding the Kids: A Practical Guide to Employing Caregivers, Baby Sitters, and Au Pairs.* New York: Prentice Hall, 1990.

Grams, Marilyn, M.D. *Breastfeeding Success for Working Mothers.* Sheridan, WY: Achievement Press, 1985.

Huggins, Kathleen, R.N., M.S. *The Nursing Mother's Companion.* Boston, MA: The Harvard Common Press, 1990.

Kaiser, Barbara and Judy Sklar Rasminsky. *The Daycare Handbook: A Parents' Guide to Finding and Keeping Quality Daycare in Canada.* Toronto: Little Brown and Company (Canada) Limited, 1991.

La Leche League International. *The Womanly Art of Breastfeeding.* New York: Penguin Books USA Inc., 1991.

Lally, J. Ronald et al. *Caring for Infants and Toddlers in Groups: Developmentally Appropriate Practice.* Washington, DC: Zero to Three, 1995.

Lin, Yeiser. *Nannies, Au Pairs, Mothers' Helpers—Caregivers.* New York: Random House Inc., 1987.

Lowman, Kaye. *Of Cradles and Careers: A Guide to Reshaping Your Job to Include a Baby in Your Life.* Franklin Park, IL: La Leche League International, 1984.

Miller, Jo Ann. *The Parents' Guide to Daycare.* New York: Bantam Books Inc., 1986.

Olds, Sally. *The Working Parents Survival Guide.* New York: Bantam Books, 1983.

Price, Anne, and Nancy Bamford. *The Breastfeeding Guide for the Working Woman.* New York: Wallaby Books, 1983.

Sissons, Brenda L. and Heather McDowall Black. *Choosing With Care: The Canadian Parent's Practical Guide to Quality Child Care for Infants and Toddlers.* Toronto: Addison-Wesley Publishers Limited, 1992.

Books for Children

Cohen, M. *Will I Have A Friend?* New York: Aladdin Books, 1967.

Conlin, S. and L. Friedman. *Nathan's Day at Preschool.* Seattle: Parent Press Inc., 1991.

Day, Alexandra. *Carl Goes to Daycare.* New York: Farrar Straus and Giroux, 1993.

Essenberg, P.E. *You're My Nikki.* New York: Dial Books, 1993.

Isadora, R. *Friends.* New York: Greenwillow Books, 1990.

Ovenell-Carter, Julie. *Adam's Daycare.* Toronto: Kids Can Press, 1997.

Oxenbury, H. *First Day of School.* New York: E.P. Dutton, Inc., 1983.

Phillips, T. *Day Care ABC.* Nils, IL: Albert Whitman and Co., 1989.

Rogers, F. *Going to Day Care.* New York: G.P. Putnam, 1985.

Tompert, A. *Will You Come Back For Me?* Morton Grove, Illinois: Albert Whitman and Co., 1985.

Important Documents

About the daycare checklists:

- Each checklist has been divided into two parts: the telephone portion and the in-person portion. You may end up moving questions from one checklist to the other, depending on how much time the daycare center director or family daycare provider is able to devote to your call or visit.

- It is unlikely that you will have enough time to ask all of the questions in each checklist. Rather than attempting to ask all of the questions, ask only those that appear to be particularly relevant to your situation.

- After your visit, re-read the checklist. You may be able to answer some additional questions based on your observations.

Daycare center and nursery school telephone checklist

Name of daycare center:

Address:

Part A—Telephone interview

Name of the person that you interviewed by phone:

Date and time of your call:

Location

Where is the center located?

Is it close to your home or place of work?

Hours of operation

What are the hours of operation?

Is there a limit to the number of hours a child can spend at the center each day?

What are the pickup and drop-off times?

Are there any times during the year when the center is closed? If so, when?

Availability of spaces

How many children are enrolled at the center?

How many children would be in your child's group?

What would the age range be within your child's group?

Are there spaces available? If not, how long is the waiting list?

Is part-time care available?

Does the center accept children on a drop-in basis?

What would happen if you needed to increase or decrease your childcare hours because of scheduling changes at work?

Are there any special criteria for admission? If it is a workplace-based childcare, are children of non-employees welcome?

Fees

What fees does the center charge for infants, toddlers, preschoolers, and school-aged children?

Are receipts provided?

Are there any additional costs (diapers, meals, or field trips)?

Are parents expected to participate in fundraising activities or otherwise financially contribute to the operation of the center?

Does the center offer discounts to families with more than one child enrolled at the center?

Is subsidized care available? If so, what are the criteria and how does a parent apply?

Is there a deposit or an enrollment fee required? If so, how much is it?

When are fees due?

Is there a fee for picking up a child late? If so, how much is charged and how soon does the fee kick in?

Is there a charge for days when your child is absent for care? What about holidays?

How much notice is required to withdraw a child from the center?

Licensing and accreditation

Is the center licensed? If not, does the state or province require that it be licensed?

What ages of children is the center licensed to accept?

Is the center accredited by either the National Association for the Education of Young Children (NAEYC) or the National Child Care Association (NCCA)?

Is the center nonprofit or for-profit? If the center is for-profit, is the owner on the premises full-time?

Staff training and certification

Have all staff members had appropriate training in early childhood education?

Have staff members had training in cardiopulmonary resuscitation (CPR), infant CPR, and first aid?

Are staff members assigned to the same children on a regular basis to ensure continuity of care?

Do staff members keep up-to-date on their immunizations?

Are criminal background checks conducted on all staff and volunteers?

Philosophies, goals, and policies

Are the center's goals and philosophies stated in writing? Do you agree with these goals and philosophies?

Are the center's policies stated in writing? Do these policies seem reasonable to you?

What does the center do to encourage ongoing staff development and training?

Does the center have a written policy on discipline which states explicitly that corporal punishment is not to be used?

Does the center have a written statement outlining its behavior management policies? Is this statement consistent with your own beliefs about what is and is not appropriate when it comes to disciplining a child?

Does the center have a written policy outlining the procedures used to resolve conflicts between parents and caregivers?

Part B—Personal visit

Date and time of visit:

Names of staff members that you met with:

Child-staff ratio

Does the center adhere to government regulations limiting group size?

Does it meet the following guidelines, as recommended by the National Association for the

Education of Young Children and the American Academy of Pediatrics?

Age	Ratio	Group Size
Birth to 12 months	1:3	Maximum group size of 6
12 to 24 months	1:3	Maximum group size of 8
24 to 30 months	1:4	Maximum group size of 8
30 to 36 months	1:5	Maximum group size of 10
3-year-olds	1:7	Maximum group size of 14
4-year-olds	1:8	Maximum group size of 16
5-year-olds	1:8	Maximum group size of 16
6- to 8-year-olds	1:10	Maximum group size of 20
9- to 12-year-olds	1:12	Maximum group size of 24

Is the group size small enough that children appear to be secure and comfortable rather than lost in a crowd?

Do the staff members appear to be comfortable with the number (and ages) of children in their care?

Safety

Are electrical outlets covered?

Are radiators covered and heaters kept away from the children?

Are there window guards above the first floor?

Are there safety gates at the tops and bottoms of stairs?

Is the surface of the floor safe and clean?

Are countertops and edges rounded and well finished?

Are dangerous materials (cleaning supplies, scissors, and so on) stored out of the reach of children?

Is the center free of such hazards as radon, asbestos, and lead paint?

Is equipment well-maintained?

Are smoke detectors used?

Is there a fire extinguisher?

Is emergency lighting properly installed and checked regularly?

Are emergency evacuation plans posted?

What is the center's fire escape plan?

Does the center conduct monthly fire drills?

Is there an updated list of telephone numbers beside the phone?

Does the center maintain updated emergency contact and medical information for each child?

What are the center's policies for handling accidents and other serious occurrences?

What are the center's policies concerning the administration of medication?

Does the center have a fenced playground?

Does the playground contain safe and age-appropriate equipment?

Is the area around and under the play equipment covered with a soft material like rubber? Are there guard rails on all elevated surfaces? Are there any sharp edges or other hazards?

Is the center appropriately insured?

Are the children well-supervised?

Are children only released to persons whom their parents have authorized, in writing, to pick them up?

Health and hygiene

Is the room well-ventilated? Is it well-lit? Is it kept at a comfortable temperature?

Is there enough open space for crawling and walking?

Is the center kept clean?

Are infant and toddler toys disinfected on a regular basis?

Are garbage cans, diaper areas, and bathrooms disinfected regularly?

Are hot running water (less than 120°), soap, and paper towels used after toileting and before and after meals and snacks?

Is smoking permitted?

Are families required to produce proof that their children have been immunized?

Is there a clearly stated policy for isolating and caring for children who become ill?

Is there a private rest area where sick children can rest?

Under what circumstances are parents called at work and asked to pick up their children?

Is there a first aid kit?

Rest periods

Are rest periods provided for children? If a child is unable to sleep, is she permitted to engage in quiet alternatives?

Are infants' individual sleep patterns respected? Can they be seen and heard while they are sleeping? Are infants left in cribs or playpens when awake?

Are the sleeping areas clean and appealing?

Do the cots and cribs conform to current safety standards?

Are there enough cots or cribs to allow all of the children to take naps?

If more than one child is using a cot or crib, are the sheets changed after one child is finished with it? Who is responsible for supplying and washing the sheets?

Mealtimes

Are the kitchen and food preparation areas hygienic?

Are meals varied, nutritious, and age-appropriate?

Are menus posted ahead of time?

Are you expected to supply food for your child? If so, is there refrigeration available?

To what extent are they willing to accommodate special diets?

How will the center support your efforts to breast-feed and wean your baby?

Are infants held while they are bottle-fed?

Are infants' individual feeding patterns respected?

Are there highchairs available for older babies? If so, are they safe and sturdy?

Are the eating areas clean and appealing?

Is mealtime pleasant and unhurried?

Does the center use nonbreakable drinking cups or paper cups?

Is food ever withheld as a punishment?

What does the center do if a child does not like a particular type of food?

Diapering and toileting

How often are diapers changed?

Are disposable gloves used when changing diapers? If they aren't, do caregivers routinely wash their hands before changing the next child?

Are the diapering and toileting areas hygienic? Is there a sink close by?

Is there a safety belt on the change table to prevent children from rolling off?

Is the diaper-change area sanitized after each use?

Are you expected to supply diapers, lotions, and baby wipes or are these items supplied?

Are the bathrooms safe and easy for young children to use?

Is there a potty or special toilet seat in the bathroom?

How will the staff support your efforts to toilet-train your child?

Transportation policies

If children are transported to daycare by someone other than their parents, is the driver licensed, qualified, and properly trained and in good health? Has he had a criminal background check?

Are field trips a regular part of the program? If so, what mode of transportation is used? Do parents have the right to refuse to allow their children to participate in field trips that are not within walking distance?

Do the vehicles that are used to transport children have seat belts and car seats that meet safety standards? Are the drivers properly insured?

Are children always placed in safety restraints when they are in vehicles?

Caregiver

Who will be working with your child?

What are her qualifications? Does she participate in ongoing professional development and training?

How long has she been working at the center?

How long has she been working with young children?

Does she demonstrate a genuine love of children?

Is she relaxed and involved with the children?

How does she relate to your child?

Does she seem like someone with whom you and your child could develop a relationship?

What ages of children is she most comfortable with?

Does she have enough time to look after all the children in her care?

Is she experienced in working with children with special needs (if applicable)?

Does she seem to possess a solid understanding of what children can and want to do at various stages of development?

Does she encourage the children to master new skills?

Does she allow them to make choices (where appropriate)?

Does she talk to the children and encourage the children to express themselves through words and language?

Does she encourage good health habits, such as handwashing before eating?

What are her feelings about pacifiers and comfort objects?

Does she offer assistance when a child needs it?

Does she react with enthusiasm to children's discoveries and accomplishments?

Does she sit with the children as they play?

Does she offer physical and verbal reassurance if a child is unhappy?

What is the rate of turnover at the center?

Will any nonstaff members be in contact with your child (students, senior citizens)? Have background checks been conducted on these individuals?

Program

What are the center's program goals? Are they compatible with your own childrearing philosophies?

How will center staff help to ease your child into the program?

Are routines clear and predictable?

How is the day structured?

Is the room set up and ready when families arrive?

Is there a safe place for your child's belongings?

Are children given a choice of developmentally appropriate activities?

Are both group and individual activities offered?

Are there a variety of activities offered (activities that promote both gross and fine motor skills as well as ones that promote language, cognitive, social, and emotional development)?

Are there sufficient quantities of art supplies? Are they within easy reach of the children?

Are the toys and equipment in good condition and within easy reach of the children?

Are children allowed to watch if they aren't interested in participating in a particular activity?

Are infants separated from older children during active indoor and outdoor play?

Are children under six separated from older children during active indoor and outdoor play?

Do the children look happy and involved in the program?

Do the children interact comfortably with both other children and their caregivers?

Does the program appear to be both organized and busy yet warm and welcoming?

Are children encouraged to take out and put away play materials by themselves?

Is the children's artwork displayed in the center as well as sent home to parents?

Is television watching permitted? If so, under what circumstances?

Does the program take into account the varied cultural and ethnic backgrounds of the children and their families?

Do children have the opportunity to speak English as well as their native language (where applicable)?

Is the program unbiased in terms of gender, income level, and physical or mental capabilities?

Are there any special features to the program?

Is the center affiliated with any religious organization? If so, how does that influence the program?

Does the center offer a formal educational program?

Do children receive two hours of outdoor play time each day, weather and health permitting?

Are they adequately supervised?

Is there ample space for all the children and equipment?

Parent Involvement

Are parents encouraged to drop by at any time? Are you welcome to phone during the day to see how your child is doing?

Are parents given opportunities to meet with other parents who use the center?

Are parents treated as partners to the caregiver?

Are parents recognized as experts when it comes to the needs of their own children?

What policies does the center have in place to promote ongoing communication between parents and center staff?

References

Is the center willing to provide you with the names and phone numbers of parents who have used the center?

Are the parents you speak with enthusiastic about the quality of care that their children have received?

Overall impression

Does the center seem warm and friendly or cold and institutional?

How does your child react to the center?

Would you feel comfortable leaving your child at the center?

Family daycare provider telephone checklist

Name:

Address:

Part A—Telephone interview

Name of caregiver (or agency representative):

Date and time of your call:

Location

Where is the family daycare setting home located?

Is it close to your home or place of work?

Hours of operation

What are the hours of operation?

Is there a limit to the number of hours a child can spend at the family daycare home each day?

What are the pickup and drop-off times?

Are there any times during the year when the family daycare home is closed? Is so, when?

Will the agency (where applicable) or your caregiver be able to provide you with backup care while the family daycare home is closed?

Availability of spaces

How many children are enrolled at the family daycare home? What are their ages?

Are there spaces available? If not, how long is the waiting list?

Is part-time care available?

Does the family daycare provider accept children on a drop-in basis?

What would happen if you needed to increase or decrease your childcare hours because of scheduling changes at work?

Fees

What fees does the family daycare provider charge for infants, toddlers, preschoolers, and school-aged children?

If you are using an agency, are there any additional agency fees? Are receipts provided?

Are there any additional costs (for example, diapers, meals, or field trips)?

What equipment, if any, are you expected to supply (strollers, highchairs, playpens, cribs, car seats, and so on)?

Does the family daycare provider offer discounts to families with more than one child enrolled at the family daycare home?

Is subsidized care available? If so, what are the criteria and how does a parent apply?

Is there a deposit or an enrollment fee required? If so, how much is it?

When are fees due?

Is there a fee for picking up a child late? If so, how much is charged and how soon does the fee kick in?

Is there a charge for days when your child is absent for care? What about holiday times?

How much notice is required to withdraw a child from the family daycare home?

Licensing and accreditation

Is the family daycare home licensed? If not, does the state or province require that it be licensed?

What ages of children is the family daycare home licensed to accept?

Is the state or provincial license posted in a visible spot? If so, is it current?

Is the family daycare home accredited by the National Association for Family Child Care?

Is the family daycare home nonprofit or for-profit?

Caregiver training and certification

Has the caregiver had appropriate training in early childhood education?

Has she had training in cardiopulmonary resuscitation (CPR), infant CPR, and first aid?

Is she up-to-date on her immunizations?

Have criminal background checks been conducted on all adults who are likely to be present while your child is present (the caregiver, her partner, any adult children or tenants, agency personnel, and so on)?

Philosophies, goals, and policies

Are the family daycare provider's goals and philosophies stated in writing? Do you agree with these goals and philosophies?

Are the family daycare provider's policies stated in writing? Do these policies seem reasonable to you?

Does the family daycare provider have a written policy on discipline which states explicitly that corporal punishment is not to be used?

Does the family daycare provider have a written statement outlining her behavior management policies? Is this statement consistent with your own beliefs about what is and is not appropriate when it comes to disciplining a child?

Are there any other businesses being run out of the home? If so, are they compatible with a family daycare operation?

Part B—Personal visit

Name of caregiver:

Date and time of your visit:

Child-caregiver ratio

Does the family daycare setting or home adhere to government regulations limiting the numbers (and ages) of children in a family daycare home?

Does the caregiver have children of her own? If so, what are their ages and have they been included in the child-caregiver ratio?

Does the caregiver appear to be comfortable with the number (and ages) of children in her care?

What is the maximum number of children she would be willing to accept?

Safety

Are electrical outlets covered?

Are radiators covered and heaters kept away from the children?

Are there window guards above the first floor?

Are there safety gates at the tops and bottoms of stairs?

Is the surface of the floor safe and clean?

Are countertops and edges rounded and well finished?

Are dangerous materials (for example, cleaning supplies, scissors, and so on) stored out of the reach of children?

Is the family daycare setting free of such hazards as radon, asbestos, and lead paint?

Is equipment well maintained?

Does the caregiver have any pets? If so, where are they kept? Do they pose any risk to the children?

Are smoke detectors used?

Is there a fire extinguisher?

What is the family daycare home's fire escape plan?

Does the family daycare provider conduct monthly fire drills?

Is there an updated list of telephone numbers beside the phone?

Does the family daycare provider maintain updated emergency contact and medical information for each child?

What are the family daycare provider's policies for handling accidents and other serious occurrences?

What are its policies concerning the administration of medication?

Does the family daycare setting have a fenced playground?

Is there a playground or park nearby? If so, is it located on a quiet or busy street? Can your caregiver get the children there safely?

Does the playground contain safe and age-appropriate equipment?

Are there guard rails on all elevated surfaces? Are there any sharp edges or other hazards?

Is the family daycare provider appropriately insured?

Are the children well supervised?

Are children only released to persons whom their parents have authorized, in writing, to pick them up?

Health and hygiene

What areas of the house will your child have access to? Are these areas well ventilated, well lit, and kept at a comfortable temperature?

Is there enough open space for crawling and walking?

Is the family daycare home kept clean?

Are infant and toddler toys disinfected on a regular basis?

Are garbage cans, diaper areas, and bathrooms disinfected regularly?

Are hot running water (less than 120 degrees), soap, and paper towels used after toileting and before and after meals and snacks?

Is smoking permitted?

Are families required to produce proof that their children have been immunized?

Is there a clearly stated policy for isolating and caring for children who become ill?

Is there a private rest area where sick children can rest?

Under what circumstances are parents called at work and asked to pick up their children?

Is there a first aid kit?

Rest periods

Are rest periods provided for children? If a child is unable to sleep, is she permitted to engage in quiet alternatives?

Are infants' individual sleep patterns respected? Can they be seen and heard while they are sleeping?

Are infants left in cribs or playpens when awake?

Are the sleeping areas clean and appealing?

Do the cots and cribs conform to current safety standards?

Are there enough cots or cribs to allow all of the children to take naps?

If more than one child is using a cot or crib, are the sheets changed after one child is finished with it? Who is responsible for supplying and washing the sheets?

Mealtimes

Are the kitchen and food preparation areas hygienic?

Are meals varied, nutritious, and age-appropriate?

Are menus posted ahead of time?

Are you expected to supply food for your child? If so, is there adequate refrigeration available?

To what extent is the caregiver willing to accommodate special diets?

How will the caregiver support your efforts to breast-feed and wean your baby?

Are infants held while they are bottle-fed?

Are infants' individual feeding patterns respected?

Are there highchairs available for older babies? If so, are they safe and sturdy?

Are the eating areas clean and appealing?

Is mealtime pleasant and unhurried?

Does the family daycare home use nonbreakable drinking cups or paper cups?

Is food ever withheld as a punishment?

What does the family daycare provider do if a child does not like a particular type of food?

Diapering and toileting

How often are diapers changed?

Are disposable gloves used when changing diapers? If they aren't, do caregivers routinely wash their hands before changing the next child?

Are the diapering and toileting areas hygienic? Is there a sink close by?

Is there a safety belt on the change table to prevent children from rolling off?

Is the diaper-change area sanitized after each use?

Are you expected to supply diapers, lotions, and baby wipes or are these items supplied?

Are the bathrooms safe and easy for young children to use?

Is there a potty or special toilet seat in the bathroom?

How will the staff support your efforts to toilet-train your child?

Transportation policies

Are field trips a regular part of the program? If so, what mode of transportation is used? Do parents have the right to refuse to allow their children to participate in field trips that are not within walking distance?

Do the vehicles that are used to transport children have seat belts and car seats that meet safety standards? Are the drivers properly insured?

Are children always placed in safety restraints when they are in vehicles?

Caregiver

What are the caregiver's qualifications? Does she participate in ongoing professional development and training?

How long has she been operating a family daycare home?

For how many more years does she intend to continue operating the family daycare home?

How long has she been working with young children?

Does she demonstrate a genuine love of children?

Is she relaxed and involved with the children?

How does she relate to your child?

Does she seem like someone with whom you and your child could develop a relationship?

What ages of children is she most comfortable with?

Does she have enough time to look after all the children in her care?

Is she experienced in working with children with special needs (if applicable)?

Does she seem to possess a solid understanding of what children can and want to do at various stages of development?

Does she encourage the children to master new skills?

Does she allow them to make choices (where appropriate)?

Does she talk to the children and encourage the children to express themselves through words and language?

Does she encourage good health habits, such as handwashing before eating?

What are her feelings about pacifiers and comfort objects?

Does she offer assistance when a child needs it?

Does she react with enthusiasm to children's discoveries and accomplishments?

Does she sit with the children as they play?

Does she offer physical and verbal reassurance if a child is unhappy?

What is the rate of turnover at the family daycare home?

Will any other than the caregiver be in contact with your child (for example, others who live in the home, agency personnel, and so on)? Have background checks been conducted on these individuals?

Program

What are the caregiver's program goals? Are they compatible with your own childrearing philosophies?

How will the caregiver help to ease your child into the program?

Are routines clear and predictable?

How is the day structured?

Is the room set up and ready when families arrive?

Is there a safe place for your child's belongings?

Are children given a choice of developmentally appropriate activities?

Are both group and individual activities offered?

Are there a variety of activities offered (activities that promote both gross and fine motor skills as well as ones that promote language, cognitive, social, and emotional development)? Are there sufficient quantities of art supplies? Are they within easy reach of the children?

Are the toys and equipment in good condition and within easy reach of the children?

Are children allowed to watch if they aren't interested in participating in a particular activity?

Are infants separated from older children during active indoor and outdoor play?

Are children under six separated from older children during active indoor and outdoor play?

Do the children look happy and involved in the program?

Do the children interact comfortably with both other children and their caregivers?

Does the program appear to be both organized and busy yet warm and welcoming?

Are children encouraged to take out and put away play materials by themselves?

Is the children's artwork displayed in the family day-care home as well as sent home to parents?

Is television watching permitted? If so, under what circumstances?

Does the program take into account the varied cultural and ethnic backgrounds of the children and their families?

Do children have the opportunity to speak English as well as their native language (where applicable)?

Is the program unbiased in terms of gender, income level, and physical or mental capabilities?

Are there any special features to the program?

Do children receive two hours of outdoor play time each day, weather and health permitting?

Are they adequately supervised?

Is there ample space for all the children and equipment?

Parent involvement

Are parents encouraged to drop by at any time? Are you welcome to phone during the day to see how your child is doing?

Are parents given opportunities to meet with other parents who use the family daycare home?

Are parents treated as partners to the caregiver?

Are parents recognized as experts when it comes to the needs of their own children?

What policies does the family daycare provider have in place to promote ongoing communication between parents and family daycare staff?

References

Is the caregiver willing to provide you with the names and phone numbers of parents who have used the family daycare home? Are the parents you speak with enthusiastic about the quality of care that their children have received?

Overall impression

How does your child react to the family daycare provider?

Would you feel comfortable leaving your child at this family daycare home?

In-home caregiver checklist

Name:

Phone number:

Part A—Telephone interview

Date of phone call:

What hours and days of the week is the caregiver available?

What are her salary expectations?

What experience has she had in caring for young children?

What was her most recent position? What were her responsibilities? What was her reason for leaving this position?

Has she had any formal training in early childhood education?

Is she certified in cardiopulmonary resuscitation (CPR) and first aid?

Does she have any health problems?

Does she smoke?

Does she have a valid driver's license and her own vehicle?

Would she be prepared to undergo a background check at your expense?

Part B—Personal interview

Date of interview:

What led her to pursue a career with children?

What does she like most about her work?

What does she like least about her work?

What age group is her favorite?

What age group is her least favorite?

What are her personal goals?

How long does she intend to continue working in the childcare field?

Is she prepared to make at least a one year commitment to your family?

Does she participate in professional development opportunities on a regular basis?

Does she belong to the local nanny association or childcare provider's network? Why or why not?

Does she demonstrate a genuine love of children? How does she relate to your child(ren)?

Does she seem like someone with whom you and your child could develop a relationship?

What ages of children is she most comfortable with? Is she experienced in working with children with special needs (if applicable)?

Does she seem to possess a solid understanding of what children can and want to do at various stages of development?

Could she recognize and deal with illness?

Does she encourage the children to master new skills?

Does she allow them to make choices (where appropriate)?

Does she talk to the children and encourage the children to express themselves through words and language?

Does she encourage good health habits, such as handwashing before eating?

What are her feelings about pacifiers and comfort objects?

Does she offer assistance when a child needs it?

Does she have CPR and first-aid training?

Does she react with enthusiasm to children's discoveries and accomplishments?

Does she sit with the children as they play?

Does she offer physical and verbal reassurance if a child is unhappy?

What is her approach to discipline?

How does she deal with crying?

What activities does she like to do with babies? toddlers? preschoolers?

Is she willing to provide you with a list of references?

Is she prepared to sign a work agreement?

Are the references you speak with enthusiastic about the quality of care that their children have received from this caregiver?

How does your child react to her?

Would you feel comfortable leaving your child with her?

FORMAL WORK AGREEMENT WITH A NANNY OR OTHER IN-HOME CAREGIVER

Childcare Agreement

This Agreement is between the following parties:

_____ (Nanny)

and

_____ (Parents)

The purpose of this agreement is to define and mutually agree upon the following terms, provisions, and conditions for the care of the following children:

_____

_____

_____

Job Conditions

Upon employment, there will be a trial period of two weeks for both Parents and Nanny to ensure compatibility.

Start Date: _____

Scheduled Work Hours:

From _____ a.m. to_____ p.m., Monday through Friday. This schedule may vary. The Nanny will be informed of any change of schedule with as much advance notice as possible.

Pay/Pay Schedule

The Nanny shall be paid $_____ each Friday unless a holiday falls on Friday. If a holiday falls on Friday, the Nanny will be paid on Thursday.

Taxes

The Parents are to withhold any mandatory taxes for which they are responsible on the Nanny's salary. The Nanny is responsible for withholding all state and federal income taxes from her own pay check.

Compensation for Additional Children

Should the blessed event of another child occur, the Nanny shall be compensated by no less than $_____/week.

Evaluation

The Nanny's performance will be evaluated by the Parents as follows:

- after the initial six months of employment
- at the end of the first year
- annually thereafter

Upon satisfactory performance of duties, the Nanny will be given a merit/cost of living increase of $_____ or _____ %.

Place of Business

_____

_____

Professional Courtesy/Due Respect

The Nanny shall be treated with full professional courtesy and the Nanny will treat the Parents with due respect.

Job Responsibilities

Specific Nanny responsibilities and duties are those relating to childcare only, such as providing loving and responsible care for the children of the family. This care includes, but is not limited to, the following:

Meals

The preparation and serving of healthy breakfast, lunch, and dinner (if applicable) to the children. In general, the meals should be a mixture of easy to make (microwaveable or ready-made) and made-from-scratch meals. All foods will be provided by the Parents. During the week, the Nanny will prepare a list of items that are needed and present this list to the Parents on Friday.

The Nanny will not be expected to prepare meals for any adult members of the household.

Dressing (including changing of diapers and hygiene)

The Nanny shall ensure that the children are properly dressed for the activities they are engaged in and the weather that they are exposed to. The Nanny may be required to give the children baths from time to time. The Nanny shall help the children learn about personal hygiene, including learning to dress themselves, potty training, brushing teeth after each meal, and so on; as well as teaching them to clean their messes when they are done playing.

Learning Activities

The Nanny will strive to teach the children proper speech, the basics of counting, their ABCs, shapes, colors, courtesy, sharing, and neatness, as their development permits.

Naptime

The Nanny shall do her best to ensure that the children get their proper naptime in the afternoon each day.

Recreation

The Nanny shall play with the children to encourage speech and personality development. In addition, the Nanny understands that there are times throughout the day when children need quiet time to play by themselves. The Nanny will ensure that all play is supervised, and that the children are never left unattended and without direct supervision.

Firm Guidance

The Nanny will ensure that the children understand that certain activities, as prescribed by the Parents, are forbidden. In no event shall the children be allowed to engage in any activity which is deemed dangerous by the Parents or Nanny. The Nanny shall be firm but loving with the children. The children are not to be spanked or hit for transgressions. Time-outs shall be used as the method for discipline. All punishment is the Parents' responsibility. The Nanny will discuss behavioral modification strategies with the Parents.

Transportation

From time to time, the Nanny shall transport the children to and from parks and special events in the Parents' vehicle. There will be no unapproved rides in any car, and no unapproved trips. The nanny may take the children on walks to and from the park, and so on.

Guidelines for Releasing Children

Under no circumstances will the Nanny release a child to any relative, neighbor, family friend or friend's parent without the Parents' direct authorization to do so. The Nanny prefers to be introduced to any person to whom she may be directed to release the children. In the event that such meeting is impossible, the Nanny will request proof of identification (such as a driver's license) before she will release any children. If such identification is unavailable, the children will not be released.

General Household Maintenance

The Nanny will be responsible for the following domestic duties, which are directly related to the care of the children:

Kitchen

The Nanny shall be responsible for daily cleaning of the kitchen area, of all highchairs and dishes that are used by the children and the Nanny. The Nanny will put dirty dishes in the dishwasher.

Play Area

The Nanny shall be responsible for daily picking-up of toys and clothes in the children's play areas.

Sweeping/Mopping

The Nanny shall be responsible for sweeping/mopping of kitchen floors (after meals, weekly, or as needed) as well as vacuuming the playroom carpet.

Garbage

The Nanny will be responsible for the emptying of the diaper pail (if applicable) only. Under no circumstances is the Nanny expected to take out the garbage, nor for ensuring that the garbage cans are taken out on trash day and removed from the street after refuse is collected.

Under no conditions is the Nanny expected to clean up after the adult members of the household.

The Nanny will never be required to clean any mess made by the Parents, including, but not limited to dirty dishes, clearing the table, washing counters and stove tops, or general tidying up.

Children's Bedrooms

The Nanny will be responsible for changing the bedding of only the small children under her care. Depending upon the age of the children, the Nanny may require that the children assist her in these duties so they learn the proper method. All children age ten and over under the care of the Nanny will change their own beds, with the assistance of the Nanny, if needed.

Children's Bathroom

The Nanny will make sure that clothes are placed in the hamper and that counters and mirrors are wiped dry after hand washing and teeth brushing.

Laundry

The Nanny is responsible only for the clothes and bedding of the children (under age eleven) directly under her care. Above age eleven, the children will assist in washing/drying laundry so they will have a thorough understanding of laundering procedures. Above age thirteen, the children will be responsible for laundering their own clothes and bedding.

The Nanny is never expected to do any laundry for the Parents nor any other member of the household not directly under her care.

Babysitting

Occasionally, the Parents will require additional babysitting. Insofar as possible, the Parents understand they must give the Nanny ample notification (preferably at least one week). On these occasions, the Nanny will be paid at a rate of $____/hour. The Nanny is in no way required to babysit beyond the agreed upon hours of duty, but understands the need for an occasional (or routine) night out and will do her best to accommodate the needs of the Parents.

The Parents understand that the Nanny will occasionally babysit for other families on Friday night or over the weekend. Parents have first option at booking the Nanny's babysitting time. If the Parents do not require the Nanny's services, and the Nanny makes plans to babysit for another family, the Parents cannot require that the Nanny cancel her plans.

The Parents agree to be a good reference for the Nanny for any new families that she may begin babysitting for during her employment with their family.

As with all families the Nanny babysits for, the Parents understand that by reserving the Nanny's time for babysitting, they are securing that time. The Parents may cancel, without any penalty, up to twenty-four hours beforehand. If cancellation is made within twenty-four hours (except by the presence of an emergency situation), the Parents understand that they are still required to pay for the time that was reserved for them and their children.

Cooking

The Parents understand that occasionally the Nanny enjoys baking and will do so in her free time only (during nap times, and so on), or at those times when the children's involvement can safely be incorporated.

Things the Nanny Is Not Responsible for and Won't Do:

- The Nanny is not a gardener. She will not weed, mow lawns, sweep patios, trim bushes, etc.

- The Nanny is in no way required to wash windows, clean garages, clean out cupboards/shelves, or offices.

- The Nanny is not a professional mover. She will not move furniture, rearrange rooms, etc.

- The Nanny will not be responsible for purchasing or delivering to any location alcohol or tobacco products, etc.

Note: The Nanny does like being able to help make life easier for the Parents. Otherwise she wouldn't be a Nanny. She is not opposed to being of assistance to either Parent with odd duties now and again, such as wrapping presents, going to the post office, grocery store, and so on, as long as it is occasional and doesn't interfere with her normal duties of childcare.

Priorities

The Parents recognize that the care for young children can be demanding. It is understood that on some days the schedule may not be adhered to, all chores may not be completed, and the play areas may not be cleaned up due to the attention the Nanny must give to the children. Care for and feeding of the children will always be the top priority.

Medicine

The Nanny shall not administer any medication, including over-the-counter medications, unless specifically directed to do so by the Parents. The Parents understand the Nanny will require a written request for administering any medicines. In addition, all prescribed medicines must remain in their original packaging with the doctor's instructions. All medicine administered by the Parents or Nanny must be logged with exact dosages and the time given so that no overdosing can occur.

Emergency Situations

In the case of any emergency, the Nanny will contact the Parents immediately. If necessary, the Nanny must not hesitate to call 911 or the Poison Control Center, prior to calling the Parents. In any emergency, if the Parents cannot be reached, the Nanny is to contact _____ (nearest relative or trusted friend). If the situation warrants immediate action or if the phones are inoperative, the Nanny may try to get assistance from the neighbors. A list of phone numbers will be posted for emergency use by the kitchen and _____ _____ (upstairs or alternative) phones.

Authorization to Treat a Minor

The Parents will sign and date two "Authorization to Treat a Minor" cards per child: one to be put on file at their pediatrician's office, the other held in the Nanny's possession. In the unlikely event of an emergency occurring when the Parents cannot be reached by the Nanny, the Nanny will be able to authorize the Doctor and the Hospital to administer any medically necessary care to the child(ren). If the Nanny is required to give authorization to medical personnel to treat the child(ren), the Parents understand that all medical care administered would be on the advice and at the discretion of medical personnel only, and the Nanny cannot be held liable or responsible for the decisions made by said medical personnel. Furthermore, the Nanny cannot be held liable or responsible for any medical bills incurred by such medical attention.

General House Rules

The rules listed below must be followed. An exception to any of these rules requires the verbal consent of one of the Parents (except in an emergency situation).

- No visitors will be permitted unless the parents have previously agreed.

- The Nanny is not required to receive any guests for the Parents.

- The Nanny will not be required to call, supervise or advise any maintenance personnel, including, but not limited to, gardeners, pool men, painters, carpet cleaners, handymen, exterminators, and so on.

- No service or maintenance personnel whatsoever will be present inside the house when the Nanny is at home alone with the children. If service or maintenance personnel are needed for repair while the Nanny is present, one Parent will be present before arrival of and through the entire visit of said service personnel.

- The Nanny is in no way responsible for work that is not completed or done because the Parents did not notify the Nanny of scheduled work or make themselves available to supervise said work.

- No long distance or collect calls will be made, except in the case of an emergency or with the prior permission of the Parents.

- Only short and occasional local calls will be made, and these shall be made during the children's nap times or the Nanny's other free times.

- The Nanny is not required to answer the telephone to take messages, nor is she required to deliver messages to callers. She is not required to receive any mail or packages, nor sign for any mail or packages, although doing so does not hold her liable in any way whatsoever if said call or package would have been refused by the Parents.

- The children are not to be taken on any unapproved rides in any cars.

- The house is to be kept locked at all times.

- The Nanny is to report any suspicious visitors or phone calls to the Parents immediately.

- The Nanny is to report any falls or injuries occurring to the children or herself to the Parents immediately.

- The Nanny must inform the Parents if she is feeling ill.

- When answering the phone, the Nanny will use the family's name (for example, "Smiths' residence"), state that the Parents are "not available," and take a message.

- The Nanny will not divulge any other information about the household, unless she has been given direct permission by the Parents to speak freely with the caller (for example, a grandparent or other relative).

- She will never indicate that she is alone with small children, and the Parents will never indicate to anyone that the Nanny will be there alone with the children.

- Both the Parents and the Nanny are to maintain a play area for the children that is free from potential dangers, (choking or strangulation hazards, breakables within children's reach, and so on).

- The Parents are to maintain a safe working environment for the Nanny at all times. This includes, but is not limited to, the following points:

- If the need for fumigation or bugspraying becomes necessary, it will be scheduled for Friday, and the Nanny will not be expected to enter the work area for at least two days. If fumigation or extermination takes place between Monday and Thursday, the Nanny is willing to watch her charges at another location for no less than two days to allow for the air to become as clear from the fumes as possible. Otherwise, the Nanny will not be expected to return to work for at least two working days, and will be paid her usual weekly salary.

- The Nanny expects to work in a smoke-free environment.

Sick Time

Obviously, health is an important criterion for this position. But on those days when the Nanny is too sick to work, the Nanny must notify the Parents by _____a.m. that morning at the absolute latest.

After the first two months of employment, the Nanny will be entitled to no less than 10 paid sick days. The Nanny shall have no less than 10 paid sick days available during any calendar year.

Vacation

After the first two months of employment, the Nanny is entitled to no less than 10 days of paid vacation time per year. This vacation time cannot be accrued from one year to the next. The Nanny agrees not to take her sick time and vacation time in sequence.

Nanny is encouraged, but not required, to coordinate her vacation with that of the Parents. But in any event, the Nanny is required to give the Parents at least two weeks notice. To the best of her ability, the Nanny will work with the Parents to schedule her vacation.

In the event that the Parents decide to take a vacation, the Nanny may be required to continue care for the children. If the Nanny cares for the children during the Parents' vacation, she shall be compensated at a rate of $_____ /night, in addition to her regular weekly salary. If the Nanny is not required to care for the children during the Parents' vacation, she will be compensated at her full weekly salary nevertheless. The Nanny must be notified of the family's vacation plans at least two weeks in advance.

If the Parents invite the Nanny to accompany them to their vacation destination, all travel-related expenses will be paid by the Parents. The Nanny's responsibilities will remain the same to the children: to maintain their schedule as best as possible while exposing them to the new environment. Under no circumstances is the Nanny required to join the family on their vacations if she does not wish to do so.

Personal Days

The Nanny will occasionally require a visit to the dentist or doctor, or may require some personal time for another reason. After the initial two months of employment, the Nanny shall be entitled to no less than five paid personal days, not to be used as or in conjunction with vacation days or sick days. Insofar as possible, the Nanny will give at least one week's notice before taking a personal day. The Nanny is not required to reveal her plans to the Parents about her personal days. The Nanny may stretch her personal days by using them in half day increments. It is understood that any additional time taken as personal time will go uncompensated.

If either Parent tells the Nanny to take the day off, there will be no pay-docking, or "making up the time" in babysitting hours or otherwise. The Nanny will not be expected to use her personal time, vacation time, or sick time to compensate for the hours given to her.

Paid Holidays

The following nine days are paid holidays for the Nanny: New Year's Day, Memorial Day, Independence Day, Labor Day, Thanksgiving Day and the following Friday, Christmas Eve, Christmas Day, New Year's Eve.

Communication

Good communication is essential. Problems and issues with the children's behavior, routine, Nanny's duties, or other matters should be brought to the attention of the Parents as soon as they occur. Likewise, if the Parents have any problems with the aforementioned issues, the Parents should bring them to the attention of the Nanny as soon as they occur. The Nanny promises to be honest and up-front with the Parents regarding all aspects of the children's care and in return asks the same of the Parents. All issues will be resolved with good communication and not recriminatory confrontation.

Notice to Quit

The Nanny agrees to provide the Parents with at least three weeks notice prior to leaving employment and the Parents agree to provide three weeks notice before terminating the Nanny, unless the personal safety of either the Nanny or the children are involved. If such is the case, the Nanny can leave employment immediately or will be asked by the Parents to leave employment immediately. Upon notice to terminate this agreement, the Nanny promises to provide as much assistance as needed to the Parents to secure high-quality childcare, and the Parents promise to be a reference for the Nanny for any future job she may seek. Upon termination of this contract, Parents will provide the Nanny with a written reference entailing job responsibilities, performance, and so on, and will agree to provide a verbal phone reference to any prospective employers. The Nanny, in turn, will provide, to any potential childcare providers, an impartial written and oral reference for the family as employers.

Amendment

This agreement may be amended in writing from time to time upon the agreement of all parties. No amendment or modification hereof shall be valid unless it is in writing and signed by all the parties.

Invalid Provisions

The invalidity or unenforceability of any particular provision hereof shall not affect the other provisions hereof, and this agreement shall be construed in all respects as if such invalid or unenforceable provisions were omitted.

Waiver

No right under this contract shall be waived (lost) merely by delaying or failing to exercise it. Consent to one act shall not be considered consent to any other or subsequent acts. Any waiver or a default under this agreement must be in writing and shall not be a waiver of any other default concerning the same or any other provisions of this agreement.

Governing Law

This agreement shall be governed by and interpreted in accordance with the laws of the State of _____. And all parties understand the terms in this contract, and understand that disregard of these terms is grounds for termination of this contract.

A signed agreement represents that the following parties mutually agree to the job conditions and description as outlined in this agreement.

Parent: _____ Date: _____

Parent: _____ Date: _____

Nanny: _____ Date: _____

This contract is reprinted with the permission of Christine Maniscalco of Life With Nanny (http://www. atmavidya.com/lifewithnanny/)and ParentsPlace.com (www.parentsplace.com). It was created by Christine Maniscalco in collaboration with other users of the Internet, and was based on an earlier template developed by ParentsPlace.com.

LETTER OF AGREEMENT WITH A FAMILY DAYCARE PROVIDER

(Date)

Dear _____:

The purpose of this letter is to summarize some of the points we have agreed upon concerning the care that you will be providing to _____ (child's name) in your home.

Fees

We agree that I shall make weekly payments of $_____, and that these payments shall be due each Friday afternoon and that you shall provide me with receipts for these payments.

We also agree that I will be required to pay for days when my child is absent from care unless

- such absence is due to the two weeks of vacation time which my family is entitled to under the terms of this agreement

- my child has been temporarily withdrawn from care due to a serious illness, in which case I will be required to pay only for the first week of care that he misses.

Supplies and Equipment

We agree that I will be responsible for providing the following supplies and equipment:

_____

_____

(for example, car seat, diapers, bottles of formula or breastmilk, baby wipes, and so on).

We agree that you will be responsible for providing the following supplies and equipment:

_____

_____

age-appropriate toys, art supplies, and so on).

Hours

We agree that your hours of operation will be from 7:30 a.m. to 5:30 p.m. My child will be dropped off at your home at approximately _____ a.m. and will be picked up by either myself or _____ (name of partner or other person responsible for picking children up) at approximately _____ p.m.

Holidays

We agree that each of us will be entitled to two weeks of holidays each calendar year, and that we will provide one another with as much notice as possible of our intention to take our holiday time.

When you are taking your holidays, I will have the option of using the services of _____ _____ (name of alternate caregiver), assuming that she is available.

When I am taking my holidays, I will not be required to pay for the days that my child is missing.

Communication

We agree to spend a few minutes talking about _____ (name(s) of children) at the beginning and end of each day, and on the last Friday of each month, when we will schedule a lengthier face-to-face meeting.

Health and Safety Issues

We agree that

- you and your partner _____ (caregiver's partner's name) will be the only adults present in the home while my child is in your care

- my child will not be left unattended at any time

- he will be allowed to play in the backyard, but not in the front yard

- you can take him to the park down the street without obtaining my permission first, but that all other outings will need to be cleared with me in advance

- he will not be exposed to any second-hand smoke in your home

- your home will continue to be pet-free

- my child will not be sent to your home when he is suffering from vomiting, diarrhea, a high fever, or any serious illness, but that it is acceptable for me to send him to your home if he has a minor head cold

- you will phone me prior to 7:30 a.m. if you are unable to provide care to my child on a particular day due to your own illness

Administration of Medication

I will provide you with a signed "Medical Consent Form" that will allow you to authorize emergency medical attention on my behalf, should you be unable to reach me.

I will also provide you with a signed "Authorization to Administer Medication Form" whenever my child requires medication. In this situation, the medication will be provided to you in its original container with the dosage information and physician's instructions clearly indicated.

Feeding

We agree that you will be responsible for providing my child with meals and snacks at the following times of day: _____.
I/you will be responsible for providing the food required for these meals and snacks.

We agree that these meals and snacks will be as nutritious as possible, and that they will not contain any of the following foods, to which my child is either allergic or highly sensitive:_____

_____.

Sleeping

We agree that you will put my child down for a nap in the crib in the playroom in the early afternoon. If he is unable to settle down for a sleep, you will encourage him to enjoy some quiet playtime instead.

Discipline

We agree that the method of discipline to be used will be time-outs and that my child will not be subjected to any form of physical punishment, regardless of the circumstances.

Diapering/Toileting

We agree that my child will be changed and encouraged to use the toilet at regular intervals throughout the day.

Outdoor Playtime

We agree that, weather and health permitting, my child will be given the opportunity to enjoy a period of outdoor playtime each morning when he is in your care.

Television

We agree that my child will not be watching television on a regular basis while he is in your care.

Other Responsibilities

We agree that you shall also assume responsibility for the following additional tasks related to my child's care: _____

_____

_____

Termination of This Agreement

Should either of us decide for whatever reason that the time has come to terminate this agreement, we agree to provide one another with at least two weeks notice.

Sincerely,

_____

Caregiver acknowledgement:

I agree to the terms and conditions set forth in this agreement.

_____ (caregiver's signature)

_____ (date)

MEDICAL CONSENT FORM

Should it be impossible to reach me in the event of an emergency, I hereby authorize _____ (caregiver's name) to take any emergency measures necessary to protect my child, including (but not limited to) arranging for transporation to the hospital by ambulance and authorizing emergency treatments recommended by the attending physician.

I understand that I shall be responsible for paying any costs incurred by _____ (caregiver's name) in the course of obtaining emergency treatment for my child.

Child's name:

_____

Date of birth:

_____

Medicare number:

_____

Health insurance company:

_____

Policy number:

_____

Preferred hospital/clinic:

_____

Name and phone number of family doctor:

_____

_____

Drug allergies or other important medical information:

_____

_____

- -

_____

Signature   Date

AUTHORIZATION TO ADMINISTER MEDICATION FORM

I hereby authorize _____ (care-giver's name) to administer the following medica-tion(s) to my child: _____

_____ (name of medication).

Start date: _____

End date: _____

Dosage: _____

Times at which medication is to be administered:

Special instructions: _____

I wish to be contacted immediately in the event that my child shows any unusual symptoms and reactions to this medication.

Signature: _____

Date: _____

FAMILY PROFILE WORKSHEET

MINI-PROFILES OF FAMILY MEMBERS

Names of adult member(s) of the household, and their relationship to the child(ren) being cared for:

Name	Relationship to child(ren)

Names of all children living in household	Ages and sexes of the children

Names of any household pets	Type of pet

Languages spoken at home: _____

Parent(s) occupation(s): _____

Ethnic/religious holidays or practices observed:

_____

_____

_____

MINI-PROFILE OF CHILD REQUIRING CARE
Name:

_____

Age:

_____

Description of special needs:

_____

_____

_____

_____

Brief description of child's physical development and challenges:

_____

_____

_____

Brief description of child's emotional development and challenges:

_____

_____

_____

Brief description of child's language development and challenges:

_____

_____

_____

Toileting routines:

_____
_____
_____
_____

Feeding routines:

_____
_____
_____
_____

Bathing routines:

_____
_____
_____
_____

Sleeping routines:

_____
_____
_____
_____

Discipline methods used with this child:

_____
_____
_____
_____

Techniques that are effective in soothing this child:

_____
_____
_____
_____

Favorite toys or activities:

_____
_____
_____
_____

Other information that you might wish to know about my child or her family:

_____

_____

_____

_____

_____

_____

_____

_____

_____

_____

_____

_____

Signature of parent   Date

Important Statistics

CAREGIVER-CHILD RATIOS FOR EACH STATE
Number Of Children Per Caregiver

State	Infants	Toddlers	Preschoolers	School-Aged
Alabama	6	8	12	22 (six- and seven-year-olds) 25 (eight- and nine-year-olds)
Alaska	5	6	10	20
Arizona	5	8	13	20
Arkansas	6	12	12	20
California	4	12	12	14
Colorado	5	7	10	15
Connecticut	4	4	10	10
Delaware	4	10	12	25
District of Columbia	4	4	8	15
Florida	4	11	15	25
Georgia	6	10	15	25
Hawaii	4	8	12	20
Idaho	6	12	12	18
Illinois	4	8	10	20
Indiana	4	5	10	20
Iowa	4	6	8	15

Kansas	3	7	12	16
Kentucky	5	10	12	15 (six-year-olds) 20 (seven- to nine-year-olds)
Louisiana	6	12	14	25
Maine	4	5	10	13
Maryland	3	6	10	15
Massachusetts	3	4	10	15 (six- and seven-year-olds) 13 (eight- and nine-year-olds)
Michigan	4	4	10	20
Minnesota	4	7	10	15
Mississippi	5	12	14	20
Missouri	4	8	10	16
Montana	4	8	8	14
Nebraska	4	6	10	15
Nevada	6	10	13	13
New Hampshire	4	6	8	15
New Jersey	4	7	10	18
New Mexico	6	12	12	15
New York	4	5	7	10
North Carolina	5	10	5	25
North Dakota	4	5	7	18
Ohio	5	7	12	18
Oklahoma	4	8	12	20
Oregon	4	4	10	15
Pennsylvania	4	6	10	12
Rhode Island	4	6	9	13
South Carolina	6	10	13	23
South Dakota	5	5	10	15
Tennessee	5	8	10	25
Texas	4	13	17	26
Utah	4	7	12	20
Vermont	4	5	10	13

Virginia	4	10	10	20
Washington	4	7	10	15
West Virginia	4	8	10	16
Wisconsin	4	6	10	18
Wyoming	5	8	10	25

CAREGIVER-CHILD RATIOS FOR CANADIAN PROVINCES AND TERRITORIES

ALBERTA

Age	Staff-Child Ratios
Daycare Centers	
0 to 12 months	1:3
13 to 18 months	1:4
19 to 35 months	1:6
3 to 5 years	1:8
5 to 6 years	1:10
Nursery Schools	
5 to 6 years	1:10

BRITISH COLUMBIA

Age	Staff-Child Ratios
0 to 3 years	1:4
30 months to 6 years	1:8
Preschool	1:10
School-age	1:10-15
Special Needs	1:4

MANITOBA

Age	Staff-Child Ratios
Mixed Age Groups	
12 weeks to 2 years	1:4
2 to 6 years	1:8
6 to 12 years	1:15
Separate Age Groups	
12 weeks to 2 years	1:3
1 to 2 years	1:4
2 to 3 years	1:6
3 to 4 years	1:8
4 to 5 years	1:9

5 to 6 years	1:10
6 to 12 years	1:15
Nursery School	
12 weeks to 2 years	1:4
2 to 6 years	1:10

NEW BRUNSWICK

Age	Staff-Child Ratios
less than 2 years	1:3
2 to 3 years	1:5
3 to 4 years	1:7
4 to 5 years	1:10
5 to 6 years	1:12
6 to 12 years	1:15

NEWFOUNDLAND

Age	Staff-Child Ratios
2 to 3 years	1:6
3 to 6 years	1:8
7 to 12 years	1:15

NORTHWEST TERRITORIES

Age	Staff-Child Ratios
0 to 12 months	1:3
13 to 24 months	1:4
25 to 35 months	1:6
3 years	1:8
4 years	1:9
5 to 11 years	1:10

NOVA SCOTIA

Age	Staff-Child Ratios
0 to 17 months	1:4
17 months to 5 years (full day)	1:7
17 months to 5 years (part day)	1:12
5 to 12 years	1:15

ONTARIO

Age	Staff-Child Ratios
0 to 18 months	1:3

18 months to 2 years	1:5
2 to 5 years	1:8
5 to 6 years	1:12
6 to 10 years	1:15

PRINCE EDWARD ISLAND

Age	Staff-Child Ratios
0 to 2 years	1:3
2 to 3 years	1:5
3 to 5 years	l:10
5 to 6 years	1:12
7+ years	1:15

QUEBEC

Age	Staff-Child Ratios
0 to 18 months	1:5
18 months to 5 years	1:8
6 to 12 years	1:15

SASKATCHEWAN

Age	Staff-Child Ratios
Infants	1:3
Toddlers	1:5
Preschool (30 months to 6 years)	1:10
School-age (6 to 12 years)	1:15

YUKON

Age	Staff-Child Ratios
0 to 18 months	1:4
18 months to 2 years	1:6
3 to 6 years	1:8
6 to 12 years	1:12

VISITOR EXCHANGE PROGRAM INFORMATION FROM THE UNITED STATES INFORMATION AGENCY

22 CFR - Part 514.31 - Au Pairs

Effective February 8, 1995

514.31 Au pairs.

(a) Introduction. These regulations govern Agency-designated exchange visitor programs under which foreign nationals are afforded the opportunity to live with an American host family and participate directly in the home life of the host family while providing limited child care services and attending a U.S. post-secondary educational institution.

(b) Program designation. The Agency may, in its sole discretion, designate bona fide programs satisfying the objectives set forth in paragraph (a) of this section. Such designation shall be for a period of two years and may be revoked by the Agency for good cause.

(c) Program eligibility. Sponsors designated by the Agency to conduct au pair exchange program shall:

1. Limit the participation of foreign nationals in such programs to not more than one year;

2. Limit the number of hours an au pair participant is obligated to provide child care services to not more than 45 hours per week;

3. Require that the au pair participant enrolls in a U.S. institution of higher education for not less than six semester hours of academic credit or its equivalent;

4. Require that all officers, employees, agents, and volunteers acting on their behalf are adequately trained and supervised;

5. Require that the au pair participant is placed with a host family within one hour's driving time of the home of the local organizational representative authorized to act on the sponsor's behalf in both routine and emergency matters arising from the au pair's participation in their exchange program;

6. Require that each local organizational representative maintain a schedule of personal monthly contact (or more frequently as required) with each au pair and host family for which he or she is responsible;

7. Require that local organizational representatives not devoting their full time and attention to their program obligations are responsible for no more than fifteen au pairs and host families; and

8. Require that each local organizational representative is provided adequate support services by a regional organizational representative.

(d) Au pair selection. In addition to satisfying the requirements of 514.10(a), sponsors shall ensure that all participants in a designated au pair exchange program:

1. Are between the ages of 18 and 26;

2. Are a secondary school graduate;

3. Are proficient in spoken English;

4. Are capable of full participating in the program as evidenced by the satisfactory completion of a physical;

5. Have been personally interviewed in English, by an organizational representative; and

6. Have successfully passed a background investigation that includes verification of school, three non-family related personal and employment references, a personality profile and a criminal record check or its recognized equivalent.

(e) Au pair placement. Sponsors shall secure, prior to the au pair's departure from the home country, a host family placement for each participant. Sponsors shall not:

1. Place an au pair with a family unless the family has specifically agreed that a parent or other responsible adult will remain in the home for the first three days following the au pair's arrival;

2. Place an au pair with a family having a child aged less than three months unless a parent or other responsible adult is present in the home;

3. Place an au pair with a host family having children under the age of two unless the au pair has at least six months of prior infant child care experience;

4. Place the au pair with a family unless a written agreement between the au pair and host family outlining the au pair's obligation to provide not more than 45 hours of child care services per week has been signed by both; and

5. Place the au pair with a family who cannot provide the au pair with a suitable private bedroom.

(f) Au pair orientation. In addition to the orientation requirements set forth herein at 514.10, all sponsors shall provide au pairs, prior to their departure from the home country, with the following information:

1. A copy of all operating procedures, rules, and regulations, including a grievance process, which govern the au pairs participation in the exchange program;

2. A detailed profile of the family and community in which the au pair will be placed;

3. A detailed profile of the educational institutions in the community where the au pair will be placed, including the financial cost of attendance at these institutions; and

4. A detailed summary of travel arrangements.

(g) Au pair training. Sponsors shall provide the au pair participant with child development and child safety instruction, as follows:

1. Prior to placement with the host family, the au pair participant shall receive not less than eight hours of child safety instruction; and

2. Prior to placement with the American host family, the au pair participant shall receive not less than twenty-four hours of child development instruction.

(h) Host family selection. Sponsors shall adequately screen all potential host families and at a minimum shall:

1. Require that the host parents are U.S. citizens or legal permanent residents;

2. Require that host parents are fluent in spoken English;

3. Require that all adult family members resident in the home have been personally interviewed by an organizational representative;

4. Require that host parents have successfully passed a background investigation including employment and personal references;

5. Require that the host family has adequate financial resources to undertake hosting obligations; and

6. Provide a written detailed summary of the exchange program and the parameters of their and the au pair's duties, participation, and obligations.

(i) Host family orientation. In addition to the requirements set forth in 514.10, sponsors shall:

1. Inform all host families of the philosophy, rules, and regulations governing the sponsor's exchange program;

2. Provide all selected host families with a copy of Agency-promulgated Exchange Visitor Program regulations;

3. Advise all selected host families of their obligation to attend at least one family day conference to be sponsored by their au pair organization during the course of the placement year. Host family attendance at such gathering is a condition of program participation and failure to attend will be grounds for possible termination of the continued or future program participation; and

4. Require that the organization's local counselor responsible for the au pair placement contacts the host family and au pair within forty-eight hours of the au pair's arrival and meets, in person, with the host family and au pair within two weeks of the au pair's arrival at the host family home.

(j) Stipend and hours. Sponsors shall require that au pair participants:

1. Are compensated at a rate of not less than $115.00 per week;

2. Do not provide more than a reasonable number of hours of child care on any given day;

3. Receive a minimum of one and a half days off per week in addition to one complete weekend off each month; and

4. Receive two weeks paid vacation.

(k) Educational component. Sponsors shall require that during the period of program participation, all au pair participants are enrolled in an accredited post-secondary institution for not less than six hours of academic credit or its equivalent. As a condition of program participation, host family participants must agree to facilitate the enrollment and attendance of the au pair and to pay the cost of such academic course work in an amount not to exceed $500.

(l) Monitoring. Sponsors shall fully monitor all au pair exchanges, and at a minimum shall:

1. Require monthly personal contact by the local counselor with each au pair and host family for which the counselor is responsible. Counselors shall maintain a record of this contact;

2. Require quarterly contact by the regional counselor with each au pair and host family for which the counselor is responsible. Counselors shall maintain a record of this contact;

3. Require that all local and regional counselors are appraised of their obligation to report unusual or serious situations or incidents involving either the au pair or host family; and

4. Promptly report to the Agency any incidents involving or alleging a crime of moral turpitude or violence.

(m) Reporting requirements. Along with the annual report required by regulations set forth at 514.17, sponsors shall file with the Agency the following information:

1. A summation of the results of an annual survey of all host family and au pair participants regarding satisfaction with the program, its strengths and weaknesses;

2. A summation of all complaints regarding host family or au pair participation in the program, specifying the nature of the complaint, its resolution, and whether any unresolved complaints are outstanding;

3. A summation of all situations which resulted in the placement of an au pair participant with more than one host family;

4. A report by a certified public accountant attesting to the sponsor's compliance with the procedures and reporting requirements set forth in this subpart;

5. A report detailing the name of the au pair, his or her host family placement, location, and the names of the local and regional organizational representatives; and

6. A complete set of all promotional materials, brochures, or pamphlets distributed to either host family or au pair participants.

(n) Sanctions. In addition to the sanctions provisions set forth at 514.50, the Agency may undertake immediate program revocation procedures upon documented evidence that a sponsor has failed to:

1. Comply with the au pair placement requirements set forth in paragraph (e) of this section;

2. Satisfy the selection requirements for each individual au pair as set forth in paragraph (d) of this section; and

3. Enforce and monitor host family's compliance with the stipend and hours requirements set forth in paragraph (j) of this section.

The *Unofficial Guide*™ Reader Questionnaire

If you would like to express your opinion about childcare or this guide, please complete this questionnaire and mail it to:

The *Unofficial Guide*™ Reader Questionnaire
Macmillan Lifestyle Group
1633 Broadway, floor 7
New York, NY 10019-6785

Gender: ___ M ___ F

Age: ___ Under 30 ___ 31–40 ___ 41–50 ___ Over 50

Education:

___ High school ___ College ___ Graduate/ Professional

What is your occupation?

_____

How did you hear about this guide?
___ Friend or relative
___ Newspaper, magazine, or Internet
___ Radio or TV
___ Recommended at bookstore
___ Recommended by librarian
___ Picked it up on my own
___ Familiar with the *Unofficial Guide*™ travel series

Did you go to the bookstore specifically for a book on childcare? Yes ___ No ___

Have you used any other *Unofficial Guides*™?
Yes ___ No ___
If Yes, which ones?

_____

_____

What other book(s) on childcare have you purchased?

_____

_____

Was this book:
___ more helpful than other(s)
___ less helpful than other(s)

Do you think this book was worth its price?
Yes ___   No ___

Did this book cover all topics related to childcare adequately?   Yes ___   No ___

Please explain your answer:

_____

_____

Were there any specific sections in this book that were of particular help to you?   Yes ___   No ___

Please explain your answer:

_____

_____

On a scale of 1 to 10, with 10 being the best rating, how would you rate this guide? ___

What other titles would you like to see published in the _Unofficial Guide_™ series?

_____

_____

Are _Unofficial Guides_™ readily available in your area?   Yes ___   No ___

Other comments:

_____

_____

Get the inside scoop . . . with the
Unofficial Guides™!

The Unofficial Guide to Alternative Medicine
    ISBN: 0-02-862526-9   Price: $15.95

The Unofficial Guide to Buying a Home
    ISBN: 0-02-862461-0   Price: $15.95

The Unofficial Guide to Buying or Leasing a Car
    ISBN: 0-02-862524-2   Price: $15.95

The Unofficial Guide to Childcare
    ISBN: 0-02-862457-2   Price: $15.95

The Unofficial Guide to Cosmetic Surgery
    ISBN: 0-02-862522-6   Price: $15.95

The Unofficial Guide to Dieting Safely
    ISBN: 0-02-862521-8   Price: $15.95

The Unofficial Guide to Eldercare
    ISBN: 0-02-862456-4   Price: $15.95

The Unofficial Guide to Hiring Contractors
    ISBN: 0-02-862460-2   Price: $15.95

The Unofficial Guide to Investing
    ISBN: 0-02-862458-0   Price: $15.95

The Unofficial Guide to Planning Your Wedding
    ISBN: 0-02-862459-9   Price: $15.95

All books in the *Unofficial Guide™* series are available at your local bookseller, or by calling 1-800-428-5331.

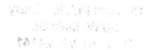

About the Author

Ann Douglas can tell you everything you need to know about childcare. Ann is an experienced journalist from Ontario, Canada whose work regularly appears in such publications as *The Chicago Tribune, Cottage Life,* and *Canadian Living.* She is also a contributor to the highly popular *Beatrice's Web Guide* and writes the "Mom's the Word" column for *Canadian Parents Online.* She recently completed a script for a television series scheduled to air on the PBS network in early 1998, and is working on a short radio documentary for the CBC.

Ann's areas of expertise include parenting, relationships, and small business. A mother of four young children, Ann is the author of the upcoming *Unofficial Guide to Having a Baby.* She has also written *The Complete Idiot's Guide To Curling* (Prentice Hall Canada, 1998); *Baby Science: How Babies Really Work* (Owl Books, 1998); and *The Complete Idiot's Guide To Canadian History* (Prentice Hall Canada, 1997).